The Law and the Prophets

NEW AFRICAN HISTORIES SERIES

Series editors: Jean Allman and Allen Isaacman

David William Cohen and E. S. Atieno Odhiambo, *The Risks of Knowledge: Investigations into the Death of the Hon. Minister John Robert Ouko in Kenya, 1990*

Belinda Bozzoli, *Theatres of Struggle and the End of Apartheid*

Gary Kynoch, *We Are Fighting the World: A History of Marashea Gangs in South Africa, 1947–1999*

Stephanie Newell, *The Forger's Tale: The Search for Odeziaku*

Jacob A. Tropp, *Natures of Colonial Change: Environmental Relations in the Making of the Transkei*

Jan Bender Shetler, *Imagining Serengeti: A History of Landscape Memory in Tanzania from Earliest Times to the Present*

Cheikh Anta Babou, *Fighting the Greater Jihad: Amadu Bamba and the Founding of the Muridiyya of Senegal, 1853–1913*

Marc Epprecht, *Heterosexual Africa? The History of an Idea from the Age of Exploration to the Age of AIDS*

Marissa J. Moorman, *Intonations: A Social History of Music and Nation in Luanda, Angola, from 1945 to Recent Times*

Karen E. Flint, *Healing Traditions: African Medicine, Cultural Exchange, and Competition in South Africa, 1820–1948*

Derek R. Peterson and Giacomo Macola, editors, *Recasting the Past: History Writing and Political Work in Modern Africa*

Moses Ochonu, *Colonial Meltdown: Northern Nigeria in the Great Depression*

Emily Burrill, Richard Roberts, and Elizabeth Thornberry, editors, *Domestic Violence and the Law in Colonial and Post-colonial Africa*

Daniel R. Magaziner, *The Law and the Prophets: Black Consciousness in South Africa, 1968–1977*

The Law and the Prophets

Black Consciousness in
South Africa, 1968–1977

Daniel R. Magaziner

OHIO UNIVERSITY PRESS ∽ ATHENS

JACANA ∽ JOHANNESBURG

DT
1758
.M34
2010

Feb 2012

Ohio University Press, Athens, Ohio 45701
www.ohioswallow.com
© 2010 by Ohio University Press
All rights reserved

Published in 2010 in South Africa by Jacana Media (Pty) Ltd., 10
Orange Street, Auckland Park 2092, South Africa

Printed in the United States of America
Ohio University Press books are printed on acid-free paper ⊗ ™

17 16 15 14 13 12 11   5 4 3 2

Portions of chapters 4 and 5 appeared in *Radical History Review*, no. 99 (Fall 2007),
and portions of chapters 2 and 3 appeared in the *International Journal of African
Historical Studies* 42, no. 2 (2009). I gratefully acknowledge the editors of MARHO,
Duke University Press, and the *IJAHS* for granting permission to reprint.

Library of Congress Cataloging-in-Publication Data
Magaziner, Daniel R.
  The law and the prophets : Black consciousness in South Africa, 1968–1977 / Daniel
R. Magaziner.
    p. cm. — (New African histories series)
  Includes bibliographical references and index.
  ISBN 978-0-8214-1917-5 (hc : alk. paper) — ISBN 978-0-8214-1918-2 (pb : alk. paper)
  1. Blacks—Race identity—South Africa—History. 2. Black Consciousness Movement
of South Africa—History. 3. Black nationalism—South Africa—History. 4. Black
nationalism—Religious aspects—Christianity. 5. Anti-apartheid movements—South
Africa—History. 6. Anti-apartheid movements—Religious aspects—Christianity.
7. South Africa—Politics and government—1961–1978. 8. Black theology. I. Title.
  DT1758.M34 2010
  305.896'06809047—dc22
                    2010019134

They were merely glad to have, at last, divine
corroboration of their experience, to hear—and it was
a tremendous thing to hear—that they had been lied
to for all these years and generations, and that their
captivity was ending, for God was black.

—James Baldwin, "Down at the Cross"

Contents

Acknowledgments

This project has its own history, going back to 1998, when I was first struck by Steve Biko's idea that "the most potent weapon in the hands of the oppressor is the mind of the oppressed." A clear-eyed, dispassionate—cynical, even?—academic wrote the pages that follow, but those words still strike me with the intensity that they once struck an idealistic college student. In the decade since then, numerous people have taught me that before understanding what Biko meant, first my own mind needed to be opened, and I want to thank them here.

Perhaps my greatest debt is to the teachers and institutions that made the journey to the PhD (relatively) painless and (frequently) pleasurable. My interest in these issues was initially sparked at Northwestern, under the tutelage of John Rowe, Michael Tetelman, Jonathon Glassman, and Ken Alder. The latter in particular urged me to consider the University of Wisconsin for my graduate studies, and I have made few better decisions in my life. In Madison, Florence Bernault, Neil Kodesh, Tejumola Olaniyan, Michael Schatzberg, Thomas Spear, and Jim Sweet offered instruction, advice, and support. My greatest debt is to Tom and Florence, who opened a space for intellectual exploration and discovery, and to my African history cohort at Wisconsin, who eagerly seized the opportunity. To me, Thursday afternoons will always be about Paul Bjerk, Kelly Duke, Sean Hanretta, Bob Houle, Dior Konate, Tim Lenoch, Gary Marquardt, Toja Okoh, Mark Pettit, Ryan Ronnenberg, Naaborko Sackeyfio, Meredith Terretta, Steve Volz, and a host of others. Being a graduate student at a public university was an often sobering experience, and I am grateful to the administrators and staff of the African Studies Program, Latin American Studies Program, and History Department at Wisconsin for greasing the skids for all those years. Thanks especially to Jim Schlender, the graduate program's MacGyver, able to fashion TA positions from duct tape and, one presumes, threats. Funding for graduate school was provided by the U.S. Department of Education Foreign Language and Area Studies Fellowship program, the U.S. Department of Education Fulbright Hays Doctoral Dissertation Research Abroad program funded the research that makes up the bulk of this book, and the Doris G. Quinn Foundation funded a generous final year write-up grant that made the exit from graduate school easier than it ought to have been.

In South Africa, my greatest thanks go to Mbulelo Mzamane, who, together with Yvonne, opened so many doors for us, including his own. Mbulelo made possible the interviews that are such a critical component of this project. Thanks also to Nkosinathi Biko for sharing both his family's history and the Steve Biko Foundation's resources with me. I enjoyed the steady and professional help of archivists across South Africa, notably at the Killie Campbell Archives in Durban, UNISA and the National Archives in Pretoria, and the National Library in Cape Town. By far my greatest debt goes to the staff at the Cullen Library's Historical Papers collection at the University of the Witwatersrand, Johannesburg. Carol Archibald and Michele Pickover welcomed me nearly every morning at 8 a.m. and never tired (at least outwardly) of my presence. They literally made this project possible. Thanks also to Andries Bezuidenhout, Irma DuPlessis, Clive Glaser, Joey Kok, Brown Maaba, Berno Schneider, and especially Shireen Ally for their support and kindness.

While in South Africa, I was fortunate to learn from another set of teachers who most likely did not realize that teaching was what they were doing. I arrived in South Africa with some theological knowledge but no real sense of what it meant. After conversations with church people and other people of faith, this was no longer the case. So thanks go to my "fathers of religion," as Soweto high school students once described their teachers—especially "Professors" Baartman, Boesak, Goba, Lamola, Mafuna, Maimela, Mayson, Mkhabela, Mofokeng, Mosala, Motlhabi, Mpumlwana, Mzoneli, Nolan, Phillip, Russell, Tlhagale, and Tshenkeng. The list goes on. I learned more about faith during our conversations than I could have in a lifetime of studying documents. Indeed, thanks are due to all 1970s activists who shared their time with me; I will always treasure our conversations. I should especially note Strini Moodley, who passed away mere weeks after our evening on the Durban waterfront. The day began with him calling me arrogant and ended with one of my most enlightening, challenging, and enjoyable interviews. I am in his debt, even if he would have undoubtedly disagreed with some of my conclusions.

Life has been a whirlwind these past few years; that this book exists at all is due to the ability of many people to keep me in my place. In Ithaca, New York, gratitude is due especially to Katie Kristof, Maggie Edwards, Karen Chirik, and Vic Koschmann—the staff and chair of the History Department, who collectively eased my transition from graduate student to professor. Both the department and the wider Ithaca community have made Cornell a great place to work. I am grateful especially to Judith Byfield, Holly Case, Johanna Crane, Duane Corpis, Grant Farred, Jeremy Foster, Durba Ghosh, Sandra Green,

Salah Hassan, T. J. Hinrichs, Stacey Langwick, Jenny Mann, Michelle Moyd, Guy Ortolano, Camille Robcis, Aaron Sachs, Suman Seth, Robert Travers, and Dagmawi Woubshet. Funding from the History Department and the Society for the Humanities Brett De Bary Interdisciplinary Mellon Writing Group program helped me to turn the dissertation into a book.

At Ohio University Press, Gillian Berchowitz has been a pleasure to work with, as have Jean Allman and Allen Isaacman. Thanks also to Tom Lodge and an anonymous reader for the press. I owe a special debt to Pamela Scully, who kindly allowed her father's painting to be reproduced for the cover, and to Oliver Hirtenfelder, who took the photograph. Nij Tontisirin prepared the map. Numerous people read and offered suggestions on the text, including Sandra Greene and the other members of the Society for the Humanities Brett De Bary Interdisciplinary Mellon Writing Group and the participants in a University of the Witwatersrand school seminar and WISER visiting scholar seminar in Johannesburg. The only way to repay Leslie Hadfield and Naaborko Sackeyfio for carefully reviewing the entire manuscript is to return the favor—and I have cleared my schedule. I knew that Katy Hansen was a woman of many talents, but her line-editing skills are beyond. She now knows the text better than I do; wherever it reads anything less than fluidly, blame my stubborn self and sympathize with her for her most onerous task.

Life is about more than academia. It is about muddy walks with the dog in January thaws and quiet moments atop rust-red dunes. (And about barstools in Madison and burritos in the Mission.) There are so many friends and family members who made this possible and made me whole; I cannot name them all. Suffice it to say that they live in Madison and Ithaca, Chicago and New York, San Francisco and Los Angeles, Iowa, New Hampshire, and Texas, in Boston and in Cleveland. They live in Columbus, Georgia, and Corpus Christi, Texas, and in Brooklyn and Queens. They live in Philadelphia, where Phyllis, Fred, and Drew are my much appreciated and much loved parents and brother, many others are members of my family, and only some are members of the Phillies.

Ryan, Chase, Jimmy, and Shane aside, the most important people in my world live in one house. For a long time, there was only one, and now there are two. Liya Reba came along four hours after I sent substantive revisions to the press, and she has benignly dictated my time ever since. Even as I write this, I am looking at her big, brown eyes and her intermittent hair (she boasts what my brother would call a "long bald"), as she sucks her thumb and tries to rip the tags from her toys. When she smiles at me, there is satisfaction beyond any book or job and the deep happiness necessary to get through both unfazed. And downstairs, I hear Katy stir. I hear her laugh, I see her smile, I witness her passion and marvel at her talent and raw intelligence. She has made this a better book; those who read it will be grateful. She has made me a better person; those who know me are in her debt. She is my world and my heart, and she knows that everything I do is for her.

This book is the culmination of a decade of life and shared experience; so much of Katy is in it that to dedicate it to her would be like dedicating it to its author—a little odd, even if she deserves it. Instead, I will beg your indulgence for only a moment more. I was an unlikely candidate for graduate school. I did not really know what it meant to study history or Africa; my application, in hindsight, was a shambles. But Tom Spear saw something in me even before I did and welcomed me to Wisconsin. In a very real sense, that one decision has made possible everything else that I love about my life. His teaching, tutelage, and support have been constants. It is with humility and gratitude that I dedicate this book to him.

Ithaca, New York
August 2009

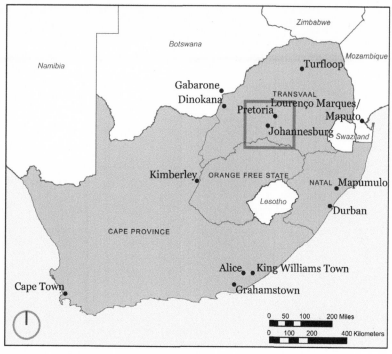

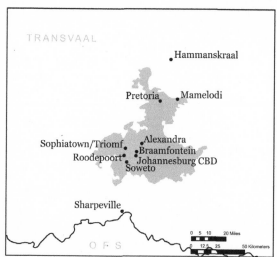

South Africa, 1968–77, showing places significant in the text

The Seventies

In 1974, nine South African activists were put on trial for terrorism. They were all officers in either the South African Students' Organisation (SASO) or the Black People's Convention (BPC)—organizations known collectively as the Black Consciousness Movement—and they were charged with threatening the peace, order, and security of the white minority–governed apartheid state. The trial stretched on for over seventeen months; it was the longest, to that date, of apartheid's innumerable security or terrorism trials. Along the way, the defendants, the state prosecutor, the judge, and other witnesses paused on numerous occasions to debate the character and political opinions of Jesus Christ.

The discussions revolved especially around a resolution SASO, the oldest of these two organizations, had passed in 1973, which described Christ as "the first freedom fighter to die for the liberation of the oppressed."[1] The resolution went on to detail how Christ had earned this reputation by associating with known Zealots, described as the anticolonial revolutionary radicals of first-century Palestine, and perhaps even the Essenes, described as an "Israeli guerilla warfare unit against the Romans." The judge asked witnesses to explain what this meant. Some demurred; others, perhaps recognizing that they were going to jail anyway, drew comparisons between the Essenes and the Front for Liberation of Mozambique (FRELIMO), whose guerrilla forces had just taken power in neighboring Mozambique. Discussions about these and other theological issues went on and on, to the point that the state prosecutor, faced with defendants who repeatedly referred to the Bible and Christ to make their case, grew frustrated. "SASO and BPC are very fond of bringing religious connotations into lots of things," he finally complained.[2] He had a point.

These young activists appeared to have drawn rather interesting conclusions about the theory and practice of resistance to apartheid, based not exclusively on politics or ideology but on theology.

Consider the plea penned by Kaborane Gilbert Sedibe, the Student Representative Council (SRC) president from the University of the North, in preparation for the trial. Sedibe explained that the charges against him were "an evil indictment . . . an indictment against God for having created me black . . . [and] an indictment against Christ for having said that I am a free man." Such evil, however, did not surprise him because "the 'son of the soil'—O.R. Tiro"— Sedibe's predecessor as SRC president—had "prophesied of these accusations against the Black man before his fateful death." Sedibe then used the Bible to rebut the charges: "God says to us in Galatians 5:1 that we must stand strong in the liberty wherewith Christ has made us free and be not entangled with the yoke of bondage. For declaring this liberty I am being charged. This should not surprise us for the word tells us in II Corinthians 2:14 that 'And do not marvel for Satan himself is transformed into an angel of light.'" Sedibe thus used Christianity against the white state that had long used that religion to justify its policies. He inverted state theology and countercharged that his prosecutors, as representatives of apartheid's law, were in fact Satan, disguised in their whiteness as angels of light. And against them he wielded the words and warnings of a recently assassinated "prophet," Ongkopotse Tiro, a student leader like Sedibe, who spoke with a righteous voice that sanctified "secular" politics. Sedibe's plea was a profound political statement in a country that disparaged those with darker skins and claimed that God's countenance shone especially on the descendants of white settlers. It was also a theological statement. Sedibe was a Christian; he knew his Bible and did not enlist the word of God without reflection. When he pleaded that "Black Consciousness preaches the freedom and liberation of the Black man from evil power representing Satan," he meant it. When he claimed that "our struggle is [a] Godly and genuine one, and as the Word of God in the Acts of the Apostles 5:39 says: 'Since it is of God, ye' i.e. forces of oppression, 'cannot overthrow it, lest ye be found to fight against God,'" he spoke in the political tongue of his time and place.[3]

This episode—adrift amid the flotsam of pretrial filings—was but one of many well-known conflicts between apartheid law and opposition prophets during South Africa's 1970s. Yet that struggle is only part of the story. Although Sedibe stood accused of fomenting rebellion against the state and thus of black opposition to apartheid as conventionally understood, his plea's structure alluded to less overt acts of rebellion. He began from a simple premise: he and his fellow accused were "advocates for the dignity of the Black man as created in the image of God." The implications of this were legion and suggestive of more than a simple struggle against a particular legal system. Black

Consciousness, Sedibe indicated, was not just a resistance ideology; it was about "dignity"—about the essential wholeness of a singular being who knew herself (or, in his language, himself) as "Black." Moreover, the "dignity of the Black man" for which Black Consciousness activists advocated came with a weighty stamp of approval, since it was in the divine's own image. Following Sedibe's plea, then, he and the others were accused of a crime altogether more fundamental than fomenting rebellion against the apartheid state. They had had the temerity to claim the existence of dignified black selves in South Africa, who were, in spite of apartheid's ideological premises, the very "image of God."

Conflicts between apartheid law and opposition prophets resonated on these multiple levels from 1968 until 1977. This period began during an ebb in the often spectacular struggles for change in twentieth-century South Africa.[4] Yet the opposition's weakness and the white minority's strength made this a pregnant pause, a time for reflection, and only after that could action be taken. This decade opened the intellectual space for a new generation of South African thinkers to explore the possibility that superficially simple statements—"I am Black," "I am a Man," "I have dignity," "I am the image of God"—might be profoundly potent. From the depths of oppression, they argued that change was not impossible but would in fact come when people had faith and hope enough to imagine their way beyond their predicament. Between 1968 and 1977, South African students, clergy, and cultural and other activists donned the prophet's mantle and spoke historical truths to the power of apartheid law. They did so first in student group meetings, in theological seminars, in sermons and newsletters and poetry; then came protests, rallies, trials, uprisings, death, and in time some sort of change. *The Law and the Prophets* is the story of this generation and about what their lives reveal regarding the potential and perils of thinking in time.

BLACK CONSCIOUSNESS AND AFRICAN INTELLECTUAL HISTORY

At the outset, I noted that Sedibe and his fellow accused were affiliated with antiapartheid organizations, which, by 1974, observers increasingly labeled the Black Consciousness Movement. That movement's history is well known. It began with the founding of SASO, an all-black student group that broke with the multiracial National Union of South African Students (NUSAS) in 1969, and emerged by the early 1970s as the critical center of internal resistance to apartheid during that decade. In the grand narrative of antiapartheid, Black Consciousness filled the gap between the 1950s and early 1960s and the younger generation of activists who emerged in the wake of the Soweto protests of June 1976. Black Consciousness leaders, exemplified by Steve Biko, inspired black South Africans with news ideas about dignity and self-worth, and these in turn inspired a resurgence in popular pressure against apartheid, despite Biko's death while in police custody in September 1977 and the banning of Black Consciousness organizations the following month. Many scholars have narrated the movement's story during these few years, and although there is disagreement about the particulars, the consensus is that between 1968 and 1977, Black Consciousness organizations and activists reignited resistance to white minority rule. They lit a fuse, as it were, that burned through the furies of popular protest in the 1980s, until South Africa's first democratic elections in 1994.[5]

The Law and the Prophets is about these critical nine years, but it does not tell the same story. The literature on Black Consciousness and the 1970s is largely limited to political science and theory, and not surprisingly, it is consumed with the question of overt resistance to apartheid. Furthermore, since that resistance eventually came—exemplified by the Soweto students who took to the streets in 1976—the literature comprises retrospectively triumphant accounts. Yet as Sedibe's plea and the religious tenor of the aforementioned trial indicate, movement histories are rather reductive accounts of this past. Sedibe cast himself as a prophet, wielding the divine revelation of freedom against the constraints of the white state. Can politics—and conventional political narratives—capture this? Can movement histories capture the story of young students such as Malusi Mpumlwana, who joined SASO in the early 1970s not because he wanted to build South African democracy but because he wanted a more human society, "a totally new reality in South Africa"?[6] White supremacy would be resisted along the way, but the change that Mpumlwana sought outpaced apartheid's laws. His recollection resonates with that of another activist, Bongi Mkhabela, who was much younger than he when, imbued with the ideas of Black Consciousness, she helped to organize the 1976 protests that made Soweto famous. She spent years in prison for her activities at that time and was crushed to discover upon her release that her world had not progressed but regressed. Although she had come of age during politics' ebb and had left prison during the flood of protest that marked the early 1980s, she remembers the latter decade as "the saddest period in our history." True, there were politics and opposition aplenty, as the flame that she had helped light was finding more fuel, but in her memory, "the place that used to be home, that used to be so embracing, so warm, was icy cold."[7] A different, less triumphant, less determined narrative connects Mpumlwana's desire to create a totally new reality in the early 1970s and Mkhabela's abject disappointment in their generation's failure to do so, despite evident political success. That too is the story of Black Consciousness, and I think that it is more true to the historical experience of those who lived it, even, perhaps, if they themselves have grown more accustomed to the teleology those other narratives developed.[8] It is a story of thought first unbounded and then bound, of ideas that became an ideology, and of what was lost along the way.

Other histories demonstrate the implications of this approach. In his justly famous study *The Cultural Origins of the French Revolution*, Roger Chartier drew our attention to what he neatly labeled "the chimera of origins." Faced with explaining such resonant historical events as the French Revolution, Chartier argued, scholars frequently read history backward to suppose "a sorting out process that retains, out of the innumerable realities that makes up the history, only the matrix of the future event." Like the French Revolution, so too do "events" such as Soweto 1976, elections in 1994, Truth, Reconciliation, and indeed the political struggle against apartheid itself impose themselves on our reading of the past, leading to studies whose fundamental assumptions privilege certain interpretations of the story before the telling. The present's finger on the scale thus yields misleading readings of the past.[9] Black Consciousness was multiple and contingent, subject to debate and change. There is disagreement about whether it was responsible for planning the Soweto uprising in 1976—but it is inarguable that the ideas, discourses, and imaginaries that inspired students to protest on 16 June belonged to the years that came before. With this in mind, I take cues from new literature on the Black Power movement in the United States that emphasizes process, not politics, and the contingent moments around which political movements cohered and fractured, thus moving beyond grand narratives that make the story triumphantly legible but less historical.[10] Subjecting Black Consciousness to a more historicist reading opens up new avenues for recapturing the late 1960s and early 1970s. In history, triumphant tales of students becoming politicians are still there—but as Sedibe, Mpumlwana, and Mkhabela suggest, they are not the only stories.

The recovery of these other stories demands inquiry into the intellectual past, a field with which African history is unpracticed at best.[11] One might speculate as to why this is so. After all, if we agree with Saul Dubow, "intellectual history is not by its nature democratic or popular," and African history has long been a discipline in search of both.[12] Intellectual history as practiced elsewhere remains a redoubt of great men (and occasionally women), and if we want to mine the African historical canon for it, the nationalist movements would be a good place to start. Amilcar Cabral, Julius Nyerere, Kwame Nkrumah, and the like remain African history's exemplary intellectuals, perhaps because their exceptionalism was in service of political transformations. Yet in *The Law and the Prophets*, I aspire to go beyond this. I do not want merely to add another statue—of Biko, perhaps?—to the Heroes' Acre of African nationalist thinkers; instead, I hope to broaden the category of African intellectual history.

The students, clerics, and artists who comprised the Black Consciousness Movement came from South Africa's small, black middle class, those privileged enough to spend time at universities and to read and reflect on their situation.[13] They were thus the descendents of previous generations of African thinkers whose ideas figure prominently in works that examine the history of African theater and poetry, journalism and academia.[14] Yet they came of age in the 1950s and 1960s, when apartheid's laws most drastically limited the prospects of access and advancement that preceding generations had sought in education. They were at once a part of the colonial, modernizing, Westernized system and apart from the dominant society that squeezed their aspirations. In this, they shared the predicament of black thinkers throughout the African diaspora, such as those featured in the work of Paul Gilroy, Robin Kelley, and Gary Wilder, all of whom lobbed critiques from positions of relative privilege and thus more stinging alienation. Just as Wilder's interwar Francophone intellectuals were prompted by their circumstances to launch an "imminent critique . . . from a standpoint internal to the existing society . . . [but pointing] to sociopolitical alternatives beyond it," so too did 1970s activists develop ways of thinking through and beyond their predicament. Interwar thinkers had developed their imminent critique through intellectual exploration, through poetry and banquets, salons and dances, all moments that political narratives tend to ignore. For his part, Sedibe used the Bible. *The Law and the Prophets* follows the examples of Wilder and others and resists the comforting temptation to track political change. Instead, it dwells on the thinking without which progress was impossible.[15]

That, perhaps, is this study's signature contribution: as intellectual history, it asserts the importance of both thinkers and their ideas. Historians have masterfully excavated the ways in which Africans have thought about political practice. They have recovered dense, vibrant political theory from beneath the weight of colonial paternalism and racist condescension and presented convincing arguments about what people must have thought at various points in the past.[16] This is what I aspire to do: to recast Black Consciousness, to show that before there was a movement, there were thinkers, activists, students at home with books and ideas who made the latter work in their particular historical context. My source base grants me access. Just as Jan Vansina upstreamed via words, I can follow ideas, track precedents, translations, domestications.[17] As Harry Nengwekhulu, a SASO founder from the University of the North, suggested, ideas were tools: "We read, man, [and then] we used to write articles on different topics . . . [and] we just wrote."[18] *The Law and the Prophets* is about the thought that went into this; it demonstrates how thinking bridged the 1960s quiet and 1970s events in a way that no movement could.

But about what did activists think? Sedibe again provides guidance here. Although he understood himself to be engaged in opposition to the state — how could it not be so, given the circumstances under which he wrote? — he was careful to note that Black Consciousness was, at its root, about the "dignity of the Black man." In the few years that followed SASO's founding in 1968, activists took none of these concepts for granted; neither "dignity," nor "black," nor "man" was assured, let alone struggle against the state. Before politics, there was self-fashioning. As a 1970 issue of the SASO Newsletter put it, members needed to ask themselves, "Who are we? What are we talking about? Where are we today? Whither are we going?"[19] These were questions designed to promote insight—into oneself, into one's circumstances, and into one's future. The various aspects that made up individuals' senses of themselves were taken apart and examined, embraced or rejected. That this later provoked a political response says a great deal about the time and place where activists lived and about the perils of intellectual exploration.

Under apartheid, identifications were politically charged. For his part, Sedibe claimed to be a black man, and following his lead, The Law and the Prophets is sensitive to the deeply gendered nature of the decade's thought.[20] Scholars have frequently noted gender's rather fraught place in the development and articulation of radical political movements across the African diaspora—and especially in the turn toward race nationalism in the 1960s and 1970s.[21] In studies of the period, most agree with Michael Gomez, who, writing about the Nation of Islam, argued that "the agenda, quite simply, was the aggregation of power and prerogative among black men; indeed, given their relative disadvantage vis-à-vis white males, the disempowerment of black women became almost essential to the creation of a sense of empowerment within the collective psyche of black men; it was certainly a route more readily available to such an end."[22] As Robert Morrell has contended, white masculinity was hegemonic across the African diaspora, and in South Africa, as elsewhere, black men frequently responded by fashioning a similarly hegemonic masculinity that was predicated on the use and control of black women.[23] To note this is not to diminish the ways in which apartheid was keyed to the "unmanning" of black men.[24] Rather, it is to open gendered assumptions, articulations, and outcomes to careful study and to reveal the multiplicities hidden within the category of black men.

After all, those Marlon Ross called "interested others"—notably black women— were deeply involved and invested in what has been largely conceived as a struggle between black and white men.[25] Young, female activists such as Bongi Mkhabela dedicated themselves to the pursuit of dignity; other women served in Black Consciousness community development organizations; women were vital voices in the seminars where thinkers first tested their ideas; some women articulated limited but potent feminist-inspired demands; and by the mid-1970s, the Black People's Convention was led by a woman. These observations disrupt generalizations about the era's gender politics. Even if the goal was the dignity of black men, black women fought for this as well: as one former activist has contended, women made "a strategic choice" to shelve specifically female concerns "in the face of opposition from a seemingly invincible white national-party state that was quick to exploit any sign of division in order to subjugate Black people even further."[26] As *The Law and the Prophets* demonstrates, such choices had histories. Much as the terms *black* and *man* were contingent and meaningful, so was the gendered pursuit of dignity muddled as well.

The contested politics of gender and selfhood resonated globally during the 1960s and 1970s. Black students in South Africa knew this, and they domesticated global intellectual currents—feminism, nationalism—and put them to work. Their context was both local and global. They came of age not only during the local lull in opposition politics that marked the 1960s but also in "the sixties," a decade that saw young people the world over effect the new left turn away from movement politics to identity politics, participatory democracy, and the politics of authenticity. It was a time when individuals' senses of themselves—when their ideas—were fashioned into tools with which to pursue postcolonial and postmodern protest. South Africans were still in the throes of their particular sort of modernity and coloniality, but they asked themselves questions in conversation with their peers and plotted an existentialist path toward a future predicated on who they were, what they were talking about, and where they wanted to go. Black Consciousness was built not with the raw materials of political Africanism or multiracialism—the ideologies with which it is most often compared—but rather at the interstices of intellectual debate and contestation about fundamental issues of being.[27]

This preoccupation with questions of existence spoke to a wider trend in African(a) intellectual history. From the 1950s on, typically white existentialism had enjoyed a fruitful tension with diaspora anticolonial and antiracist thought. Thinkers from Jean-Paul Sartre to Albert Camus, Frantz Fanon, and Aimé Césaire collectively probed the historical production of racial and other identities and debated the appropriate response. Not surprisingly, each of these thinkers featured at critical moments in the development of Black Consciousness ideas. Yet African intellectual history was not merely derivative of European or American intellectual history; South African students, for example, developed their ideas in a dramatically different context than their French or American peers—or even their Afro-American ones. All asked questions about "freedom, anguish, dread and responsibility," but in South Africa in particular, the "teleological question of black liberation" and the actions necessary to realize it loomed.[28] Let me be clear here: this teleology is of a different order than that of the triumphant antiapartheid tomes. It is more eschatological than anything else, concerned not with how the very particular struggle against apartheid would end but with the undetermined ending the *SASO Newsletter* suggested—"Whither are we going?"—within a context where going somewhere was a pressing need. Indeed, South African black thought during the early 1970s was frequently less about explicit resistance to apartheid and more about fundamental ethical questions regarding how one should live in service of the future.[29]

Such ethical questions have often been the purview of prophets, and *The Law and the Prophets* traces how South African thinkers developed their unique political philosophy. The three chapters that constitute part 1 first set the historical and intellectual stage and then follow the construction of the Black Consciousness idea-set from student seminars to the *SASO Newsletter* from roughly 1968 until 1972. That time period—as well as many of the characters and ideas prominent then—also figures in parts 2 and 3; in order to better situate later events within my new reading of Black Consciousness, part 1 disaggregates Black Consciousness thought in order to cast its details into sharper relief.

The three chapters in this part trace how students and other activists worked diligently to define and embody new black selves, even as they begged the question of what those selves would do. By the mid-1970s, however, new pressures and contingencies helped to effect a reconciliation of sorts between consciousness-raising and the pursuit of political power. Activists met these new challenges with another set of ideas about progress and change, ideas that had also developed over the previous years and were drawn, as Sedibe demonstrated, from Christianity.

LIBERATING CHRISTIANITY THROUGH FAITH AND HOPE

Here is another Black Consciousness story. In 1967, a multiracial group of South African students met at Grahamstown to form a new ecumenical Christian group premised on "race relations rather than race separations."[30] Black Christian students flocked to join this new organization, which shared the name University Christian Movement (UCM) with its American counterpart, ensuring that it soon had a black majority. In time, however, the importance of race relations within the UCM was gradually eclipsed by believers' efforts to interpret Christ's specific message to South Africa's black oppressed. By dint of choice and circumstance, these explorations moved in a particular direction, as evidenced by the tone of a funeral held nearly a decade after the Grahamstown meeting. A SASO activist had died under mysterious circumstances in police custody, but the preacher did not bemoan his death. Instead, the minister hailed it as a "majestic closing of a career of public service." "Christ's death is the prototype of all deaths that are a mask of victory," he continued, and so, like Christ, the dead activist had actually won.[31] South Africa's Christ covered a great deal of ground during the seventies: it was Christ whose love brought people of all races together; it was Christ who had a particular message for singularly oppressed black South Africa; it was Christ who died on the cross and taught that death was worth it.

South Africa's Christ thus tells another story, which part 2 explores in the context of the development of Black Consciousness thought in part 1. Black Consciousness initially begged off the question of the future, yet the question of liberation, however defined, remained. Lewis Gordon's recent study of Africana existentialism hinges on Christianity as the link between existentialist inwardness and the black quest for liberation; similarly, for South Africans Christianity was an essential and intrinsic tool. I will suggest that there are numerous reasons for this, some perhaps in keeping with Slavoj Žižek's stubborn insistence that Christianity contains vast, if typically unrealized, revolutionary potential. The faith plots an absolute break with the past and places hope in the future, he and others contend, and it therefore offers a revolution so total, so complete, as to be entirely free of teleology.[32] Black Consciousness philosophy probed the future in this undetermined Christian way; students counseled each other to prepare the people for "the day of reckoning" when black South Africa might "rejoice in the knowledge that we have been architects of our own future."[33] "No nation can win a battle without faith," Steve Biko wrote, and through faith came hope that change was not "an eschatological myth but an achievable goal."[34]

Such religiosity might not surprise us. After all, Gordon's quick turn to black Christianity to explain black philosophy is one of many recent moves in that direction. In African studies, the interpenetration of the political, the religious, the cultural, and the ethical has long been noted and is now enjoying a bit of a revival.[35] South Africa's Christ was carried on the shoulders of reams of theological and political critique, in conversation with similar trends around the world. As such, the seventies offer a privileged vantage point from which to watch this multifaceted process unfold and to observe thinkers engaged in the quintessentially modern project of self-fashioning, with tools—faith and hope—that secularization had been supposed to render out of date.

It is not exactly novel to note this. The Christian tenor of black South African politics stretches back to Tiyo Soga's nascent Africanism in the mid-nineteenth century—and perhaps even beyond, to his prophetic antecedents Nxele and Ntsikana.[36] Christianity has been an essential component of South African nationalisms—both black and white—from turn-of-the-century Ethiopian irruptions through Garveyite prophets in the 1920s to Anton Lembede's theologies of blood and territory to Sedibe's plea. Yet too much of this literature falls back on the language of anthropological curiosity—asking "Isn't it remarkable?" rather than the more satisfying "How did it work?"[37] *The Law and the Prophets* is less interested in noting that the sacred and secular were interpenetrated than in seeing how Christianity worked in late 1960s and early 1970s South Africa.

In what follows, I endeavor to listen to actors' explanations and understandings of their beliefs, aspirations, and actions. Recall Sedibe one last time. His tone was just so Christian, so assured in its faith in God and Christ and in the belief that the revelations revealed in scripture meant something. Scholars beyond African studies—and indeed, all people concerned with faith's often contentious role in public life—can learn a great deal from such sincere efforts to understand and apply revelation in the world.[38] *The Law and the Prophets* strives to be careful not to turn the Christian faith into a shorthand to talk about something else, as in other studies where the label *Christian* is applied in discussions about how people changed the way they dressed or began to handle money.[39] Rather, as J. D. Y. Peel has reminded us, "the redemptive sacrifice of Christ does not imply double-entry book keeping or vice versa." If Christians are "irreducibly" Christian, we need to go where they are and were, to note that about which they spoke and wrote, and to see in the 1970s how the path from nineteenth-century conversion to twenty-first-century Pentecostalism was long and jagged, full of fits and starts and constant debate.[40]

The three chapters of part 2 elaborate on the development of Black Consciousness in part 1 by tracing South Africans' engagement with the Christian faith and Christian theology during roughly the same time period, the late 1960s and first years of the 1970s. This process led clergy and lay Christians—and even unbelievers—to look without flinching at the faith's history and failings in South Africa (and Africa in general) and to discard and reassess according to their moment's demands. Like their SASO counterparts, Christians affiliated with the UCM and other organizations read widely and vigorously translated ideas from the United States, Europe, Latin America, and elsewhere in Africa. In time, this process led many to a total redefinition of the Christian faith in the South African context, from one complicit in colonization and dispossession to a message of assured liberation, in spite of the manifold bonds of the present. Biko had argued that victory was a matter of faith, and *The Law and the Prophets* probes the past to consider how and whether this was so.

THE POLITICAL TURN

But critically, such faith came "in spite of" of present circumstances. Søren Kierkegaard argued that this was the very essence of faith, which meant "to see the sword hanging over the head of the beloved" but still to live with joy.[41] In the late 1960s, the theologian Jürgen Moltmann agreed and then added an eschatological dimension. Faith knows what it knows to be true, Moltmann wrote, "and hope awaits the time when this truth shall be manifested."[42] The movement from faith to hope was a progression in time and space, from fraught present to as yet unknown future, from the land of Pharaoh to the land of milk and honey. The point was to look forward, to hope in spite of the present—which, in 1970s South Africa, meant in spite of apartheid and in spite of politics.[43]

Keeping faith can be costly, however, as one more Black Consciousness story illustrates well. Onkgopotse Abraham Tiro was born in the northern Transvaal village of Dinokana in 1945. He attended government schools in his home-town, in Soweto, and in Mafeking, with breaks to work when money was short, and he was a diligent and enthusiastic lay leader and preacher in the Seventh-Day Adventist Church. In the early 1970s, he matriculated to the apartheid-mandated university for Sotho-, Tswana-, and Pedi-speakers at Turfloop, where he joined SASO and became SRC president. In this capacity, he was asked to deliver a speech extolling education to parents, students, and government-appointed administrators; instead, he raised his voice against the inequities of Bantu education. He was expelled from the university for these sentiments and moved to Soweto to teach high school math, advise a Seventh-Day Adventist youth group, and organize for SASO in Johannesburg. Government pressure pursued him, and he soon left for exile in Botswana. He died there, killed by a parcel bomb in early February 1974. Tiro had been Sedibe's "prophet," the "son of the soil" who foretold future trials, and he had helped to determine activists' responses. It was Tiro who introduced the resolution discussed at the outset of this introduction, which hailed Christ as the "first freedom fighter to die for the liberation of the oppressed." Perhaps he had had this example in mind when, shortly before his death, he wrote and urged those still in South Africa to remain fearless and hopeful in spite of setbacks. His organization was part of a movement by that point; self-fashioning and ethical critique were increasingly part of a bounded ideology known as Black Consciousness. As Tiro's example demonstrates, where there was politics, there would be suffer-ing, and there would be setbacks.

By the mid-1970s, whether by design or by accident, the Black Conscious-ness Movement was swept into the antiapartheid struggle, with the ideological conflict and violence that that entailed. Violence befell narratives as well, forcing faith and hope in a "totally new reality" to give way to the far more limited, if laudable, goal of ending apartheid. To be sure, faith still had a role to play—graveside orators celebrated activists killed by the police, declaring, "Lord, we are sure we shall win, because You are on our side"—but political setbacks and political determinations reduced the struggle's scale.[44] Part 3's chapters move the story from the late 1960s and early 1970s to its end in 1977. I first trace the theory and practice of spreading what activists referred to as the gospel of Black Consciousness. Ideas become ideologies as they move from mouth to mouth and tract to tract; they freeze, as it were, because frozen, they are blunter tools, more easily wielded in political trenches. Part 3 most explicitly gives the entire study its title, as prophets associated with the Black

Consciousness Movement faced the law in protests, strikes, streets, court-rooms, and funerals and assumed the form familiar from the grand narrative of the struggle against apartheid.

Yet this encounter—and the study's title—can be read in a second, more insidious way. When the Black Consciousness Movement joined the political struggle to end apartheid, it lost the truly revolutionary potential Žižek saw in Christianity. Apartheid limited its opposition's dreams. The system's laws would bind South Africans for only two decades more; the idea that ending those laws had been the goal all along has lasted far longer. As the seventies dawned, activists had sought to raise consciousness, to transform identity, to preach and instill dignity and confidence worthy of the image of God. By decade's end, they comforted themselves with the notion that dying to end apartheid was worth it because to do so was to be like Christ.

In what follows, I have sought to rediscover and explicate the thinking that attended this process. I have done so by mustering both old and new sources. I interviewed nearly sixty former activists during many months of formal research in South Africa. Many of my informants had been prominent Black Consciousness and Black Theology activists—such as Barney Pityana and Allan Boesak. Many more are somewhat less well known, including Anne Hope, a Christian Institute (CI) employee who spent critical months training Biko, Pityana, and others in radical pedagogy during 1972, and Tau Mokoka, a University of the North dropout who organized for SASO's Pretoria branch between 1972 and 1977. Typical interviews lasted between one and two hours, during which time I asked my informants open-ended questions about their backgrounds, their activism, and their reflections on the past. As I found myself working through the density and depth of the Black Consciousness ideas that I had recorded, it became more and more apparent that those ideas were the story and that by tracking changes there, I would be able to see this period in new ways.

Thankfully, archival and published sources offered ample documentation with which to complement and complicate these reflections. I have revisited whatever records are available for this period, but it was especially invigorating to find new sources, especially the bits and pieces hidden in the archives of church groups and other organizations, as well as the press and government archives. Although the National Archive holdings on Black Consciousness are rather scant, evidence collected during the law's pursuit of these prophets is not. This study opened with a trial, the records of which stretch across thousands of pages of argument, debate, and supporting documentation. I wallowed in sources such as these like a pig in the muck, in pursuit of what people thought they were doing as they went about their lives during this decade. What has resulted is a less determined narrative, which follows a generation of activists as their struggle gained momentum and human warmth was lost along the way.

It is almost inappropriate to note this. Such conclusions test the limits of scholarly objectivity, and what is more, they depress somewhat by refusing to accept the triumphant tale that is typically told.[45] But no one can study the struggle against apartheid objectively; it is a human story brimming with pathos and emotion, and that is what I imagine draws us to it in the first place. These Black Consciousness stories are not intended to undermine such tales of change with their contingent endings and alternative ways of remembering the past, merely for the sake of historical accuracy or cynicism. Rather, these stories seek to restore to tales of change some of the possibilities that have been lost, the dreams that had motivated a generation, at least for a moment. Here, the very words of the title—*The Law and the Prophets*—resonate on another level. They come from Christ's Golden Rule, from the Sermon on the Mount's summation of humanity's accumulated wisdom: "So whatever you wish that men would do to you, do so to them; for this is the law and the prophets." This law is altogether more fundamental than those of any legal system or movement, but these others have the power to make people forget that this is true. We thus have a great deal to learn from the dreams, trials, and histories of prophets.

PART I

⌐

Making Black Consciousness

When Steve Biko assumed the presidency of SASO in 1969, he was twenty-two years old. Born in 1946, he later wrote that he had "lived all my conscious life in the framework of institutionalized separate development." Apartheid had been a constant: "My friendships, my love, my thinking and every other facet of my life have been carved and shaped within the context of separate development."[1] Part 1 explores the ramifications and effects of this fact—or at least the perception that this was the case—on the generation of students and activists who made Black Consciousness.

Chapter 1 better situates this process within larger historical narratives, first in terms of the mechanics of 1960s politics and education and then, following the lead of Rob Nixon and others, within the more particular narrative of black South African thought under apartheid.[2] Finally, it considers the immediate impact of these years on the first generation of student activists, through their experiences of both apartheid and the education system. Most contend that they came of age during a lull in antiapartheid politics, but as we shall see, it was more a period of reassessment rather than a full stop. That being said, black politics did more or less yield the stage during the 1960s, and an array of ostensibly multiracial liberal groups came to the fore. Chapter 2 recounts how nascent black student organizations began to challenge the liberal ascendancy and thereby opened the space for the more fundamental critique that became Black Consciousness. The chapter continues by showing how, in their interpretations of this break, SASO activists began a new process of self-identification, as men and responsible adults.

Chapter 3 covers the period between 1968 and 1972, during which Biko and other activists founded SASO and began to explore what the organization was for. To that end, they considered fundamental categories of identification— notably race—and developed a political philosophy that called for neither liberation nor power but consciousness. Thus, between 1968 and 1972, political practice was not a matter of protest, of public struggle, of slogans and trials.

Rather, as Biko's colleague Strini Moodley wrote near the end of these four years, it was about the "projection of the beingness."[3] Read this way, Black Consciousness offered a unique sort of politics; it was not something you did or believed, it was something you were.

1 ꗑ Sophiatown after the Fall
The Sixties

A SMALL, undistinguished house sits at 111 Ray Street, near Johannesburg. In its ordinariness, it offers mute testimony to failure. This area is the suburb known once again as Sophiatown—"once again" because only recently has this suburb regained its birth name. For generations, the neighborhood was known as Triomf—from the Afrikaans word meaning "triumph"—a name linked to its history. As Sophiatown, the neighborhood was founded in the early twentieth century as a "freehold" township, and it had been one of Johannesburg's only multiracial and relatively free spaces. The so-called triumph was the apartheid state's destruction of this space by the end of the 1950s; as apartheid dictated, Sophiatown's inhabitants were separated according to racial groups, with their neighborhood bulldozed and Triomf erected in its place.

Which brings us to the small house with its attached garage and neat fence of black spikes. It hearkens back to a well-remembered part of both Sophiatown's and South Africa's history, where *Drum* writers held forth with Can Themba at his famed House of Truth. In the years since the neighborhood's destruction, Themba's home has figured prominently in the writing of historians, memoirists, writers of fiction, and others who have memorialized and lamented the rise and fall of the "Sophiatown Renaissance" during the 1950s. Themba is a wonderful character, and the renaissance makes for lively stories.[1] But the problem of its end looms. The building at 111 Ray is no longer the House of Truth, nor is the rechristened but still predominantly Afrikaans Triomf truly Sophiatown. The black spot's residents failed to stop the destruction of their homes, just as in Sharpeville's wake, it was apparent that the Pan-Africanist Congress (PAC) and the African National Congress (ANC) had failed to stop apartheid.

Sophiatown was a rallying point for antiapartheid agitation during the 1950s, but in the end, rallies and protests achieved little—a momentary release, author and Sophiatown resident Bloke Modisane remembered, "that left us exhausted and limp."[2] By 1960, the ANC and PAC were banned; by 1964, their leaders were imprisoned or in exile and the struggle, it seemed, had stilled. The university students of 1968 were teenagers in 1960. Some counted political activists among their family members; others had grown up in Sophiatown and similar places and remembered with anger the removals, police raids, disillusionment, and frustration that marked its final days. Sophiatown after the fall is the critical intellectual context for understanding what the pre-1968 failures meant to those students who sought to begin again in the years that followed. The state's triumph was black South Africa's defeat; the failure to save Sophiatown and similar places—and the helplessness that defeat engendered—was the context in which the Black Consciousness generation formed its political and mental consciousness. In this chapter, I first set the political and institutional context in which Black Consciousness developed, and then I consider the less overt but perhaps more resonant memories and experiences that students took with them to the university.

LIBERAL POLITICS AND GRAND APARTHEID

In the wake of the 1960 bannings and subsequent imprisonment or exile of African political leaders, black voices more or less ceded the mantle of opposition to self-described liberal political groups that plotted multiracial reform against white exclusiveness. Embodied by Alan Paton's short-lived Liberal Party and the National Union of South African Students, liberals agitated against the moral bankruptcy of the apartheid regime and called for "nonwhites" to be integrated into the (white-dominated) political and economic system. Liberal politics, however, failed to slow apartheid's further development during the 1960s. Instead, Sophiatown, Sharpeville, and subsequent defeats cleared the stage for Grand Apartheid—Prime Minister Hendrik Verwoerd's master plan for the final and total separation of the country's peoples. Sophiatown's demolition was only one famous example among thousands of similar actions. All told, hundreds of thousands of people fell victim to the Department of Bantu Administration's planning during the 1960s, and by that decade's close, the apartheid idea reigned. The government moved ahead with plans for Bantustan independence, after which South Africa was to be not one country but many—one rich, powerful white republic ringed by black, poor, and ostensibly independent nations.[3]

The government similarly restructured other areas of South African life, especially the education system. In order to redefine "appropriate" education for Africans and other nonwhites, the National Party effectively transformed instruction at the primary and secondary levels. The Department of Bantu Education seized control of African education from the country's many missions, and at the tertiary level, the government introduced the Expansion of University Education Act in 1959.[4] This act had three major functions. First, it made it illegal for nonwhite students to attend white universities such as the University of Cape Town (UCT). Second, it gave the government control of the University of Fort Hare—the Africans-only, mission-run university at which leaders such as Robert Sobukwe and Nelson Mandela had been educated—and reserved it for Xhosa–speakers. And third, the act established four ethnically divided universities, in keeping with its policy of "separate development" both between white and black and within the nonwhite community: the University of the North (Turfloop) for those speaking Sotho-Tswana and other Transvaal languages, the University of Zululand for Zulus, the University of Durban–Westville for Indians, and the University of the Western Cape for Coloureds.[5] Finally, the act increased government control over education by empowering the state to set the university curricula and the minister of Bantu administration to appoint administrators. True to its name in some sense, the act did increase especially African enrollment in universities: from 811 in 1961 to 4,601 in 1970.[6]

Yet whites still dominated the student scene. The 4,600 African students plus about 4,000 Coloureds and Indians were but a fraction of the 46,000 white students spread among the English- and Afrikaans-speaking universities. Moreover, even though the number of white students represented only a very small percentage of South Africa's 3.7 million whites, inclusive nonwhite numbers were an infinitesimal one-third of 1 percent of the total nonwhite population of over 18 million.[7] Given these demographics, many black tertiary students joined the National Union of South African Students, just as many black political leaders joined the Liberal Party. This organization's liberal credentials were well established. NUSAS's leadership aspired to political influence and courted the government's displeasure (and sometimes repression) by organizing protests for academic freedom and inviting politically conscious speakers to South Africa. (For instance, New York senator Robert F. Kennedy visited South Africa at NUSAS's invitation.)[8]

Despite these liberal pretenses, however, NUSAS's leadership reflected the realities of South Africa's student population. The NUSAS executive remained white during the 1960s—only twelve nonwhites served on the NUSAS board through 1967, compared to fifty-four whites, and only whites had served as the organization's president or vice president. Although it reflected the demographics of the universities, the racial makeup of NUSAS was politically problematic for an organization that was among the most overt opponents to the state and claimed a mandate not only from the schools, where whites were in the majority, but also from the general population, where they most decidedly were not.[9] This situation created conflicts once black students discovered their voice.

The tenor of that voice, however, was in question. Apartheid put students and other aspirant intellectuals in a bind. Consider the aforementioned Can Themba. Themba reputedly boasted that he knew no African language, and in his writing, he flourished his mastery of English like a rapier. One might doubt the former claim, but the intent is telling. The "African Bourgeoisie" was well established by the 1950s.[10] These individuals were the descendants of nineteenth-century converts—teachers, ministers, lawyers, and clerks, many of them university educated, and testaments, in a sense, to the oft-ridiculed British "civilizing mission." Apartheid fell on them with a particular harshness. Denied citizenship in the modern state, they were instead categorized as "natives," "Bantus," or "nonwhites." Like the rest of African society, they were to be denied visions of the "the green pastures of European society in which [the native] is not allowed to graze."[11] To compound matters, people such as Themba and Modisane fared little better in subaltern discourse, where their urban manners, English language, and aspirations marked them as "situations," condemned to be forever out of place. As Themba lamented when he stood on the cusp of exile and was faced with Sophiatown's destruction, intractable political conflict, and no hope for the future, "The dilemma is so complete! . . . What can I do?"[12] For students forced to train at "bush colleges" and seemingly destined to staff Bantustan bureaucracies, the dilemma was complete indeed.[13] Given this state of affairs, it was not surprising that writers such as Modisane and Themba—particularly the former—obsessively chronicled their own emasculation and infantilization under the apartheid system.[14] They formed their senses of self through their legal and material circumstances, as the law's classification of, and control over, their bodies was accompanied by frustration, hopelessness, and ultimately submission, whether to alcohol (in Themba's case) or flight to an uneasy exile (for Modisane).

By the late 1960s, however, a new generation of black thinkers had learned from their elders' missteps and insisted that their minds would not be classified, nor their bodies labeled. In the 1950s, Modisane had only halfheartedly participated in protests; they offered no more than a momentary release, he reflected, before the overwhelming sense of futility returned. Black Consciousness inverted this; rebellion in fact and in theory would not feel futile because it was an essential and internal part of an individual's sense of self. By thinking of themselves in new ways, students argued that they could create something new: they would no longer be bodies to submit and be controlled but subjects conscious of, and with faith in, themselves as beings who would rebel.[15]

Before considering where student thought ended up, we must first consider what black students took with them to the university. Like students everywhere, they arrived at their segregated universities with more than books and trunks of clothes. Unlike students elsewhere, however, their "internal baggage" comprised familial memories of protests and experiences of apartheid, traditions of resistance and acquiescence, conflicted feelings about attending government-run schools, and the pressures and responsibilities of being among the first in their communities to receive a tertiary education.

The students of 1968 were high schoolers or younger when the ANC and PAC were banned. Many were too young to remember the political struggles that accompanied the early years of separate development and had grown up in a world where apartheid and its cognates—forced removals, Bantu Education, job reservation—were simple facts. In their memories, the silence that attended their high school years was deafening. They recalled the years after Sharpeville as a "lull," "a time of silence," a period "of profound astonishment" in which *politics* was a dirty word and people "bottled it all in" for fear of banning, imprisonment, or worse.[16] The imprisonment and exile of ANC and PAC leaders left the black population with a "political vacuum," which remained unfilled. "People were waiting for leaders to emerge," Fanyana Mazibuko remembered, but few were willing to risk the consequences that politics entailed.[17]

Even if not explicitly discussed, apartheid politics structured students' lives in ways both obvious and subtle. Future activist Nkwenkwe Nkomo's run-ins with the system stretched from his childhood in the late 1950s, when, clutching a bag of chips, he wandered into a whites-only park in the East Rand town of Benoni while his father picked up supplies for his employer. Perhaps more remarkable than the signs reading "whites only" (which he did not understand) was the specter of a fellow African—a municipal employee—quickly stepping to block his path to the open swing set.[18] At the age of five, he could affirm another activist's assertion that "apartheid . . . was a political system that you could not ignore."[19]

For Saths Cooper, the system's impact was more subtle but equally telling. At the Indian community-organized schools in Durban, the quality of education was often high, for job reservation laws meant that the best and brightest of his parents' peers could do little other than teach. Students thus benefited "from frustrated physicians, frustrated nuclear physicists," and the like who had become teachers. However, the cost of their frustrations was painfully evident. Bottled aspirations led to obvious and frequent alcohol abuse, codified in the community's cliché that one "drank like a teacher." Images of drunk, frustrated physicians in the classroom, though not as blatant as a placard and municipal employee conspiring to reserve swing sets for whites, could nonetheless mark a mind.[20]

Despite apartheid's limitations, families and communities continued to place their hopes in education. Steve Biko attended both the Catholic Church's Mariannhill school and the University of Natal Non-European Medical School (UNNE) with the support of funds raised by his community in King William's Town's Ginsberg township. (That their funds earned him fame but not a degree was duly noted by his neighbors.)[21] More commonly, degrees translated into respect and even a modicum of fame. Johannesburg's *World* newspaper gave the University of the North's annual commencement ceremony a two-page spread, complete with pictures of the graduates and lists of every student who received a degree. Political leaders were commonly known by their academic achievements: young Sobukwe devotees hailed him simply as "Prof" for his teaching days at the University of the Witwatersrand, and the *World's* readers followed the fortunes of "Zululand's erudite leader," Gatsha Buthelezi.[22]

Given their prominence, most students were pressured to keep their studies apart from their politics. Buthelezi may have been erudite, but in fact he had been expelled from Fort Hare for political activities; by the 1960s, South Africa's prisons were filled with former students turned expellees turned politicians. As Africans' enrollment at segregated universities expanded during the 1960s, many relied on scholarships from governmental and other sources, some of which stipulated that "the students agree to keep well out of politics."[23] Many parents had similar expectations. After SASO was founded in 1968, for example, many of its early fund-raising efforts were interspersed with requests to financially support students such as Fikile Jolobe, formerly of the Natal Medical School, now that "his family [will] have nothing to do with him."[24] Thandisizwe Mazibuko, another former student at the medical school, witnessed his father blame himself for having decided to name his son "love the nation"; the elder Mazibuko was a teacher who aspired only to further his son's chances in life. "He couldn't take it" when his son was expelled, Thandisizwe recollected, and it took him years to forgive his son.[25]

In some respects, however, schooling had always been political. Following the advent of Bantu Education, the simple decision to support a child's further education was a political choice for parents. For some, the government's intrusion into the education system and its manipulated expectations meant seeking solutions beyond Bantu Education's reach. Thus, Chris Mzoneli's family shipped him off to Swaziland where he could continue his mission education unabated, just as Mbulelo Mzamane's father did with his son—the father himself was a veteran of the Sophiatown struggles. But such decisions often cost more than familial separation. While a lecturer at the interdenominational Federal Theological Seminary (or Fed Sem), for example, Desmond Tutu was denied the principal's position in part due to concerns that his logging "more than 9000 miles a year" in transporting his children between Alice and Swaziland was already too great of a strain.[26]

The future leadership of SASO was stocked with graduates of the country's shrinking array of mission schools, individuals who had "voted with their feet" to avoid apartheid education and demonstrated the politically conscious backgrounds from which student leaders emerged. Those parents with the means to do so tried to circumvent the system as best they could. Steve Biko attended first the Church of Scotland's Lovedale College and then the Catholic Church's Mariannhill institution with support from the local community. Others, including Malusi Mpumlwana, a future colleague of Biko's at UNNE, attended St. John's, an Anglican school in the Transkei. Malusi's future wife, Thoko Mbanjwa, was sent by her father—a Congregationalist priest—to the American Board's Inanda Seminary near Durban. Other examples abound, from the aforementioned Thandisizwe Mazibuko, who overlapped with Biko at Mariannhill, to Barney Pityana, who had earlier studied with Biko at Lovedale.

No matter what sort of school they attended, many remembered it as a politicizing place. Nkwenkwe Nkomo's uncles taught him to work to protest the Republic of South Africa's advent on 31 May 1961.[27] "The government . . . gave us little flags at school to celebrate the Republic and some medallions, the kind of things that we could pin on and stuff like that. And my job," he said, "was to take the flags and burn them and get these medallions and throw them into the storm water drains." The same day burned itself into twelve-year-old Thandisizwe Mazibuko's consciousness as well because "authorities [at his school] had given medals in commemoration of 1961. We had the medals and they were given to all the schools kids and the flags [and] . . . on that 31st of May we had to sing the [apartheid national anthem] Die Stem." He and his classmates were small and "we didn't know anything," but his teachers and principal refused the command. The latter "just threw [the flags] away, dumped them somewhere and we were never given the flag . . . there was excitement in town and we were wondering why we are not given these [flags] and it didn't make any sense to us. But later we began to understand what was happening."[28] Thus, even though 31 May 1961 was fast becoming "holy" as a symbol of the ascendant Afrikaner nation, Mazibuko and Nkomo's elders demonstrated that an alternative analysis was possible.[29]

Such open displays of politics were rare, however, and widespread paranoia encouraged less overt political "training." Throughout the sixties, teachers used what Cooper called "laconic exclamations"—well-chosen words whose meaning some students were able to follow.[30] For students in missionary schools, critique was born from teachers' instructions to question received wisdom, whether from teachers, society, or the Bible. Future theologian Bonganjalo Goba's teachers imparted politics through the exegetical setting: "It was in these bible studies where you could begin to ask questions," he recalled, "[a missionary] would simply say, it was not by God's design that you should be sitting in this [segregated school], it is man's making, it is a sinful situation." By encouraging students to ask questions of the Bible, missionaries gave Christianity a politically cutting edge. "When you began to engage the scriptures, you could then begin to see a real contradiction between what was being said in the scriptures and what was happening in the world," he remembered. Critical reading led to critical consciousness, and students at mission schools thus gained perspective beyond the apolitical education their parents sought.[31]

Teachers in government schools also found ways to engage their students politically. Tshenuwani Simon Farisani said a teacher in his state-run school in Venda called apartheid Satan and objected especially to how the devil clipped students' aspirations. "Shall we all be teachers and nurses and clerks and labourers?" he asked, "I want my boys to fly in the air!"[32] Tau Mokoka recalled less lyrical but nonetheless critical sentiments from his high school teachers in Mamelodi, near Pretoria. His history teacher, for example, pointed out that Afrikaners wrote the textbooks and that not one had anything positive to say about Africans. Tau also remembered his principal reporting upon returning from a trip, "If you want to know that your room stinks, go out and come back." Tau laughed when he told me this. Although many students were mystified by the principal's comments or chose to ignore their history teacher, he said, "those that listened very well . . . got the message."[33]

As with their parents' decisions surrounding government schools, students' political consciousness faced the challenge of deciding whether to attend government-controlled universities.[34] Barney Pityana attended the highly politicized Lovedale preparatory school; while there, he noted Fort Hare's failed efforts to remain independent of government control. Pityana was expelled from Lovedale for his political activities and ended up finishing high school at a township school outside Port Elizabeth. Upon reaching matric, however, he chose not to seek further education. His parents' hopes for his education had been irrevocably dirtied by the government's control over the universities, he reasoned. Students at Fort Hare had recognized this as early as 1960, a year after the government took control of their university when they had dissolved the Student Representative Council rather than sanction the government's involvement.[35] Seeing this, Pityana decided not to attend Fort Hare in the first place.

Similarly, community activist Mogobe Ramose's politics propelled him to take classes at the nonresidential and thus ostensibly unsegregated University of South Africa (UNISA) rather than submit to segregated education. "I have no reason to condone what is created for me without prior consultation with me," he explained. Such iconoclasm could work the other way as well. The remnants of the Congress Alliance urged Indians in Durban to refuse to attend the segregated University of Durban–Westville, but just as Ramose sought independence from the regime, cultural activist Strini Moodley rejected instructions from banned groups whose politics had failed to stop apartheid and went to school anyway, citing the need to define his own perspective.[36]

What students took with them to their universities mattered. Whether guided by political principles, whether choosing to stay at home or leave to attend an inferior university, Pityana, Ramose, and Moodley demonstrated in their accounts how individuals grappled with the implications of their choices in those defining moments.[37] Years later, a group of parents protested their children's expulsion from the University of the North. Their children were politicized, the parents conceded, but it was the system's fault, since "the students at this University are Apartheid Babies—born, sucked and fed on apartheid. They know no other feed, no other upbringing, no other life."[38] Their lifetimes had coincided with separate development, Bantu Education, and the destruction of Sophiatown. These were the circumstances that shaped future activists, their aspirations and experiences, their political consciousness, and their willingness to question and challenge the nature of their world. Their parents, families, and communities—and the laws under which they lived—helped them to pack more than their trunks. Sophiatown had fallen and men such as Modisane and Themba had fled, yet the quest to define oneself remained. At the university, this quest intensified and grew heated, as black students found their ostensibly segregated world still dominated by whites.

2 ∽ "Black man, you are on your own!"

Black Students, White Liberals, and Adulthood

BY 1968, black students' displeasure with white dominance of student politics led first to blacks-only meetings, and then to the creation of the exclusively black student organization SASO. Years later, John Sebidi, a Catholic priest and SASO supporter, described that organization's founding as "a hefty attempt at severing . . . the 'psychological umbilical cord' that held the black man to the slow-moving liberal band-wagon."[1] All told, this severing took about a year, starting with a blacks-only caucus in 1968 and culminating with the inauguration of the new organization, with Steve Biko as its first president, in 1969. Many of the people discussed in chapter 1 participated in this process, and many more were attracted not only to the political theater of rejecting white liberals but also to later iterations of what that meant.[2] After all, Sebidi's image does more than sketch a political transition; it speaks of a transformation that was both a birth and about being an adult, being able to stand on one's own and reject infantilization at the hands of whites. In this chapter, I consider the break with white liberals and then explore the intellectual implications of the SASO slogan, coined by Barney Pityana, that gives this chapter its title.

NO MORE TEA PARTIES

In May 1968, NUSAS called a meeting to respond to racial tensions between the University of Natal's Pietermaritzburg and Non-European campuses. At that meeting, UNNE representative Steve Biko was among NUSAS's most vocal supporters. He rose in support of a resolution to disaffiliate from the whites-only Pietermaritzburg campus on the grounds that the latter's decision to host a racially exclusive graduation was in violation of "the basic principal of the National Union which . . . [is] non-racialism."[3] Biko represented black students—nonwhites in the parlance of the time—whose numbers could not dent whites' dominance over student affairs. At this meeting, they clung to the status quo of 1960s opposition politics. Faced with racialism, a rejection of the liberal's multiracial ideal, Biko and his SRC pledged "to continue to work relentlessly for the realisation . . . of the principles for which the National Union stands." It was, Saths Cooper later put it, testament to the "single common characteristic amongst both black and white student leaders of the time . . . the rejection of racism and the common fear of being branded as racist." To be politically legitimate meant being "colourless."[4]

Yet "colourlessness" had its problems. Black students made up an increasingly large proportion of the national student body, but NUSAS remained, in Craig Charney's evocative phrase, a "black body with a white brain." Its white leaders supported worthy causes, "ideas such as academic freedom, the rule of law, human rights as contained in the UN Charter, etc.," but their claims to speak on behalf of the disenfranchised majority were more problematic.[5] This situation could not stand—especially at the end of the 1960s, the decade of African independence, which, despite setbacks in southern Africa, had seen the emergence of strong, self-possessed leaders across the continent. Nyerere, Nkrumah, Kenneth Kaunda, and others—all of their ideas were available; there was "a whole host of heroes we identified with," Biko remembered.[6] These were leaders of independent countries, self-confident men who did not just parrot the UN Charter but actually controlled seats in the UN General Assembly. If they had cut off the far thicker colonial umbilical cord, surely nonwhite South African students could do the same.

The white leaders who had supported the UNNE's protest against racialism were predictably appalled by blacks students' decision just a few months later to meet without them. After Duncan Innes, NUSAS's president, protested to Biko, the latter responded gently, stating only that NUSAS had "neglected" nonwhite centers and that nonwhites wanted a place to talk in private. He went on to assure Innes that the meeting was in no way a rejection of "the healthy and liberal ideas that [have] been made by student leaders in this country."[7] Indeed, SASO's early communiqués seemed to apologize for the organization's existence. "SASO is *not* a national union and has never claimed to be one," Biko wrote in December 1969; it offered "no competition" to NUSAS. Instead, the nascent organization claimed only the desire "to make the nonwhite students accepted on their own terms as an integral part of the South African student community." Their methods might appear strange—after all, multiracial contact was fundamental to liberal South Africa's agenda—but on the surface at least, it seemed that integration was still the goal.[8]

Yet even though SASO's language appeared conciliatory, with its nod toward one undivided "South African student community," some black students were beginning to question whether they and their white colleagues had the same aspirations. Multiracial student meetings grew increasingly polarized throughout 1969. That year, conflicts surfaced at NUSAS meetings and at meetings of the multiracial and ecumenical University Christian Movement (to which many SASO and NUSAS members belonged). There was a fundamental conflict of interest, the UCM secretary reported: "It seems that the white students within the UCM are primarily in search of a theological identity, . . . [whereas] the non-whites in UCM, more particularly the African group, feel a greater need for political identity." Part 2 of this book addresses the question of theological identity; here, we note the changing context for student group discussions. Black students were in search of a political identity, and many soon concluded that the rejection of multiracialism was the most "pragmatic" way to realize that goal.[9]

The UCM was the critical context for this shift. It was at the UCM's meeting in 1968 that nonwhite students first decided to form their own organization, a fact noted by UCM's general secretary, Colin Collins, who claimed that UCM consciously "founded" SASO.[10] This move was an abrupt departure from the UCM's own roots, as an organization founded to promote "race relations, not race separations," but after 1968, "polarisation" between black and white became the rule.[11] Collins's successor, Chris Mokoditoa, put it this way: "We started polarizing, saying that you have different tastes, we have different tastes, we have different objectives." A politics of fundamental difference entered the multiracial UCM, as it had NUSAS. There was no longer one student body but different bodies working on different levels. "We want[ed] liberation of the black person," Mokoditoa continued, and whites "wanted academic freedom, liberation of the schools."[12] It came down to a difference of perspective.

As Barney Pityana explained, his ANC-aligned student group at Lovedale had set a precedent. There, high school students saw no divide between their student and activist identities; for them, there was one "agenda for liberation . . . and we saw ourselves as part of that." For blacks, the need for a political identity was paramount, and now this attitude had spread to the tertiary institutions that sent representatives to NUSAS congresses. "NUSAS . . . wanted . . . to champion what they called purely student issues and concerns and we were saying that's not possible," Mokoditoa recalled. Rather, "our view was that . . . [although] we are operating from a student base, . . . black students . . . can never separate themselves from what society was demanding outside." Blacks did not have the luxury of distinguishing between their student and political selves—the law made this impossible. For Pityana, Mokoditoa, and others, these different perspectives doomed multiracial solidarity.[13] Stanley Ntwasa, a SASO delegate and future UCM leader from the Federal Theological Seminary, put it best: "When Black meets Black, . . . they know they have so much in common." There could be no such assurance when black met white.[14]

During its early years, SASO used this insight to develop a cogent critique of liberalism and propose a new paradigm for student—and black—politics. The first step was to reject liberalism. Whites were different, SASO activists argued, and even the best among them viewed blacks patronizingly, as charity cases. "The white liberals always knew what was good for the blacks and told them so," Biko wrote in 1970. Multiracial relationships in NUSAS and elsewhere were not between equivalent human beings but between token blacks and guilty white consciences in search of succor.[15] Biko sharply criticized "tea parties" at which black students were paraded around like trophies—"the more tea-parties one calls the more of a liberal he is and the freer he shall feel from . . . guilt." These sorts of relationships did not benefit blacks: they were for and about whites and for and about whites' feelings, so that when white liberals voted for opposition parties, they could feel "that [they are] not like the . . . the others." Liberals were able to escape from apartheid—their tea parties helped them forget the "eye sore spoiling an otherwise beautiful view." Like Ntwasa, Biko argued that this marked an insurmountable wall between black and white. White liberals could retreat to backyard tea parties to forget apartheid race relations; blacks were "unable to escape."[16]

Other student leaders took Biko's critique further. For Harry Nengwekhulu, liberal groups such as NUSAS not only were misguided but also were the "most dangerous organisations that you can ever come across in South Africa," all the more so because they claimed to be morally superior than the less conflicted Broederbond or National Party. "We don't recognise them, we've got no respect for them," he asserted.[17] Liberal whites saw the black community as a charity, and as another speaker at a SASO rally contended, "we regard [that] as an insult to our dignity."[18] White students were particularly guilty of dabbling in black oppression: "They [were] not seriously looking for radical change," Malusi Mpumlwana explained. "They [were] just experiencing an opportunity to be different," to play radical before graduating and being "absorbed into their fathers' businesses."[19]

SASO's criticism of liberals was a particularly potent issue in 1970, when Helen Suzman's Progressive Party sought to pick up more seats in the whites-only Parliament. Liberal media, including the *Rand Daily Mail*, followed the party's progress with glee. The "Progs" gained a few seats—at the expense of the opposition United Party and the larger-than-ever National Party majorities—and won banner headlines such as "TRIUMPH!" and "IT'S A PROGRESSIVE KNOCK-OUT!"[20] The black liberal media's response was much the same. The *World*, the paper with the largest black readership, was edited by M. T. Moerane, "a gentle old black liberal" who had been a member of Alan

Paton's recently defunct Liberal Party.[21] This paper celebrated the Progressives' electoral fortunes, declaring that any "swing from the Nats means hope for us."[22] Moerane's faith in liberals was bolstered when "more whites than ever" voted Progressive—even though the Nationalists swept the country. A cartoon summed up this perspective well. In it, Jojo—"the most popular man in the townships"—stood off to the side waving a "Helen" pennant while a group of jubilant (white and whiskered) Progressive Party supporters marched with Suzman on their shoulders. Jojo told his readers that his only regret was "that I could not have voted for Helen too."[23]

Such sentiments proved SASO's point. Electoral politics were an arena in which the "white brain" lorded over "black bodies," just as happened in NUSAS. Jojo stood off to the side, on the "touchlines" in South African parlance. Biko rejected this state of affairs and retorted that "blacks are tired of standing at the touchlines to witness a game that they should be playing."[24] They would rather ignore the game altogether.[25] To Biko, the Progressives were irrelevant; they were only the latest in a long line of whites who had sought to control black aspirations. Just as blacks founded the PAC at the end of the 1950s in order "to be their own guardians," so too did SASO strive to wean students from the liberal teat.[26] For too long, activist Bennie Khoapa argued, liberals had "hood-winked" the black population. He contended that like the Congress of Democrats who had stolen the Freedom Charter, NUSAS and the Progressives had now stolen the political agenda.[27] Instead, in the late 1960s, the time had come for blacks to "do things for themselves and all by themselves."[28]

Many liberals—both white and black—responded with alarm. "This exclusivity indicates what an evil and late hour it is for South Africa in its race relations!" warned *Pro Veritate*, the Christian Institute's ecumenical journal.[29] M. Radebe, an avid contributor to the *World*'s letters page, concurred. The black man's only hope was in a "united front" with white "moderates," he argued; "anti-white liberal Africans" were only adding more fuel to the "fierce flame" of racial hatred in the country.[30] SASO's emergence upset the consensus that opposition to apartheid was only legitimate when "diverse," and many worried that SASO was playing into the government's hands. In March 1969, white NUSAS members at the University of Natal tried to attend a UNNE Student Representative Council meeting, only to be booed out with hoots, catcalls, and sarcastic cries of "Hello baas" and "Hello missus." Liberal whites needed "to confront their racialism," the local NUSAS chairman declared.[31] The government was gleeful, and state-funded Radio Zulu went so far as to hail SASO for furthering separate development. The state's approval put the final stamp on what Neville Curtis, a NUSAS leader, called SASO "racism." What did SASO want liberals to do? asked former Liberal Party leader Alan Paton—"Emigrate? Join the National Party?"[32]

The answer to Paton's question was, more or less, nothing. Although some SASO leaders suggested that whites should concentrate on their own communities, most simply declared liberals' actions to be of little consequence. Liberal politics had gotten nowhere because the liberals' analysis was wrong. Biko explained this through a new understanding of the dialectics of political progress. For liberals, he argued, the thesis was apartheid, the antithesis multiracialism, and the synthesis "very feebly defined." But for SASO, South Africa's problem was more fundamental than the racial system. The thesis was worse than state-imposed segregation; instead, it was "white racism and therefore the *antithesis* [must] be a strong solidarity amongst the blacks on whom this white racism seeks to prey."[33] Only then might the synthesis of truly nonracial society emerge. Some whites, among them Peter Randall—a former employee of the paradigmatically liberal South African Institute of Race Relations (SAIRR)— took this analysis at its word. He admitted finding this new antiliberalism "scary" because it "threatened much of what I believed in. But I did hope [that] the separation . . . [was] a temporary phenomenon until we can all get together in a non-racial society."[34] If, as Biko and others argued, racism meant the will to dominate, blacks could not be racist—instead, they were countering racism and opening a space for a more humanistic, nonracial society.

At the close of the 1960s, SASO gained momentum, and polarization became the order of the day. Whereas in 1968, Biko had assured NUSAS of his support and noted that SASO offered no competition to the multiracial body, by 1970, SASO withdrew its recognition of NUSAS. After what the *World* called secret meetings with SASO leadership—including "Steve Diko"—NUSAS "abandoned [its] claim to represent Africans."[35] A year later, SASO's president informed his NUSAS counterpart that he could have nothing to do with him, since any cooperation between the organizations "would . . . adversely affect Saso."[36] Antiliberalism spread beyond student circles. At their 1970 conference, some ministers of the African but liberal Interdenominational African Ministries' Association of Southern Africa, or IDAMASA (which had long preached "racial tolerance among all racial groups"), began to preach black solidarity against whites, a development the general secretary of the multiracial South African Council of Churches (SACC) noted with concern.[37]

By 1970, SASO's past president "Diko" was indifferent to the student organization he once championed. NUSAS could "take what policy it likes on SASO," he said, "whatever you do won't hurt us."[38] If only blacks could understand blacks and if only black solidarity could effectively counter white racism and move toward a synthesis, then liberalism was truly dead and its remnants merely shadows. In SASO's opinion, NUSAS, the Progressives, and tea party liberals were illegitimate products of white racism, complicit in apartheid and unworthy of attention. By 1970, SASO had completed its break with liberalism.

Biko's dialectics showed a new way forward. "We wanted a totally new reality in South Africa," Malusi Mpumlwana suggested, one created by blacks.

Yet in many ways, their critique of liberalism was beholden to the politics of the mid-1960s. It still revolved around whites and focused on the appropriate strategies with which to confront the racial state. But students keenly felt the need to go further. If the political struggle was going to begin again, it could not merely re-tread old paths. The desire for a new reality demanded that activists rethink the nature of politicized lives.[39]

BLACK MEN, BLACK WOMEN

SASO's decision to separate from NUSAS had not come, activists claimed, without "deep thinking and . . . thorough analysis."[40] Reflection and intellectual exercise were central to SASO's evolving program and organizational ethos: "Man has always been a storehouse for ideas and innovations to make the world he lives in a betterplace [*sic*] for himself. In the face of apparently insurmountable problems, man seeks to conquer by working out ingenious schemes designed to get him out of the doldrums."[41] With the emergence of SASO, it was now time for "we as a people . . . to indulge unhindered on self-reflection, on self-definition."[42] A speaker at SASO's 1971 General Students' Council (GSC) warned delegates that "nothing is more dangerous to a country than uncriticised ideas [and] dogma which must not be disputed" — apartheid was dogmatic, as was liberalism.[43] Recognizing this, SASO held "formation schools" in which it reviewed the past and sought innovative responses to the present. Activists published thought pieces of lesser and greater sophistication, and above all, they engaged South Africa's identity politics in the search for a new approach to the obvious problems of black life in South Africa.

This effort began with a basic assumption: that blacks were men. In a paper published in 1972, SASO president Barney Pityana repeatedly called for "the Black man [to] realize that he is on his own"[44] — *man, he, his.* By forming SASO, Pityana indicated that student activists had opened a space to be men. Indeed, even a cursory glance through SASO records demonstrates that "manhood" was perhaps the most basic element of nonwhite student identity. "Man" used ideas to make "his" world a better place for "himself." Thought helped "him" plot a way out. Gendered language was fundamental to SASO's conception of its project, both in what it struggled against and what it hoped to be.

Activists argued that apartheid did more than merely oppress blacks; South Africa had long done that. Apartheid law was more insidious. Blacks had been oppressed under the Union government, Biko wrote, "but they were still men."[45] Now, in the years since apartheid's advent, the black individual had become a mere "shell, a shadow of a man."[46] The state constrained black students' possibilities, another activist wrote, and left students "hemmed in and castrated. In fact they feel that they are . . . eunuchs."[47] As long as apartheid persisted, so too did the specter of castration. Take, for example, reactions to the 1972 banning of former UCM traveling secretary Stanley Ntwasa. "Politically 'Stan' is no more," the SASO *Newsletter* mourned: "A black brother has joined the swelling ranks of Black political enuchs [*sic*]."[48] This worked the other way as well. Opponents to apartheid, such as "Anti-UBC [Urban Bantu Council]" who wrote to the *World* from Dube, mocked Africans who collaborated with the system as "castrated men" who "have lost their manhood."[49] Possession of the male sexual member was political shorthand. If you were oppressed and did nothing, you never had it; if you were banned, you had lost it; if you collaborated, presumably you did not deserve it in the first place.

As the scholar Cynthia Enloe noted, "Nationalisms have 'typically sprung from masculinized memory, masculinized humiliation and masculinized hope.'"[50] Manhood anxieties plagued oppressed black communities—and often prompted male activists to seek out power in the only place available, namely, their relations with black women.[51] Indeed, SASO demonstrated these tendencies in its earliest days. On page seven of the inaugural edition of the SASO *Newsletter*, activists published a short, biting piece entitled "The Chemical Analysis of a Woman," sandwiched between a discussion of racial polarization and a tour of SASO's member campuses. The tone was set at the outset: the element's "atomic wt.: accepted at 120, though known isotopes vary from 100 to 180." (This reflected South Africa's then ongoing transition to the metric system.) The so-called element's "physical properties" were volatile: "[It] boils at nothing. Freezes without reason . . . all varieties melt with proper treatment . . . [it] exhibits magnetic properties especially in the presence of noble metals," for example, diamonds and gold. What is more, an element's "uses" were "chiefly ornamental," and it was "seldom found in places requiring mental exertion like lecture theatres, parliamentary buildings, etc."[52]

The relationship between male feelings of emasculation and a concomitant ill treatment of women is an old trope in South Africa. Bloke Modisane's memoir, for instance, makes this explicit. Images of emasculation pepper the book. Apartheid "castrates," Modisane wrote, and he responded by sleeping with every available woman, so that "perhaps one day I might earn the respect and admiration of at least one man." The hierarchy here is clear: although the white state denied the black male member, women allowed Modisane, through sexual conquest, to prove "myself to myself." It is no wonder that one critic suggested Modisane's *Blame Me on History* might just as well have been named "Blame Me on Masculinity."[53]

As the "Chemical Analysis" satire indicates, despite their determination not to replicate the intellectual failings of their predecessors, SASO leaders too had lapsed into tired tropes. Female students had been among the earliest members of SASO; they had participated in the deliberations that led black students to separate from NUSAS in 1968; they studied, collaborated, and debated with similarly minded men who, in other contexts, repeatedly stated their faith that intellectual activity would overcome the morass of apartheid politics. Yet here, women were mocked as creatures of instinct incapable of "mental exertion." Not surprisingly, the gender politics of Black Consciousness were a frequent subject in memoirs from the era as well, most prominently that of Mamphela Ramphele. Black Consciousness was a male-dominated environment, she recalled, and a woman had no choice but to rely on "aggression" and "intimidation" to offer her opinion: "As a woman, an African woman at that, one had to be outrageous to be heard, let alone taken seriously."[54]

Some have been willing to forgive SASO's lapses. To cite one example, in their introduction to a recent edition of Biko's writings, Malusi and Thoko Mpumlwana contended that the student leader's exclusive use of male pronouns revealed only that he was "a product of his time."[55] Rather than judge with history's sharp glare, these writers protested, we ought instead to read in a silent *and woman* (or the inclusive *people*) appended to *black man.* "Unequivocally, Biko was a product of his time," Julian Kunnie wrote. "Had he lived today, I am convinced that he would be deeply sensitive to the question of the oppression of women, the cornerstone of all revolutionary movements."[56] Other recent defenses have taken this notion further. Former Black Consciousness activist and later woman's rights activist Oshadi Mangena has argued that Black Consciousness is wrongly included in the rogues' gallery of black nationalist organizations with bad gender politics. She has insisted that Black Consciousness ought instead to be celebrated, as women played a prominent role at SASO's founding. She pointed to the election of Winnie Kgware, a woman, as the first president of SASO's affiliated Black Peoples Convention in 1972—making the Black Consciousness generation the first to boast a multigendered organization with a female president.[57] And if Black Consciousness did lack a fully articulated gender analysis in spite of this, so be it. The times had called for black South Africans to focus their attention on the political problem of race above all. Black women knew this, and as Asha Rambally, another former activist, has contended, they made "a strategic choice" to shelve specifically female concerns "in the face of opposition from a seemingly invincible white national–party state that was quick to exploit any sign of division in order to subjugate Black people even further."[58] The political problem of liberation—from racism, from liberalism—came first.

These justifications, especially the idea that SASO discourse was a product of its moment, obscure the choices that had been available to activists at the time. All sorts of intellectual currents washed over South Africa during the late 1960s and early 1970s, and among these was the gathering force of international feminism. The UCM, which had incubated SASO, was an enthusiastic proponent. Beginning in 1970, UCM conferences referenced ongoing debates about women's liberation alongside the group's well-established concerns about race relations and religious transformation. By 1971, sentiments such as "black liberation includes women's liberation or it will not be liberation at all" were common, and the annual UCM conference at Camp Jonathan in Natal made feminism a central concern.[59] There, activists discussed new trends in global thought on gender; they performed short, guerrilla-style theater pieces illustrating the various levels of oppression faced by women; and, most prominently, they devoted their Sunday worship—a centerpiece of UCM conferences—to publicly confessing that male oppression of women was equal to white oppression of blacks.

This worship was a remarkable statement of feminist consciousness, especially as it came at a conference attended by both white and black South Africans, including many SASO members. Entitled "Freedom Is More" and written by UCM theology director Basil Moore, the worship was in the form of a play with three parts—the first entitled "An Israelite in Egypt," the second "A Black in South Africa," and the third "A Woman in Society." Each character took a turn delivering a monologue to the audience, and as the play unfolded, each endured a dehumanizing experience at the hands of an oppressive authority figure—respectively, a slave master, a white police officer, and a husband. The details of these experiences mattered less than what they revealed—that, in the woman's words, an Israelite in Egypt, a black in South Africa, or a woman in society was not human but "an object. A role. A machine. A non-person."[60] Moreover, Moore seemed to cast women's concerns as more fundamental than those of either Old Testament Israelites or modern-day black South Africans. After all, the latter two groups' oppression came in the context of a particular, limited historical experience, but the site of women's oppression was at once timeless—society in no particular time or place—and universal—the commonplace of domestic life. In this worship, she had the last word, all the more resonant for being unexpected. As we shall see, the radical strand of the Christian South African community was well prepared to relate Exodus to apartheid, but to have a woman declare, along with her counterparts, "I have a name. It is important to me. You will hear it, know it, feel it" was something new.[61] Here, UCM activists were trying to make change bigger than South Africa, to propose that human liberation involved transformations more fundamental than those related to local history and politics.

But this was a controversial idea. Indeed, as Rubin Phillip, a former UCM activist and SASO vice president remembered, feminism was seen as too universal at a time when the particular—represented by the middle character, the black man in South Africa—was considered a much more pressing concern.[62] Almost immediately, South Africa's dominant narrative reasserted itself; Freedom '71 was the UCM's last conference in part because of increased government repression and in part because SASO's emergence cast ever larger shadows over the multiracial mood. Reports suggest that Freedom '71's breakout sessions and discussions were racially polarized, just as they had been since SASO's founding. Only days after Moore proposed that one organization might address all of these concerns, the UCM decided the time of the unified movement was over, and it resolved instead to become a "federation of concerns and projects," namely, Black Theology, white consciousness, and women's liberation.[63]

Black student activists largely did not share Moore's sense that women's liberation was either as pressing or as fundamental as black liberation, nor did they believe it was equivalent to it. "We must appreciate that we are Black first and then women," a speaker at a SASO meeting asserted only months after Freedom '71.[64] Black men agreed. As Dan Mogale, a former activist in SASO's Pretoria branch told me, "the orientation and the context [of the struggle] has got to be correct." Feminism and women's liberation might be laudable in some contexts, but South Africa could "not be just . . . like any other feminist movement, feminist in the very European perspective because we were . . . in Africa . . . we are not saying women's issues are not actually important to us but we want to say they cannot be brought in the same way they are understood in the European context."[65]

Given the UCM's calls for feminist awareness, the divergent paths taken after the 1971 conference suggest that instead of being unquestioned, "context" was a choice that SASO activists made. As the UCM yielded to SASO, black activists opted for a "monist" approach to politics, which "prioritize[d] one form of discrimination over others."[66] Indeed, as former activist Deborah Matshoba revealed in a recent interview, the stakes of the choice had been discussed and explicit. She recounted that when she and other female SASO members proposed to found a women's student organization, which would affiliate with SASO, the latter organization's (male) leadership cautioned that to do so would be to divide the opposition. "If you are a WSO, you are not SASO," Biko contended, and both organizations would be weaker for the split.[67]

Under apartheid, the political liberation of black men was the preeminent concern and correct context for struggle. Rather than downplay this fact, we can learn from it. Women could not go it alone as women; that aspect of their identities was deemed secondary. But this did not mean that they had no role. Instead, to return to Moore's play, yes, the oppressed did have a name, an identity by which the oppressor would be forced to recognize them—and Pityana's call to "black men" demonstrated what that was.

I will return to Bloke Modisane's memories of the 1950s for a moment. His deployment of masculinity did not stop with gender; in at least two pivotal episodes in his memoir, he invoked gendered language to talk instead about age. Both episodes involved the police's ability to demand information at will, one involving Bloke's father, the other himself. In the former instance, he witnessed his father quietly accede to both a pass raid and an impertinent young white police officer. His father was reduced; he was not a man, he was a boy. This experience—and Bloke's awareness of its meaning—was not enough to stop the younger Modisane from doing the same in similar circumstances. When making his way from Houghton to Sophiatown without a pass late one night, Modisane himself played a child upon encountering white police—successfully enough that a white policeman (again, a young one) rewarded him with a playful kick on the bottom. He was a schoolboy in short pants once more. Far from being a man, he was not even an adult.[68]

Activists in the 1970s knew this predicament well. Police raids, activist Bongi Mkhabela recalled, "turned your father into a little boy." Readers of the *Rand Daily Mail* compared black South Africans unfavorably to American "Negroes," since the former had "the mentality of an adolescent."[69] In a society abounding in the infantilization of the majority of the population, maturity was a potentially potent issue. Simply advancing in years did not assure maturation; Modisane was chronologically an adult, but he had stooped to play a boy. SASO took this issue on directly, asserting that after breaking with liberals, blacks would no longer accept "being treated as perpetual under-16s." "On his own [without whites] the black man wishes to explore his surroundings and test his possibilities," Biko wrote. The language here is striking—far from being perpetual adolescents, blacks were, Biko envisioned, independent agents, "exploring" and "testing." The university was the suitable context for this, and a sense of maturity and responsibility valorized the campus as an arena within a broader struggle.[70] Because student and broader political identities were indivisible, campus rules (such as restricting opposite sex entrance into dorms, banning alcohol at campus functions, and segregating year-opening "rag" or charity fund-raising festivals) necessitated a political response—not just because they were unjust but also because "we were arguing that we were not secondary school kids."[71] Away from their parents, apart from white liberals, they felt their lives were their own.[72] SASO rhetoric rang with *selfs*—the "self-reflection" of thought; the "self-definition" of identities; the individual who must lift "himself and his community" "from the doldrums," shoulder "full responsibility," and build "self-reliance."[73] SASO called its supporters to confidently assert adult identities, to assume maturity in their own minds and in their dealings with other people.[74]

The assertion of adulthood was a departure from the tradition of South African politics, as exemplified in the "young Africa" of Anton Lembede, Robert Sobukwe, and the ANC Youth League. In 1949, Sobukwe shared his vision of "Africa re-born, African rejuvenated . . . young Africa" with Fort Hare's graduating class.[75] For the Youth Leaguers, the future was boundless and open. Despite the dawn of apartheid in 1948, the ANC had its Program of Action, the United Nations was dedicated to ending colonialism, and surely Africa's brightest days lay ahead. When SASO held its first GSC twenty years later, however, both the struggle against apartheid and postcolonialism had landed with a thud. South African students remembered Nkrumah's overthrow, Biafra, and Idi Amin. During its initial run, the SASO *Newsletter* frequently published critical stories about postcolonial Africa. In a 1972 interview, Biko mentioned to Gail Gerhart that he had admired Oginga Odinga. His choice was instructive, since Odinga had emerged as chief critic of the postcolony. His book, *Not Yet Uhuru*—prefaced by an exiled Nkrumah and available through the African Writers Series—ended with a stinging indictment of once young Africa: "School-leavers become the unemployed and the unemployed become the bitter men of the streets. The jobless, the frustrated, the peasants starving on the land, will endure much hardship, but how much more and for how long?"[76] Sobukwe's African future was now long past, and cynicism came easily. It was time, as SASO rhetoric had it, for the people to grow up.

For the new generation of black activists, the first sign of this new maturity would be acknowledging their complicity in their own oppression. Modisane blamed apartheid for his castration, but in the early 1970s, activists blamed all those who had allowed white South Africa into their heads—to wit, themselves. "The most potent weapon in the hands of the oppressor is the mind of the oppressed," Biko wrote, and his organization called blacks to repent for the "sin" of allowing themselves to be "misused."[77] Indeed, when, as one black student put it, "the potent truth is that the oppressed contribute 70% to their oppression and the oppressors only 30%," psychological analysis and self-criticism was necessary.[78] The terrain of struggle was the mind, and the focus was inward. SASO offered a "psychological intervention," former activist Saths Cooper has suggested, and its goal was to "instill a sense of confidence in ourselves and our destiny." Having rejected liberalism, the activists' desired target was not political change itself; it was a matured mind-set. To build a "better tomorrow," "self respect and self confidence" needed to be the foundation.[79]

And in this effort, during the late 1960s and early 1970s, SASO considered women as capable as men. As Mangena and others asserted, female activists were prominent participants in SASO seminars and conferences; they acted in the organization's plays and helped to coordinate its community programs. This is revealing because, according to SASO's evolving philosophy, none of these activities could be undertaken without the radical critique and responsibility that distinguished "men" from "boys."[80] When male SASO activists flocked to the all-girls Inanda Seminary near Durban to organize the students there, they put the lie to their own newsletter's dismissal of women's intellectual potential. Thoko Mpumlwana was a student at Inanda in the early 1970s, a time when the first generation of SASO leadership was being trained in the Paulo Freire method of adult education and cultural action (about which more later). She did not know this yet; all she knew was that people such as Saths Cooper, Strini Moodley, and Barney Pityana helped Inanda's students with their theater and their poetry during frequent visits to campus. Under their guidance, student productions became "much more relevant" and female high school students grew increasingly "aware."[81] SASO opened a political and intellectual space in which women could participate; they too could be "black men," on their own, responsible, and mature.

The determination to be responsible adults demonstrated how SASO's break with NUSAS and white liberals was more than a political and strategic move. By claiming to be on their own, students and other activists asserted the right to define who they were and who they wanted to be. The severing of the umbilical cord about which Sedibe wrote was the first step toward a political renewal. Biko's new dialectics held that white racism needed to be countered with black solidarity, something that could only be achieved by rediscovering the manhood and maturity that apartheid denied. On its own, attaining maturity was challenging enough. But there remained the pressing need to respond to a society in which life's possibilities began and ended with race.

3 ⌒ The Age of Philosophers
Becoming "Black Consciousness"

THE FIRST years of the 1970s were not calm ones at the University of the North. Turfloop's government-appointed rector sounded the alarm as early as 1971, when his brief attendance at a student arts festival left him "concerned" for what "the organisation known as SASO" might do. Subsequent events proved him right, and on two occasions over the next three years, student agitation led the university authorities to expel the entire student body. Such efforts made no real inroads against student militancy, however, and finally, in 1974, the government convened a commission of inquiry to find some way to calm the campus. It was a foregone conclusion that the commission would blame the outspoken students who supported SASO and propagated its Black Consciousness ideology. Yet the commissioners injected a note of caution. It was not the young organization's fault entirely, they argued, but more of a structural problem: blacks fit uneasily in any university, since "universities grow from the cumulative stores of knowledge amassed, recorded and applied over centuries. For most of the Black peoples a written language and the recording of facts are a very recent development." According to the commission, SASO members were totally unsuited for intellectual endeavors; was it a surprise, then, that the organization's "Black Consciousness ideology" had proved "totally irreconcilable with the age-old Western sciences which are fundamental to all [of] us in all countries?" Universities were cradles of thinking and exploration, poised on the brink of the new. All countries would thus be well served by universities and their cutting-edge ideas. But not so black South Africa. There, the past reigned, and it was not fair to expect students who "come from homes where their parents are living as their ancestors lived 200 years ago" to appreciate the university experience.[1]

The commission blamed Black Consciousness ideology for being "irreconcilable" with the good, progressive, Western traditions at the heart of the university. During the years between black students' withdrawal from NUSAS in 1969 and the commission's sitting, Black Consciousness had crashed its way into South African politics. Both its detractors and its supporters knew what they were watching: black exclusivism grappling against white apartheid, with the country's multiracial future in doubt.[2] Black Consciousness was a political stance in opposition to the state; not surprisingly, then, state appointees thought it inimical to the success of a state-run university.

Yet far from being inimical to the university, the commission's Black Consciousness ideology—with its capitalized B and C—was fundamentally of that context. The capitalized ideology had begun lowercased and low-keyed, with students reading, debating, and wondering about who they were and what that meant. This chapter seeks this more obscure phase before the "capitalization" of their conclusions. In chapter 1, we saw that the commission's vision of students' backgrounds was flawed. In chapter 2, we saw young people claim to be mature adults, on their own. Now, we will follow students through the first generation of black consciousness thought, as they completed the turn away from white liberalism and developed their own perspective.

The Black Consciousness that students developed underscores the irony and ignorance of the commission. SASO adherents were antiwhite, at least in some sense, and proud of their black identities: that much was true. But Black Consciousness ideology was very much a product of the Western academic tradition, of individuals critiquing, sifting, and thinking forward into the future. Indeed, David Attwell has argued that Black Consciousness was a quintessentially modern project, in that its adherents were engaged with the "currently governing concept of what it means to be a subject of history."[3] The name that the commissioners attached to their more fully developed ideology betrayed their aspirations. What could be more modern, subjective, individual—indeed, even Western—than "consciousness"? But theirs was not an uncritical movement toward the white world, as had been the dominant trend in black South Africa's engagement with modernity during the 1950s.[4] Rather than ape white society, Black Consciousness thinkers rejected it and defined for themselves "what it meant to be a subject of history." They were autonomous shoppers in the marketplace of ideas, helping themselves to concepts whether white or black, African or African American, "Third World," European existentialist, or American New Left.

Black Consciousness thinkers drew on this variety of sources to develop a new perspective not just about political engagement—with liberals, without liberals, and so forth—but also about the nature of living as responsible beings, agents, and conscious selves at the end of the globally tumultuous 1960s.

Their ideas were by turn original and plagiarized, confusing and simple, so-phisticated and crude. They called for "more human" relations and advocated total racial separation to defeat separate development. Their conclusions were often abstract and aloof but appropriate to an era that theologian and lecturer Manas Buthelezi has described as "the age of philosophers." From 1968 to 1972, the clash of racialisms in whose shadow the commission sat remained in the future. There was little in the way of political activity, and apartheid rested more or less unchallenged; if black students chafed under white control, their irritation was kept hidden. Scholars have cast this period as the prologue to the more "political" explosions soon to come. Yet I side with Bishop Buthelezi, not claiming their future as our past but watching as students projected them-selves forward into as yet unwritten time and called for consciousness to meet the myriad responsibilities the end of the present would surely bring.[5]

BEING "BLACK"

Pityana called for "black men" to be on their own. I have suggested that using "men" was a conscious choice signifying maturity as much as masculinity. But what did it mean to be "black"? South African students in SASO were only the most recent people of African descent to work through issues of iden-tification and categorization. As Mark Sanders has explored, the writings of Biko, Pityana, and other activists betray their familiarity with the works of the Martinican theorist Frantz Fanon, and at first blush, Biko's dialectics (black solidarity to counter white racism) recalls Fanon's discussion in *Black Skin, White Masks*. But there were critical differences. In *Black Skin, White Masks*, Fanon had bemoaned Jean-Paul Sartre's dialectical analysis of Négritude, the Afro-French cultural and political movement. In particular, Fanon re-jected the philosopher's description of Négritude as the "weak-beat"—the antithesis—that opposed white supremacy and that would ultimately give way to a nonracial synthesis. Such dialectics failed to respond to selfhood crises in the now, Fanon charged. For his part, however, Biko employed dialectics remarkably similar to Sartre's to defend his understanding of blackness against charges of racialism. Sartre had written that Négritude "is intended to prepare the . . . realization of the human in a society without races." Fanon rejected this: "My . . . consciousness does not hold itself out as a lack. It is."[6] But Biko sided with Sartre, casting black solidarity—casting blackness—as a response to white racism. Only when the dialectic is complete, he wrote, could South Africa "reach some kind of balance—a true humanity."[7]

There are multiple ways to read this translation. Perhaps Biko misunderstood Fanon; perhaps he saw Sartre's dialectics as something useful and missed Fanon's critique; or perhaps he understood perfectly well and simply made the determi-nation that South African politics needed both antithesis and synthesis, the one now and the other in the future—the envisioned true humanity. But what did this mean for SASO's understanding of "blackness?" At the most superficial level, black identity emerged from "a lack" experienced by those without rights or place in white South Africa. Early on, SASO employed the language of the state—identifying itself as an exclusively nonwhite group working on behalf of nonwhites—but by the second GSC in 1970, this negative definition was condemned as a "denial of self-respect to the majority of South Africa's people." The term *nonwhite* cast being white as the aspired-to norm and separated those who had attained the status from those who had not. SASO resolved to use *Black* instead.[8]

Yet despite this shift in language, at least in some respects, the meaning remained the same. The SASO Policy Manifesto, agreed to at the third GSC in 1971, defined its Black constituency as "those who are by law or tradition, politically, economically and socially discriminated against as a group in the South African society."[9] Biko later expounded on this to Gail Gerhart: SASO, he said, "is not a movement for Africans, not a movement for Indians, for Coloured people; it's a movement for people who are oppressed."[10] Race was contingent: it was formed through the historical experience of oppression in a particular context. "Skin colour itself is insignificant," a SASO sympathizer explained, "what is important is what the skin actually signifies in sociological terms."[11] Blackness was limited to "those without the franchise" and was thus aimed at a constituency beyond individuals of "African" descent.[12] Pityana's call to black men was a call to adults without ancestors. Blackness was entirely of a particular historical moment; family and pigmentation did not matter—a historically constructed ontology vis-à-vis the extant state of oppression did.[13]

For some in the so-called black community, this stance was too much of a stretch. Many Indians and Coloured nonwhites interpreted blackness as Africanism by another name. Debates surrounding the use of "black" soon spread beyond student circles. In 1972, for example, the Coloured Federal Party contested Coloured Representative Council elections on the issue of using *blackness* in response to the opposition Labour Party's qualified embrace of the term. Federal Party officials suggested that by embracing the word *black*, its opponents had "stated that we must all live together." "Do you want to live in Soweto?" they asked; "We don't want to live in Soweto."[14] The Labour Party's David Curry protested that blackness functioned as a "self-awakening . . . not a colour identity," but the Federal Party won the election.

Fears of Africanism were perhaps not unfounded. This was the 1970s, after all, and Indians in particular could look north with concern. Idi Amin was well covered in the South African press, both for the spectacle he presented and for the obvious propaganda lesson the government wanted to draw from the Ugandan story. The editors of the *SASO Newsletter* reported that Indian students were pointing "to what is happening to the North of us as the example of what lies in store for Indian people in this country."[15] In response, SASO condemned Amin's actions yet urged minorities within the black community to keep their eyes on the goal of opposing white rule.

Two years later, however, SASO's position evolved in an instructive way. Although the newsletter still declared that Amin was "as guilty as the white-man in South Africa," now there was a lesson to be had. The article contended that members of Uganda's Asian community had considered themselves more British than Ugandan. They had "refused to see themselves as part of the soil of Africa" and thus abetted their dispossession. The article urged South African Indians to embrace blackness, but the language of the article—especially the reference to the soil of Africa—hearkened back to a more timeless Africanism within the supposedly historical "black."[16]

Yet SASO adherents refused to call themselves Africanists. They rejected claims such as that of Anton Lembede, the Youth League luminary, who had declared that "non-European unity . . . [was] a fantastic dream which has no foundation in reality."[17] Instead, SASO used Africa in a very particular way. The concept of soil was a central element in Lembede's and other African-ist thought, yet neither land dispossession and recovery nor birth or blood figured prominently in this phase of South African activists' discourse. But the notion of Africa still mattered and helped to refine what it meant to be black. Biko's vision of the future was to "reset the table in an African way." "On the whole, a country in Africa, in which the majority of the people are African, must inevitably exhibit African values and be truly African in style," he explained.[18] But this did not mean that only Africans could be involved in the struggle. Africa was the terrain on which the struggle occurred, but being African was less important than being black; blackness was attuned to the demands of conscious life in the particular time and space of apartheid South Africa. Biko's dialectics best expressed the contingency of blackness, as SASO activists understood it. It would, at a certain point, yield, vanishing beneath nonracial, "true humanity." It was preoccupied with the now of apartheid and what that meant for the future, not retrospective ties of soil and blood. Black selfhood was contingent, topical, and limited, no matter how the table might one day be set.

Students, another activist explained, were not "nostalgic" for the "pure" Africa that had existed before Jan Van Riebeeck; they demanded instead "the birth of a new creativity."[19] This distinction was politically important. Students attended colleges divided by ethnicity and were ostensibly citizens not of South Africa but of states limited to similar sorts of non-Western, premodern, "tribal" peoples. Yet students knew themselves as quintessentially modern products of universities. SASO's 1971 declaration of students' rights made this explicit: "All peoples have an undisputable claim to what has been contributed universally by mankind in terms of knowledge."[20] Referring to "Africa" might help to bolster Africans' confidence in themselves and lessen their reliance on whites as part of the ongoing production of maturity, but "Africa" unquestioned and poorly defined could only take students so far. Postcolonial disappointments rendered such easy politics problematic. In the age of Hastings Banda's visit to Pretoria, "people are much more critical now," Biko told Gail Gerhart. Solidarity could not be based on soil or skin color; it was based on what one was doing and how one carried oneself vis-à-vis the pressing problems of existence.[21]

A close reading of one of Biko's essays helps illustrate what it meant to be black versus African. In August 1971, he delivered a paper to a group of African ministers in which he picked and chose his way through various meanings of African culture to arrive at one more appropriate for the political challenge facing his community. He opened with the observation that "African" culture did need not mean "pre–Van Riebeeck." Africans still existed, and African culture perforce did as well. His subject, Biko continued, was "the modern African culture," which was "a man-centred society": "We believe in the inherent goodness of man. We enjoy man for himself." African society was humanistic; it was therefore in keeping with the dialectics that held "true humanity" as his philosophy's end. Yet although humanistic African culture contrasted with Western "technological" culture, the former was not to supplant the latter. The dialectics still ruled here, and in his envisioned future, "Africans can comfortably stay with people of other cultures and be able to contribute to the joint cultures of the communities they have joined." Africa had taken part in the broad processes of global history, and humanism would show the way: "We believe that in the long run the special contribution to the world by Africa will be in this field of human relationships. The great powers of the world may have done wonders in giving the world an industrial and military look, but the great gift still has to come from Africa—giving the world a more human face." This essay critiqued the West and celebrated an aspect of an imagined African culture. In the process Biko envisioned "Africa" as moving from the particular to the universal, through the historical present into the envisioned future.[22]

Biko's most obvious source here was Kenneth Kaunda. Biko cited the Zambian president and freely adopted his language. Zambian independence, Kaunda had written, was a triumph of "self confidence . . . and the man-centred society" and demonstrated that "Africa's gift to world culture must be in the realm of human relationships." Kaunda's tone doubtlessly appealed to Biko as well. Kaunda was a devoted nationalist and a proud African who wanted to contribute to indivisible human society He acknowledged setbacks but rejected pessimism and looked forward. Kaunda's Africa had changed.

Western colonialism had made inroads—some worthy, others less so—but the potential for a united human community remained. Kaunda rejected the either/or model so popular with apartheid theorists and Bantustan leaders. "Balancing a budget" was not African or European, he wrote, it was merely done in the right or wrong way—and in the realm of human relationships, the African way could be the right way for all people.[23] Kaunda's spirit was easily translated to the new self-conceptions for which SASO called. To Biko, humanism was not only an African trait; he also cast it as the essential under-pinning of black society. Collectively, then, black South Africans lived in a way "opposed to the highly impersonal world in which Whitey lives."[24]

At this point, Biko's analysis turned away from Kaunda's example; it is doubtful, after all, that the august postcolonial statesman would have referred to "Whitey." Biko's cheek marked a departure. Elements of Kaunda's Africa applied to SASO's "black," but in the land where "Whitey" still ruled, Biko needed more. Here, he transitioned to a discussion of the "modern black cul-ture" that SASO was fashioning, exemplified by "soul [music] . . . with its all engulfing rhythm." His imagination set out from South Africa. Soul music, he contended, "immediately caught on and set hundreds of millions of black bodies in gyration throughout the world." Critically, this culture moved in a particular direction; it had a "defiant message 'say it loud! I'm black and I'm proud.'" Through James Brown's defiance, Biko arrived at "our modern culture." Blackness shared humanism's concern with human relationships and its desire to contribute to a universal human future. But blackness, in its moment, spoke in an unequivocally political voice about a specific political situation: "This is a culture that emanates from a situation of oppression . . . [it] is responsible for the restoration of faith in ourselves and therefore offers a hope in the direction we are taking from here."[25] Just as Paul Gilroy reflected that the African diaspora's "music . . . contributed to [his] sense of racial self," so too did black South Africans refract soul music to define a defiant racial solidarity in their unique circumstances. The diaspora imaginary helped Biko fashion a particular voice, which moved from African to black, from human relationships to putting Whitey in his place. Modern black culture, he con-cluded, emerged from the particular tension of defiance amid oppression. Black culture was thus of a moment, not eternal but existential.[26]

Cast in this way, black culture—and blackness more generally—liberated. A year before addressing the ministers, Biko had ended another essay with an extended citation from Sekou Touré, to the effect that cultural forms were relevant only when they contributed to "the great battle of Africa and of suf-fering humanity."[27] In all likelihood, the use of Touré's words was another idea adapted from Frantz Fanon, who had prefaced his famed essay "On National Culture" with the same citation. In that essay, Fanon urged "native intellectuals" to do more than celebrate past and faded glories. "All the proofs of a wonderful Songhai civilization will not change the fact that today the Songhais are underfed and illiterate," he charged. Being underfed and illiterate was what mattered today; such historical conditions were what Fanon called the "seething pot" of the oppressed's reality. The intellectual could reify cultural surfaces, could make the "sari . . . sacred," but this would not free the people from the seething pot. Culture, like consciousness, is tricky—the intellectual wishes to "attach himself to the people, but instead he only catches hold of their outer garments. And these outer garments are merely a reflection of a hidden life . . . perpetually in motion." The intellectual, then, must be on the move as well. Selves were made in struggle, and intellectuals needed to join the "fight for the liberation of the nation," for "there is no other fight." This is what Touré meant; that Biko lifted his words from Fanon demonstrates his allegiance to the idea.[28]

It was not enough, therefore, for Biko's blacks simply to sing along with James Brown. Oppression called on intellectuals to fashion a defiant response. In Fanon's time, Négritude poets and thinkers had embodied philosophical defiance. SASO noted this and published David Diop and Leopold Senghor in early editions of the newsletter.[29] Yet, there were other choices, and by the early 1970s, SASO had found new favorites from the United States, who wrote that "my beauty is the blackness of this land" and delineated America's tragedies.[30] The newsletter's own face changed to reflect this transition. In 1970, its covers had been crudely drawn by hand, and in 1971, they ranged from "tribal" art to abstract images. By January 1972, however, SASO had settled on an easily interpreted symbol: a black hand clenched in a fist.

SASO's opponents quickly attacked both this choice and SASO in general for being "borrowed" from black America and therefore inauthentically South African. The government banned T-shirts bearing the fist and asserted that the idea of blackness "was introduced to South Africa from America."[31] One disaffected SASO member, former president Themba Sono, went so far as to expose what he called the "import doctrine" by juxtaposing selections from SASO's writings with others from the United States.[32] He dismissed the organization's leaders as mimeographs, charging, among other things, that the SASO Policy Manifesto, the organization's clearest statement on South Africa's future, did little more than reproduce one of Charles Hamilton and Stokely Carmichael's more celebrated quotes from *Black Power*. In 1967, Carmichael and Hamilton had written that Black Power "rests on a fundamental premise: Before a group can enter the open society, it must first close ranks." Sono demonstrated SASO's debt to this: "SASO accepts the premise that before the Black people should join the open society, they should first close ranks." And beyond these textual congruences, in critics' minds, SASO's most obvious debt to black America was that it described its African, Indian, and Coloured constituency with Afro-America's word. Black Consciousness, it was argued, was "substantively a foreign doctrinal thesis whose only affinity with the local realities is that it has been articulated . . . by people whose *skin* share [*sic*] the same *color*." Far from marking a creative response to South African realities, Sono and others charged, SASO's understanding of what it meant to be black was merely derivative.[33]

They had a point. As with Biko's use of Kaunda, SASO activists did not exactly respect copyright. They often wrote, as Mark Sanders put it, "in and out" of sources, using quotation marks in some cases and allowing the illusion of their own authorship to rest unchallenged in others.[34] Indeed, once one is familiar with the sources of SASO thought, the writings can read like an endless succession of purloined phrases, ideas ripped from one context and (often inappropriately) applied to another. But it was not so simple as the government and other observers inferred. Activists copied, but they also translated; they read words from one context and wrote them into their own.

In 1972, for example, Bennie Khoapa, the head of the SASO-affiliated Black Community Programmes, delivered a talk at the University of Cape Town in which he explained what SASO meant. This talk was biting and eloquent and almost entirely lifted from an article by Lerone Bennett, published in a special issue of *Ebony* magazine, entitled "Which Way, Black America? Separation? Integration? Liberation?" (in August 1970). Bennett's appeal was obvious: his politics were right on—and he could turn a sharp phrase.[35] But Khoapa edited. He cut out overt references to the United States, as well as any other obviously "foreign" elements from his own speech. These edits made for the occasional head-scratching phrase, as when Khoapa castigated "integrationists," who "believe that the words in the books mean something."

What books? What words? He did not say but only went on to a different subject. Bennett, however, had been explicit: "Words in the books mean something. But racism is not a matter of the Declaration of Independence or the Decalogue or the Sermon on the Mount." We can understand that the Declaration of Independence reference would have given Khoapa away. But why leave out the Ten Commandments and Christ's most famous sermon? One can only guess, but clues are found in the other phrases that Khoapa omitted. Bennett had argued that integrationists missed the root of racism— which "is a matter of labor, productive relations, money and power." He thus dismissed the "great ideas" of the Declaration and the Bible as rhetorical distractions from the real issues at hand. Khoapa was happy to borrow freely from what the American described as a "philosophy of liberation" and to join his denigration of integrationists' rhetoric, but he was not ready to follow him down the path toward a more concrete, political economy critique. For Bennett's "philosophy" was also a political program; he and other American Black Power advocates wrote in the wake of the civil rights movement's dismantling of superficial segregation but failure to ameliorate economic circumstances. It therefore made sense that he would move from ideals to practical matters. Bennett talked about marshaling black America's economic power first—as a "preparatory stage"—to ultimately restructure the system. This effort, he warned, would take a very long time. Khoapa agreed that his was a "preparatory stage . . . [and that] our task is to prepare for 10, 15, and 40 years" into the future. Yet without the economic critique (or a readily available *Ebony*), Khoapa seemed to be saying that a philosophy of liberation was the preparatory stage, which called for people to unify, organize, and put faith in transformation but did not call for the marshaling of economic resources as Bennett had done.[36] In South Africa, racism and apartheid were the problems, and Khoapa proposed "struggle," not economic strategies, as the solution.

This single act of translation allows us further inside SASO's developing thought. South Africans students were undoubtedly attracted by the American example and language, but the contexts were not the same, and even minimal picking and choosing demonstrated the different way that they understood what it meant to be black. Ideas encountered in books were tools, whether they spoke about gender, about maturity, about Africa, about the meaning of independence, about the definition of blackness, or, following Fanon, about the necessity of struggle. Readers manipulated the ideas to their own ends—not the other way around. "I always go to find something from a book," Biko said. Another activist confirmed this, noting that students "read selectively, looking for particular quotes, ideas rather than entire philosophies." Ideas were inanimate until an agent with a particular experience and perspective sought them out and deployed them.[37] It has been commonplace to note South African Black Consciousness's symbolic debt to American Black Power, but here, I am interested in learning from the erasures, elisions, and translations.[38] Gilroy described the black diaspora as a "counterculture of modernity" precisely because its aesthetic output, attuned to defiance, refused to respect the boundaries set by dominant society.[39] Just as I will show how Black Consciousness's faith-infused politics rejected the narrow strictures of "rational" political practice, so too might we argue that activists' use of text appropriately violated modernist, legalistic notions of intellectual property and propriety.[40] "Liberating blackness" was fashioned in conversation with "oppressive non-whiteness"; similarly, South African activists used the materials of the modern world—copyrighted books, trademarked ideas—to make their response to it, in whatever ways they saw fit. How they did so is of paramount importance. That Khoapa copied is not particularly interesting, but that he made the decision to edit Bennett's discussion of the economics of racism is. Following his example, we can see what it meant that SASO activists chose "consciousness," not "power," to describe their project. Biko picked his way through books, including Carmichael's; surely, then, he had noted the role that consciousness played there. "A new consciousness among black people," Hamilton and Carmichael wrote, "will make it possible for us to proceed." It would provide a "sense of peoplehood" from which progress would come.[41]

In *Black Power*, consciousness came first, before the overall study turned to the future. Consciousness was the foundation from which power would come. Yet Biko's world was very different from Carmichael's. *Black Power* reflected on community organizing and planned concrete steps; it was not necessarily a philosophical tract. In African America, consciousness was the beginning, not the end. In South Africa, however, the potential for community-oriented democracy did not yet exist.[42] There had been no civil rights struggle and no Voting Rights Act, however flawed those might have been. There was just apartheid, "a situation from which [we] are unable to escape at any given moment," to which black South Africa needed to respond. This is why a philosophy of liberation mattered more than the raw materialism of economic change. Maturity was one step, historical and defiant blackness was another; together, these cultivated a radical consciousness, an "attitude of mind and a way of life" from which the future could be built.[43] By naming this attitude of mind "Black Consciousness," SASO activists staked their unique claim.[44]

The name took a while to develop. As late as 1971, a thorough report on a SASO formation school described progress on the questions of black identity, "black personality," a black man's "sense of security and belonging," and the power of "self-respect and self-confidence." Yet nowhere did the term *Black Consciousness* appear. Where it did appear in other articles, it shared spaced with *Négritude*, *African existentialism*, and other favorites. All these shared a concern with "mind power," as one student leader put it, and could be interchangeably deployed. Students were involved in a philosophical project in keeping with the latest intellectual trends; just as existentialism spoke of "being," so did SASO's "African existentialism" argue that "being cannot be non-Being. Black cannot be non-White."[45] Soon, though, activists had arrived at the term *black consciousness*, which, by 1972, earned capital letters for both words. The concept retained the meanings of its ousted competitors. Black Consciousness was "a superior philosophy" and a "supremely cultural fact." Its appeal was evinced by the students who attended GSCs in increasing numbers, founded theater and poetry groups, and attended formation schools where debate over its meaning was a recurrent theme. Nowhere did Black Consciousness suggest the "movement" with which it would later be wed. It was "mind power," and all other sorts of power were, at least for the moment, hypothetical.

The use of overtly existentialist language to define Black Consciousness—such as Strini Moodley's definition, cited earlier, about the "projection of the beingness"—suggests a final element of this "liberating philosophy."[46] We have seen the thinking that helped to define Black Consciousness—that students were men, adults, and black. We have yet to consider what Black Consciousness was *for*. As with Biko's modern black culture that responded to a situation of oppression, consciousness called beings (and being) to struggle, if not to a movement per se. Projecting one's beingness meant translating with Khoapa and Biko, to turn others' calls for concrete economic and political change in the future into calls to live in a particular way in the South African present.

SASO activists made this distinction by marking time. At a winter 1970 formation school, students debated the applicability of Carmichael's suggestion that "before a group can enter the open society, it must first close ranks." They disagreed, on the grounds that they did not want an "open" society but a completely new one. Here, however, I am concerned not with their translation but with their conclusion that the new society would come—"at some stage."[47] The future was not their purview. A year later, Biko told Gail Gerhart that he and his peers could not see past "stage 1" of their project, which was about spreading the "awareness that makes black people reject feeling inferior." "Who will be responsible for steps 2 and 3, I don't know," he admitted, nor did he know what those steps might be.[48] That same year, a speaker at the SASO GSC made this attitude toward the future even more explicit. "We may not reach [our] goal today or to-morrow," he said, "we may not reach it in our life-time." This last line reads as a rejoinder to the previous generation's political methodology. The ANC had promised "freedom in our lifetime" and had failed to deliver; SASO promised instead only a new "way of life" and "attitude of mind"—and argued that awakened consciousness would prove to be the "the renaissance of the 20th century." The future was far off and opaque, but SASO's language was clear. Theirs was a more immediate terrain of struggle—bounded by the space between the ears—that would, in the end, shape lives.[49] Attaining new adult selves through Black Consciousness was the first step. Until this goal was achieved, the future was unthinkable.

Black Consciousness thinkers thus set strict conditions for the resumption of political protest. They urged a calm probing of, not a hasty rush toward, the political future. The ramifications of this approach have been multiple, especially—stepping out of history for a moment—considering questions about what has and has not changed since 1994. Most often, we measure historical change in movements, programs, and processes, in events that take a material shape. But early 1970s Black Consciousness measured change in an intangible way, for which it is more difficult to account. Change was about self-awareness and the rejection of inferiority complexes. It was measured in individual selves accepting that their blackness was an existential reality and that consciousness demanded they move toward the future, without knowing exactly what it entailed.

In its abstraction, this approach nodded toward the global student Left. Like their peers in the United States, Europe, and elsewhere, SASO activists grappled with basic questions about "human relations and value," and they called for a "philosophical reconstruction" in an entrenched world.[50] Biko and his peers "looked uncomfortably" at their time and place and asked fundamental questions of human relationships and identifications, just as the Students for a Democratic Society had in 1962 in Port Huron, Michigan.[51] The person and the personal relationship were their immediate concerns, even and especially since those too were constrained by the enforced failings of human relations in apartheid society. As Barney Pityana put it, the "question of . . . the future was not relevant for black people." Instead, to be black was to be "concerned with the present situation . . . dreams of the future would obscure the need of the present."[52]

More than anything else, SASO was anchored in a sense of the present—discomfort and discontent with the way things were. It was concerned with being, and it begged off the past, looked warily toward the future, and judged the present by its relevance to a struggle that claimed little beyond the need for change. Relevance was what mattered. Students were sent to other students bearing only the assurance that "he is relevant, she is relevant"; authors could be white or black, as long as they displayed "relevance in terms of how they viewed the world." The language of relevance determined how sources were used as well. When going abroad or reading foreign sources, for example, students were cautioned "not to copy" (although, as we have seen, some did) but instead "to glean that which they think is relevant for us." Relevant, of course, had its opposite, and just as in American New Left circles, where *irrelevant* was "the most dreaded of words,"[53] in South Africa there were "relevant black men and irrelevant black men," "highly irrelevant" Bantustan leaders and government functionaries, and, above all, Black Consciousness advocates who challenged the "irrelevant and therefore misleading" promise of future integration into white society.[54]

"I have lived all my conscious life in the framework of institutionalised separate development," Biko wrote in 1970.[55] Apartheid shaped lives and structured the experience of existence; in Black Consciousness, the system met an opposing consciousness, not a call for political or economic redress but an alternative analysis that promised a solidarity of beings grounded in time and space. The present demanded a new perspective, and student activists read, wrote, and looked into themselves to forge this. Where they had once been eunuchs, they projected themselves into the present as men. Where they had once been Bantu, nonwhite, or simply African, they defined and inhabited the new identity of black. And where they had been inert, they argued that the act of self-definition and the assumption of personal responsibility would yield struggle.

Yet on its own, Black Consciousness was not the broader "new" that South African students sought. During SASO's first four years, students turned away from the future and worked in the present to fashion new beings who, by definition, were supposed to push forward. Overt political opposition to apartheid had failed, and a lull had ensued. SASO sought to remake the population, to awaken it to responsibility, to patiently and methodically rebuild the people's capacity for struggle as "black men." But these philosophical injunctions could not help but be wedded to concrete historical demands, despite students' attempts to keep this at bay. Khoapa had edited the material out of his speech, but apartheid still structured black South Africans' material realities. South Africa was not the United States, where overt, juridical oppression had yielded to the more subtle, if still strong, racism against which Black Power struggled. SASO brought philosophy into conflict with politics, but in South Africa the political solution—the political definition of the liberated future— was obvious. There was a very concrete goal out there, even if speakers warned that it was a long way away. SASO was involved in stage one, but in the very act of self-definition, Black Consciousness adherents acknowledged the looming weight of stages two and three. To be black was not only to be a man, to be responsible and defiant. Black Consciousness was a philosophy of liberation for people who were discriminated against by law, for those "without the franchise." By becoming consciously black, Biko wrote, "you have committed yourself to fight."[56] What would conscious blacks fight for in the still uncertain future? That would be up to them.

PART II

~

Emergent Gospel

Religious talk pervaded the production of Black Consciousness. It was sometimes rhetorical, as in the recollection of a Cape Town activist that Fanon's *Wretched of the Earth* was known as the "the Old Testament" or as in BPC activist Nkwenkwe Nkomo's frequent description of SASO and other Black Consciousness activists as "prophets . . . bishops . . . ministers [and] evangelists."[1] Yet it often went beyond mere rhetorical convention to suggest that religious — primarily Christian — ways of thinking underpinned activists' political approach. "I wish to state that black consciousness must be tackled by its advocates as a religion," an unnamed author reported. "We believe in it, we think it is right." The philosophy needed "disciplined protagonists" — missionaries — who would "convert" others: "This is a kind of evangelism that must work in converting people to the truth [and] we need this . . . almost as badly as the colonialists needed missionaries."[2] This was seen in their sources as well. Biko's "Africa" was adapted from Kaunda's concept of African Humanism, and especially from the Zambian president's discussion of the "holiness" of human relationships. "Humanisms" were widespread during the 1960s, and Kaunda had carefully distinguished his own version from "existential humanism," calling it not only African, but "Christian." Faith in the Christian God was the appropriate "faith for men" because, he argued, it was "faith in people."[3] This was the language that Biko lifted to describe "modern black culture." Faith in people and in the sanctity of relationships, which manifested the divine, was what Africa would give the world.

Activists did approach Christianity warily; after all, the religion had come to South Africa accompanied by conquest, guns, and economic exploitation. Black Consciousness thinkers argued that missionaries not only had abetted material conquest but also were to some extent responsible for the psychological ailments afflicting black South Africa. "The white missionary described black people as thieves, lazy, [and] sex-hungry," Biko charged, and "equated all that was valuable with whiteness." African traditions were disparaged, "described as . . . pagan and barbaristic." Conversion strained societies, and as pressure increased, local peoples were "stripped of the core of their being and estranged from each other [and Africa] became a playground for colonialists." Christianity in South Africa was exemplified by the apartheid state, Biko suggested: both were "cold and cruel," with "stern-faced ministers" blaming blacks for their "sins" while failing to relate "vices to poverty, unemployment, overcrowding, lack of schooling and migratory labour."[4] In the face of this, SASO concluded that an entirely new set of values was necessary. Why, then, did they continue to think about the production, content, and spread of these values in a Christian way?

There is an answer, a seemingly simply one, which is in reality quite complicated and opens new lines of inquiry: because they were, by and large, Christian. Many had attended mission schools, many more came from longstanding Christian families, and many quite simply believed. Take, for example, Nkwenkwe Nkomo, who peppered his memos with references to Black Consciousness as "good tidings," "gospel" and "manna." We met in his office in Sandton, where he was serving as group chairman for one of South Africa's largest advertising firms. Surely, I asked him, this practice was merely rhetorical. He shook his head: "There are three influences that shaped my life: the church, scouting, and the liberation movement. And it is a bit difficult to say where each one started, it was . . . seamless." Leaving scouting aside, this answer stuck and the record bore him out.[5] On trial with the rest of the Black Consciousness leadership in 1974, he was twenty-two years old and already an established lay preacher, albeit of a particular sort: "I was delivering a sermon . . . and I chose as my text Ezekiel 37, the dry bones. And in my sermon I likened the Black people in this country to the bones that Ezekiel talks about and I said that we, the people, would come and lead the people of God to bring like like [sic] Ezekiel, and I made mention of the . . . Ezekiels in the Black community . . . Thereafter the elders called me and told me not to speak politics in church."[6] He was confused. It was not politics to him: it was the Christian message, unadulterated, and it needed to speak to the world.

The interpenetration of politics and religion was commonly observed during this period. In 1969, John Mbiti of Kenya wrote that "Africans are notoriously religious [and] religion permeates into all the departments of life so fully that it is not easy or possible to isolate it." Mbiti was arguing for renewed attention to "African traditional religions" in service of the postcolonial project.[7] In keeping with his movement's methodology, SASO's second president borrowed Mbiti's words. "Black people are notoriously religious," Pityana wrote in 1971, and religion "permeates" the "depths of life." Yet rather than call for attention to "traditional religions," Pityana instead called for attention to the "church," to the ways in which the study of Christianity "is a study of black consciousness or self-awareness. In the context of the black community, the two themes are intertwined."[8] For Pityana, as for Nkomo, religion was indistinguishable from the rest of life. Ezekiel spoke to young black South Africans. Biko sharply critiqued the church; yet he still wrote that he did "not question the basic truth at the heart of the Christian message."[9] It remained only to figure out how this truth could be rescued and revealed—not to write Christianity off, but to right it. Black Consciousness called South Africans to faith in themselves and in the promise, ultimately, of a future. Its adherents compared it to a religion and called it the "gospel." What did this mean to people who believed?

The three chapters of part 2 work through the religious counterpart to SASO's ostensibly secular philosophy. The narrative first loops back to the mid-1960s to consider church-state relationships during that decade and then traces Christian critique of apartheid in the early 1970s. Just as SASO's philosophy of liberation broke with the political theories of the past, so too did black South African Christians open a space for a radical rethinking of the faith. I follow this through the various forms that influenced South African Christians: ostensibly secular theology, African theology and, most resoundingly, Black theology.

4 ⌁ Church, State, and the Death of God

A Prolegomenon to the Black Messiah

SOMETIME AFTER February 1974, the Black Consciousness–affiliated People's Experimental Theatre (PET) organization circulated a collection of poems and short theater pieces. It prominently featured a poem entitled "Casualties" by Roli Karolen, which compared Abraham Tiro, who had recently been assassinated in Botswana, to Jesus Christ. As Karolen explained, both Jesus of Nazareth and "Tiro of Dinokana" lived short lives, preached truth, suffered, and died. The poet equated Jesus's Sermon on the Mount with the words the young South African was best known for: "a graduation speech [that] made headlines." "Prophet, Martyr and Hero to your people / Settlers adopted Jesus of Nazareth and called him God / Whitey rejected Tiro of Dinokana and called him Terrorist," Karolen declared. Six years after the founding of SASO, his poem demonstrated the degree to which resistance politics had become Christianized and sanctified. He called upon the followers of both Tiro and Jesus to recognize their bond: "that Blessed are the Jews who lived with Jesus / Blessed are the Blacks who shared with Tiro / Sacred are all those who keep up with struggle / Of the son of David and the son of Azania." These were not idle words, nor did they offer a thoughtless comparison. By the middle of the seventies, political rhetoric had assumed a Christian aura, and Christ had in turn been incarnated in the cauldron of South African politics.[1]

This melding was by no means inevitable. Despite the profusion of Christians in SASO; despite the long history of missionary advocacy and mission school–educated Africans resisting industrialization, segregation, and the expansion of the apartheid system; and despite the outcry of international church figures such as Trevor Huddleston at the fall of Sophiatown, the mainstream Christian church's critical voice in South Africa was far from assured in the late

1960s.[2] A 1968 memo from UCM's organizers captured the tenor of the time. Since theirs was "a religious organization," they explained, "it is concerned with Man's relationship to God."[3] They had founded UCM to initiate a traditional discussion of faith, in which God was apart from human experience and Christian students were called "to love, trust and hope in God, Father, Son and Holy Spirit."[4] Although it advocated multiracial fellowship, the UCM's constitution was not altogether different from the teachings of the government- and apartheid-supporting Dutch Reformed Church (DRC), which taught black seminarians little more than to "accept that you are a sinner, you are saved by grace, and you have to be grateful for salvation. It didn't say anything about what was happening [in the world.] It wasn't applied."[5] By tracing the changing perspective and debates over the appropriate role and context for the Christian voice in the late 1960s and early 1970s, this chapter shows the steps that led from the sacred relationship between individuals and God to the sacred struggle of Jesus of Nazareth and Tiro of Dinokana on earth.

In the process, I lay the intellectual groundwork beneath a forthcoming concept: the promised "Black Messiah." To understand the marriage of faith in politics and faith in God in 1970s South Africa, we must detour from student struggle to consider wider debates about the relationships between church and state that conditioned this discourse's emergence. There, one can explore the theological structures and concerns that prefaced calls for sacred struggle. DRC seminaries may have taught their students not to apply theology to the world, but that church's history and connection with National Party politics demonstrated that Christianity was already intimately involved in its own sacred struggle for "Christian nationalism" in white South Africa. Thus, the unfolding relationship between church and state and between faith and politics cannot be understood without first considering the fraught premise of Christian opposition to apartheid in the first place.

The chapter then considers alternate Christian voices during the 1960s and explores the development of moral and religious opposition to apartheid at the decade's close. The actors involved—from the Catholic Church to the South African Council of Churches (SACC) to Beyers Naudé's Christian Institute and the Study Project on Christianity in Apartheid Society (SPROCAS)—are familiar from the secondary literature. But where other scholars have focused largely on the political maneuvering behind church-state relations, I instead consider the intellectual content behind such wrangling—the theological language and concepts that underpinned Christians' attempts to apply their faith. What, for example, did Naudé's calls for a "confessing church" mean in the South African context? How did such calls resonate? On what traditions did they draw? By the close of the 1960s, church people from the UCM and elsewhere were increasingly translating radical theological trends from outside

South Africa into their own political context, where ideas found debate, favor, and critique.[6]

In 1959, the minister of Bantu administration declared, "God has given a divine task and calling to every People in the world, which dare not be destroyed." This divine task, as he described it, corresponded closely with the extension of separate development across South Africa. Each "national group," he declared, had "an inherent right to live and develop . . . the personal and national ideals of . . . every ethnic group [, which] can best be developed within [the] . . . national community."[7] We might write off these words, spoken at a time when the government's segregating policies were continuing apace, as a rhetorical device designed to separate black people from their remaining land. However, the words had a theological and historical logic of their own.

It was and is commonplace to hear the National Party government described as Christian. As NP loyalists saw it, their 1948 election only validated the fact that they had been selected "by God to bring Christianity and civilization to the African continent." For its part, the DRC provided clerical credence to government affairs. Soon after the 1948 election, the DRC declared its virtually unequivocal support for the doctrine of separate development.[8] In the face of its subsequent expulsion first from the World Council of Churches (WCC) and eventually from the World Alliance of Reformed Churches, the DRC clung fast to its belief that the Bible "does leave room for organizing the co-existence of different nations in one country through the policy of separate development."[9] The head of the DRC was half-jokingly referred to as "the second most powerful man in the country" and the church itself as the "National Party at prayer."[10]

This situation had important implications for the role of Christian identity in public discourse. Events such as the battle of Blood River were sanctified as the Day of the Covenant, with the Afrikaner defeat of the Zulu transformed into the "victory of Christianity over barbarism."[11] Each year, on the battle's 16 December anniversary, the country shut down to mark the Afrikaners' unique, Abrahamic relationship with God and God's attentiveness to, as Prime Minister John Vorster put it, "the power [of] positive prayer."[12] Such co-opting of religion did not stop with government-sponsored celebrations. It took stranger form in 1972, when Interior Minister Connie Mulder argued for a bar on the entrance of atheist immigrants into the country—"no matter how good their qualifications might be"—and even if they would bolster the white *volk*'s numbers.[13]

At first glance, DRC theology appears to hearken back to its Calvinist roots. Like their Puritan cousins in the Massachusetts Bay Colony, the Dutch Reformed and French Huguenots who arrived in southern Africa over the course of the seventeenth and eighteenth centuries subscribed to a theology of election and predestination, holding that humans were sinful and fallen, that they were saved only by the grace of God, and that those saved—the elect—should demonstrate their faith through well-ordered living in a community of their peers.[14] Yet Calvinist communities did not necessarily lend themselves to the discourse of "separately developing nations" on which apartheid was based and to which the DRC nodded its approval. For Dutch Reformed theologians at the University of Stellenbosch during the nineteenth century, Calvin begged updating.[15]

DRC theology sailed from the Netherlands replete with stern Calvinist injunctions about sober living and rigid comportment, as well as racially tinged ideas about the Curse of Ham. However, once in southern Africa, that theology developed along uniquely southern African lines.[16] Events such as the Covenant, the Great Trek, and the long decades of resistance to British imperialism came to constitute "the sacred period of Afrikaner history," each step demonstrating how faith in an "active, sovereign God" had been rewarded through God's unique relationship with a "national elect." This "civil religion," as T. Dunbar Moodie called it, was further strengthened in the fire of the South African War, the formation of the National Party, its electoral victories, and ultimately the almost messianic emergence of the independent Republic of South Africa in May 1961.[17]

Faced with the plurality of South Africa's peoples, theologians drew attention to the lessons of Genesis 11 and wrote about the necessity of preserving the distinctions God had sanctioned by destroying the Tower of Babel. Shelving Christ's claims that "in me there is no Jew or Gentile," the DRC followed the lead of the prominent Dutch theologian Abraham Kuyper, whose "neo-Calvinism" proclaimed that God's will manifested itself in the maintenance of "diversity of nations, tongues, etc."[18] Like Kuyper in the Netherlands, Dutch Reformed theologians at Stellenbosch and elsewhere rejected the so-called liberalizing tendencies of English missionaries, which edited God's rule by establishing separations between church and state and spoke about the "one world" of the Christian communion.[19] Neo-Calvinists drew attention instead to Paul's Epistle to the Romans, in which he wrote that "in the single human body there are many limbs and organs, all with different functions" and urged early Christians to "use the different gifts allotted to us by God's grace."[20] Kuyper took this description of Christian individuals and applied it to nations. It was unchristian and unnatural to declare the one world of the Christian communion, since "each ethnic group was . . . an organism which formed part of the body of humanity. As an organism a people had a rhythm and a law of its own expressed in its language, history, biological composition and locality."[21] DRC theology wrote Calvinism's faith in God and direct relationship between the divine and the individual onto the larger scale of the volk's history, with the community's struggles to maintain linguistic and ethnic purity providing further evidence of its election. Humanity was one body, yes. But according to developing neo-Calvinism, mankind maintained its distinctiveness by having different nations, different peoples, and even different churches participate in their unique and separate relationships with the divine.

Over the course of the late nineteenth and early twentieth centuries, neo-Calvinism became DRC orthodoxy. The church maintained distinct "cultures" and "social spheres" between the white and Afrikaner-dominated DRC, the Coloured Dutch Reformed Mission Church, and the African Dutch Reformed Church in Africa, presaging its approval for separate development when at last the nominally secular state caught up.[22] These differences required the DRC to carefully communicate its theology to its "daughter" churches, whose election was far from certain. Whereas white DRC theology developed through a reading of God's grace, as seen in the rough-and-tumble of the community's political history, DRC seminaries and government schools cautioned that this should not be so. Black students were taught that that Afrikaners were a chosen people, who "were where they were because God wanted them there, and that [we blacks] were where we were because God wanted [us] there." This was as far into politics as Dutch Reformed church people were willing to go.[23] More typical, recalled Allan Boesak, who studied at the DRC Mission Church's seminary for Coloureds at the University of the Western Cape during the 1960s, were white professors who taught only a "pietistic version of Reformed theology that equipped you in all sorts of ways to talk to people about heaven and about sin and about damnation, but not about the real issues that would face them and certainly not raising the question of how this faith could be applicable to social, political and economic issues."[24] When he tried to invite the DRC radical Beyers Naudé to campus in 1965, seminary authorities banned him and instead drafted a local DRC dominee to preach on "what is a liberalist?"[25] Similarly, African students at the DRC's seminary at the University of the North—where DRC priests were the only churchmen allowed on campus—essentially took dictation from their white, Afrikaans-speaking overseers.[26] They were "indoctrinated" in a theology that made it seem "as if the world didn't exist." This was the preferred Reformed tradition for producing nonwhite priests: not Calvin's experiments in Geneva, nor Kuyper's organisms and spheres (although that assuredly found its moments), nor politics lived through one's faith. It was a theology of the individual, a sinner grappling alone with faith in God, with the sheer weight of lessons unapplied to the world suggesting that, as one black DRC seminarian put it, "if at that time people had said to me, the DRC was the National Party at Prayer, I would have said no, but what do you mean?"[27]

Undoubtedly, politics structured the historical development of DRC theology, from its neo-Calvinist roots through its electoral successes, restrictions on atheist immigration, and annual celebration of the "power of positive prayer." Yet politics belonged to a chosen people; to others, faith was to remain personal, not public, and such individuals were concerned with the conflict between sin and grace, not church and state. To liberal observers, the DRC was a perversion, an inappropriate misreading of the Bible that threatened the entire Christian enterprise. As the government took control of English-speaking mission schools, politically conscious blacks easily concluded that Christianity itself "was in fact in alliance with our oppression. That face of Christianity people knew and understood."[28] In his time, Kuyper opposed the modernizing state and advocated a more godly politics. Like its theological inspiration, the DRC demonstrated that faith was inexorably in politics—and by the 1960s, it had been for a long time. Still, as some Christians began to apply their faith to worldly affairs, others debated whether it was appropriate to do so.

"A POLITICAL PROGRAM
WHICH CHRISTIANS OUGHT TO SUPPORT"

In 1942, William Temple, the archbishop of Canterbury, joined the discussion about his church's appropriate relationship with politics. World War II was under way, further eroding humanity's faith in its modern world. The Vatican was silent as German Christians were elevating Hitler to messianic status. And in England, Temple had to ask whether the church had the "right" to "interfere" in political affairs.[29] Temple's answer was that the church should comment if and when God's "natural order" was upset or had undergone some revision. Twenty-seven years later, his basic conclusion rang true for Christian activists who were considering the course of the Study Project on Christianity in Apartheid Society.[30] Run jointly by the SACC and CI, SPROCAS did not seek to impose Christian solutions or Christian policies on South Africa; it sought instead to study the problem and find out what Christian "ethics" had to say about the South African situation and in turn what effect apartheid had had on the church. As if invoking a patron saint, SPROCAS enclosed copies of Temple's *Christianity and the Social Order* to the church people and laity who comprised its six commissions, asking anew the question of whether there was "a political program which Christians ought to support."[31]

If such a program existed, the liberal church people who stocked the SPROCAS commissions undoubtedly rejected the notion that apartheid was it. Liberal Christians in the country's English-speaking churches were appalled at the DRC theology of separate spheres and "national" communities. Even if segregation was desired by both blacks and whites, liberal opinion held that it betrayed "the New Testament principle that the Church is the one body of Christ in which the races are to live in reconciliation and unity with one another. A resort to segregation would be a relapse from this biblical principle to the pagan principle that 'birds of a feather flock together.'"[32] Apartheid was, as Catholic bishop Denis Hurley put it in 1964, "immoral," and Christians had to reject it.[33] His Anglican counterpart, Alphaeus Zulu, agreed, insisting that "members of different branches of Christ's church in this country must gather to listen to the Word of God together without consideration of race or colour." As cited earlier, this call for "different Communions and Cultures" to come together was precisely what the UCM wanted to achieve, and in apartheid South Africa, a multiracial gathering was political.[34]

Yet there is quite a cognitive distance between Christians making moral pronouncements on politics and Christians making politics the duty of the church. It was one thing to comment and quite another to present an alternative theological vision that thoroughly intermingled the world and the Word, as the DRC seemed to have done. True, some English-speaking churches did seem defiantly political. The Catholic Church, for instance, had refused to cede control over its six hundred schools to the Ministry of Bantu Education, and Bishop Hurley himself served for a time as the president of the quintessentially liberal South African Institute of Race Relations.[35] This intransigence won the Church supporters and even converts among the black population. In the eyes of Chris Mokoditoa, the UCM's general secretary, the Catholics' refusal to give the government their schools demonstrated that "they were devoted to teaching the black man." Similarly, Mokgethi Motlhabi, UCM Black Theology director, felt drawn to Catholicism for no reason other than because "it seemed that in our township most of the educated young people were Catholic." This reputation worked to the church's advantage, which, some observers suggest, had been the Church's intention all along.[36]

Regardless of its motivation for keeping its schools, the Church's "devotion" did not readily translate to a consistent and overt political stance. In fact, the maintenance of the schools often provided Catholic church people with a ready excuse for not engaging in political activity. Despite charging that apartheid was immoral, Hurley supported officials at the Church's St. Francis school when they refused to host a multiracial UCM meeting. He wrote, "There were many objections to . . . inter-racial meetings" that previously had been held at St. Francis, and he worried that such events would lead the government to curtail the Church's missionary efforts "in the native reserves."[37] A St. Francis school representative's response to Colin Collins, then the UCM's general secretary, was even more direct: "I cannot imagine how you can risk prejudicing a school like St. Francis of vital importance to thousands of children who have nowhere else of any value to get their education in order to house yourself and your ineffective lunatics for one week."[38] Furthermore, many of the Church's teachers and mission priests were foreign, and persistent fears of deportation often led the National Bishops' Conference to comply with the government, even to the point of refusing to publicly condemn one of their members who expressed satisfaction with apartheid.[39] The Catholic Church was not alone in this. Other churches faced similar challenges at their remaining mission schools, and they generally preferred to reserve comment on political matters rather than risk losing foreign teachers and the last vestiges of mission education in South Africa.[40]

During the 1960s, then, English-speaking church authorities typically conceded the theology-politics debate to the DRC's extant achievements, and most black Christians accepted this state of affairs. At its 1968 conference, the IDAMASA invited its members to consider "questions which concern all members and ministers of Religion to-day," namely, "Illegitimacy, Alcoholism and Marriage," and a reader of the country's widest circulating black newspaper worried that African Christians were growing "luke-warm" in their faith because there was "too much sleep . . . to little fasting and self-denial" and, critically, "too much conversation in the world."[41] Black ministers warned schoolchildren that calls for equality were sacrilegious in that they demonstrated "the sin of envy," and they asked their congregations to pray for those whose politics made them "a tool of the devil."[42] However, some black Christians rejected the church's apolitical stance. The Catholic Church's "fence-sitting" amid spreading oppression led Bokwe Mafuna to give up his dream of becoming a priest. While at seminary in the mid-1960s, he asked himself, "Could I truthfully stand in front of a congregation . . . and say to them, you must turn the other cheek?" He concluded that he could not and dropped out.[43] Too often, for both the institutional church and individual believers, being Christian meant subscribing to the "mentality of everything is fine" when it was anything but.[44]

By the late 1960s, however, this situation was beginning to change. In late 1968, the Theological Commission of the South African Council of Churches released its "Message to the People of South Africa," which linked Christian responsibility and the South African political situation. It asserted that "Christians are called to witness to the significance of the Gospel in the particular circumstances of time and places in which they find themselves," and it argued that this necessitated speaking out against apartheid.[45] The Message offered a thoroughly scriptural critique of apartheid: whereas the Nationalist government offered salvation (of race, of nation) through its policy of separate development, the Message countered that "salvation in Christ exposes the falsity of hope of salvation through any other means."[46] Apartheid was a "false idol" that was owed no loyalty. With the Message, liberal Christians asked white South Africa "to whom or to what are you truly giving your first loyalty, your primary commitment? Is it to a subsection of mankind, an ethnic group, a human tradition, a political idea; or to Christ?"[47] The Message was specifically tailored to appeal to whites; it did not claim to speak to or for blacks. As David Thomas has suggested, it was among the last products of South African liberalism, a defense of the ideal that there was no inherent difference between white and black, and it was thus a political move in a place where politics was reserved for the minority.[48]

Christian critique continued immediately after the Message when the SACC and the Christian Institute inaugurated their study project, charged to demonstrate where and how "our present social order [is] . . . opposed to Christianity."[49] SPROCAS's six commissions assessed apartheid's impact on everything from the church to education to politics, all based on the faith "that Christ calls us to integration and unity rather than segregation and disunity."[50] Despite calls for integration, however, the composition of SPROCAS's commissions demonstrated the whiteness of the enterprise, for out of more than 120 members, only 14 were black.[51] That being said, SPROCAS's published reports offered comprehensive critiques of South African society, hoping to tweak the white electorate's morality. SPROCAS supporters believed that, so tweaked, South Africa would change. Unlike blacks in SASO and elsewhere who were increasingly questioning the entire premise of white South Africa, liberals did not want to believe that their country was beyond redemption; as late as 1971, SPROCAS supporters saw progress in rumors that the minister of Bantu education had instructed another official to read SPROCAS's education report and identify which recommendations "could be . . . put into effect immediately and which over the long term."[52] Writing to Peter Randall, SPROCAS's organizer, the general secretary of the Presbyterian Church judged the story "most encouraging."[53] Such tales proved fleeting, however, and in retrospect, Randall would be unable to point to any of the study project's concrete accomplishments.[54]

However, the study project did yield at least one subtle yet arguably more important result in that it renewed debate on what it meant to be a Christian. In response to the "Message to the People of South Africa," DRC supporters leaped to defend their particular faith. When SPROCAS demonstrated the fallacy of linking apartheid to Christianity, the DRC paper *Woord en Daad* dismissed the project as "clear evidence of the liberalistic, humanistic, secularistic life-view"—an unchristian enterprise and therefore unworthy of response. Another Afrikaans editorial page refused to agree that "apartheid cannot be coupled with Biblical truth" and accused the commissioners of playing electoral politics: "If suspicion and doubt can be sown about this [truth, then] voters can be uprooted from this Christian foundation" and vote against the system. It was an ugly and unsavory prospect but not surprising, given "the way these people [SPROCAS members] reason."[55]

Christianity's role in electoral politics came to the forefront again in 1970, when many SPROCAS commissioners and other church people published *Twelve Statements: A Christian Election Manifesto* in a variety of media. On the eve of parliamentary elections, the *Statements* contended that "it is the Christian's duty to contribute by his vote toward the establishment of a government . . . in accordance with the Biblical commandments of truth, justice and love." True Christians ought to support a political program because it furthered "the law of love given by Christ."[56] The signatories of the *Statements* did not go so far as to advocate for a particular political party, but their attempt to influence politics was too much for some Christians. Thus, a *Pro Veritate* reader in Cape Town felt that the *Statements* chastised Afrikaners, and he was not "prepared to moralize in this way over so many of my fellow Christians." Another sneered that the *Statements* gave Christians no choice but to vote for the Progressive Party.[57] Like SPROCAS and the "Message" that preceded it, the *Twelve Statements* were designed to change how "Christianity" was deployed in politics—by using scripture to measure South Africa's realities against the demands of the Gospel. With these efforts, Christian activists argued that politics could and rightly should be judged by faith.

Other Christians had already made this leap. In September 1963, for instance, Beyers Naudé, the dominee at the Aasvoëlkop DRC congregation in Johannesburg, had resigned rather than step down from his position as editor of the Christian Institute's ecumenical theological journal, *Pro Veritate*. Naudé was a rising star in the DRC, but faced with the choice of abandoning his congregation or the journal—which had emerged as one of the few Afrikaans voices against apartheid—Naudé chose the latter. He was "deeply concerned by the violation of the gospel by the church," he told the congregants, and felt the need "to confront it" with the Gospel's truth.[58] Preaching from Acts 5:29—"Peter replied for the apostles: 'We must obey God rather than men'"—Naudé presented his choice as being between obedience to God or obedience to the authority of the church and, by extension, the state it supported. He admitted that "some will say, is it not sheer audacity to draw an analogy from this [biblical] story to the situation in which we find ourselves today?" But he concluded that if God's revelation was still true for the world, he had no choice.[59] As John De Gruchy explained, this was a classic reformed "confession," a theological statement that commented on present practices in light of scripture; it meant that "you publicly said what [scripture] meant in terms of [the] issues of the day," whatever political consequences that might entail.[60] Confessing Christians sanctified the whole world by drawing attention to God's rule everywhere, by returning to scripture and appealing to an authority undeniably higher than that of a single church.[61]

By the turn of the 1970s, there were increasing calls for a Christianity outside of the church—or rather "across all Churches," and beholden to none—where faith would be involved in political struggles, "in every aspect of society." According to the editors of *Pro Veritate*, the promise of reform faded as the "Message to the People of South Africa" and SPROCAS failed to provoke "worth-while change." They instead urged Christians to form a "confessing community" to confront the system.[62]

In fact, such confrontations were already taking place. Throughout the early 1970s, church organizations such as the UCM and CI actively courted government censure, and in time, the government reacted with investigations, bannings, and arrests. By March 1971, the conflict had grown so tense as to catch the attention of Bob Connolly, the *Rand Daily Mail*'s cartoonist. In one sketch, he depicted the security branch raiding a house in a white suburb. Through the picture window, we see a worried man holding a sign identifying himself as an "atheist." As a nonbeliever, the caption declared him "immune" from police harassment.[63] In the summer of 1971, Johannesburg saw the dean of its Anglican Cathedral arrested and charged with abetting the banned ANC; police raids at the homes and offices of UCM and CI leaders;[64] the banning of a Catholic priest who had written an exposé of conditions in a "resettled" community; and Alphaeus Zulu, the Anglican bishop of Zululand, charged with a pass offense while attending a UCM seminar in Roodepoort.[65]

This intermingling was too much for some. Politics, with its rounds of public denunciations, security raids, detentions, and angry protests, was dirty, a *Rand Daily Mail* correspondent charged, and the minister who "would use the sacred desk to express his political persuasion . . . [brought] reproach on the precious and holy name of Christ and of his cause."[66] Such a response was exactly what the government wanted from its white citizens, and the state reinforced these charges by linking local confessing clergy who preached the "social gospel" with global organizations such as the World Council of Churches and other "spiritual terrorists" who aimed to destabilize the state.[67]

It was clear that by the early 1970s, the conversation had progressed significantly from the time when UCM described itself as religious and therefore concerned with "man's relationship to God." Yet in some sense, the terms of the debate remained the same: politics was something that Christians did or did not do, ought to support or ought not to. The church could either comment correctly or be quiet; church people could either advocate a "social gospel" or concern themselves with Christ's "real message."[68] For many, church was still church, faith was still faith, politics was still politics, and whether you agreed with it or not, appending *social* to *gospel* blurred but did not erase the line.

To some, however, the connections between faith and politics were clearer. A. Z. Mzara, a *World* reader, offered his take early in 1969. As he saw it, the problem was with a way of thinking that "[takes] human nature, chop[s] it up into various blocks, as we do with wood and talk[s] of a person being either a politician, a theologian or an economist." Debating over who can do this or who cannot do that achieved little, as "the human being is simultaneously political, religious, social and economic." Christians lived on earth with all men, Mzara concluded, and were therefore "concerned with situations where man is found." There was no appropriate place for Christian activity, save everywhere. If human nature was whole, rather than being exclusively about God, scripture or concerned with debates for or against the "social gospel," being a Christian meant engaging all of society, wherever people were found.[69] In his letter, Mzara blurred conceptual lines in search of wholeness. It was not yet the poet Karolen's "sacred" blacks in struggle, but by sanctifying the entire world as a site for action, a space was opened for the proclamation of the earthly Black Messiah.

THE MIDDLE OF THE CITY

Mzara's challenge resonated with an ongoing global theological debate. Even as the "Message to the People of South Africa" declared that "Christ is our master . . . to whom all authority is given," this image of Christ and God sitting in judgment over human affairs was being revised.[70] The sixties saw repeated discussion about the divine's exact position vis-à-vis people's social lives. Was God interested, as the Confessing Church taught, but distant from humanity, up there somewhere, a constant moral hand on the tiller whose steering people could mimic? Or was the divine actually incarnated into human actions, not distant but "imminent . . . in persons . . . in political struggles, struggles for freedom"?[71] A vocal group of Christians the world over were increasingly seeing divinity incarnated in human affairs. In South Africa, the 1960s and early 1970s saw individual Christians and groups delve into political things. This challenged Christians, especially in the UCM, to consider the more fundamental reorientation of the faith itself. As Cedric Mayson, a CI staffer and Methodist priest suggested, students recognized that "God [and] theology were also involved in the whole problems of society and [theology] had to [be] widened from that point of view." Beginning within the UCM, this "secularizing" of the religious soon resonated across the population.[72]

From the onset, white UCM activists had a soft spot for "relevant" faith. At the inaugural conference in 1967, students gathered into multiracial work groups and concluded that Christianity needed to embrace "language and thought forms" that would "have some meaning for those not skilled in scholastic philosophy or 17th and 18th century theology." The students called on the churches to update the "cultural trappings" of religious services to make more room for "creative spontaneity."[73] UCM officers responded. At conferences and branch meetings, they moved away from staid, tradition-bound worship to what Basil Moore, UCM's first president (and later director of theology), called "worship happenings"—"spontaneous expressions about what it means to be a Christian."[74] These "happenings" typically involved poetry readings, dance, music, and visual art as well as "confession"—"outbursts of frustration at being members of an unjust society"—and a period known as "do your own thing." The focus on spontaneity directly corresponded to students' desire for creative worship services, which would comment on events beyond the sanctuary.

Indeed, as early as 1968, some UCM officials were explaining their practices in terms of South African political realities. Young South African Christians, Moore contended, did not want to be "temporarily suspended from the human race and society during their period at University." Rather, they wanted their religious experience to speak directly to lived life; to that end, the happenings typically included discussions of a certain piece of scripture in light of current-day experience, intending to make "our faith fresh, stimulating, relevant, and, most important, our own."[75] *Relevant* was the UCM's watchword. This focus courted criticism, including what Moore deemed "weird and wonderful" stories in the media and letters disparaging the organization for too closely linking the Gospel to modern life. But the UCM pressed on with the conviction that it was possible to build a new community and foster a relevant faith.[76]

Just as worship bridged the sacred space of the sanctuary and the "secular" world, UCM theology urged Christians to live their faith every day. The UCM's inaugural service bemoaned that Christians "have tried to confine Christ within our ecclesiastical structures . . . and have refused to follow Him out into the world."[77] Worship was safe but ineffective when left inside the sanctuary. To counter that, UCM named their magazine *One for the Road*, to give Christian students "a liturgical setting within the secular."[78] Secularization, a Catholic member wrote, "is sweeping across the world at a tremendous rate," and it was a trend that Christians needed to embrace. Rather than lament the decline of the sacred, "Brother Cairns" continued, "we as Christians must respond to his [Christ's] teaching and inspiration in order to make the world truly secular." As he saw it, "Christians" who found it sinful to relate the Gospel to the modern, secular world had based that judgment on a fundamental misapprehension of Christian tradition, in this case, the edict that Christians be in the world but not of it.[79] He retorted: "We must be fully in the world which is good because it was made by God." If everything good—all science, all knowledge, all reason—came from God, then it was Christians' sacred responsibility to embrace the secular.[80]

By embracing the modern as godly, advocates of secularization had found a cutting-edge faith. It was "radically different," in that it "defie[d] the old divisions between sacred and secular."[81] Indeed, like Mzara, the UCM sought to change the meaning behind the very terms *sacred* and *secular*. Secularization furthered the cause of the modern experience; it sanctified the whole of life as currently lived and kept Christians' eyes locked on the world around them. "God is no longer 'up there,'" Colin Collins wrote, "and Christ is as much in the concrete jungle of the cities as he was in Galilee."[82] Secular faith meant fully aware subjects working in a world made free by the breaking down of old structures. Whereas Beyers Naudé had used scriptural standards to judge the DRC, the UCM's theology focused as much on people's day-to-day experiences as on interpreted scripture. It celebrated the world around it, the diversity of the South African population within the city, which UCM defined as modern and thus opposed to "inefficient, anti-urban, anachronistic [and] blasphemous apartheid."[83] Rather than look backward to scripture, UCM read forward. Revelation, activists argued, was ongoing, in the growing "concrete jungles" and increasingly technological world. Now mattered.

The UCM's language—particularly regarding the tension between the city and apartheid—reflected the thinking of Harvey Cox, a Harvard divinity professor who, in his 1965 *Secular City*, urged Christians to see the "secularizing" world as evidence that humankind was finally prepared to assume the responsibility given to it by God. The word *secular* itself supported his argument: it came from the Latin *saeculum*, meaning "this present age," and, Cox argued, only by focusing energy in the present would people succeed in building God's liberated kingdom.[84] He differentiated between *secularism*—indeed, between all *-isms*—and *secularization*, claiming that the latter was "almost certainly [an] irreversible process" that would result in more openness, not an ism-esque dogma beneath which people could hide.[85] For Cox, the central message of the Gospel was a call for people to become "mature and responsible stewards" of the world by constantly seeking social change—Trotsky's "permanent revolution" expressing God's will through "permanent conversion."[86]

Cox mocked anti-Christian zealots such as Bertrand Russell and die-hard Communists as "quaint anachronisms" whose shrill claims about the death of God ignored the fact that God's death was a laudable process deserving of Christians' applause.[87] Indeed, he suggested that Christians take the discourse further to ultimately lose religion by speaking about God in a "political way":

We speak of God politically whenever we give occasion to our neighbor to become the responsible, adult agent, the . . . man God expects him to be today. We speak to him of God whenever we cause him to realize consciously the web of interhuman reciprocity in which he is brought into being and sustained in it as a man. We speak to him of God whenever our words cause him to shed some of his blindness and prejudices of immaturity and to accept a larger and freer role in fashioning the instruments of human justice and cultural vision. We do not speak to him of God by trying to make him religious but, on the contrary, by encouraging him to come fully of age, putting away childish things.[88]

As did Black Consciousness, Cox called Christians to adulthood, to maturity, and he promised that, once there, the kingdom would pay social dividends. "The religious quest is ended," he proclaimed, "and man is freed to serve and love his neighbor."[89] Faith was concerned with human relations, and politics was its business. The UCM was convinced. In early 1968, its leaders arranged for a hundred copies of Cox's book to be shipped from Detroit.[90]

Cox, however, was only the latest voice in a continuing discussion about the nature of faith in the world. Cox's challenge to "speak of God politically" was in many ways a 1960s' refinement of a generations-old quest for "religionless Christianity." Naming his predecessor, Cox wrote that "we must learn, as Bonhoeffer said, to speak of God in a secular fashion and find a non-religious interpretation of biblical concepts."[91] Dietrich Bonhoeffer was the German Confessing Church's best-known theologian, but his thinking did not end with confronting the state. As World War II raged, Bonhoeffer affirmed a faith thoroughly embedded in human societies, irrespective of church or politics. He rejected as "immature" the concept of God the father, in whom we place our faith and who in turn benevolently explains the gaps in our knowledge.[92] This was a mere "garment of faith" that humans needed to cast aside; instead, Bonhoeffer called for the Word to be "preached concretely, in the midst of historical reality." Bonhoeffer's theology built upon Paul's lesson that faith in Christ had breached the wall between people and God. With Christ, circumcision no longer marked a covenant with the divine, nor did a curtain separate worshippers from the holy of holies. In the 1930s, Bonhoeffer updated this for a world "come of age," an adult world, a mature humanity. "Freedom from [circumcision] is also freedom from religion," he declared. So-called secular theology needed only the Word in the world, experienced and applied in history.[93] Bonhoeffer argued that God's incarnation in Christ had insinuated divinity thoroughly and completely into human affairs. Christ was "the Lord of the World," and Bonhoeffer smashed any qualitative difference between the universe and the divine. Thus, he did not preach what Karl Barth had deemed the absolute difference between God and the universe or the "God of the gaps" or the deus ex machina; instead, he urged his church to stand "not at the boundaries, where human powers give out, but in the middle of the village."[94]

Secularization, as conceived of by Bonhoeffer and others, promised the continued "interpenetration" of the sacred and the profane, a process that had begun with the Incarnation and moved from Paul, through the Reformation's rejection of "communities of the sacred" in favor of "unlimited sovereignty," to fleeing Pietism, stoic Calvinism, Weberian capitalism, and so forth.[95] Protestant theology decorporatized the faith experience and placed it with people, not institutions. Whereas pre-Reformed Christians were "passenger[s] in the ecclesial ship on its journey to God," Charles Taylor wrote, after the Reformation, "each believer rows his or her boat." Bonhoeffer took this notion one step further, begging individuals to put down their oars and realize that they had arrived. He described this as the church standing in the middle of the village, but Cox's preferred "city" is a more fitting analogy. As the UCM realized, Cox's term evoked the now, the quintessentially modern experience of living as individuals among masses of the same. Christ elevated love of neighbor equal to love of God. How neighbors loved each other, how they gathered together, how they fought over and shared space—this was politics, and following Bonhoeffer's and Cox's lead, it called for faith.

Catholic seminarian Mokgethi Motlhabi found Bonhoeffer's and Cox's "religionless" theology more compelling than the Christianity taught by his teachers. "I felt we were somehow enslaved by religion," he recalled, and this new theology offered more personalized "situation ethics"—a way for faith to guide a "decision in accordance with the needs of the situation."[96] Motlhabi's response was a common one, especially in the UCM, where some suggested that even the word *Christian* smacked of an orthodoxy that had no place in apartheid South Africa. Recalling Collins's correspondence with Denis Hurley, the archbishop of Durban may have been thankful that he had demurred from hosting Happening '69, because by that time the very notion that the movement was a Christian endeavor was under attack. In 1967, the UCM constitution had claimed to bring together Christians of "different communions" to testify to their "unity in Christ." By 1969, that clause was suspect because it "implied a faith which some UCM members do not share." In spite of the prominent "Christian" in the movement's name, delegates worried that a constitution in the name of Jesus Christ prejudged the outcome of their experiences in the movement. UCM, they contended, was about searching, not certainty.[97]

This debate challenged the movement's Christian identity.[98] If secularization was a goal and could be seen as God's will, was "Christianity"—the institution, the religion—still necessary? The UCM leadership recognized this dilemma and in response distributed an explicit discussion of its evolving theology in preparation for the Encounter '70 conference. In it, Moore turned UCM's theology on its head, suggesting that it began not from the Word as revealed in scripture but in "the things which the Movement is in fact doing and saying." Theology did not guide Christians' actions; their actions determined what Christians got from their theology. He conceded that God remained important in Christians' lives, but in the spirit of *Secular City*'s God, he contended that God could no longer be seen as the "sole initiator and sustainer of Christian action; [instead] men are free and responsible agents." Worshipping the liberal's God and debating his place in politics was irrelevant, for "it is man who is of religious significance, and this religious significance is defined not in terms of what he knows about God, but in terms of what he makes of his world."[99] At Happening '69, Christian language was retained to serve certain "fundamentals," but within a few months, UCM's only fundamental was the truth of human life and action, a far cry from its foundational claims to bring together the various races to witness to the "purposes of God."[100]

In a follow-up article in the UCM newsletter, Moore demonstrated his debt to Bonhoeffer. According to Moore, the German had earned the company of Luther, St. Thomas Aquinas, Jesus, and Moses by demonstrating that Christians need not explain the world "in terms of 'God'" but that God might be known in terms of people's actions in the world.[101] "God"—now set in quotes or, as Moore favored, replaced with "it"—was a way to read human life, history, and potential: "It is a way of evaluating everything that has been and is in terms of what could be."[102] One knew God by reading the past to assess the present and find hope for the future. The divine was in "liberating experiences," Moore wrote, and the Christian's job was to see these extended further across and deeper within human societies.[103] In many ways, Moore more thoroughly secularized the religious experience than had Bonhoeffer or Cox. By seeing people as having religious significance and denoting the "religious" as whatever people make of the world, Moore went beyond lauding "God's" death to declaring it more or less irrelevant.

The UCM's position did not want for detractors. If God was dead and if people were of religious significance, what possible purpose did faith serve? For J. Erasmus, a Methodist minister from Beaufort West, such theology could not be Christian; it was instead a "denial of Christian faith."[104] Ted Simpson, the principal at the Anglican Seminary at Fed Sem, accused Moore of abandoning theology in favor of "sloganeering" and "parody." Removed from its "scientific" moorings, he contended, UCM's theology threatened to cross over to ideology and thereby lose the credibility that came with being "Christian."

Worse still, Simpson charged Moore with a lack of originality. He accused Moore of stealing his ideas not directly from Bonhoeffer but from Bishop John Robinson of England, whose book *Honest to God* had, in 1963, first spilled secular theology into the public arena.[105] Moore did owe Robinson his gratitude.[106] Indeed, Bonhoeffer's fame was at least in part due to the popularity of the Englishman's book, which went through eight printings in its first year of publication alone. In it, Robinson offered a vigorous response to a perceived crisis of faith in the English church, based on evidence showing "active support for the churches" in that country nearing that of the Soviet Union. Many felt that scientific and other advances meant "there is no room for [God], not merely in the inn, but in the entire universe."[107] Robinson, a bishop from South London, sought salvation in the efforts of Bonhoeffer and other theologians, notably Paul Tillich of New York's Union Theological Seminary, to redefine the experience and purpose of Christian faith amid the "secular strivings of our day." Like Bonhoeffer, Robinson focused on the Incarnation, when God through Christ "entered into the human scene, one who was not 'of it,' and yet lived genuinely and completely with it." Christ had begun the "interpenetration" of spheres, and now it fell to Christians to complete the work—not by praying cloistered or shuttered in their sanctuaries but by "penetrating through the world to God." The divine was on earth, met in love and in human relationships. Robinson concluded that "prayer and ethics are simply the inside and the outside of the same thing": how you carried yourself in your relationships with people (Motlhabi's "situation ethics") determined the content and the quality of your "religious" experience.[108]

Moore followed Robinson's argument this far. Yet even though Moore knew Robinson's work and perhaps stole from his conclusions, what he did not steal reveals a great deal about his circumstances, namely, the pressing need to bring the divine even more concretely into South Africa's corner of the world. For his part, Robinson never turned "God" into "it," as Moore had done. Rather, Robinson built upon the work of Paul Tillich to find a new place for the transcendent in Christian faith. He drew on Tillich's notion of God as the core of a person—neither "out there" in the rapidly shrinking beyond nor entirely internal to humanity but rather straddling the two, being within us by virtue of being "above . . . the limits of our imagination."[109] God dwelled at imagination's limits, around outer edges that we do not know exist because we cannot conceive of them. To believe this was to demonstrate "absolute faith" in the "God above God," a faith that needed modernity's doubt to allow the believer to consider the absurdity of faith in God and yet believe in spite of all the evidence to the contrary. Like Bonhoeffer's, Tillich's faith required maturity, the courage to abandon the theistic God who "has disappeared in the anxiety of doubt." Faith in God was a fact that only people living ordinary, secular lives—with no God the father, with no miracles—could affirm.[110]

Moore and the UCM chose not to follow Tillich's lead. Believing that, as an English socialist journal wrote, Tillich's spirituality was on a path to "sentimental meaninglessness," the UCM clung more easily to the horizontal axis of the imminent-transcendent divide. God existed not in spite of the evidence to the contrary but as "the true structure of [human-made, human-run] reality." Moore made God concrete, seeing "it" exclusively in human affairs. "It" was not something a mature person sought but something that a mature person "did" by participating in "ethical behaviour," choosing and living to bring more liberating experiences into the world. The use of *liberating* is instructive; like Cox, Moore traveled the byways of secular theology to speak of God in a political way, to bestow the once divine's name on the human quest for "peace [and] justice." In South Africa, there could no longer be debate over the appropriate role for Christian action. Neo-Calvinists might not like the end result, but, like the DRC's, secular theology's God was at home in human affairs and thus truly sovereign over the world.[111]

Moore's own version of secular theology was not readily accepted by the black students, who made up the bulk of the UCM's membership. Many had watched secular theology's spread with a combination of concern and boredom. "The secularization debate became very long-winded for me," a Congregationalist member from Fed Sem remembered. It was a "diversion" from pressing needs that, despite the rhetoric, failed to "affect the people on the ground."[112] For Gabriel Setiloane, a Methodist minister and proponent of indigenous "African Theology," it was pernicious—yet another foreign concept designed to separate the black man from his God. "We are smothered to death by Western theologies," he wrote, "vying with each other in seeking so much to cut God to size that some have now actually got rid of Him (I mean the *God is dead* thing!)."[113] Setiloane's critique points to a larger problem with this theology, one that the UCM began to confront within its own ranks. Who was it for? And was it appropriate for South Africa?

Whereas Robinson used Bonhoeffer to respond to "man who gets on perfectly well without religion," Barney Pityana used John Mbiti precisely because the "black man is notoriously religious."[114] Indeed, in South Africa and elsewhere in the global theological community, secular theology was guilty of cultural bias in assuming that its particular version of disenchanted modernity reigned supreme across the world.[115] As the South African theologian Albert Nolan put it, many black South Africans "had perfectly traditional ideas about God—except that God wasn't on the side of whites."[116] This disconnect proved the undoing of secular theology in South Africa. By the time of Happening '69, delegates knew that the movement's rainbow claims belied serious fissures just beneath the surface. The UCM newsletter described it: "It seems that the white students within the UCM are primarily in search of a theological identity, . . . [whereas] the non-whites in UCM, more particularly the African group, feel a greater need for political identity in the wider sense." The latter group's search, the unnamed author concluded, "is not primarily a theological but a pragmatic one."[117] Despite these divides, the article was entitled "Creative Tensions." The movement hoped to go beyond such disagreements and emerge stronger for their airing. To these ends, UCM structured its next conference, Encounter '70, around small, multiracial discussions—"encounter groups"—in which to further seek the divine in the neighbor.

However, encounter groups lasted "about ten minutes" before black students demanded that UCM begin discussing the country's political situation in earnest.[118] The conference report ably summed up the disconnect: "Many blacks felt that it was totally unrealistic in the South African context to expect blacks to trust other people, either white or black, so implicitly that they would expose themselves and their real feelings and intentions. . . . They asked what relevance it had for them. . . . They were not faced with the primary problem of deepening inter-personal relations but of . . . liberating their oppressed people."[119] For Chris Mokoditoa, a delegate and UCM's last general secretary, encounter groups were well-meaning but "too theoretical and too irrelevant," a reflection supported by the report's conclusion that "for many blacks the primary concerns are social and political and . . . it is in the solution of the problems in these areas that the hope lies for being fully human, and thus for inter-personal relations." South African society and secular theology showed no signs of solving political problems, and in light of this failure, Encounter '70 closed with a "sharp confrontation between black and white members."[120]

Yet to end the chapter with this confrontation would be to diminish what secular theology had accomplished—and to miss how its exposition, discussion, and even rejection had transformed the relationship between faith and politics for many South African students. Secular theology had opened new possibilities for articulating what it meant to be a Christian, and even its critics bear witness to its legacy. In the early 1960s, Bokwe Mafuna could not imagine standing in front of congregation and being true to himself. Yet by decade's close, he was redefining his Christianity, based on the knowledge that "most people who truly are seeking God but are unable to find to him [fail] because they look for him or her or it in books, in institutions, and in people *other than themselves.*"[121] Through faith in themselves and, through that, in others, true Christians might find God. Tillich, Bonhoeffer, Moore—and indeed, Calvin and Luther—would have approved. Further, despite Setiloane's concerns, secular theology freed Christianity from its marriage to either Dutch Reformed or mainstream English church politics. By directing believers' attentions to their communities and to their own lives and urging them to see the truths, pitfalls, and promises inherent there, secular theology helped to separate the Christian faith from its European trappings. The rector of the Lutheran Theological College at Mapumulo was fond of describing mission Christianity as a loaf of bread, wrapped in a plastic bag. For too long, he said, "someone who may think that the plastic bag is part of bread may find himself eating it," with "indigestion" the result.[122] As the 1960s turned to the 1970s and as the meaning and function of Christianity was revised, secular theology opened the possibility of a renewal, a rediscovery of the bag-free nourishment that Christ offered. This in turn opened the space for even more radical manifestations of faith.[123]

Many of Robinson's British readers had feared that the "heretical outpourings of Bonhoeffer, Tillich and other alien agnostics" would lead the next generation to unbelief. Yet the implications of Robinson's injunction to link prayer and ethics, as well as Moore's call to seek God through liberating experiences, resonated differently among people to whom both God and liberation were real and pressing concerns. Many blacks did reject "alien" secular theology as the most recent plastic bag, but its ideas opened a space to explore a still more relevant faith. From both within and without the UCM, blacks instead sought something more intrinsic, a faith that was not foreign but that, as Sabelo Stanley Ntwasa memorably put it, came "from my guts."[124] In the 1930s, Dietrich Bonhoeffer contended that "the promise of the Messiah is everywhere alive in history"; by the turn of the 1970s, girded with theology, South Africans were anticipating a messianic age.[125]

5 ⮑ Christ in Context
The Changing Face of Christianity

BUT WHAT did a faith from a young, black, South African student activist's "guts" look like? It depended. Ideas depend on identities—on who thinkers think they are and on what they think they are trying to do. In the 1970s, some argued that a less "foreign" faith required little more than replacing white leadership with black; others thought that the transformation had to be far more profound, with changed leaders portending more fundamental reassessments of faith. Some attempted this reassessment by looking to "traditional" African "religious" practices—the use of quotes implies the difficulties they encountered there—and others looked instead for a sacred road to a hoped-for political future. Secular theology might have been dismissed as foreign by some black South Africans, but its insights were keenly felt. It had made the case for the divine's infusion across and through people's earthly lives. In seminars, essays, and discussions, black South African Christians soon set out to determine for themselves what that meant. This chapter continues to unpack their efforts to link Jesus of Nazareth and Tiro of Dinokana, political and religious faith.

The critique of Christianity did not end with the acceptance or rejection of secular theology, nor did it cease with more representative leadership within the mainstream churches. Instead, just as Western theologians adapted their faith to fit emergent postmodernity, so too did Africans interrogate Christianity's place in postcoloniality. They probed the boundaries proscribed by mission and participated in what Lamin Sanneh has described as the further "translation" of the faith.[1] African Theology resulted from this effort—a school of theological thinking that strove to respond to the particular needs, experiences, and conditions of a certain "Africa."

Yet African Theology's Africa could not mean the continent as a whole. It was largely an interpretation of God's word designed for postcolonies, for independent countries in search of roots from which new nations might grow. But what about the unfree Africa, where local people had no power? Africans in places such as South Africa had a different perspective compared to Africans in independent nations. They were not yet in a position to look backward; what lay ahead was far more pressing. As we shall see, this marked a critical distinction between the African Theology that arose in independent Africa and what came to be called Black Theology in South Africa. The latter was about context, which in the usage of the time meant not just where you were but where you were going. As John Parratt explained, theologians in independent Africa sought a more culturally conditioned, "indigenous theology," whereas their still-colonized counterparts in South Africa increasingly looked to a "contextual theology," focused not on the past but on the challenges of the now and especially "the struggle for human justice" plotted into the future.[2] African Theologians such as John Mbiti were uncomfortable with the not-yet, but South African Christians—driven by necessity—charged forward.[3]

Yet Barney Pityana's casual borrowing of Mbiti's language suggests that South Africans still heard African Theology, and we must heed its insights in order better to understand South African departures. This chapter opens with debates over so-called Africanization, the indigenizing of power well under way in most of Africa but more politically problematic in its southern tip. As Michael Hardt and Antonio Negri asked in a different context, what does demographic change mean when fundamental power relationships remain the same?[4] In the late 1960s, South African Christians' demands for more control over their churches only corrected part of the problem. In the Bantustans, the African faces on the wall and flags flown over "independent" capitals belied actual power relationships; in church affairs, Africanization only achieved so much. Faced with the pressing demands of context and the future, South Africans first turned elsewhere in Africa and then to the diaspora, specifically to black America. There, they found a more overtly political faith known as Black Theology, which shared their concerns with the historical contingency of blackness and the enduring necessity of liberation. As South African church people began to develop their own voice, they interwove this latter insight with secular and African Theology. As SASO had done, church people carefully picked their way through both their sources and themselves, wielding the strands of identity, political imperative, and perceived context to talk about both Christ and Tiro.

"OUR CHURCH HAS LET US DOWN"

In January 1970, a group of black Catholic ministers publicly claimed more rights within their church. Representing the St. Peter's Old Boys Association—a name that neatly played on the Black Consciousness coming-of-age narrative (as well as the Catholic Church's blacks-only seminary north of Pretoria)— they condemned the Church for treating them "like glorified altar boys," like ecclesiastical children, "in spite of our ordination." They went on to accuse their church of shrinking before apartheid politics—yet they neither called for a fully integrated priesthood nor threatened to leave the fold. Instead, they urged Catholics to stop "living in a make-believe world," contending that "if we have to have apartheid, we might as well insist on our own rights under it." Their demands were simple: more black priests in black parishes and more black control over parishes' administration. "We prefer," they concluded, "to manage or mismanage ourselves."[5]

The Old Boys had a good case. Their alma mater was reserved exclusively for black students, yet it boasted only one black lecturer among its eight-person staff; white foreigners ran township parishes, with black priests serving only as adjuncts; and black Catholic students in nearby Johannesburg were forced into government-run schools, as the Catholic Church ran only one school for blacks compared to twenty-two for the much smaller white population.[6] Like the rest of black South Africa, black Catholics were thus woefully underserved by white authority. Since the Church was "not really orienting us to manhood and adulthood," the Old Boys claimed this role for themselves. Yet the Old Boys did not search for a path outside the Church; rather, they emphatically wanted further in. Preaching "realism," they claimed for their community what little apartheid purported to bring—the right to develop separately, to "rediscover [our] personality and [our] identity . . . to develop all [our] faculties—mental, physical, aesthetic." And they doubted "whether [we] can achieve this in the midst of White people."[7]

This was Africanization, a process set off by independence and Vatican II and, by the late 1960s, well under way in independent Africa. Africanization's supporters contended that churches needed to increase African representation and authority. A representative church would undoubtedly have a majority African clergy, they argued, but this was of necessity, not rebellion; such changes, one of the Old Boys explained, were for "the good of the church." Only African priests could further "indigenize" the Catholic faith and thus ensure the Church's continued existence in South Africa.[8] Africanization was in a sense akin to affirmative action in postapartheid society: pictures on the wall change, but the fundamental power relationships remain the same. This is not to say that such changes—whether in mainstream, separatist, or nineteenth-century Ethiopian churches—meant nothing. But Africanization was change to a point and no further. If the church's theology and political perspective were conservative, so would they continue to be, only now with different people in charge.

This seemed like a reasonable demand. The *Rand Daily Mail* printed the Old Boys Asssociation's declaration in its entirety, and its editorial page nodded its support through a cartoon, which showed a priest's collar inscribed with "white collar jobs" above a caption that read "Reserved for whites."[9] Similarly, the *World's* Percy Qoboza, himself a noted Catholic, penned a long investigative report that cited widespread disillusionment among township Catholics.[10] Other churches noted the discussion and scrambled to protect their reputations. The Anglican Church already boasted two black bishops and assured its parishioners that continued pay disparities between black and white priests would soon end.[11] White authorities at the interdenominational Federal Theological Seminary noted the spread of Black Consciousness among the student body and called for the hiring of more black chaplains and, if possible, a black seminary president. (However, the bishop of Cape Town viewed this as impossible at the time, noting, "[Even though] I see the advantage of having an African . . . he must be a man who will measure up to the job.")[12] Given the press, it was not altogether surprising that in 1972, the pope nominated a black man, Peter Buthelezi, to fill a temporary vacancy as bishop of Johannesburg. Notably, a black Catholic group marked this with flyers pressing beyond demographics to the "socio-economic conditions of the Black man."[13]

This last incident marked the fault lines within Africanization efforts. What was Africanization's desired end? Was the selection of Peter Buthelezi enough? Or was his presence only preface to more fundamental changes? Just five years before, after all, the notably "liberal" Methodist Church had elected Seth Mokitimi its first black president, yet some black Methodists grumbled that nothing had changed.[14] Just as SASO members critiqued independent African leaders regardless of skin color, so too did many black Christians chide newly elevated church leaders for not being black enough, in the Black Consciousness sense of the term. In a report to a conference of black churchmen, for example, Rubin Phillip sharply criticized the Anglican Church's efforts to become more demographically representative. "The blacks that we elect . . . are not really people of the right calibre," he insisted. Instead, they were either "white puppets or very antiquated in their ideas and attitudes." There were black faces on the wall—and then there were real black men. Africanization could not stop at what Mapumulo rector Makhitini described as "window dressing" and still declare a meaningful victory.[15]

This marked a fault in Africanization, with some Christians suggesting that black faces mattered only if they changed people's experiences in the pews. After all, the Anglican Church had a long history in South Africa and scores of trained African ministers to show for it, but at the dawn of the 1970s, Anglican minister Rubin Phillip suggested that its services "could have been in England apart from singing a few vernacular songs." There was nothing particularly African about the practice of the faith. Former SASO activist and Ethiopian Episcopalian bishop Malusi Mpumlwana agreed, tracing this back to the late nineteenth century when his own church broke from the Anglicans, partly in response to white missionary control and especially in reaction to the worship's stubborn Europeanness. Late nineteenth-century parishioners had wanted to worship in a more African manner by including local elements—a different sort of Africanization than that discussed so far.[16] Ethiopian Episcopalianism had been locally grounded and evolved, modified in a way that both the Catholics who picketed Buthelezi's installation and Phillip suggested; it moved beyond black faces to new practices, whether social or liturgical.

In the 1960s and early 1970s, the latter practices emerged as the most immediate arena for change. Clement Mokoka was one of the Old Boys and a parish priest outside Pretoria. There, in the late 1960s, he earned a reputation for pushing against the edges of traditional Catholic practice: "Clement Mokoka . . . would stand on his pulpit and say to his congregation—hey—the traditional indigenous doctors also know—don't go to them at night when I don't see you. You can go during the day. There is nothing wrong with it. And he would even say to them, if you want to go because a child got sick at night and you have no way, come and wake me up and I will drive you there."[17] Predictably, these statements earned criticism from white church authorities, as well as from parishioners who for so long had been taught that such activities meant "we are going back to heathenism." Yet Mokoka insisted that many others felt comfortable with a Catholic priest volunteering to drive parishioners to the local community healer, and still more approved of incorporating traditional ritual practices, such as root burning, into the liturgy. (After all, did not the Church instruct the use of incense?) Their goal was to further indigenize the Church, not to pervert it. "Africans should be at peace with the gospel," Mokoka told me, and they needed to figure out how best "to express ourselves as a community at prayer."[18]

Like SASO activists, priests wanted not only to exert control over their institutions but also to mold them, to figure out what shape they ought to take; Biko himself had charged black priests with turning the church "into one we cherish, we love, we understand and one that is relevant to us."[19] This call resonated especially in Catholic circles, where the Second Vatican Council had opened the liturgy to local languages, among other reforms, in hopes of both limiting the distance between priest and congregation and in general furthering the religion's enculturation. Mokoka and his peers felt Vatican II's effects while at seminary. There, teachers had shelved old texts in favor of the council's communications, and students debated the implications of changes at the top. In Mokoka's opinion, the ethos of the place shifted after Vatican II:

"The sense we got . . . was that the Church is ours and we have to be responsible for the Church." That was in fact the crux of the Old Boys' argument—that Africans "must take the Church on our shoulders." Buti Tlhagale, who also trained during the late 1960s and early 1970s, echoed this in language Abraham Kuyper would have recognized. After Vatican II, Tlhagale insisted, "Catholicism [did] not mean having a monolithic way of looking at things; without diversity, there probably wouldn't be salvation. God created us different and that's how we're going to be saved—in our own uniqueness, in difference."[20] Seminary students' experiences of the late 1960s thus corresponded with that of their bush college peers. In both settings, responsibility was the byword, with decisions to be made no longer by "ecclesiastical children" but by mature adults, on their own. Tlhagale's ideas echoed the DRC's to some extent, except that he did not suggest that salvation was reserved only for the elect. Rather, salvation was available for everyone in their uniqueness. All one had to do was to recognize and figure out how best to earn it.

AFRICAN THEOLOGY AND THE PROBLEM OF "RELIGION"

In 1968, St. Peter's alum Smangaliso Mkhatshwa issued an early call for "Africanisation of the church," in which he claimed not to be dismissing the church but instead advocating for its further implanting in African soil.[21] In 1970, he signed the Black Priests' Manifesto with the rest of the Old Boys and insisted that it was not hated "racialism" that drove him but the Vatican itself. Mkhatshwa and the Old Boys explained that the pope had charged Africans with giving the Church "that precious and original contribution of Négritude which she needs," and that was what Africanization was about: finding the "African soul" within Catholicism.[22] This presumed that the universal message of the supposed "world religion" necessarily had and needed to find its local realization. Scripture enjoined Christians to translate their message, and Europeans had proven adept at doing so. As independence dawned across the African continent, some Christians called for the cessation of foreign missionary activity; with the rise of decolonization, the missionary legacy was undergoing revision, and the faith needed its local readers to take over.[23]

This was a continent-wide process. West African theologians searched the precolonial past for spiritual material, and their historian counterparts shunned histories of mission for more locally oriented church histories. In East Africa, thinkers such as John Mbiti—whose words we have already seen co-opted to the Black Consciousness cause—interrogated Christianity's interaction with local faiths, while Southern Africans such as Gabriel Setiloane cast doubt upon the entire premise of "comparative religion" in the colonial context. South Africans heard these conversations and occasionally interjected. But translation is a complicated process, as the scholarship on it reflects. Some have argued that it was complete and total, that Christianity had insinuated itself into African thought patterns and set off irreversible change.[24] Others have argued the opposite, that Christianity was in fact domesticated to African realities and ways of thinking, not the other way around, and that missionaries remained oblivious all the while.[25] Others more lyrically have described the process as the "pulling," both "together and against one another," of the (distinct, if adjacent) "component pieces" of a "multi-colored woolen cord."[26] Theologians lacked the benefit of hindsight as they tried to figure out where they were, yet their conclusions regarding these debates were instructive in their time—and they remain so in our own. Like Western secular theology, African Theology frequently pressed against the edges of both Christianity and religion and offered the potential to radically reinterpret both. This was liberating for some, jarring for others, and for many South Africans still not enough. Translation had to go on.

If the pope urged African priests to insert the "African soul" into their faith, then Mokoka's openness to local ritual practices made theological sense. True, some parishioners echoed missionaries' historical concerns about backsliding into heathenism, but with Africans' assumption of responsibility, others argued that "traditional" practices offered insights. Or so Buti Tlhagale insisted when, while still at seminary, he wrote the rector to suggest that Catholic priests be allowed to study anthropology. Anthropology interrogated local cultures, and, he said, "we're asking that our culture be taken seriously and that we begin to be taught our own culture so that even theological categories should be in terms of our own African culture." Biko had blamed missionaries for demeaning local practices as ritual and barbaric; now, Tlhagale suggested that missionary institutions ought to help students rediscover what was lost. "There's nothing as exhilarating as beginning to understand yourself, your culture, who you are, what makes you," he observed, and the time had come for theology to reflect this.[27]

The new theology sprang from the African experience. Chris Mzoneli was a student at the Lutheran Theological Seminary at Mapumulo when he began to reflect on African traditions in light of biblical texts. There, he became convinced that "Africans are . . . closer to the gospel." "If one talks about heaven and earth for example, [about] the narrowing of the gap between secular and sacred, African-ness . . . is like in the Old Testament . . . there was never a time when Yahweh was not there." This was, he explained, why African Christians always favored the prophets: because Isaiah and his peers did not reflect a "secular division."[28] Like secular theology, Mzoneli's African-ness did not respect the modern world's boundaries; instead, it encroached upon them, by turning secular theology on its head. Bonhoeffer's notion of the Incarnation saw spirit and flesh linked, through Christ, and cast into the secular world. This consecrated political affairs, and it gave faithful purpose to man-come-of-age. Yet Mzoneli meant something different. Spirit and flesh were linked, true, but as the prophets attested, the divine was still the actor who was intensely involved in the world. There was no God-above-God here; there was simply Yahweh, present, and Africans seemed closer to that truth.

Buti Tlhagale expanded on this point by turning, like Bonhoeffer, to the singular moment of the Incarnation. African culture, learned through anthropology, was the path toward salvation through uniqueness because God/spirit had become Christ/flesh: "God came into this world, assumed the values of this world, and therefore assumed the cultural values of *all the cultures under the sun*" (emphasis added). Christ was white; Christ was brown; Christ was European; Christ was African. All cultures offered the opportunity to experience the divine, and revelation was pervasive, simultaneous, and ongoing. Secular theology had rejected both deist notions of God as watchmaker and theist notions of a God out there somewhere who helps explain things we cannot, in favor of God as a divine presence pervading the world through the Incarnation, secularizing, and humanizing. Tlhagale, Mzoneli, and others contended that if this was the case, then the divine existed and had always existed in culture, and therefore African ways of communicating with the unseen (venerating ancestors, cleansing rituals, and the like) bore God's thumbprint and God's approval. Africanist faiths such as Mpumlwana's had long justified themselves through ancient Ethiopia, St. Augustine, and Psalm 68. They need not have. Now, all religious practices, properly understood, communed with Christianity's God—the revelation had been revealed to all the world's cultures at the moment of Incarnation.[29]

This conclusion did not speak well of missionaries who had fashioned themselves as Christ's great messengers in Africa. They now stood accused of brainwashing the local population, and they were held responsible not only for abetting colonialism but also for the colonization of Africans' minds by denigrating what were in fact legitimate African religions.[30] African theologians concluded that missionaries had been too heavy-handed, arrogant, and blinded to appreciate the very real, vibrant, and faithful African societies surrounding them. They had sown discord, and now, in the late twentieth century, African theological thinkers exacted revenge. It is telling that in 1971, when Lawrence Zulu, a lecturer at Fed Sem, delivered a paper that lauded the bravery and accomplishments of nineteenth-century English missionaries, it was met with dull disapproval.[31] It was not a good time to be a missionary.

Or, for that matter, a Western-oriented Christian. For some, the logic of simultaneous revelation freed the faith from its historically tight embrace of Western society. If there was a true Christian core out there, then the new theology needed to "tear open" the faith's "Greek Roman thought forms and modes of expression . . . in order to get to Christ."[32] Some white Christians protested that eliminating those "thought forms" in fact eliminated the historical Christ, and they pleaded, perhaps disingenuously, that since Christianity "has never been influenced by the Anglo-Saxon or Nordic ancestral beliefs of the white people," it was inappropriate to incorporate the ancestral beliefs of black people. Others doubted whether anything purely African continued to exist centuries after colonization.[33] But African theologians maintained that local peoples' ways of thinking about the divine had been and continued to be relevant.

Having dismissed missionaries, African theologians turned to so-called traditional faith in search of ways to improve Christianity. John Mbiti's *African Religions and Philosophy* exemplified this approach. In it, Mbiti, a Kenyan, Anglican priest, and Cambridge PhD, put the lie to charges of heathenism with a sophisticated and wide-ranging discourse on various aspects of African religion. Trusting, pace Emile Durkheim, that the study of religion actually meant the "study of the peoples themselves in all the complexities of both traditional and modern life," Mbiti held up African beliefs about God, the past, the future, redemption, and salvation against a typically mute but assumed Christian counterpoint. One was not necessarily better than the other; rather, before testing the waters of comparative religion, the point was to establish African religion as a fact undeserving of denigration.[34]

Judeo-Christian monotheism was always there, however. The fourteen references to God in Mbiti's table of contents alone demonstrated his allegiance to the language missionaries had brought. He argued that, without exception, all Africans "have a notion of God" and that "African soil is rich enough to have germinated its own religious perception" of the ultimate divine. Further, echoing the foregoing discussion of biblical precedents, he defined this "religious perception" in language reminiscent of ancient Israel's monotheism-affirming Sh'ma: "Every African people recognizes God as One." His premise was a simple one: following the logic of simultaneous revelation, it was evident that Africans had known God before the advent of colonial and missionary rule.[35]

Yet even if the divine was one and if African soil originated ways of approaching it (or *him*, at the time), Mbiti described the religious nature of African societies in a way that rendered the human-deity relationship somewhat problematic. Reminiscent of secular theology's description of a world infused with divinity, in African societies "the whole environment and the whole time [is] occupied by religious meaning, so that at any moment and in any place, a person feels secure enough to act in a meaningful and religious consciousness." Religion saturated life. It was continuous, with "neither founders nor reformers," and absolutely fundamental: "An ontological phenomenon; it pertains to the question of existence or being." Religion was wherever Africans were (in the most profound sense of the word), and this put a particular weight on African societies. If religion was pervasive, then it did more than function as a representation of that society, as Durkheim would suggest. Rather, it was the society. "Traditional religion," Mbiti wrote, manifested itself in "traditional solidarity, in which the individual says 'I am because we are and since we are, therefore I am.'" The bonds between the community were eternal and religious — or at least they had been until missionaries came and shattered the ideal.[36]

And it was an idealization. Despite their desire to move forward, both African Theologians and Black Consciousness thinkers typically gazed upon precolonial society with little cynicism. In chapter 3, we saw Biko describe an "unindividualistic" and "man-centered" society pervaded by God; his particular source might have been Kaunda, but it could easily have been Mbiti as well. Indeed, Biko's successor as SASO president, Barney Pityana, cited the Kenyan in an extended meditation titled "Old Value Systems and Concepts," which he presented to a SASO formation school: "The tribal community was tolerant and accepting. People were valued not for what they could achieve but because they were part of the others. Their contribution, however limited, to the material welfare of the village was acceptable, but it was their presence and not their achievement which was appreciated. The tribal community was an inclusive society. The web of relationships . . . were widely spread."[37] The critical difference between such ideas and secular theology is this: whereas secular theology plotted modern, decorporatized human relationships as the potential site for a new earthly divine, such descriptions of idealized African societies and intellectual innovations like African Humanism and African Theology placed the particular genius for divine human relationships in Africa's social past and, by extension, its future.

This insight marked a further departure from secular theology — away from the individual and toward the collective. In this, theologians found biblical precedent. In 1971, Bonganjalo Goba presented a paper to a UCM seminar that compared Africa's "corporate personality" with ancient Israel. The concept, he explained, referred to the "social consciousness of the people [and] the solidarity which existed and which seemed to govern [their] whole existence." In both Africa and Israel, the individual mattered less than the whole, from which the individual "derived his character." In Africa, as in Israel, relationships determined identity, and those relationships in turn structured how one approached the divine.[38] Over time, biblical analogies of this type became less important, and Africans' supposedly unique cultural genius for human relationships, manifested in society, ontology, and religion, stood more frequently on its own as Africa's great gift to the world.

This was the goal for which Biko had called — "a more human face" — and it was at the heart of African Theology. This was the faith — the godliness — that students and church people found in Mbiti-penned essays in South African Christian journals. This was the enduring African core of Christianity that inspired Setiloane (like Mbiti, an ordained minister) to sustain a monograph-length argument about the image of the divine among his people, both before and after the missionaries arrived. This same logic compelled him to publish pieces about rituals such as the Nguni *ukubuyisa*, which brought the "dead into vital participation with the living" and whose incorporation in Christian funeral rites would further indigenize its practice.[39] It was how a mid-twentieth-century African minister and university professor might express his faith.[40]

Buti Tlhagale argued that Incarnation made African cultural elements religiously viable, and in human relationships, a variety of thinkers found divinity. But to what extent was African Theology necessarily "Christian"? Theologians were ambivalent about this; for his part, Mbiti argued that traditional African religions had "remained fairly stable" despite Islam, Christianity, and colonialism. Moreover, he insisted that the essence of Christianity—with its orientation toward the future, toward the millennium, toward Christ's return—was in fact foreign to the traditional African worldview. Time served as his main intellectual tool, and in African societies, he argued, time was about the "here and now," not the "hope for a future" that marked Christianity. Indeed, he regarded the introduction of the future warily: "[The] new discovery of the future dimension, is not a smooth one and may well be at the root of . . . the political instability of our nations. In Church life this discovery seems to create a strong expectation of the millennium" and, with that, an otherworldliness that distracted people from the "challenges of this life." He did acknowledge change, and he noted with some satisfaction that Christianity had carried "world revolutions" in technology and communication to the continent—but he maintained that these were "dangerous," even if "dynamic."[41]

Yet even though Mbiti approached Christianity a bit warily, his was a Christian theology. It did not trace God's word as specifically revealed through approved scriptures, but it was in keeping with the trends of its era. It was an exegesis of society, not of scripture, much as Cox had urged in a different context. It was thus an instrument designed to further Christianity: to Africanize where Cox and Moore called for secularizing. Recall that Setiloane introduced ukubuyisa in hopes of Africanizing Christian ritual. This was the essential first step but not the last: Africans "still await the rediscovery that life is one—and that it is one no longer under the old customs, but in Christ," he wrote.[42] Mbiti agreed. In the last section of his celebration of African religion, his personal mission shone through. Traditional religion deserved respect and elevation on par with the other religions of the world, but like "Islam and the other religious systems [it was] preparatory"; these were perhaps "essential ground in the search for the Ultimate . . . but only Christianity has the terrible responsibility of pointing the way to that ultimate Identity, Foundation and Source of being."[43] The responsibility was terrible because it promised dislocation and change, loosening the moorings that had bound societies. It was terrible but essential, and as Mkhatshwa suggested, it fell to Africans to push their faith further, to indigenize, acculturate, and assume the grave responsibility of finally making the religion live in Africa.[44]

Critically, African theologians achieved this by unsettling the post-Enlightenment logic that separated the religious and secular spheres. Translation into local idioms demanded that they do this, Setiloane argued, since "there is actually no African word to translate 'religion.' At best it is translated as 'a people's ways' or 'customs.' Religion is something lived and practiced, not discussed and talked about."[45] Religion as a category did not exist, he argued. And if it did, the totality of a people's ways—their entire social being—made establishing boundaries and definition difficult. Mbiti's research led to similar conclusions: "Religion is a difficult word to define," he wrote, so "I do not attempt to define it," opting instead to explain that "for Africans it is an onto-logical phenomenon; it pertains to the question of existence or being."[46] How far we are from sacred practices and ritual; now, we have come to being, the totality of existence, combined through African Theology with the vitality of human relationships and, as in secular theology, a pervasive faith, every day of the week, in the church of the world.

In its time, African Theology hoped for a more complete faith, a founda-tion from which Africans might ultimately understand, "accede to and accept the teaching about God's revelation in Jesus Christ."[47] It was this approach to Christianity that Black Consciousness thinkers encountered on the pages of the same journals in which they published; it was these ideas that Barney Pityana "borrowed" to describe the necessity of a particular approach to poli-tics. It was the religion to which SASO's "Committee On: What Is Worthy of Preservation from Our Past" signaled its approval: "Blacks believed in the community—in the existence of a God."[48] It was a religion that saw divinity and community inexorably intermingled in lived life in this world, with spirit and flesh made one in society, again and again.

Yet South African activists gave this a final twist, which would undoubtedly have unsettled Mbiti: as one author put it, "black consciousness must be tackled by its advocates as a religion: we believe in it, we think it is right."[49] This was a singular understanding of religion. It was entirely in the present— not what "we have believed" or "you have believed" but "we believe." And it was the subjective interpretation of a particular community—"we [the agents] think it is right." That was the final piece of "religion" in the South African context. In African Theology, it was being, relationships; here, it was further refined as something strongly held, something believed in by a historical community in a particular moment. Was it God? Maybe, in a sense. Rules, dogmas, church institutions? Potentially, but probably not. Faith? Given this definition, there could be no more appropriate term.

Faith can be defined as subjective belief and, following Kierkegaard (and Karen Fields), as active belief.[50] But if faith was subjective and active, then it was continually subject to translation. South Africans have participated in our discussion thus far. Tlhagale offered the logic of the Incarnation; Goba, Phillip, and Mzoneli referred to the specific African genius for relationships; and Biko and others agreed that missionaries' mistakes needed to be undone before an appropriate faith would emerge. Their participation, however, did not signal their complete approval of African Theology. John Sebidi, one of the Old Boys, agreed with Mbiti that Africans were "'Animal Religiosum' [and] for this reason all [their] problems will basically be religious, moral problems." In his priesthood, he traded black shirt and white collar for brightly colored Afro shirts, and like Mokoka, he embraced a range of ritual practices under the category "Christianity." But there, he departed from the African Theology model: "I make no bones about it," he wrote in 1968, "justice and love, the dignity of man, essential equality and freedom of all men, brother of all in the fatherhood of one God etc. ought to be the type of preaching that is thundered, without apology, from our pulpits." Nuns and priests ought to stand on the "picket lines for racial justice, . . . [as] evangelists, telling modern man what the Gospel says."[51] As an Old Boy, Sebidi believed in acculturation, indigenization, and the exegetical potential of African societies. Yet in the South African context, translation continued. Although student activists paused at the dawn of the 1970s to look backward, "to the heritage of our forefathers," they needed a faith rooted in an explicit temporal purpose: "roots to anchor [us] firmly in the midst of a militant struggle."[52] Struggle meant now and future, and that demanded that the community develop a different sort of faith.

African Theology posed a trio of problems for South African activists. First, at the most superficial level, its celebration of Africanness was politically untenable in the quest for wider black unity, and it came perilously close to supporting apartheid's thesis about the absolute difference between whites and Africans. Second, although it was antimission and critical of Western theology, it approached politics — struggle — tentatively, at a time when Black Consciousness defined new identities based entirely on relevance and defiant "projections of the beingness." Third, questions about African Theology's Christianity suggested intellectual fault lines. When Biko wrote that he did not "question the truth at the heart of the Christian message," how did he understand what that was? Was it simultaneous revelation? Or, pace Sebidi, did he understand the Gospel to mean "justice and love" and hope for the world's conversion to those ideals? We must still consider how this group of Africans—who fashioned themselves black—both engaged African Theology and cast about, again, for a faith they felt in their guts.

David Chidester has argued that the apartheid government approached religion following the logic of separate development. Every national group had its own appropriate religion, "separate, hermetically sealed compartments into which human beings can be classified and divided."[53] Apartheid perverted postcolonial ideologies of cultural pluralism and cultural relativism into a set of boxes into which peoples neatly fit. African Theology might elevate African "traditions" to exegetical prominence in Kenya and elsewhere, but in South Africa, where young teachers in training were sent to colleges built to resemble precolonial villages as if "normal rectangular buildings were . . . not good for our Bantu psyche," cultural reification was a rather problematic enterprise.[54] As Manas Buthelezi explained: "An African Theology tied to a past tradition [or] heritage smacked of something similar to the Government's attempt to link the political future of the Black man to past traditions and institutions." It was presumptuous, he continued, to assume how much of the past people would allow to dictate their future.[55]

Besides, this was the era of Black Consciousness, with the term *black* politically defined to include all those oppressed by the system, not only those who had met missionaries on the frontier and seen their religion undermined. Soweto Urban Bantu Council member David Thebehali demonstrated the particularly South African political problem caused by African Theology. He expressed his support for that theology's "de-brainwashing" project, for its potential to give Christianity "the relevance for human affairs that it needs to do or have." But he warned that South Africans would not be able to exploit its full potential because Black Consciousness meant that "you must be able to justify the same thing for the Indians, for the Coloureds, if you are going to use [it]." He continued: "That is where I see these tensions and contradictions coming in. Because we've taken a base that is too broad."[56] He supported African Theology and worried that South Africans would not fully benefit from its insights because of Black Consciousness. Yet even as he worried that blackness was "too broad," he attested to its gathering strength.

Still, South African blackness implied more than oppositional solidarity. It was predicated on a willingness to struggle—in fact, more than a willingness but rather a beingness attuned entirely to the political project. This implied a perspective on the future, something that, as we have seen, African Theology—and SASO—approached warily. Mbiti thought that his Christian faith provided the one true path, superior to all other "preparatory" belief systems. Yet he worried that it had bequeathed a future dimension and concomitant instability to Africa. To the South African theologian Manas Buthelezi, Mbiti's hesitation reeked of "nostalgia," amid pressing day-to-day and today-to-tomorrow concerns.[57]

Within Black Consciousness, there was, of course, a role for political nostalgia. De-brainwashing in the name of Africanness was a potent act in the wake of colonialism, but it required a politics of a different sort. By the 1960s, South Africa abounded with African Independent Churches (AICs) that combined Christian and traditional rituals and beliefs. These churches, in the words of an AIC theology syllabus, represented a Christianity "deeply rooted in African soil" but also one that typically denied secular theology's innovations and maintained sharp distinctions between the affairs of God and the political affairs of people.[58] Moreover, as seen earlier, even Mbiti worried that where future-oriented Christianities existed, they were otherworldly and millennium-oriented and thus distracted from the challenges of lived life. From this perspective, AICs might have embodied African Theology's insights, but vis-à-vis South Africa's manifold challenges, they offered the correct perspective on neither the present nor the future.

And there was still that dogged question about Christianity as a category. Black Consciousness adherents tended to come from rather traditional Christian backgrounds, as distinguished from traditionally African ones. Many were educated in the theological struggles of their Catholic, Anglican, and other churches of the mission era and disapproved of calls to leave them. Black Consciousness activists were thus modern and opposed to cultural reification that benefited the political status quo, all elements that seemed in conflict with African Theology. Yet its ideas resonated, and South African observers had to note that it offered a successful translation of the faith to African circumstances. The challenge, then, was to make it effectively South African as well.

Across the Atlantic, black American theologians were grappling with a similar set of questions. In 1964, Joseph Washington published a provocative analysis of what he called the black religion, in which he challenged the widespread assumption that "Negroes are authentically and historically rooted in the Christian tradition."[59] Rather, he contended, civil rights struggles actually proved the opposite—that blacks had embraced a "folk religion, [a] militant identity for the purposes of justice," which failed Christianity's test of conversion and reflection on the word of God.[60] This militant folk religion might earn political victories in this world, he cautioned, but in so doing, it risked reducing Christianity to earthly affairs. Washington's sources revealingly lacked still-evolving secular theology, but his polemic posed a challenge to those who saw racial justice as an inexorably Christian cause. The civil rights movement had already been challenged by the Nation of Islam's charges that its Christian faith was a slave religion, a tool of the white devil. Now, ministers had to defend their other flank from charges that their ideas were not in fact rooted in Christianity.

James Cone, a young theology student at Garrett Seminary in Evanston, Illinois, wanted to combat Washington's premise but was quickly frustrated. Because Washington had defined Christianity as interested exclusively in "the faith and creeds of the Church," Cone later wrote, his conclusions were entirely appropriate.[61] More frustrating for Cone was that such conclusions were in keeping with the conservative, church- and salvation-oriented theology he was learning in graduate school. Faced with the twin problems of political and religious relevance, Cone and other young black theologians set out, as Bonhoeffer, Robinson, Mbiti, and others had done, to redefine what Christianity meant in their particular context. They did so by focusing on an area where African Theology lagged: on the person and actions of Christ.

The ideas that resulted became known as Black Theology, a name demonstrating the theology's close relationship with the burgeoning Black Power movement of the late 1960s. Indeed, from its earliest iteration by a group of black churchmen in 1966, Black Theology was at once theological and unapologetically political. Black churchmen, in a statement by the National Committee of Negro Churchmen, expressed the "conviction that Jesus Christ reigns in the 'here' and 'now,' as well as in the future," and if Christ reigned here, if Christ was active now, then Christians needed to be "for human justice in the places of social change and upheaval where our Master is already at work." As Mississippi simmered and ghettos burned and as the world courted revolution and change, the "Master" was at work. This contention transcended charges that the civil rights movement was not Christian; instead, these churchmen proposed that the movement revealed the essence of Christian faith.[62]

The statement was inflammatory, but its signatories begged the question of its underlying logic. It fell to Cone, who by the late 1960s was a professor at Union Theological Seminary, to make the reasoning explicit.[63] His study *Black Theology and Black Power* was published in 1969; in it, Cone offered a sustained, systematic, radical black counterpart to theological innovations earlier in the 1960s. His political stance was clear. Black Power, he declared, was "the most important development in American life in [the twentieth] century." It represented, at long last, the authentic description of "what the black man feels in the white world." Just as Biko described the absurdity of black lives under apartheid, Cone asserted that American blacks experienced "misery in a disorderly, an irrational and unpredictable world, [where they are] oppressed by the absurdity of the disparity between the universe as [they] wish it to be and as [they] see it." Summoning Paul Tillich (his colleague at Union), Cone insisted that Black Power reflected the "courage to be" in spite of America's absurdity. Through it, the black person "affirms his being in spite of those elements of his existence which conflict with his essential self-affirmation." Tillich had used the "in spite of" model to affirm the God-above-God; here Cone embodied it, black pride and power "in spite of" white society.[64]

For Cone, Black Power was an existentialist-inspired, inward-facing process. Thus, riots were not violent nihilism but "an assertion of the dignity of all black people," the outward face of the internal production of pride in spite of oppression. But Cone was above all a Christian, and he was concerned with another level of inward activity, the production and maintenance of faith. At the outset, he challenged himself, asking, "Is there any relationship at all between the work of God and the activity of the ghetto?" and, more politically salient, "[Is] Black Power compatible with the Christian faith, or are we dealing with two utterly divergent perspectives?" His conclusions were remarkable. In light of Black Theology, Cone suggested that Black Power ought to be seen as nothing short of "Christ's central message to 20th century America."[65]

Cone substantiated this spectacular statement by departing from both secular theology and African Theology. Following Karl Barth, he asserted that Christianity's uniqueness was its focus on one person and its faith that one person was the key to theological reflection. One needed only to turn to scripture to assess whether the Black Power project of dignity-in-the-face-of-oppression passed the scriptural test. Christology—the theology of Christ—was that key.[66] About Christ, Cone was unequivocal: "Jesus' work is essentially one of liberation." Cone proceeded to set out the theological proof behind the claim that the "Master" was currently at work for justice. He began from the same place as Bonhoeffer and Tlhagale—the moment of the Incarnation, when God took on the values of this world. According to Bonhoeffer, this sacralized the village; according to Tlhagale, it validated culture(s). For Cone, the historicity of the Incarnation was the point. God had become human as a disenfranchised Jew under Roman occupation, and the Gospels told the political story that followed. Christ had preached that the last would be first; he had challenged both the Jewish and the Roman status quo, and he had been killed, with the mocking political title "King of the Jews" (not, notably, "otherworldly-millennium-bringing-messiah") inscribed above his head. In history and belief, Cone argued, Christ offered "the poor man" the freedom "to rebel against that which makes him other than human." This was not escapism or simply culture and human relationships validated by the divine. It was the divine through Christ, condoning and perhaps compelling earthly acts of rebellion.[67]

Cone's hermeneutic linked Christ's specific first-century experience with Cone's present age. Christ had come to an oppressed and colonized people, whose experience marked him and shaped his preaching. Black Theology would do the same. "Thinking of Christ as nonblack in the twentieth-century is as theologically impossible as thinking of him as non-Jewish in the first century," Cone contended. Christ's preaching revealed that he had taken Jewish suffering seriously; so too Black Theology began "from the perspective of black enslavement," in order to show how riots and outward expressions of black inwardness represented the twentieth-century version of God's call for "creative love." Cone delineated the difference between the calls of mainstream

American Christianity (and the civil rights establishment) for "love" in integration and peaceful nonviolence, which he dismissed as "cheap grace," and what he saw in the riots—"God's grace . . . the radical identification with the neighbor." God demanded an active love, and Christ in Palestine was the precedent. Accepting Christ as "the very core of one's existence" demanded demonstrating "a radical identification with all men." This preoccupation with the neighbor hearkened back to Cox—but Cone incarnated the theory into a particular set of political relationships: blacks and whites and the ongoing struggle. It was in that context, imbued with active love, that the believer would proclaim "the Good News of freedom by actively fighting against all those powers which hold men captive."[68]

Amid the riots, amid racism, amid Vietnam and continued oppression, Cone made this call even more explicit. Christ was here, in this present age, judging church and society. "The coming of Christ means a denial of where we thought we were. It means destroying the white devil in us. Reconciliation to God means that white people are prepared to deny themselves (whiteness), take up the cross (blackness) and follow Christ (black ghetto)." Black Theology moved with the urgency of nineteenth-century slave preachers, he wrote, who taught "not patience but impatience, not calmness but protest." Impatience with the present and movement toward the future was the essence of Christianity. Where Judaism had looked backward, to the trials of previous generations, he explained that Christianity instead focused on the present, on what Christ *is* doing, and on the future, when his kingdom would surely come. "To look into the future is to grasp the truth of God," Cone wrote, and in twentieth-century America, the black liberation struggles had gotten it right. Now, in the late 1960s, Black Power represented active love to the oppressor; it was evidence of God's grace, Cone argued, and would prevent the "mistaking of worship"—surface, superficial ritual—for deep, active, and abiding "faith."[69] This language sounded like Cox, and it sounded like Tillich. It was trendy—but Cone animated the trends. If secular theology produced prêt-à-porter ideas about the consecrated world, Cone actually tailored the theories and wore them into the battles contested there.

Some African observers worried that these ideas were too radical and unsettling, unsuited to the postcolonial construction project the diaspora needed to support. "Black Theology is a painful phenomenon in the history of the Church," John Mbiti wrote, because it grew out the particularities of African American history, not from the "spontaneous joy in being a Christian." Mbiti argued that Black Theology was embittered and polarizing when it spoke ill of white people and sanctified the suffering of blacks. Cone might have redefined love by drawing connections between historical contexts, but the end result was an "excessive preoccupation with liberation." Notwithstanding his own suggestion that African Theology needed to concern itself with lived life, Mbiti fretted that Black Theology was too earthly, too wed to the goal of political change. "When the immediate concerns of liberation are realized, it is not at all clear where Black Theology is supposed to go." It offered Christ and context, but no culture beyond liberation, no ethic beyond liberation, no church beyond liberation—everything else was "subservient to the overriding emphasis on blackness and liberation." Black Theology, Mbiti concluded, perhaps regretfully, was "an embarrassment to Christianity."[70]

Cone felt otherwise. Of course Black Theology was preoccupied with liberation, he wrote with Gayraud Wilmore in 1972; black religion in the United States had always been about the dialectic between oppression and liberation.[71] It might appear excessively political, but that was where American black Christians were, and it was where the first-century Jews who followed Christ had been. Black Theology was a contextual theology, and it was exactly what it needed to be.[72] Rather, to Cone, it was African Theology that was flawed. Too often, he wrote, "including Africa meant excluding the Christian identity in black religion." Christianity was about Christ's intervention in human history. Culture was useful, but history was paramount. "History is the place where we struggle to be human," he asserted, and "culture is the tool we develop in order to defend the integrity of our humanity." In the late 1960s, black Americans were enveloped in struggle. And, as in South Africa, any culture that was not about struggle distracted from the pressing demands of the present.[73]

In this, Cone's defense/critique resonated with the response of many South Africans to African Theology. Indeed, South Africans began from the same place. John Sebidi had issued his call for preachers to "thunder" from the pulpits while Cone was still formulating his ideas. American Black Theology was born of the diasporic experience, of the dialectics of slavery and freedom, liberation, and oppression; these had South African cognates. As David Attwell suggested, "Apartheid seems to have turned its own citizens into cultural exiles."[74] Black South Africans were not where they had once been nor near where they desired to be. It was not surprising, therefore, that an informal poll of Fed Sem students overwhelmingly favored Black Theology's contextualization over African Theology's indigenization. The "Gospel of liberation can be translated and adapted for one's situation," one student wrote. "[When we] contextualize, . . . [we] make [Christianity] relevant to our life situations."[75]

Yet even though South Africans were in ways similar to the diaspora, they were not in fact cultural exiles. Rather, they were where and what they were, and that, for lack of a better term, was South African. They defended Cone's theology with African Theology's underlying logic, arguing that Cone's contextualization was actually Mbiti's translation, only taken a few steps further. "I and others from South Africa *do* Black Theology," Desmond Tutu informed

Mbiti, "which is for us, at this point, African theology." The latter worked in some contexts, but elsewhere, where the Gospels still spoke and Christ still worked, history and translation would continue.[76] South Africans gave American Black Theology an African twist. The missionary impact needed to be undone. Manas Buthelezi wrote, "It is a well known psychological fact that an honourable past can serve as a source of inspiration in moments of despondency." This would in turn lead to a future-oriented faith: "The past very often gives content to the kind of faith a person has about his destiny."[77] Other South African Christian thinkers picked up this thread. "Throughout Africa," Mokgethi Motlhabi and Steve Biko wrote, "African theological concepts are being re-examined . . . to eradicate imprisoning notions of the Christian religion so that its message for them in their situation can be discovered."[78] Situations differed, but insights passed between them. Blacks rejected the division between the sacred and secular in favor of a faith that saturated the "wholesomeness of life . . . no set days of worship, no distinction between . . . 'church' and . . . 'world.'"[79] Faith, Biko wrote, was "manifest in our daily lives. We thanked God through our ancestors before we drank beer, married, worked . . . we would obviously find it artificial to create special occasions for worship."[80] This was African Theology, thrust into practice as part of the Black Consciousness project. It was "an opportunity for our theologians to prove themselves, to help restore God to our people, who died with the coming of the missionary and is still being crucified."[81]

Thus, we have arrived at the brink of something original: a South African voice that spoke of culture, politics, and history and embodied Christ in a specific community's sufferings and aspirations. This was a Christ enveloped thoroughly in culture and in the manifold absurdities of context. American Black Theology offered South Africans the possibility of restoring Christ to African Theology. Its proponents believed in history. They believed that a man named Jesus had come into a situation, lived, taught, and died and that in that history lay lessons for the future. Now, theologians were prepared to update and reframe that message for a different time and place. Jesus had asked difficult questions of first-century Palestine; so too would he pose problems for twentieth-century South Africa.

There was a pressing need that he do so. South African believers worried that Christianity was losing support, and, as Biko put it, "the only path open for us now is to redefine the message in the bible and to make it relevant to the struggling masses." Relevance was quintessentially and simply existential—freed from the past, Black Theology focused on the now and soon, on a particular community of black people engaged in a particular struggle. Next came the method: "Christianity is an adaptable religion that fits into the cultural situation of the people." Translation, following the connected logic of African and secular theology. Faith is a means of reaching the divine; the entire world is God's; and the sine qua non is culture, earth, society. Finally, the outcome—adopting a political attitude: "Black theology seeks to depict Jesus as a fighting God."[82] Reflection/action, spirit/flesh, faith/history, sacred/political. Intellectual innovations were undermining assumed oppositions between sacred and secular, the world of God and the world of people. Black Theologians and Black Consciousness activists wanted to break these pairs apart and smash them into wholes. This was, Cone wrote, the "tearing/healing power of Christ" that stirred revolutions.[83] So it had and so, activists fervently prayed, would it again.

6 ⤳ The South African Voice
From Black Theology to the Black Messiah

IN AUGUST 1970, Aelred Stubbs, an instructor at St. Peter's Seminary at Alice, wrote to the Anglican bishop of Kimberley and Kuruman to request that a student be temporarily excused from his studies. Since his arrival at the Anglican section of the Federal Theological Seminary in 1969, Stanley Ntwasa had been a challenging student. "Extremely critical of the institutional church," he was nevertheless training to become a priest. In his second year, he was nominated for the seminary's Alan Paton writing prize due to his fiercely original thinking—even if he expressed it in "English . . . careless to the point of impertinence." He drank too much, often in the company of SASO agitators from neighboring Fort Hare, yet he showed a grasp of doctrine comprehensive enough to excel at his courses. In spite of (or perhaps because of) these contradictions, his instructors and peers thought him a liberated person, living true to the dictates of developing Black Consciousness. "It is in fact difficult for me . . . to write coolly about Stanley," Stubbs noted, since the young man displayed the rare ability to project absolute "independence [yet] can still feel and display affection for a white man." Ntwasa was headstrong, fiercely intelligent, and complex; he was also difficult enough to be remanded to Wilgespruit Ecumenical Centre for "sensitivity training" early in 1970. Yet Stubbs still expected that "he may . . . make an important contribution to the life and witness of the Church in South Africa."[1]

In 1970, this contribution was intended for the UCM, and Stubbs requested that Ntwasa be granted leave to serve as the organization's traveling secretary. The UCM was deep in the throes of secular theology, and Stubbs hoped that Ntwasa might have a tempering influence, with his theological "orthodoxy" serving as a "corrective to some of the UCM output." Like many black students, Ntwasa had displayed impatience with the UCM's tortured expositions; he was brash but had a firm grasp of doctrine and was, in both his teacher's and the bishop's opinions, well suited to the task. Ntwasa was granted leave and moved to Johannesburg to work with Moore, Collins, and Justice Moloto, the UCM's first black president. There, as in Alice, Ntwasa's attitude earned immediate comment. Where blacks were supposed to yield the sidewalks to whites, in Braamfontein Ntwasa stalked his territory, frequently bumping recalcitrant office workers into the street.[2] The UCM had offices in Pharmacy House with a number of other organizations, whose employees were not always pleased to share supposedly segregated toilets with a young, black theology student. As Ntwasa's assistant, Mokgethi Motlhabi, remembered, on one occasion Ntwasa was confronted by a white woman upon exiting a whites-only toilet. He paused in front of her and demonstrated his way with scripture: "Ntwasa simply looks at her and says, *in my father's house there are many toilets*!!!"[3] Ntwasa was, in short, the defiant, relevant, liberated man for whom Black Consciousness called.[4] In his letter to the bishop, Stubbs had noted that Ntwasa's duties at UCM would include "a great deal of reading in 'black theology.'" Ntwasa's actions demonstrated that regardless of his supposed orthodoxy, he certainly had the temperament to embrace the radicalism for which Black Theology called.[5]

Ntwasa's arrival in Braamfontein coincided with Moloto's presidency and a shift in UCM's rhetoric. In his presidential address to Encounter '70, Moloto rebuked the charge of Christianity's irrelevance. He conceded that the faith's translation had provided enough "thou shalt nots" to render it inscrutable to a person for whom "priority number one . . . is shelter, food and water," but he stopped short of dismissing it. Rather, he focused delegates' attention on "Christ's mission in this world [, which] was one of liberation." To Moloto, "if the UCM should be Christian, it should be about liberation." In one phrase, Moloto redefined what it meant for UCM to claim the Christian faith. No allegiance to commandments was required, no abstention from sinful behaviors, no belonging to an ecclesiastical body — "if the UCM should be Christian, it should be about liberation." Opponents to apartheid, he reasoned, ought to side with Christ, who "identified with the politically and economically disinherited [and] became practically and explicitly critical of the system imposed by the secular rulers." Moloto preempted criticism, claiming that UCM's new stance did not constitute a religious organization playing politics but was instead the reasoned position of a Christian organization concerned with "reality."[6]

Given this new perspective, it was not surprising that Ntwasa, Moloto, and other black Christian activists turned eagerly to James Cone. "We in South Africa have read with tremendous interest and excitement your recent publications on 'Black Theology,'" Ntwasa wrote Cone in January 1971, adding, "Your works have certainly set in motion a radical re-think of Christianity in our fascist country."[7] Ntwasa was perhaps flattering the American; after all, Ntwasa's own organization had been involved in rethinking its faith for nearly four years. Regardless, in Cone's work, UCM found a name for the more political theology expressed by Moloto. Ntwasa announced that UCM was organizing a national seminar on Black Theology, to be held outside Johannesburg in March 1971, and it planned to hold follow-up seminars throughout the country. UCM also planned to publish a book on the subject, to "provide black preachers with an invaluable study document." The UCM leaders had hoped to invite Cone to participate in the national seminar, but they were realistic: the government was unlikely to grant him a visa, and the organization lacked the resources to get him to South Africa in any case. Instead, Ntwasa asked Cone to send a taped address, "which would serve as an introduction to the Seminar." He left the tape's content up to Cone but hoped for "something on the world-wide oppression of people of colour and thus the world-wide significance of 'Black Theology.'" This international focus would provide a needed balance to the seminar's content, which, Ntwasa noted, would obviously lean toward the theology's local application.[8]

Cone agreed, and in early March, a group of church people and laypeople gathered in Roodepoort to listen to the American's tape and debate its meaning for South Africa. Over the next months, UCM held a half dozen follow-up seminars across the country, attended by student activists, seminary students, current and future bishops of the Anglican Church as well as soon-to-be Catholic bishops, lay activists, future prisoners, future guerrillas, and even avowed skeptics such as Harry Nengwekhulu. These events drew derision from some and praise from others. Black Theology earned coverage in the country's newspapers and theological journals, and there was much teeth gnashing about its implications for South Africa's politics and Christian faith.

South Africans' engagement with Black Theology soon went beyond the organizational and political context. As the letter to Cone made clear, South Africans were self-consciously translating an international voice into a local idiom; in their discussions, they manufactured a distinctively South African faith that crossed between the individual and the collective, the sacred and the secular, the nationalist and the humanist, the biblical and the existential, the personal and the prophetic. This faith dealt with issues of identity and issues of belief and, with the wider context always present, ultimately erased the fine line between religion and politics. Context ruled: the theology was not reserved for seminars but instead was meant for publication and eventual deployment by an army of preachers, designed to impact the country's slowly resurgent politics. To be a black South African and to have faith in Christ—or in the

Black Messiah, a spirit that was not quite Christ—was to have faith in politics and in the evolving prize toward which students turned prophets pointed.

DIVIDED GOSPEL

Cone may not have known it, but his invitation to the national seminar came rather late. The initial call for papers was made toward the end of November 1970, with a follow-up sent to participants in early January. In this second call, Ntwasa laid out the seminar's rationale: "Christian theology from the perspective of the black man is not new in South Africa . . . [but] the current revolution in theology internationally has brought the theological perspective of oppressed people into the heart of church councils and seminaries."[9] The national and follow-up seminars promised to bring a particular perspective and a particular politics to the South African churches, namely, the perspective and politics of the oppressed. Given this framework, it seems the invitation for papers was more of a directive, and it included instructions to write on a particular theme, lists of suggested readings, and an essay penned by UCM theology director Basil Moore, entitled "Towards a Black Theology."[10] This chapter first explores the deployment and reception of Black Theology, before moving on to consider how South African theologians raised their own issues and moved toward their own version of a relevant faith.

From the outset, Black Theology was supposed to bring theologians out from their "detached academic hothouses to grapple with . . . pulsating human problems."[11] Theologians were expected to question the ecclesiastical status quo and theological precedent, while keeping an eye on the political prize. The structure of the national seminar revealed this. It began with background, including the Cone tape, and then moved on to denser content papers and devoted the third and longest day to the future. Through theology, the oppressed looked forward. Although none of the seminar papers took politics as their expressed subject, the discourse framing the event demonstrated, as had Cone, that Black Theology was inherently political.

Political and divisive. No whites were invited to the seminar, even though at least one—Moore—had been instrumental in laying out its agenda. As at SASO's first meeting, just over two years earlier, whites' omission demonstrated the major shift that had occurred. The Christian Institute had offices near UCM; CI officials had trusted in multiracialism and, like Moore and Collins, had signed the "Message to the People of South Africa" and sat on SPROCAS committees. But now, through their journal *Pro Veritate*, CI activists suggested that with Black Theology, UCM had gone too far. Black Theology's exclusivity, the editors wrote, "indicates what an evil and late hour it is for SA in its race relations!" It was one thing for a student group to claim tokenism and go its own way; it was still another for black students in the UCM to reject secular theology as irrelevant in the quest for a political solution. But now, this ecumenical, multiracial organization was condoning a racially exclusive conference based on the premise that theology—the interpretation of God's word—could be "black." The editors protested: "Christ's gospel knows no exclusivity on the grounds of . . . colour." To suggest otherwise smacked of racialism, and they charged UCM with failing to heed Christ's "'new commandment' [that] love conquers everything." In Christ, they argued, there could be neither Black Power nor White Power but only "God's power, *love's* power."[12]

The idea of a "black" theology circulated in the mainstream press as well. A reader of the *Rand Daily Mail* rejected the concept entirely: "I read that at a seminar of African clergymen there was a clamour for 'Black theology'— whatever that may be," he wrote. Black theology, as he understood it, assigned a race to Christ and in doing so wed divinity to sullied human sociology. "God belongs to no race, colour or nationality," the writer argued, "so theology is simply theology."[13] Other readers picked up this thread. Denise Goodwin, from Rustenberg, was troubled by the conclusions reached at the Transvaal regional seminar, especially that Black Theology was a "reflection on God in the light of . . . black experience." This, Goodwin claimed, did "not seem any different from white-dominated churches solely concerned with the future of the white man." The theologians and activists assembled at the Transvaal seminar justified their project with Jesus's reading of Isaiah, as told in Luke 4:18: "The Spirit of the Lord has been given to me, for he has anointed me. He has sent me to bring the good news to the poor, to proclaim liberty to captives . . . to set the downtrodden free." According to Black Theology's exegesis, Christ had been a liberator, and therefore, a theology with overt political intentions was in line with Christ's teachings. Goodwin disagreed, pointing out that, according to scripture, Christ had in fact earned his audience's ire once people perceived that "he was not a liberator of nations but a liberator from sin." A theology in light of black experience hearkened back to Black Consciousness's concern with relevance. In its critics' view, however, it inappropriately linked scripture and the present day and was therefore as wrongheaded as DRC dominees' stories of God's chosen people's Exodus from the nineteenth-century Cape.[14] Members of white, Afrikaans-dominated churches had aspired to the status of chosen people; they had in effect written themselves into the Bible and in so doing used religion to justify their position and their politics. To some, Black Theology threatened to do the same.

White readers were not alone in their concern. The Transvaal Black Theology seminar was held at St. Peter's, the Old Boys' alma mater, which had just hosted debates over Africanization. Mokgethi Motlhabi was a student there while the seminar was going on and recalled that he and other students wondered, "How can theology be black or white? There is only one theology." Calls for more control over church affairs were one thing; claiming racially exclusive interpretations of God's word was another thing entirely.[15] An editorial in the *World* noted that first SASO and now Black Theology demonstrated that "we are going black." "Going black" meant becoming confident and self-reliant, and it was a good thing: "The black man in this country has accepted the fact that his salvation lies in his own hands." Still, in an atmosphere poisoned by race, the *World* hoped that Black Theology was just a "transitional phase" on the path to a "united South Africa."[16] This view was not altogether surprising: M. T. Moerane, the paper's editor at the time, was a former member of the Liberal Party and an occasional critic of SASO. Although he sought to fashion his paper for the new black voice, the goal of an undivided South Africa—and an undivided Gospel—died hard.

With these debates in the press, government attention was inevitable. In *Honest to God*, John Robinson suggested that it would take at least two generations for academic innovations such as secular theology to reach the man in the pew.[17] But even though Robinson was criticized and perhaps even branded a heretic, his theology did not run afoul of the law. This was not the case in South Africa. Instead, during the weeks and months immediately following the UCM's call for a national seminar, Black Theology was—sometimes intentionally, sometimes not—the subject of urgent debate and widespread coverage, by both the press and the state security apparatus.[18] In the supposedly Christian state, Christian debates were political matters. This media coverage of Black Theology undoubtedly helped to raise its profile in a way that church seminars could not.[19] The national seminar had come at the height of the church-state confrontation discussed in chapter 4, only two weeks after Security Branch raids on UCM leaders and other church activists.[20] So it most likely surprised no one when police raided St. Ansgar's seminary at Roodepoort early in the morning before the conference's final day. Unfortunately for the Security Branch, during the raid the police arrested the Anglican bishop Alphaeus Zulu for failing to produce his pass. Zulu was not only the presiding bishop of the ostensibly self-governing Zululand but also one of only two black Anglican bishops in South Africa and a governing president of the World Council of Churches. Further, he had been arrested in his pajamas. His detention prompted an "angry outcry" from the churches.[21] Even the conservative Afrikaans press joined in, slamming his arrest on the grounds that he was one of the few WCC leaders who "strongly opposed . . . the recent WCC decision to provide guerillas in Southern Africa with financial assistance."[22] Faced with an onslaught of criticism, the Roodepoort town clerk released the bishop on his honor and instructed him to produce his pass to the magistrate in his home district. For his part, the clerk was unrepentant. "This is something that happens from time to time," he explained, "we have . . . bishops and all sorts of people involved these days."[23]

It was ironic that the raid netted Zulu. He not only was a critic of the WCC but also had connections in Bantustan politics (which would lead him to a seat in the KwaZulu "parliament" upon his retirement) and was ambivalent about the possibilities of South African Black Theology. In his opinion, it was too American, too wrapped in Cone's efforts to "find a theological basis for the Black Power Movement." Cone's work was "sincere" and "consistent" within the American context, but Zulu worried that the South African effort lacked "sufficient understanding [of] Black Theology in the U.S.A." American Black Theology, Zulu claimed, was a theology only for the "oppressed black man" in that country; therefore, its utility in South Africa was limited.[24] Zulu was an Anglican bishop who believed in the universal Gospel; for him, Black Theology might help address lingering racism in church structures, but its theological value was less certain. "Some exponents of Black Theology give the impression that theology should be the handmaid of the black revolution," he later wrote. This sort of thinking chafed because "according to Jesus Christ, no one will ever know when the day of judgments [will come] or its matter of coming." Were a "black revolution" to come, it would be a political judgment, a threshold crossed in the community's political history, but in Bishop Zulu's opinion, such an event could not be Christian.[25]

One wonders, therefore, about Zulu's reaction to the invitations penned by Ntwasa and Moore. After all, the UCM officials had made it clear how they envisioned—and attempted to structure—the initial articulation of South African Black Theology. The themes, as Zulu noted, were the "Theology of Hope" and the "Theology of Liberation," both of which evoked earthly concerns.[26] Black Theology was a deeply politicized enterprise, made more so by government's heavy-handed attention to the national seminar. Such overt politicking, however, only scratched the surface of the theological reasoning behind Black Theology. Ways of thinking and hermeneutical critique fit less neatly into newspaper columns, but they still structured the rhetorical spectacle in the papers. Black Theologians were South Africans, they were blacks, and they were political. Yet they were also Christians, concerned with scripture, biblical precedent, and the implication of Christ's universal message of love in lived lives. What theologians justified publicly therefore needed justification within their own circles and minds. How could theology be colored? To what extent did calling theology "black" repeat the DRC's mistake, sacrificing relevance for politics, the world of men for the word of God? They were Christians—so what of Zulu's warning that they not follow Cone toward a purely political day of judgment, lest they lose Christ along the way?

"BLACK IS BEAUTIFUL FOR GOD HAS MADE IT STUPENDOUSLY BEAUTIFUL"

Black Theology was capacious, as it had to be in order to bridge the gap between Biko's "more human face" and black South Africa's political aspirations.

It inspired seminars, public debate, numerous publications, transnational dialogue, and, by the mid-1980s, its own journal. It counted future archbishops and Nobel Peace Prize winners, future prisoners (for reasons both laudable and decidedly less so), and, as we shall see, future martyrs among its exponents. It had its own traditions of critique and a variety of schools of thought whose adherents often did not (and do not) see eye to eye. And in the more easily apprehended terrain of politics, Black Theology played a central role in reconstituting political discourse in 1970s South Africa. It bridged the personal and the political through the medium of faith. By following the themes explored by its proponents, we see how they explained their situations and prospects and how they thought through Christianity to understand life under apartheid. Black Theology was born of relatively free reflection; however, such unguarded exploration was short-lived, evidenced by the police lurking at seminars. This chapter does not offer Black Theology's full story but instead explores the concerns, contexts, and ideas that helped to develop faith from Ntwasa's gut.

Attendees at the national seminar received South Africa's first explicitly titled treatise on Black Theology. It was written by a white man, who was not invited to attend. Basil Moore understood that his authorship of "Towards a Black Theology" was odd, and he apologized for "the unbelievable impertinence of writing this article." Yet he felt compelled to write it: "I am angry because I am sick of being treated as a white man." Just as "blackness" determined all life for those with darker skins, so too did "whiteness determine . . . my being as a man. South Africa defines and circumscribes my responses to whiteness and not my being as a man." In this way, Moore set the context for Black Theology's emergence in South Africa. It was born from emotion—anger—and existentialist concern with how apartheid limited an individual's being. Moore evoked Cone, who had also fired existentialism with the heat of conflict. Indeed, as we have seen, only a year before Moore had translated secular theology to the South African context, with the critical modification that God ("it") was known through "liberating experiences." Apartheid constrained being, and now faith was seen as the path to liberation.[27]

However, as suggested by Cone, to move forward theology needed first to look backward. Moore agreed that knowing Christ meant knowing Christ's context, what his words meant "against the back-drop of [his listeners'] beliefs, needs, aspirations, etc." Christ's message, Moore wrote, was heard in time and space: "If you want a relevance tied to no time and no place then you don't want Christ." Here again, like Cone, Moore noted the specifics of Jesus's historical moment, with language that easily alluded to ongoing conflicts in Southern Africa. "The 'calm hills of Galilee' were alive with guerilla fighters, plotting, scheming and acting for freedom," he insisted. Christ lived in a land where the "politically dispossessed" were engaged in a "violent fight for free-dom."[28] He walked Galilee and saw political prisoners nailed to crosses. He had a Zealot in his party and surely understood what these things meant.[29]

Theology therefore needed to demonstrate how Christ had responded to the "pressing issue[s] of his day." Moore suggested that Christ's truth too often had been obscured by conservative orthodoxy but that it was still possible to retrieve.[30] Take the Sermon on the Mount. Moore insisted that its many promises were not opiates bidding the "wretched poor" to wait with patience. Rather, Christ was appealing to believers to look inside themselves, to affirm themselves in recognition that every person "has value simply by being loved by God." Although such therapeutic language might appear benign, Moore argued that it was politically potent, for with it, Christ had lit "the danger-ous fire of [the people's] sense of dignity and worth as human beings." Such an awakening made oppression intolerable.[31] Moore's Christ thus spoke in language similar to that of Black Consciousness. The Sermon on the Mount, Moore argued, had been what Saths Cooper called a "psychological interven-tion" in the minds of the oppressed. It had assuaged the fears of "the last" with the promise that they would be first; this was Biko's "stage 1." Moore made the allusion explicit: "Jesus fits the situation of South African blacks . . . [and] the Roman rulers fit the situation of South African whites."[32]

Yet where extant Black Consciousness thought demurred from answering the question of what came next, Moore's allusive theology carried the liberat-ing process beyond the first stage. According to Moore, Christ had first done what Black Consciousness was doing, and then he had gone further to demon-strate in his own struggle that "to be human is to find something worth dying for." Christ's revolutionary message had been obscured by later Christians, but his actions and fate spoke loudly enough. Moore turned to Pilate's choice between Barrabas (whom he described as a Zealot leader) and Jesus to make his point: "Imagine the South African premier thinking he could realistically get away with it if he decided to let the people decide if they wanted a harmless Zionist preacher released or Robert Sobukwe. If the Prime Minister wanted the Zionist released he never would have given him the unfair competition of Sobukwe. He would need at least a Mandela if he wanted the people to have a live option. So the question: 'Barrabas or Jesus' itself indicates that Jesus was somewhat of the same ilk." Read this way, Christ did not die for his people's sins; rather, his death was a state-sponsored assassination, the politi-cal outcome of a political trial in a time and place of heated conflict. Jesus was a political prophet rightly compared to men like Sobukwe and Mandela, leaders of political struggles who had suffered for their cause. By citing them in his theology, Moore entertained the questions that SASO begged: those that asked about violence and revolution, about suffering and sacrifice. He concluded that the true church comprised those who held faith that quiet affirmations of dignity would swell to protest and that true Christians were "up to their necks in the struggle" or they were not Christians at all.[33]

Cone had employed scripture to sanctify the political struggles raging in black America, but there were not yet any such struggles within 1970s South Africa, where student activists still spoke the language of consciousness, not power. Moore, however, was interested in political struggles, and with Black Theology, he projected the community into the unknown political future. Since much of what Christians knew about Jesus was muddled, he traded divinity and salvation for what could be—at least in his opinion—unequivocally known: "Jesus was an agitator."[34] Moore's Black Theology, expressed in a South African political idiom, naturally followed his description of God/ it manifested in political struggles. South African society fostered a crisis of being, an angst-ridden context within which Christians needed to struggle. Jesus-the-agitator had known violence, known revolution, courted the company of rebels and the opprobrium of a (not coincidentally) European empire. He knew the way.

Moore's essay got around. It was included with the invitations to the national seminar, and both South African and international church people regularly wrote to the UCM office to request copies.[35] Many were troubled by what they read there, just as Bishop Zulu had been after the seminar. Don Morlan, a former American missionary to South Africa, lauded Moore's essay as "one of the most stimulating theological reflections that I have seen during the last three years," but he nevertheless worried that Moore had too closely overlain biblical and political truths. Equating Christ and blacks in such an unequivocal way implied, in Morlan's opinion, that "one must be black to be Christian." The political struggle might be necessary, but it could not come at the expense of Christ's universal message. Indeed, Morlan continued, by so closely aligning Christianity and politics, Moore came perilously near to declaring "that only the oppressed could be among the faithful." He accused Moore of casting political suffering in too positive a light. Jesus did speak about poverty and oppression, but "not all" in his party were poor. Rather, the apostles had shared not political or sociological designations but "a strong . . . desire for a new society." That had been enough then and ought to be now.[36]

Many black South Africans shared Morlan's concerns. Attendees at the national seminar, for example, agonized over whether it was appropriate to analogize from the biblical experience to the apartheid experience.[37] Ntwasa worried that Cone had too tightly wedded Black Theology and Black Power, an approach that was simply not broad enough in a world where "many other people are oppressed."[38] Where Cone and Moore seemed intent on the absolute authority of political liberation, Ntwasa contended that South Africans chafed under a glut of authority and instead needed a "theology of freedom and liberation, . . . not a theology of authoritarianism." Theology, he insisted, was about "being human," about "how people relate to each other" and the pursuit, "ultimately, of human unity."[39]

Ntwasa had carried the label of orthodoxy to his appointment with the UCM, and at first glance, his critique does rebut Cone's (and Moore's) more radical theology. Yet *orthodoxy* is a fluid term. Moore's essay might have failed to engage questions of divinity and salvation beyond the political horizon; this was novel theology, and so too did Ntwasa embrace modern questions of being and humanness and the process of racial liberation. Indeed, even as black South African Christians such as Ntwasa partially turned away from Moore's and Cone's more overt racial and political ideas, their "orthodoxy" embraced new insights into the "humanistic" issues that Jesus had spoken about. True, this was a concern that Moore and Cone shared; as the former noted, Jesus had taught that "every person has value simply by being loved by God." But for Ntwasa and others, this was only a starting point. Given the manifold limitations of black life in South Africa, the question of God's love was the most pressing.

Another Federal Seminary student from Kimberley expressed this idea best. In a letter to the UCM office, Drake Tshenkeng opened with a weighty question: "Why lord! Why! Did you make me black?" Given the manifold evidence of black people's benighted position in the world—and especially in South Africa—this was perhaps theology's most urgent problem: if God was good, why did bad things happen? God had created man in his image and God was master of the world, yet apartheid made black existence intolerable. Where, then, was God?[40] South African Black Theology's first task, therefore, was to ask why God had "creat[ed] black people black."[41] Ntwasa elaborated on this in a paper presented to a number of Black Theology seminars. Where blacks had once sought to develop senses of themselves through participation in multiracial organizations, they were now called to embrace their blackness, recognizing that their creator had consciously made them so. Yet this provoked unsettling questions. "What we as blacks want to find out is whether our position as third-rate persons is a deliberate creation by God," Ntwasa wrote.[42] It was not yet time for the political Messiah of whom the Gospels told; black theologians needed first to address the problem—and the promise—of Genesis.

The Bible's first book resounds with direct communication between God and God's human creations. Take Genesis 22:1: "After these things, God tempted Abraham, and said to him: Abraham, Abraham. And he answered: Here I am." Black Consciousness argued that such confident declarations of "I" were beyond many black South Africans. As Ernest Baartman, a Methodist preacher and early exponent of Black Theology, explained, Black Consciousness and Black Theology both began by asking "Who am I?" to the self, the community, and especially to the "Creator." Jesus demanded this task. His Golden Rule required believers to love others as they loved themselves; "self-affirmation" was thus the key to the Gospel and where liberating theology began.[43] Like Black Consciousness, Black Theology sought to develop an "I" who could then recognize and approach others of equal value.[44]

The idea that God had not made a mistake when creating black people became manifest in activists' physical and stylistic choices. By 1972, it was common practice for both men and women to reject their so-called Christian names in favor of more African ones. "Some of us switched over to the use of our African names," Ramphele recalled, "instead of the 'slave names' we had hitherto used."[45] Invectives against black women's use of wigs and skin lighteners were another obvious manifestation of this way of thinking. The prominent poet James Matthews, for instance, bemoaned his 'sister's' "face smeared with astra cream / skin paled for white man's society." Such behavior rendered the oft-cited slogan "Black is beautiful" "as artificial as the wig she wears."[46] Majoba, from Port Elizabeth, agreed, in expressly creationist terms: "It is a great shame that about 3/4 of African women use Wigs. God did not make a mistake when he gave us short curly hair," he wrote to *Drum* in late 1971.[47]

Rather than try to emulate whites, black women in particular were called on to take pride in their God-created selves. Contrast Matthews's "sister" with his "woman," for example: "Proudly she walks, a sensuous, black lily / swaying in the wind / This daughter of Sheba . . . My woman wears her blackness like a Queen."[48] Female activists such as Nkosazana Zuma, a SASO member from the University of Zululand, remembered rejecting the idea that "we have to be whiter and have straighter hair to be human beings."[49] Women cultivated new fashions to manifest these self-aware, adult selves—Afro haircuts instead of wigs, black skin instead of bleached, and, as Matshoba and others noted, hot pants instead of more moderated wear.[50] For outspoken women associated with Black Consciousness and Black Theology, fashion was the external manifestation of confidence in one's self and affirmation of one's creation. In her hot pants and Afro, the black woman was as much a child of God and as much a "man" as Ntwasa had been when he commandeered Braamfontein's sidewalks. She was "being what God created us to be, BLACK human beings," and God did not make mistakes. "Coming from the hands of a perfect Being we are therefore beautiful," a *Drum* reader concluded, "BLACK is beautiful . . . the term reconciles the BLACK man with himself."[51] So it could be with women as well.[52]

But if God had not made a mistake, how did activists explain the black existential condition? For Ntwasa, the answer was politics and history: "an artificial fabrication of the truth by power-hungry people, whose motives are authority, security, wealth and comfort."[53] Blackness was historically contingent; thus, to say that God created black and that black was good was, in some sense, to wed blackness—and, via blackness, God—to the historical conditions of apartheid and oppression. Theologians explored this tension by distinguishing, once more, between being "black" and being "nonwhite." The latter was Ntwasa's "artificial fabrication," Manas Buthelezi wrote, which held that people of color "were created in the image of the white man and not of God." Black Theology, by contrast, cast aside the false idol of nonwhite, becoming, as Buthelezi described it, "a theology of the Image of God." Nonwhites did not know their creator and were not free. Blacks were liberated.[54]

The progression from nonwhite to black moved forward in political time and backward in biblical time. It undid history to bring about the reunion of "the black man and his God" about which Biko wrote. Widely circulated images helped embody this. The cover of the quickly banned *Essays on Black Theology*, for example, showed a black man chained by both his arms and legs yet smiling joyously as a white mask fell to reveal his features. In a lecture delivered a few years later, Buthelezi directed his audience's attention to a similar drawing published in *Pro Veritate*, showing a man peeling off whitish skin, his "natural" hair and serious, dark features emerging from behind a false face complete with grotesque toothy grin, bulbous nose, and artificially straightened hair. Given Black Theology's progression from nonwhite to black, it is worth noting the attention paid to this black man's muscles. To be the image of God was to be virile and robust, especially in contrast to the dandified nonwhite, with his rather effeminate curls pasted to his forehead. In Black Theology, the image of God was a manly one, with a stern, serious expression.[55]

But being made in God's image carried with it certain responsibilities. To be black under Black Theology meant to look unflinchingly at a history in which the color "represents poverty, disinheritance, all that is ugly and soiled," while at the same time working to change this reality. "[I have] God-endowed dignity," Congregationalist theology student Bonganjalo Goba wrote in *Pro Veritate* in 1971, and through Black Theology, "[I am] look[ing] at myself with honesty" for the first time. The interplay between external conditions—the white world, poverty, oppression—and self-conscious insight led to faith that "Christ is redeeming my blackness." Goba suggested that only by reflecting on this process would black people truly understand that "black is beautiful for God has made it stupendously beautiful."[56]

Goba's conclusion had multiple implications. For some, it suggested that blackness was in some way superior and therefore akin to whiteness under colonialism and apartheid.[57] For many others, however, the idea that God had made black beautiful demanded further interrogation. If God made black beautiful but not necessarily "better" than white, then what did it mean to be black? Biblical exegesis offered a historical explanation. Throughout the Old and New Testaments, communities suffered and were redeemed. Jesus had suffered; blacks were suffering. The Israelites had been enslaved; apartheid ruled. Separate development was like "the Tower of Babel."[58] "The Church is white," Barney Pityana explained, "it tells us 'white Caesar can do no wrong.'"[59] Through inference and analogy, Christ's blackness was affirmed as a historical and political condition.

Yet just as Bishop Zulu worried that South Africans were merely transplanting a black American framework, so too were some South African thinkers uncomfortable with analogizing the local with the biblical. Thus, to Mokgethi Motlhabi, comparing the Israelites to South African blacks was both dangerous and functionally meaningless. Motlhabi accepted that God was multiple and that theology looked different from different vantage points, but he could not accept the retelling of the Exodus narrative set in South Africa's townships and Bantustans. The people in the Bible "had their own lives." "You can't use examples from the stories of other people and claim that you know, because God liberated the Israelites, therefore he will liberate me." Rather, Motlhabi gradually came to feel that Christianity—with its reliance on biblical precedent (witness Jesus's repeated reference to Isaiah and other prophets)—did not provide an adequate hermeneutic for interpreting God's role on earth. "The Bible is not the only story," he asserted, and Black Theology "needed to be broader" than Christianity.[60] That blacks were created in God's own image did not necessarily mean that God had covenanted with them, as had happened with the Israelites. To Motlhabi, the reality of apartheid's evil could not be explained away by looking only to scripture.

However, many South African church people and activists found the Bible to be an effective and righteous way to explain the plight of South African blacks. To Simon Maimela, a Black Theology activist at the Lutheran Mapumulo Seminary, the Bible clearly revealed the liberator God's intentions for his beloved black community. Yet to Maimela, "God does not always act directly. So we should lay the blame where the blame should be laid—at the middle persons," whether pharoah, pharisee, or settler.[61] This notion hearkened back to Ntwasa's explanation that blacks' "third rate" status was the fault of "power-hungry" people, not God. Lay blame where blame ought to be laid—not with divine displeasure but with white racists at play in history. Earthly evil had human explanations. A God who was neutral to blacks' concerns or who sanctioned apartheid was impossible to imagine: "For God to qualify to be God to me and to qualify to the extent that God would command my respect to be worshiped can only be a God who loves and who does good. . . . Otherwise, that God could only be the devil. And so for me that's the distinction. If God is God, I expect God not to do something that can be done by the devil."[62] In this, Black Theology was remarkably similar to Mark Chapman's interpretation of

African American Christianity. Questions about God and evil should be and often were asked, Chapman argued, but in the end, black American Christians believed that there was "a moral order in the universe that leaned in the direction of justice."[63] As Cone put it, "faith in Christ . . . does not explain evil; it empowers us to fight against evil."[64] Maimela and other Black Theologians saw nothing wrong with using the Bible to illuminate their own community's struggle. The Israelites had fought for justice, Christ had fought for justice, and the UCM, in its theology seminars, fought for justice.

Yet unlike in African American Christianity, where Exodus was the dominant scriptural analog, South Africans from Moore to the Calvinist theologian Allan Boesak focused instead on the Gospels. Black South Africans were conquered, not exiled. Unlike African Americans, they did not sing sorrow songs about returns, about freedom from bondage, about the return to Zion. Instead, they looked to the Messiah's promise of another age, to the not yet, not the once more. For his part, Boesak went further than both Cone and Moore by arguing that the Bible mattered more than present-day experience: "I don't think the experience can be the only thing, because if it's only the experience, experiences change, experiences are too fickle, experiences are too subjective . . . we need something more fundamental, something more . . . sustainable than just our experiences." Black Theology's hermeneutic too greatly privileged the present day, but scriptural stories had universal applications that, when correctly understood, were even more powerful. "The Word came to slaves and so it is an oppressed people to whom God speaks and with whom God is working and on who's behalf God is working." Therefore, Boesak argued, theology could remain faithful to scripture and still speak to a particular moment's experience and a particular community's dreams of liberation.[65]

Although Boesak claimed his perspective was more faithful to the Bible than that of either Moore or Cone, he ended up with the same argument, asserting that God's incarnation in Christ, correctly understood, was about liberation. "Jesus came and lived in this world as the Oppressed One who took upon himself all the suffering and humiliation of all oppressed peoples," he wrote in the 1970s. This, then, was the Gospel truth: Jesus "lived on earth very much the same way blacks are forced to live. He has made their life his own, he has identified himself with them, he is the Black Messiah."[66]

THE BLACK MESSIAH

The idea of the Black Messiah has long circulated in diasporic communities. At times, it was embodied in a particular person, a savior—from Marcus Garvey to Nelson Mandela.[67] The trope of the one who would lead the people to the promised land has been repeatedly taken up on both sides of the Atlantic, perhaps most famously by Martin Luther King Jr. on the eve of his assassination.[68] The metaphor was often mixed: it could refer to a Jesus-like character, a suffering servant who promised redemption and salvation whether in this world or the next, or to a Moses, a more political actor who had led his people from one expressly earthly condition to another. In 1970s South Africa, as we have seen, people spoke less of the historical event of the Exodus and more about the messianic age still to come; thus, Boesak's Black Messiah was definitively Jesus Christ.

But which Jesus Christ? Dwight Hopkins explained that Black Theologians in both the United States and South Africa wrestled with two very different sets of ideas on the subject: one was the "Jesus of history," the other the "Christ of faith."[69] In other words, when Boesak and others hailed Christ as the Black Messiah, did they mean that he was actually, in pigmented fact, of color? Or in keeping with Black Consciousness's more complicated understanding of the term, were they in fact urging faith in the Christos, the spirit, almost, of the "Oppressed One," whose politics made him "black"? What sort of faith was faith in the Black Messiah? To answer these questions, we need to revisit the relationship between religion and politics, explore how South Africans used theology to address issues both divine and earthly, and consider how this process structured this era's political faith.

Boesak's Jesus was "black" in the qualified sense. Boesak preserved the quotes, bracketing the term in order to make it clear that he did not mean that Jesus had been literally black-skinned. By the 1970s, this was an important distinction to make and a difficult one to keep. Like Boesak, Manas Buthelezi wrote often about seeing Christ as "black," in light of the then dominant meaning of blackness. But, he said, "I wouldn't be too much excited in talking about the Black Christ, that Christ is Black. No! He was Jewish!" There were black people in the Bible, but both Boesak and Buthelezi made it clear that they did not count the historical Jesus among them.[70] Yet nuance could easily be lost. Tau Mokoka was a Black Consciousness activist and layperson who used Black Theology in community organizing. He borrowed from Black Theology, he told me, by "arguing that God is black, that actually Jesus was black!"[71] The black Jesus of history found his way into popular culture as well during the 1970s, as when, in 1973, the visiting American Billy Graham caused a sensation by noting that Jesus "probably had a brown skin."[72] Ironically, South African liberal (and corporate) culture at times adopted this idea, as when, commissioned by Johannesburg's *Star* newspaper, South African artist Larry Scully painted a "Madonna and Child of Soweto" to raise funds for a black educational program. Harry Openheimer bought the painting and donated it to the Regina Mundi Cathedral in Johannesburg's largest township. Its dark-skinned Mary and ebony Baby Jesus earned pride of place above the altar, and from there, they watched the church play an increasingly politicized role in the months after 16 June 1976.[73] Collectively, these incidents begged the question: Was Jesus actually black?

Albert Cleage, a prominent Black Theology exponent from the Shrine of the Black Madonna in Detroit, said yes. He taught that the "Jesus of history" had been black, no qualifications or caveats necessary, and that therefore Christ was unquestionably the Black Messiah. "We are concerned . . . with the actual blood line," Cleage wrote, and "Jesus was born to Mary, a Jew of the tribe of Judah, a non-white people." Jesus was black, only to have his lineage twisted to serve the interest of white "gentiles." Cleage went even further. Following the combined logic of creation in God's image and American racial thought, he argued that "God himself is black." "In America, one drop of black makes you black, so by American law, God is black, and by any practical interpretation, why would God have made seven-eighths of the world non-white and yet he himself be white?" The premise, Cleage concluded, was "simply not reasonable."[74]

For his part, in *Black Theology and Black Power*, James Cone acknowledged that his account would be criticized by those who argued that "Christ is above race." Yet to Cone, "society is not raceless, any more than when God became a despised Jew." He wrote: "White liberal preference for a raceless Christ serves only to make official and orthodox the centuries old portrayal of Christ as white . . . for whites to find him with big lips and kinky hair is as offensive as it was for the Pharisees to find him partying with tax-collectors. But whether whites want to hear it or not, *Christ is black, baby*, with all of the features which are so detestable to white society." The historical Christ lurks in this citation (whites would find the "big-lipped" Christ as offensive as "it *was*" for the Pharisees), but the historical Jesus was not Cone's subject. Instead, the American focused on where the Christ of faith was in Cone's own time. Given the company that he had kept in the past, Cone concluded, it was none other than Christ with the "black face and big black hands" whom passersby saw "lounging on a streetcorner."[75]

The South African theologian Boesak found fault with aspects of both Cleage's and Cone's Christ. "It seems to us that the literal color of Jesus is irrelevant," Boesak wrote of the former, and although he agreed with Cone that Christ "was not white in *any* sense of the word," he still bristled at the image of the street corner Jesus. To Boesak, there had only been one Jesus, and he had not lounged on street corners; rather, he had led struggles in first-century Palestine. It was these struggles that had turned the Jesus of history into the Christ of faith. Like Cone, Boesak mediated between the two, but he argued that the latter, as the Black Messiah, transcended time. Christ is not here now, but his inspiration was felt: "[He] has made [blacks'] life his own, he has identified himself with them."[76] One did not need to incarnate Christ in the townships because, given what he meant for history and faith, he was already there.

Boesak wrote in the late 1970s to defend a Christian's involvement in politics, but he was also careful to preserve a theological understanding of a Black Messiah whose relevance was not limited to politics. His purposes thus accorded with Biko's when, years earlier, the latter used theology and existentialism in his presentation to a Black Theology seminar. In his "Black Consciousness and the Quest for True Humanity," Biko challenged theology "to describe Christ as a fighting God, not a passive God who allows a lie to rest unchallenged." Like Boesak, Biko did not suggest that Jesus had been black. His race was irrelevant. His actions were what mattered. Christ was relevant; he fought. He was thus "black" in the historically conditioned, existential sense of the term. Black Theology for Biko was therefore a simple affair. It needed only to to pay attention to what the Christ had done and would do: fight.[77]

Christ was an animated existentialist, much as Black Consciousness called blacks to project their beingness in a way attuned to struggle. But for what did he fight? And, by extension, for what were blacks supposed to struggle? "We have set out on the quest for true humanity and somewhere on the distant horizon we can see the glittering prize," Biko claimed. The goal was abstract and vague, but it was also big and grand and total—true humanity, a new reality that would be fundamentally different from the morass of human relationships evident in apartheid society.[78] This was a particular vision of a messianic age, even if it lacked the specific label. Back in 1968, Basil Moore had justified the UCM's "worship happenings" with claims, from Judaism, that with the messianic age, a "new . . . community of spiritual, ethical and social righteousness would come."[79] In his paper, Biko embraced this idea that a messiah would bring new ways of being human. Students had already issued the "prophetic cry . . . Black Man you are on your own!" and now they assumed the Messiah's mantle: "We shall be in a position to bestow upon South Africa the greatest gift possible—a more human face."[80] We have seen this construct before. It belonged to Kenneth Kaunda, who had talked about human relations as Africa's great gift to the world. Indeed, Biko had used the construct elsewhere in the same way.[81] Yet now, at this theology seminar, the focus was no longer the whole world or a continent but within a specific nation. And its agents were called by name: the "we," being Biko's peers, his audience, his generation. Black Theology's universalism was to be found through its local agents—not as chosen people but as apostles and missionaries of the fighting Christ. They had been anointed.

This sense of mission soon wound its way into Black Consciousness discourse, and within a year, it acquired a name. Initially, the Black Messiah retained some of Biko's abstraction—not quite but in some sense Christ, not exactly students, not quite ready to declare for political liberation but definitely moving in that direction. Local theologians began with a remarkably disembodied and undetermined vision of a Black Messiah. In 1972, the Black People's Convention held its first annual meeting. Its interim president—an independent church leader named Mashwabada Mayatula—explained what the moment meant: "I am grateful that today we begin to open the first page in the history book of the newly resurrected Black nation in SA. At long last, the LIBERATOR, namely, the promised Black Messiah, 'the very God of the very God' has come. He has freely given us what we prayed for . . . the HOLY SPIRIT—the 'Spirit' of Black Consciousness, of Black Solidarity and Black unity." Christ did not feature here, nor, for that matter, did any recognizable political leader or even political ideology. Instead, Mayatula called his audience's attention to a "spirit," the mood of the "resurrected" black nation. Those collected there were given a mighty task—they themselves were either "liberator," the "Black Messiah" of prophecy, or at the very least evidence that that spirit had come. This was a fortuitous moment at which to hail the Messiah's advent: the emergence of the BPC demonstrated that what the people had prayed for—consciousness, solidarity, and unity—was at hand and that the movement toward liberation was well under way. In this context, even without reference to "race" or a specific political future, Mayatula's Black Messiah marked Black Theology's public shift away from the self-affirmation of Genesis and toward Moore's and Cone's preoccupation with political liberation.

Mayatula's Black Messiah was similar to but not quite Christ, in the same way that the biblical precedent in Exodus and the Gospels was, following Boesak, similar to but not identical to blacks' trials in the townships. Put another way, although the Son of Man was not a card-carrying member of BPC, the BPC, in its political task, was a latter-day revelation of the Son of Man, Mayatula continued. The Black Messiah, he explained, was the same "word of God . . . that once caused deliverance of Israelites from the House of Bondage." Faith had done this before and would do it again. His rhetoric blended the political promise of Exodus with Christianity's gendered and anthropomorphized savior. "One may ask, 'Who is this Black Messiah?' . . . He is the Holy Spirit of Black Consciousness and Black solidarity. He is our power." This last sentence sticks. "Power" was wielded infrequently in Black Consciousness talk. Its use here helps mark the transition at stake: from individual Consciousness, through Theology, to talk of collective power, to what this new mood would do—but without noting what the object of that power would be.[82]

Subsequent translators have had trouble explaining what Mayatula's Messiah meant within the context of the struggle against apartheid. Some thought that with the term, Mayatula was actually anointing himself or his organization. Others embraced a more abstract notion. BPC's national organizer,

Nkwenkwe Nkomo, described the Black Messiah not as a specific organization nor a specific person nor Christ but as a feeling, a nondetermined entity to which activists were "faithful disciple[s]."[83] To Nkomo, the Black Messiah was the spiritual underpinning of Black Consciousness, separate from a particular political program.

Within a few years, however, this distinction was lost. In his final address to the BPC, Mayatula's successor, T. S. Farisani, employed his training at the Lutheran Church's Mapumulo Seminary to great effect. He recalled a recent morning when, on the cusp of waking, he had had a vision in which, while soaring far above the earth, he had seen a "pale man, holding the sun in his hand." The light-skinned demon had captured the source of light and turned its rays to his advantage. There were thirteen rays, and each bore a resonant word or phrase: "apartheid, oppression, suppression, torture, bannings, Robben Island, Central Prison, Security Branch, Bureau of State Security, discrimination, injustice, inequality of man and Homelands." Farisani watched, transfixed, when a great storm rose up and swept away both the pale man and the "thirteen abominables." One can easily imagine the passion with which he described what came next: "On the horizon I saw a Blackman with his legs apart, his mouth wide open, the sun in his hand, with sheaths of rays folded, shouting . . . as [the] sunray sheaths unfolded. JUSTICE, EQUALITY, FAIRNESS, UNITY, LIBERATION. . . . The man grew taller, the sun rose higher and higher and the shouts grew louder and louder as the golden words [became] clearer and clearer."[84] Farisani recognized the "Blackman" and greeted him on behalf of BPC: "SIYABONGA [We thank you] BLACK MESSIAH!" Returning to earth—and his audience—Farisani explained what the vision meant. It was the Black Messiah's turn to hold the sun, and the rays told the tale: the specific horrors of apartheid would "soon" be replaced with the worthy promises of political liberation. He wished his audience the "POWER, SOLIDARITY, PERSISTANCE AND FORTITUDE" to make it so.[85]

So incarnated, Farisani's Black Messiah marked yet another step in Black Theology's march from Genesis through the Gospels and onto South Africa's streets. Farisani's imagery was reminiscent of Biko's "glittering prize," but where the latter was open to interpretation, Farisani had specifics. In the messianic age, there would be no apartheid but equality, no more (political) oppression but (political) liberation, no more Robben Island but justice. The faith implicit in the talk of a messianic age was there, as was the prophecy and vision of things as yet unseen. But however thundering the rhetoric, only apartheid, the system, and its agents were being swept away, and in the end, one group of people (here embodied in the transition from pale to dark men) still held the sun. Whereas Ntwasa had critiqued Cone for too great an obsession with power and authority, here we see clearly that Farisani's Black Messiah was in control. But was his control the more human face of which Ntwasa, Biko, and other activists spoke? Black Theology still used language that tended toward the abstract, toward confidence in things unseen and futures unknown, but it was beginning to develop a platform. What sort of faith did this theology entail? Belief in Farisani's virile Black Messiah stemmed, as Biko had suggested, from the premise of a "fighting God," and in Farisani's mind, it was clear that God struggled in the present age, in the present politics. Here, it seems, was the theology that Bishop Zulu worried would make Christianity little more than the "handmaid of the black revolution."

Yet to accept the critique and move on in search of political history is to elide a critical element of Black Theological discourse. Even if it had arrived on the brink on political struggle, Black Theology was not just politics. God had created the world, God was ultimately responsible for human affairs, and God could fight, but if apartheid was the fault of men, not God, then there was an almost Barthian gap between God and people's actions. Stubbs's assessment of Ntwasa was correct: Black Theologians did tend toward a more conservative theism, especially when compared with the UCM's faith in the totally diffused "it." Despite their embrace of humanism, black thinkers did not go so far as to completely overlay themselves and the divine or cast God as an actor in their affairs. When, for example, authors of a 1970 SASO report reminded activists that "God is not in the habit of coming down to earth to solve people's problems," they managed to preserve both knowledge of God's existence and separation from earthly events. God might sanction human affairs, but outcomes were a human responsibility.[86]

Ntwasa's explication of the "concept of the church" in Black Theology demonstrated the tension that inhered here. Ntwasa argued that belonging to a "church," to a community of believers, meant filling the middle ground between divine and earthly action. He reserved a place for the triad of beliefs— belief in Jesus, belief that he is the son of God, and belief that he came to redeem mankind—but he described how human actors needed to embody their faith through action, not belief, thus filling the space God had left for human initiative. If to be Christian meant to "live and die with Christ," Ntwasa argued, then "to die with Christ is not to have a spiritual experience of Christ, but . . . to fuse [one's] life with Christ's [so] that it takes on the quality of Christ's life and death. . . . It is therefore to share the quality of being totally engaged in the struggle against evil—against anything that binds people." Belief was not enough to qualify for membership in Ntwasa's church; instead, its members were "those whose lives are perceived to have the quality of Christ-in-his-struggle-against-human-bondage. It is thus the company of liberators, or it is not the Church." Ntwasa walked a fine line here. He obviously wanted to preserve an element of the transcendental—Jesus as Son of God, the redeemer of humankind—yet his "church" had strict entrance requirements: either the company of liberators or not the church at all.[87] The vertical was briefly mentioned, but the horizontal was underlined.

That is why Biko's "glittering prize" is so interesting. Black Consciousness and Black Theology called for a change far beyond a sociological or political shift, while retaining the necessity of both. Yet within a few short years, Biko's God had evolved into Farisani's more programmatic Black Messiah; similarly, Black Theology's transcendence gave way to a profoundly earth-focused faith. As Ntwasa had done, St. Peter's seminary lecturer Anthony Mabona struggled to preserve the tension between vertical and horizontal faith. His subject was worship: "Anyone who does not believe in a transcendent deity and in the reality of the eternal Kingdom cannot worship in a Christian sense." Here, Christian faith was reserved for those who believed in transcendence, not those who "lived and died with Christ." Yet even to Mabona, worship had a goal, an end. It was not just about opening oneself to experiences of the divine but about "developing correct attitudes towards things and towards men"; it was not about "the ghostly elevation of ideas" but about the terrain of action.[88]

Mabona was a Catholic. We might therefore have expected that, to him, worship meant both faith and works. Yet even the resolutely Calvinist Boesak shared Mabona's understanding of enacted faith. Theology, Boesak explained, did not mean teasing out God's word in search of the correct way to approach the divine. Rather, theology was "faith active in the world," and faith in turn was "the action of love within history." Actions constituted faith, and therefore, faith was historical. Believers were encouraged to cultivate "sensitivity" to what God was doing in the world, as Boesak demonstrated in his use of Exodus to interpret the Bible's liberating content, and then act accordingly. This was faith—and without history and sociology and politics, it could not exist.[89]

To this point, I have clung to a rather conventional organizational framework, jockeying between the "religious" and the "political" to show how Christianity was incarnated in the struggle against apartheid and how in turn we might better understand how theologians and activists believed secular strivings worked toward salvation. This framework, which governs much of the historiography of nationalist or religious movements, is no longer adequate. Black Theology was about politics, but it was not just about a nation; it was about an approach to God, but it was not only about religion. Cedric Mayson, a Christian Institute employee and *Pro Veritate* editor, suggested that Black Theology "wasn't an attempt to be a religion, it was an attempt to grasp an understanding of the theological and spiritual truths in the human communities that underlaid . . . struggle."[90] Black Theology was deeply Christian because its adherents were but even more so because they consciously turned to Christ's revelation in scripture to plot their own way forward. Charges that Black Theology failed some litmus test of true and godly faith were largely irrelevant when faced with the "truths" of this specific human community. Why? Because of exchanges like this:

> Bokwe Mafuna: Every pastor and priest is faced with the same problem, that with all his background of theological and philosophical training [he] has to talk to ordinary housewives and the unemployed and sinners and drunkards who are part of his congregation and he's got to try and articulate the wonderful revelations that he thinks he has got in his head. . . . And sometimes they doze off in the pews listening to a very boring sermon, which might be bordering on the truth, but it is because the poor man or the poor woman had to be working late, night shift, whether as a prostitute or as a driver. And just the difference in the experiences in their world, there is such a huge chasm, and yet they are all concerned about the same things, about truth, about redemption, about liberation, about the equality, and the interdependence of human beings.
>
> Daniel Magaziner: The situation you describe, were there people who were able effectively to really bridge it? You use the example of the priest, someone who . . . thinks he knows and then is able to actually say to people who have been working and say this, translate it?
>
> BM: Has it ever happened?
>
> DM: Yeah, that you know of?
>
> BM: Jesus the Nazarene.[91]

In this conversation, Mafuna explained precisely what I had failed to grasp in my research on Black Theology: how my quest for conceptions of divinity and my often clumsy probing of the line between sacred and secular failed to grasp the way in which 1970s activists understood life's "wholeness." The training and philosophy and abstract beliefs were part of it; "ghostly" ideas also had a role to play, whether they came from the Bible, from tradition, from African Humanism, or from Western existentialism. But in the final accounting, it came down to assumptions about the nature of human beings—that political ideals such as liberation and equality mattered and that the most effective faith soldered ideas and ideals together and made people move—and that was what Christ had done.

Biko was undoubtedly this era's most famous political thinker, and therefore, his views are useful in clarifying this argument. He was not a well-known Christian. Indeed, his assumption of a salaried position in a South African Council of Churches organization drew protests from the SACC's general secretary, who worried "as to his relationship . . . to the Church."[92] Yet not only did Biko participate in the UCM and in Black Theology seminars but, as we have seen, he also capably expressed his own need for a relevant faith. Writing to a minister and friend after being banned to King William's Town in the mid-1970s, Biko hinted at the Black Messiah's lineage. Religious truth, he wrote, "lies in my ability to incorporate my vertical relationship with God into the horizontal relationships with my fellow man." Segueing smoothly from secular theology to Black Theology, he suggested that this was precisely what the opponents to Roman-occupied Palestine had achieved through the "advent" of their messiah. Biko sought that same unification—of the godly, the human, and the liberating—in Black Theology. Through it, he wrote, "I have felt better protected from becoming completely agnostic." Biko agreed with Ntwasa and Boesak but also with Mabona and Zulu: he too did not want to let go of God, to completely sacrifice transcendence for politics. History would have made it easy to do so. ("My God," Biko lamented, "if I have to view Christ as . . . so conservatively interpreted at times . . . I find him foreign to me.") Yet he still maintained the transcendent by plotting a fundamentally transformative path, toward a "distant horizon."[93]

Yet Biko's theology—and Black Theology in general—was undermined by the creative tension within itself. No matter how carefully believers trod, Ntwasa's conclusions left marks: the church was the "company of liberators" or it "was not the Church." Given Christianity's history in Africa and its varied roles in the continent's benighted south, the Christian faith was inextricably in and indistinguishable from politics. "We live in the world of politics, in the world of events, in the world of . . . many things [and] this life has to be addressed [in its fullness]," Motlhabi told me.[94] Christianity had come with missionaries, it had abetted conquest, and it had helped to impose "foreign" rule. Now, Biko tasked the revolutionary not only with exposing this complicity and undermining history's ill effects but also with restoring "faith in life amongst all citizens of his country."[95] Keeping faith in life was what mattered. When Biko appealed to "my God" to bemoan Christian South Africa's conservative Christ, he was expressing his own belief that faith could and needed to fight in South Africa's political world. Having traveled the political path from liberal to secular to the eve of the Black Messiah's arrival, Christianity was no longer foreign; it was not an instrument or cover but instead intrinsic and essential, something without which the hoped-for future would not come.

Like their counterparts in UCM, SASO activists had cultivated this religiosity from the beginning, when students approached Manas Buthelezi and asked him to help to develop a Black Theology for South Africa. They had defined *black* as an attitude and a way, a being attuned toward an undefined struggle, to which theology added a sense of self that was proud to have been made in the image of God. Students thus embraced the certainty that religion brings: "We believe in it, we think it is right." There is orthodoxy and dogma aplenty there. In our conversation, Manas Buthelezi speculated that students had come to him as a shield, thinking that if "you can have a meeting of your activist hotheads and then you invite a pastor to address them—that would give some kind of cover."[96] Yet in the early 1970s, as the national seminar revealed, Christian meetings were often more politically fraught than student meetings. I offer another hypothesis: that if the students were looking for a cover, it was from themselves. Students eschewed political talk during those early days—it was still stage one, time to focus on the distant horizon and not on the "black revolution" about which Zulu worried. They drew themselves instead to faith, as if predicting Achille Mbembe's argument that "if there is one thing the religious points to, it is . . . to the category of possibility—the belief that things are not condemned to always be the same."[97]

The promise of change is inherent in Christianity, and I think that was what South African students wanted to find. And although they initially denied it, ultimately their Black Messiah could only be about politics, about themselves, about that experience South Africans call simply The Struggle. Black Theology grew out of an oppositional context, and from the outset, perhaps without meaning to, its subscribers gave it a political purpose. Through theology, they found and created faith in themselves as a generation and a community, as prophets and disciples, and indeed as manifestations of an epoch's messiah; through theology, they moved from the "I" of reflection to the "We" of action. Thus, they hoped to replicate that most miraculous of events: transforming ideas into actions and, as another epoch's messiah taught, in turn transforming their world.

PART III

᠊᠊᠊᠊

The Movement

Hindsight casts the shadow of the Black Consciousness Movement over these efforts to unpack the thinking and experiences that structured blackness, consciousness, and faith in the late 1960s and early 1970s. Similarly, by 1972, the shadows of political liberation and more easily narrated politics began to loom over the realm of intellectual inquiry and creativity. This study's third part follows Black Consciousness as it made its highly contingent progress from ideas to ideology and from reflection to movement. Chapter 7 traces the theories and processes that set the stage for this transition, as Black Consciousness activists thought about and tried to spread their ideas. It begins by introducing the concept of conscientization, an idea developed by the Brazilian educational theorist Paulo Freire. The concept was exported to South Africa around 1970 and was eagerly embraced by SASO and UCM activists. Conscientization was based on the idea that the oppressed needed to develop their own critical faculties rather than have some vanguard force an ideology upon them. As the chapter demonstrates, however, this concept shifted by the mid-1970s, as Black Consciousness conscientization became more dogmatic and straightforwardly ideological.

This transition was the result of the theoretical's encounter with the empirical; concientization became politicized as the result of sometimes intentional "accidents," which saw activists associated with Black Consciousness thought drive their organizations toward confrontations with political foes—both non-whites and the state—even as some members argued that it was not yet time to do so. Chapter 8 narrates critical junctures along the road toward the political horizon, beginning with the founding of the Black People's Convention in late 1971 and 1972. These events—which included university strikes, protests against Bantustan leaders and the apartheid government, well-publicized trials, and ultimately the 1976 Soweto uprising—all had intellectual, emotional, and physical costs, and the last chapter of *The Law and the Prophets* considers how ideas of suffering, hope, and faith evolved to match changing political circumstances. The political furies of the mid-1970s bore little resemblence to the relative quiet that had conditioned the development of Black Consciousness and Black Theology, and the believers' theology—especially their image of Christ—responded to this. By 1973, Christ was not the harbinger of a "more human face," but a freedom fighter whose death had brought his people's liberation that much closer. As setbacks mounted and suffering increased, so too did the rhetorical relationship between activists and Christ, as martyrs whose deaths promised that an oppressive system's end was near. Chapter 9 closes this study with readings of sermons preached at activists' funerals between 1974 and 1977, and suggests that the wedding of suffering and death to hope and victory was among the most enduring legacies of Black Consciousness and Black Theology.

7 ⤙ "I write what I like"

Conscientization, Culture, and Politicization

OVER THE course of 1971, Basil Moore and Stanley Ntwasa collected papers from 1971's Black Theology seminars to be published in South Africa under the title *Essays in Black Theology*. Like their editors, however, the essays were banned after a brief run. Two years later, from exile in Great Britain, Moore published the collection with the title *Black Theology: The South African Voice*. The latter title was altogether more appropriate. Developing the black community's voice was the most lasting concern of Black Consciousness thinkers. Activists believed that South Africa's problems would begin to be solved if and when blacks were "capable of entering into dialogue with white members of this country as equals who speak from a position of strength rather from a position of weakness."[1] Separation from sympathetic whites was explained in terms of the cultivation of this voice; with activists having established their own organizations, the letters page in the *SASO Newsletter* now invited readers to "Speak Black Man!" Steve Biko's famed columns in the same publication made this so explicit as to be easily overlooked. In a society where blacks were perceived as a faceless, voiceless, and inarticulate gaggle, there was untold power in writing "what I like."

To this point, I have focused on the small group of thinkers and activists who were instrumental in crafting Black Consciousness and Black Theology. I have traced how they developed their voice, from the advent of SASO through the cultivation of the uniquely "South African Voice" that spoke of Christ's liberating message for their country. By 1971–72, members of this group knew and spoke of themselves as blacks in the image of God; with their voices and pens, they had, as Biko wrote, "started on the road towards emancipation."[2] Speaking and writing are powerful acts, especially under a political system that constrained the vast majority of the population's capacity to do either and in a society where, in the late 1960s, an estimated 60 percent of the population over the age of ten was considered functionally illiterate.[3] Black Consciousness thinkers and activists trusted in the power of creative talk; they were the youths who had eagerly flocked to high school debating groups to argue that the pen is mightier than the sword, the literate vanguard who first read and then cultivated the ability to write about the issues that mattered to them.[4] The problem was with the rest of black society. How could the vast majority become new selves, with a voice?

Issues of literacy, writing, and other cultural activities had been among the UCM's earliest concerns. Beginning in 1968, activists discussed the need for a widespread literacy program. Led by Colin Collins, the UCM organized workshops on literacy training, and numerous students spent their vacations teaching African workers—often the staff at their universities—the rudiments of reading and writing, typically with materials from the Johannesburg-based Bureau of Literacy and Education, a nongovernmental organization that worked closely with the Ministry of Bantu Education.[5] UCM activists cited these efforts in a 1969 appeal to the Transkei government for permission to work on adult education in that territory, even as activists' ideas about literacy were beginning to change. By then, UCM's Literacy Committee was considering recent and more radical methods from the United States and elsewhere. Foremost among these was Paulo Freire's method of literacy and cultural education. By late 1969, Freire's unattributed influence was obvious in an essay that rejected the Bureau of Literacy and Education both for its complicit relationship with the Ministry of Bantu Education and for its methods. Whereas the bureau was accused of treating adult students as "vacuums" to be filled by "teachers," UCM imagined its adult students as thinking subjects who "even though . . . unschooled and illiterate, have knowledge, wisdom, insight and creativity."[6] As Freire's South African translators explained, literacy was not just about being able to read censored newspapers and exploitative labor contracts; instead, true literacy was about the construction of autonomous selves. Freire called for teachers not to preach but to listen, not to enforce ideology but to conscientize—a crude English term translated from the Portuguese *conscientiçazão*. As UCM found itself under attack in 1971 and 1972, its members voted to transfer the literacy project's resources to SASO. Given Freire's resonance with their own ideas, it made sense that SASO activists approached Anne Hope, a former Freire student and a friend of Collins's, and asked her to train them in Freire's method.

Conscientization is undoubtedly a familiar concept to many students of South African politics. From the mid-1970s through the 1980s, South African activists used this term to describe the process of spreading political awareness. As such, conscientization was linked to protest, and a community's readiness to engage in political struggle was seen as the degree to which it had been successfully conscientized. This chapter weaves in conscientization as a theme in order to show (1) how activists transformed a pedagogical concept into an ideological one, and (2) how ideas about subjectivity and voice moved through literacy and cultural creativity to call for a politicization of the personal—new South African selves who spoke with one voice about one subject in particular: life under apartheid and the demands of struggle.

"CONSCIENTISATION IS MY MISSION"

When SASO leaders approached Anne Hope in early 1972, she was only too happy to offer her services. "I thought he [Freire] was the answer to all the problems," she told me, and she felt that "anyone who was a bit awake" would embrace the Brazilian's method.[7] Over the course of 1972, Biko, Pityana, and other Black Consciousness activists met with Hope every other month to learn how to apply Freire's insights to their situation. Freire's ideas resonated with Biko, who had once plotted self-reflection as the critical moment, after which "you have committed yourself to fight."[8] As such, he sketched a direct relationship between reflection—critical thought—and action; this was the same dialectical relationship that was at the heart of Freire's conscientiçazão. Freire defined the term as "critical self-insertion into reality" by the oppressed. The agent was critical here; to be conscientized was not simply to be made aware but to make oneself aware. Freire's English editor elaborated on this, noting that conscientization was the "process by which men, not as recipients but as knowing subjects, achieve a deepening awareness both of the socio-cultural reality which shapes their lives and of their capacity to transform that reality."[9] Conscientization thus was the process by which students would educate themselves to become "selves" and then, once they had achieved critical consciousness, work for societal transformation. Critical consciousness was primary; as Freire put it, the individual's "reflective presence" humanized the world and made political progress possible.[10]

We must be clear about the roles prescribed here. The politically conscious few were not the agents in Freire's scheme. Instead, they were facilitators who were supposed to create the conditions under which conscientization—"self-insertion into reality"—might occur. Freire's method was indeed methodical, as Hope explained: it began with a slow, painstaking process of conducting "listening surveys" among a target population, used to plot the best way to "encode" people's own language, symbols, and epistemologies. The goal was to impart not revolutionary consciousness, but consciousness itself and to trust that the people's "awakened" consciousness would make political change inevitable.[11] Listening surveys meant going to the people. Malusi Mpumlwana recalled spending his weekends while enrolled at the UNNE going to shebeens (unlicensed bars) around Durban not for entertainment but for research. He and other SASO members at the medical school focused on areas, such as Gandhi's Phoenix Settlement, that were plagued with undeveloped infrastructure and poor sanitation. There, activists, in keeping with both Freire's teaching and the dictates of Black Consciousness ("Black man, you are on your own"), endeavored to inculcate the "self-help spirit" rather than solve the people's problems. Following Freire, Mpumlwana recollected, "our agenda was to try and build a mass capacity of critical consciousness" from which "action [would] flow." This was neither charity (ridiculed as the redoubt of white liberals) nor overt politicization. Rather, Mpumlwana instructed, the goal was "critical consciousness . . . what I call 'bright-light' consciousness," as opposed to mass consciousness.[12]

That was Black Consciousness true to its roots: thinking, analyzing, but not determining. Telling people what to believe was not the point; as another UNNE student put it, "We did not say, look, we have come to teach you about Black Consciousness," but rather, "We were doing Black Consciousness, we were enacting Black Consciousness there."[13] The emphasis was on slow, methodical work in order to help people generate analysis and only then to interrogate and act against the roots of their situation. Mpumlwana recognized the inherent political dangers: "The best way to mobilize and galvanize people is not to make them all critically conscious, but is really to get them all to follow," he told me. That was what previous political movements had done, with spectacular results. The willingness to follow marked "mass" consciousness, and Mpumlwana conceded that it "actually is better for political organization than critical consciousness. Because [with] critical consciousness, people might actually not get anywhere."[14] Indeed, Freire's theory offered no guarantee that the people, once conscientized, would act appropriately. Nor did Freirean patience satisfy more radical critics. Poverty was a pressing problem at the Phoenix settlement and around South Africa, and more materially inclined white radicals roundly condemned SASO for wasting its time on listening sessions while people continued to die from disease.[15]

Criticisms aside, the way in which the concept of conscientization linked antideterminaton and faith in inevitable change fit comfortably with the rest of the Black Consciousness philosophy. To SASO activists, their emphasis on conscientization distinguished themselves and their activities from more conventional politics. Clement Mokoka, a Catholic priest in Pretoria, worked closely with that city's SASO branch, known as the Pretoria Students Organisation (PRESO). Nowhere in his discussion of concientization did the question of politics come in; rather, the focus was on people "talking . . . and we would send some students to go just to town with the workers and try to listen to what they are talking about."[16] Former UNNE student Aubrey Mokoape scoffed at the notion that the Phoenix development project was in fact groundwork for a Black Consciousness political party. "It was not as if we were out for a membership drive," he told a Pretoria court.[17] This antipolitics idea of conscientization was at the center of Black Consciousness activists' self-conception of their not-quite-politics-yet-still-political project. "Our idea was not a political party, our idea was conscientization of society," Mpumlwana insisted. "We already had political parties and that was not the point. It's not about an organization, it's about . . . how you treat yourself, and how you relate to your environment."[18] Indeed, as with SASO's early critique of postcolonial politics, political parties were not to be trusted. They indoctrinated, Strini Moodley explained, and "indoctrination implies that you have a particular philosophy . . . or value system that you wish to impose upon a people, whereas conscientisation implies . . . you believe that it is not for me as an individual to [impose] things upon another individual."[19] To do so would be to deny the being of the other, to treat people as mere "receptacles" to be filled by some all-knowing teacher.[20] No, Moodley continued, the important thing was "to make the other individual appreciate from his own point of view and through his own analysis of the society what is wrong with society. I am not going to tell people this is wrong and that is wrong or you must do this . . . rather than impose something, you raise questions in the minds of people."[21] In this sense, conscientization carried on the process we saw in chapter 1, when those who became Black Consciousness activists recalled their own 1960s experiences with teachers, peers, or books and how they began to ask questions of the sources and draw their own conclusions. Conscientization was "consulting the mind"; it was listening to the people and raising questions, in hopes that "they would think."[22] Imposing doctrine from above could create mass consciousness, as both Freire and Mpumlwana explained, but doing so was antithetical to the dialogic, reflective processes implicit in conscientization.

This tension proved hard to maintain. The righteousness of orthodoxy was put down in SASO thinking, but just as freethinking Christianity could result in right-thinking Black Theology, so too was the potential for proscribed doctrine a possibility. After all, our definition of Black Consciousness as religion ("we believe in it, we think it is right") contained within it not just a strong assertion of the collective's subjectivity but also the assurance that followed belief. As Freire envisioned it, conscientization was to be open ended. The dialogue might have a desired end, but those in the already-conscious vanguard were not to "impose" their opinion on the subject. It is striking, therefore, to hear Oshadi Mangena, another Pretoria activist, describe her understanding of the process. "[We] always talked about the three c's," she told me: "You make them aware first so the first C stands for conscientization.

I think it was something from Paulo Freire—Conscientise. Then you can cooperate or collaborate with the people who agree with you. But if when you have conscientised them they still do not want to go the right way, then you confront them. That's the third C."[23] This language invoked Freire, but marked a departure from his ideas. By confronting those who "do not want to go the right way," South African activists were claiming that they held the answer; theirs was the right way, and by implication, other ways were not.

This sense of mission undermined and eventually collapsed the dialogic tension that Freire had maintained. This change was in some sense a by-product of evolving political circumstances. Indeed, even as activists embraced Freire's method and worked diligently to listen and develop codes with which to approach the wider population, some worried that activists had politics too much on the mind. "Their codes were too radical," Anne Hope recalled, "and they raised anxiety in some of the people they were working with."[24] Consequently, conversations could veer away from dialogue to pressure. Dan Mogale and Simon Mashiangwako, PRESO activists, demonstrated this; when they spoke of conscientization, they described it as a sort of exclusive knowledge or insight that they and other activists possessed. Conscientization, they suggested, was wielded to force people to action, and information was "our key conscientization tool," not to help people ask questions but to "make people move." As with Mangena's example, cited earlier, their account of conscientization was more doctrinaire, more politicizing. Although activists employed the Freirean idiom of "codes" and "developing" consciousness, they did so to force confrontation, to "make people move" in a particular direction.[25] Indeed, in an undated article delivered to a SASO general student congress, Vic Mafungo made this other use of conscientization even more explicit. Freire's term, he explained, meant "making blacks aware of the need for liberation."[26]

Conscientization was increasingly used as a euphemism for what in another context might have been called simply *politicization*. In the late 1970s, reflecting on the importance of the Black Consciousness Movement, one former activist conflated the two terms. Movement supporters "must continue to politicise people, to conscientise, [at] which they have been very good," he contended.[27] Black Consciousness leaders themselves seized on this: the 1970s, Mosibudi Mangena insisted, revealed the "liberatory, conscientized . . . political energy in the country that saw the beginning of the decline of the system."[28] Conscientization thus moved beyond the realm of the slow creation of awareness to signify concern with liberation—and not only that. It was also about cultivating a perspective on politics that was associated with a particular group that knew the way.

Given the religiosity pervasive in Black Consciousness thought, it is not surprising that activists spoke about conscientization in terms of conversion.

When asked how God justified conscientization, Rev. Simon Farisani, who we earlier saw prophesize about the Black Messiah, answered without hesitation. He cited Matthew 28:18–20, Christ's "Great Commission," which instructed, "Go ye into the world and speak to the people, teach them everything that I have taught you."[29] This was a remarkable statement. The Great Commission had long served to justify European mission, of which SASO and Christian activists were not great fans. Yet here, a Black Consciousness leader embraced mission's logic, even if cloaked in Freire's language. This was a critical admission. A hierarchy of knowledge rested at mission's core: missionaries knew and believed that others needed to know what they knew. The mission encounter has been called a long conversation, but it was a conversation in which one side repeatedly claimed to have a monopoly on universal and eternal truth. Although empathy and political sympathy might lead us to embrace Black Consciousness's particular righteousness, we should note how its embrace of mission marked a final departure from a faith in change rooted in dialogue to one rooted in orthodoxy. Conscientization meant conversion; it meant recognizing those who could "be converted into the kind of black people we'd like to have in the struggle" and dismissing those who could not.[30] This was a different sort of Black Consciousness—not something enacted in self-help schemes and concomitant awareness but an object to be wielded. "I believe we should propagate Black Consciousness as a philosophy," a Johannesburg area activist told a court in the mid-1970s, "because the Black people need an . . . ideology in order to bind them together, so that they know what they are fighting for."[31] For this activist, Black Consciousness did not mean projecting one's beingness as a creation of God; Black Consciousness meant instead an ideology and a political movement.

AN AESTHETIC INTERLUDE

This transformation suggested that Anne Hope was right to worry that SASO's codes were too radical. Students were trained in the Freirean method and attempted to utilize it across 1972, but literacy programs never took off in the way she and others had hoped. Although there were some successes—PRESO in particular enjoyed great success, albeit with children more than adults—Hope later reflected that most activists used Freire's methods "much more in theater" and other potentially politicizing venues.[32] This was a progression that Freire's own theories supported, as he wrote that following encoding and conscientization, the arts would "gradually cease to be a mere expression of the easy life of the affluent bourgeoisie and begin to find their inspiration in the hard life of the people."[33] A quick survey of the decade's cultural politics supports Hope's assessment that this was what Black Consciousness cultural activists had sought to achieve. The 1970s saw not only a political and theological resurgence but also an effluence of artistic production. From poetry published in SASO's newsletter and other media to the increasing popularity of township theater and the musical stylings of Lefifi Tladi, Phillip Tabane, and others, black South African culture enjoyed a renaissance of a particular sort in the early 1970s.[34] New cultural output reflected the Black Consciousness aesthetic: as a mid-1970s magazine put it, given the circumstances of black life, "we cannot waste our time on comical dramas" and escapist fantasies. Rather, since "we live in times of war where a Black man cannot stop thinking of his liberation," art, like philosophy and theology, needed to be a relevant part of the evolving conscientizing project.[35]

As the decade progressed, popular culture emerged as the critical arena in which activists, students, and others cultivated black South Africa's voice and spread Black Consciousness's ideas. We have seen evidence of this already in the poetry that compared Tiro to Christ and elsewhere. The SASO Newsletter's turn away from Négritude poets to black American poets had marked a critical break, and so did its prominent publication of works by South African poets, some unknown and others (including Mafika Gwala, Mandla Langa, Sipho Sepamla, and Mongane Wally Serote) who were already earning reputations for their Black Consciousness–infused verse.

License was not granted to acclaimed poets alone. Teachers at high schools, such as Morris Isaacson in Soweto, wrote poetry "from the heart" and disseminated it to their students, who in turn were invited to create and share their own works.[36] Given their proximity to SASO's nerve center in Durban, Thoko Mbanjwa and other students at Inanda Seminary were well positioned to receive the message of conscientized artistic creativity. As we saw in chapter 3, teachers there invited local activists to assist in the students' English and drama lessons. These activists, Mpumlwana noted, "would come and do poetry with us, they would read poetry—and relevant poetry and not Byron, Wordsworth and so on, but much more written by South Africans, written by themselves." Activists would then "encourage us as well, after having small discussions, to write. And we would write and read . . . the thoughts we had."[37] Individuals crafted their own voices, but the injunction to create relevant art typically ensured that the end product reflected either the poet's experiences under apartheid or the gathering momentum of renewed struggle against the state. After all, as the prominent Black Consciousness poet James Matthews later wrote,

> I wish I could write a
> Poem
> Record the beginning of
> Dawn
> The opening of a flower

At the approach of a bee
. . . Then I look at people
Maimed shackled, jailed
The knowing is now clear
I will never be able to write
A poem about a dawn
. . . Or a bee.[38]

This aesthetic was not without its critics. Some felt that black creativity was being stifled by an overemphasis on the real over the lyrical. Richard Rive, the famed Coloured novelist and poet, for one, bemoaned the new poetry in a harsh review published in *Pro Veritate*. "Black Consciousness poetry in South Africa is . . . mediocre," Rive wrote; "the writing is of a highly polemical nature, hysterical, screaming and declamatory." He understood that the era's poets were trying to both describe their experiences and plot a way forward, but the manner in which they did so "becomes a mere listing of grievances interspersed with shrieks for revenge. This type of poetry, obsessed as it is with its message, impairs literary excellence." To live up to its name, he concluded, poetry must "go deeper and beyond any special pleading at any particular time." Ultimately, he concluded that "what [Black Consciousness poets] are producing is not poetry."[39]

What Rive and other critics failed to appreciate, however, was that Black Consciousness artists were not interested in timelessness but strove instead for a radical timeliness. As Strini Moodley explained, "a true artist cannot extract himself from his own experience and . . . talk in objective universal terms." This was a situational aesthetic, and just as theologians had defended their contextual theology, so Moodley argued that Western ways of thinking had obscured this essential truth about cultural production. He suggested that the ancient Greeks had turned to theater "to communicate an experience . . . that the entire community was faced with"—in other words, the politics of the moment— and thus black theater was in keeping with this precedent. The aesthetic response to the moment was what mattered. Although Moodley did periodically celebrate black artistic traditions, his aesthetic demanded something of the now.[40] Even as nationalist Africa was undergoing the cultural turn away from politics, Black Consciousness thinkers such as Moodley instead aligned their cultural politics with Fanon and Freire, arguing that the "cultural revolution" was made with the "seething pot," not the sari's faded and irrelevant glories.[41] If this meant that new black art, literature, and theater therefore tended to be didactic and repetitive, so be it. "Black writers are preoccupied with politics," Mbulelo Mzamane told a gathering of black intellectuals in mid-1976, and for that they made no apologies.[42]

This preoccupation with political voice was not without its risks, and art often courted government repression, just as theology had done.[43] In the early 1970s, PRESO activists used their church contacts to bring a play entitled *She Lied* (the "she" was a white woman who lied about a sexual encounter with a black man) to schools around Pretoria, and they recalled numerous occasions when police raids followed the final curtain.[44] Similarly, in the spring of 1973, Johannesburg-based cultural activists associated with the People's Experimental Theatre performed Mthuli ka Shezi's play *Shanti* to packed houses and enthusiastic audiences on university campuses and in township venues such as the Donaldson Orlando Community Centre (DOCC).[45] The Security Branch was less enthused and repeatedly raided performances. Few arrests were made, although on one occasion, officers apparently "removed the cast's equipment, including a wig."[46]

It is no wonder that plays like *Shanti* garnered the government's attention. Written by a prominent SASO leader, the play was especially radical, even for the Black Consciousness aesthetic, in that Shezi's characters pursued a political program that went far beyond Black Consciousness's more tentative moves in that direction. *Shanti* was the story of the forbidden love between two students, Thabo, an African, and Shanti, an Indian. As the plot unfolds, they reflect on love and on blackness (and on their impending exams), until Thabo is arrested, escapes, and flees to Mozambique, where he dies fighting with FRELIMO guerrillas. Interspersed with this, Shezi wrote long monologues peppered with Black Consciousness rhetoric, delivered by the main characters and their Coloured friend, Koos. To take only one example: at the play's outset, Koos encapsulates recently developed thinking with words that stage directions indicate were addressed directly to the audience:

> Shall I be so easily impressed by parliamentary speeches that the Coloured comes immediately after the White, then follows the rest? Your kind, Shanti, then Thabo's. Are we three not components of Blacks? Are we not Blacks, suffering what we do in degrees? Are we not all Black, who shouldn't only be proud but who should also guard against contamination by induced inferiority complex? Yes, I am Black and inferior to no man . . . I am Black. Black like my mothers. Black like the sufferers. Black like the continent.[47]

Audiences responded to these ideas. At the trial of activist Eric Molobi during the mid-1970s, numerous witnesses testified to repeatedly viewing Shezi's play. It resonated, one said, as a "dramatical portrayal of things I had been thinking about." *Shanti* was widely considered "a play that none can afford to miss."[48]

Shanti's evident success was testament to culture's utility as a means to spread Black Consciousness ideas and conscientize the wider populace. The play's unique content also helped to ensure that popular culture became wedded to ideological correctness, to the expression of Black Consciousness's particular voice, not that of the still-inarticulate audience. Plays, poems, relevant art and music—all helped to get the word out, even if this approach was not exactly what Freire and Anne Hope had intended. Shezi wrote the play sometime before his own death under mysterious circumstances in late 1972. (See chapter 9.) Its plot—especially the playwright's apparent support for armed struggle, à la FRELIMO—was controversial, and as we have seen, the government's response was heavy-handed. What is notable in this regard is that although *Shanti* contained various Black Consciousness–influenced elements, its precise political agenda was one that neither SASO nor any other Black Consciousness organization shared. Rather, activists staged it at least in part because it had been "Shezi's wish . . . but unfortunately he died before he could do so." Charged with pushing a revolutionary program, actors pleaded, "We are only fulfilling a dead man's wish."[49] The government was not interested in such defenses and used artistic endeavors to charge activists with political agitation.

During the trial of the nine Black Consciousness leaders with which I opened this study, the state repeatedly cited *Shanti* as evidence that SASO and BPC leaders were not merely the cultural activists and intellectuals that they claimed to be. *Shanti*, the government charged, proved that Black Consciousness was "inflammatory, provocative, anti-white, racialistic, subversive and . . . revolutionary."[50] The defense attorneys' two-pronged response was deeply ironic, in that their efforts to forestall a harsh judgment necessitated that they downplay two fundamental tenets of Black Consciousness thought: that revolutions began in the mind and that appropriate culture was inherently political. First, SASO and BPC's lawyers called an expert "on ethnic nationalism in South Africa," who testified that "far from being 'relevant' [*Shanti*] is about the political and ideological belly-gazing of three young intellectuals." Students' claims aside, it was, in his expert opinion, highly unlikely that such philosophical reflection could provoke a revolution. In their own testimony, the defendants pursued the other tack. Asked whether *Shanti* "showed the true meaning of Black Consciousness," Zithulele Cindi demurred; the play was hardly worth discussing, he suggested, because it "did not have the stage craft that is necessary, [nor] was [it] up to the standards in theatrical terms."[51] How could the play be revolutionary, he innocently asked to the court, when it could hardly even be considered a play?

This defense was a strategy to fit the occasion, and evidence suggests that testimony such as Cindi's did not reflect what activists actually believed. Indeed, before the charges were filed, Black Consciousness publications had hailed *Shanti*, as had the *World's* reviewer and the witnesses in the Molobi trial. The play's easily interpreted message, its declamatory action that functioned to publicize Black Consciousness thinking, its rigid adherence to Black Consciousness talk (if not the philosophy's as yet ill-defined political program)— all had been worthy of celebration. *Shanti* was no "apologetic" play, activists crowed, nor was it a "token protest play . . . that merely says we are oppressed and leaves it at that." Whereas township playwrights such as Gibson Kente were deemed "comical" and escapist and protest theater like that of Athol Fugard was dismissed as intended for whites, activists deemed *Shanti* to be defiantly Black Consciousness. More than a play, PET concluded, it "gives positive direction to blacks."[52]

But what exactly was this direction? Was it toward armed struggle, as Thabo's trajectory suggested? The expert witness had charged Shezi's characters with irrelevant "navel-gazing," but as we have seen, the intellectual history of the 1970s resounded with faith that navel-gazing was a radical activity. By the time PET and other groups staged *Shanti*, the popular notion of voice had evolved. No longer concerned with cultivating individuals' subjectivity toward indeterminate ends, Black Consciousness–infused popular culture instead offered itself as the articulate vanguard that represented the people's voice. In a critical moment in the play, Thabo is in prison, reflecting on his and his people's predicament. As Koos had done, he turns to face the audience and urges them: "Sing on, my Black brothers, sing on. . . . Speak up and demand an answer. Speak up and say your say. You faceless millions! Speak up, you images of God!"[53] Thabo spoke in Shezi's voice, in Black Theology's voice, in the voice of the *SASO Newsletter's* injunctions to speak. Cindi might not have found it good theater, nor, perhaps, would Freire have judged it appropriate conscientization, but interrupted by the ovations of a packed house, it was undoubtedly good politics.

In this way, culture paced the progression from dialogic conscientization to didactic politicization, just as state incursions would help to transform nebulous Black Consciousness into a movement that confronted the system. Theories of conscientization were rooted, like Black Consciousness itself, in the mellowed philosophies of the late 1960s. But by the early 1970s, the pot was beginning to seethe and culture delivered an altogether more strident response, one consumed with the problem of liberation. A mid-1970s high school poet shared these concerns. "Conscientisation is my mission," he wrote, but that was only the beginning: "Bantustanism? That's praying for more oppression / White racism? I'm gonna squash that pretty soon . . . Black liberation is sure my goal / [A] free and just society will be the end-product."[54] Thought has occupied our attention for a while now, even as action has repeatedly threatened to take the stage. The twinned questions of conscientization and culture did not evolve in a vacuum; along the way, they related to those who were confronted and converted and those who could never be, to the aesthetic challenge of the now, and to the political problem of the not yet. By the time Security Branch raids robbed *Shanti's* cast of their equipment, the period reserved for reflection was closing. The age of philosophers was nearly past and the age of politics ascendant.

8 ⌇ The Age of Politics
Confronting the State

THE BLACK Consciousness Movement did not assume the mantle of 1970s opposition to apartheid unopposed. The poet cited in the last chapter pledged to struggle against "white racism"—this was obvious. The challenge of "Bantustanism" was less clear, as was the memory and current role of previous liberation movements. Over the course of the early 1970s, Black Consciousness activists considered the legacy of the PAC and ANC and debated among themselves the correct course of action regarding the ostensibly independent black "republics" that the government championed. In these discussions, activists manufactured Black Consciousness the Movement, not the epistemology or philosophy, culminating in 1972 with the establishment of the Black People's Convention, the first expressly political black organization since 1960.

SASO had previously eschewed direct political confrontation, but as it morphed into the Black Consciousness Movement, both internal and external conflict ensued. In this regard, I agree with James Brennan's recent reflections on German political theorist Carl Schmitt in light of African political history. "The process of defining enemies and constructing purge categories constituted a politics of enmity," Brennan wrote, "or what Carl Schmitt holds to be the fundamental feature of the political, the distinction between friend and enemy."[1] This held for Tanganyika in the 1950s, and in the 1970s, South African activists began to "sort the non-whites from the blacks," with blacks defined as the conscientized few who embraced their blackness in the way the Movement deemed appropriate.[2] As the philosophy turned Movement began to name its friends and call out its enemies, the state took an increasing interest in its activities, which helped to drive events along, even as some activists worried that their organizations were moving too quickly past "stage one."

Soon, events spun out of Black Consciousness's control. Conversations that started on isolated college campuses moved into cities, protest rallies, courts, and ultimately township streets following 16 June 1976. Black Consciousness ways of thinking changed in the course of things, and it was this contingent process of ideological maturation and confrontation that eventually saw the Movement ascend the 1970s.

BLACKS AND "NONWHITES"

At the outset, 1970s activists demonstrated little interest in supplanting previous liberation movements. "We already had political parties and that was not the point," Mplumlwana told me.[3] Indeed, SASO had prided itself on counting both ANC and PAC members in its ranks.[4] For his part, Barney Pityana saw no conflict in remaining an ANC supporter even while founding SASO. "We needed to be a new movement that acknowledge[d] the ANC and other organizations," he remembered, but also brought "a new cadre of young people into a consciousness of themselves that [was] not defined by where they had been or whatever loyalties they had." Thus, in SASO, people such as Biko—whom Pityana and others described as PAC—could share space with ANC loyalists.[5]

In fact, although SASO was skeptical of nationalist movements and what they could and could not achieve, during its first few years it never claimed to have taken over from previous organizations. In 1971, for example, when the SASO Newsletter covered Malawian president Hastings Banda's visit to South Africa, it excoriated him for not meeting black South Africa's "true leaders"—not SASO but those "who are either in Robben Island, in exile or in banishment."[6] Even after forming BPC, prominent leaders such as Mandela and Sobukwe remained highly regarded, even if Black Consciousness activists claimed that, in Mandela's case, they respected him in spite of his organization.[7] Black Consciousness activists often described themselves as placeholders for the more established organizations: activists celebrated "the history and achievement of the black movements" that preceded SASO and suggested that they were merely trying prepare "the mind of the people" for the struggle that the ANC and PAC would rightfully bring. The latter organizations' had a "practical" project, activists suggested, whereas SASO's was a "philosophical one."[8]

Questions of placeholding and intent sometimes undermined Black Consciousness's legitimacy, especially within exile circles. As activists left the country for a variety of reasons during the 1970s, they encountered ANC members who dismissed SASO and its philosophical project as a "baby organization of confused people."[9] Indeed, despite SASO's efforts to valorize student politics as an arena of struggle, others rejected its emphasis on philosophy as the immature or underdeveloped product of youth, especially when contrasted to the maturity signified by ANC materialist "practicality." In some sense, then, SASO leaders such as Biko, who demurred from accepting responsibility for the "stages" following conscientization, helped to create the image of Black Consciousness as something to be grown out of.[10]

Yet many did not accept the notion that there were two conversions—one leading from apathy to blackness, the other from Black Consciousness to some higher stage of political awareness. Biko might not have been interested in making a political party, but that did not stop him from indirectly attacking other parties' failings. In the 1950s, Africanists had critiqued the ANC for being beholden to white communists; in the 1970s, Biko described it as controlled by "liberals." During the Congress movement's heyday, "the white liberals . . . knew what was good for the blacks and told them so," Biko charged. Perhaps demonstrating his latent PAC sympathies, he concluded that "it was only at the end of the fifties that the blacks started demanding to be their own guardians."[11] In this, Biko seemed to favor Africanism, but activists just as frequently critiqued the PAC, particularly for its failure to include Indian and Coloured victims of white racism. As Black Consciousness ideas coalesced into a movement, activists argued that they were headed in a new direction, toward neither "multi-racial overtones [n]or [a] totally African image."[12]

With the work of conscientization well under way by late 1971, some activists believed that it was time for Black Consciousness to stake its unique political claim by forming an "adult" complement to SASO and thus demarcate Black Consciousness from older movements.[13] This proposition was hotly debated. Biko and Mpumlwana, for instance, argued that stage one was nowhere near complete. Various older civic activists agreed, and suggested that spreading Black Consciousness called for a "super cultural organization," not a new political party.[14] But other SASO activists agitated for a new organization and decided to kick-start it in December 1971 by hijacking a meeting at the Donaldson Orlando Community Centre in Soweto, where M. T. Moerane and other prominent African leaders were planning to form a cultural group.[15]

At that meeting, the "elders" were surprised when "the youngsters of the SASO, who have been preaching Black consciousness since 1968," asserted that blacks did not "need another cultural organization." Instead, SASO activists put forward a resolution that called for the formation of a political party.[16] Moerane protested and advocated a countermotion that called for the meeting to proceed as scheduled; he was heckled and his motion defeated. Various elders disavowed the proceedings. Both Moerane and Ellen Kuzwayo, for example, asked the record to indicate their nonparticipation. (Kuzwayo, a social worker and frequent critic of apartheid—and later a prominent opposition leader—claimed that her "professional ethics" precluded her sanctioning of a political organization.) The meeting went on, only it was now run by SASO members and supporters, who introduced resolutions to form an explicitly political organization.[17]

These resolutions—particularly the first, which justified a political party, and the second, which actually formed the Black People's Convention— demonstrate how Black Consciousness established its political voice vis-à-vis previous movements. First, SASO delegates rejected Moerane's protest against the inclusion of Indians and Coloureds; this new black political organization was to subscribe to SASO's definition of race. Having dismissed Africanism, delegates charged that the cultural organization under discussion also betrayed an "apparent positive attitude towards multiracialism." "Multiracialism is a pie in the sky," the resolution read, and thus a distraction while "there is an urgent need for the formation of a Political Movement" to be based on "the only viable ideology towards our salvation . . . Black Consciousness."[18]

This conclusion—that Black Consciousness was the only viable ideology— was surely disagreeable to many, a fact that SASO activists seemed to acknowledge in their first resolution, which spoke in the name of "we the delegates of SASO." But when the time came to form an organization, they demonstrated no such modesty. In a clear rejoinder to the PAC and the ANC, the assembly declared that only "the banner of Black Consciousness" could truly "articulate the interests of all Black People in this country." To that end, the delegates called for a black people's convention to be held the following July, and they resolved to have as their "primary objective the total liberation of all Blacks."

This primary objective was also the least defined. Liberation and its frequent companion freedom are fluid concepts. True, the resolution did cite the desire to "negate and oppose vigorously the politics of unrepresentative white regime designated to perpetuate slavery and servitude," but in terms of particulars, such as the ideals in the Freedom Charter, the BPC was vague.[19] In this sense, the decision to pursue politics through the BPC was SASO's philosophical approach in another form. Its program to "oppose vigorously" and "negate" racism resonated with SASO's existentialism-infused calls to negate nonwhiteness and assume an oppositional stance. This was the same call for being political, only now made under the banner of overt, aboveground politics.

There was one indication, however, of a more immediate political program within the resolution, which in turn opened the possibility of more concrete policies and actions. Almost as an afterthought amid bold calls for "total liberation," the delegates declared that "this body [will] work completely outside the system-created platforms."[20] This meeting took place at the DOCC, a frequent site of Soweto Urban Bantu Council meetings; whereas the PAC and the ANC were phantoms, with no overt presence in the country, system-created platforms were very real and very influential during the early 1970s. By countering not only previous liberation movements but also the erstwhile

politicians who ostensibly represented Africans' interests, Black Consciousness engaged in South African politics for the first time. Adherents rejected
collaboration and thus put teeth in their philosophical distinction between
blacks and those unworthy of the name. As Schmitt suggested, so began the
universal political practice of naming allies and enemies, pointing out those
in the community who were "with us," who were "against us," who were conscientized and converted, and who needed to be confronted.

Of course, such charges had been commonplace in both ANC and PAC
rhetoric. Yet it was still a risk for Black Consciousness to level them, since
Bantustan politics and personalities enjoyed relative influence and a good
amount of positive coverage in both the black and white presses. When Bantustan presidents met with the Vorster government, for example, *Drum* crowed
about "the day *our* leaders marched to Pretoria." One leader in particular, the
prime minister of Zululand, Gatsha Buthelezi, received the lion's share of
the praise.[21] Readers of the *World* lauded him as "a born Genius" and "Chief
Gatsha—our hero," and others warned his potential opponents that "he wields
an indestructible weapon—the truth and the words of God."[22] Buthelezi's
own résumé seemed to make an exceptional case: he had been very publicly
expelled from Fort Hare for political activities, and even though he worked
within the system, he used his position of (relative) authority to publicly
denigrate apartheid. Buthelezi was popular and influential, and even as Black
Consciousness activists began to nip around the edges of Bantustanism, they
approached him warily.[23]

Still, their concern with authenticity and relevance demanded that they
mark those leaders, however prominent, who were considered inauthentic
and irrelevant. Again, an American idiom found favor: Malcolm X's famed
distinction between "field niggers" and "house niggers," or, as the latter were
more commonly known, "Uncle Toms." Such terms could be used positively,
as when SASO's University of Zululand branch reported hosting "S[ipho]
Buthelezi[,] a local field-nigger."[24] It was more common, however, for Ameri-
canisms to be used to admonish. In Black Consciousness rhetoric, "Toms"
were those who failed to project their beingness in the correct way. Readers
hammered a Coloured man who protested against being called black, for
example, by declaring him "one of those light-skinned Uncle Toms who are
trying to identify themselves with Whitey."[25] African Americans could be
subject to such aspersions as well. Students held a brief meeting with U.S.
representative Charles Diggs in 1971 but were not satisfied with the congress-
man's responses to student concerns. Although Diggs was a prominent African American politician and an advocate for black South Africa, the *SASO
Newsletter* reported that he "was considered much of an 'Uncle Tom' when he
replied cautiously to students' questions on topical affairs."[26] Along the same

lines, the black American entertainer Percy Sledge's visit to Johannesburg in 1970 generated some of the earliest name-calling of the Black Consciousness era. Sledge slept in a whites-only hotel; played to segregated audiences; endorsed Johannesburg, apartheid's model city, with his highest praise ("It's the most to be in this burg!" he told reporters); and lent his name and image to a white-owned downtown furniture retailer ("I dig you the most that's why I can recommend the Percy Sledge Health Mattress and Bed set").[27] For his sins, the poet James Matthews declared Sledge little better than a clown—the purportedly "big black cat from America" who in truth wanted nothing more than to be "a pseudo-white" or, as Matthews put it then, "pinky."[28]

Name-calling was far more effective locally, and the borrowed American terms eventually became linked most often to Bantustan politicians. One *World* reader wove a seamless narrative linking black American and black South African history to deride a visit by Bantustan leaders to the United Nations: "In the 17th century, the slavemaster took Tom, gave him a little education, dressed him well and made the others look up to him. Then he used him to control the other slaves. The same strategy is being used today, by the same White slave masters. They take a Black man, give him 'Bantu education,' make him a celebrity and then let him lead the Blacks. Now we have our 20th century Uncle Toms." Uncle Tom thus became a repeated trope of attacks against those "stooges" and "puppets" who preached "Bantustan politics."[29]

In keeping with Black Consciousness's lineage, activists also generated their own derogatories. White society's language proved especially popular. Blackness required an appropriate existential attitude, so Bantustan leaders remained "Bantus" or, more frequently, "non-whites."[30] The latter term was the favorite way of describing any dark-skinned people or groups who failed Black Consciousness's test. The Coloured Labour Party and Natal Indian Congress (NIC) were initially seen as allies; the Labour Party embraced "black," and NIC leaders peopled SASO symposia and community development projects around Durban.[31] By 1972, however, both the Labour Party and NIC had fallen out of favor, and SASO activists dismissed them as "non-whites" for criticizing SASO's political stance on collaboration and participation in segregated "elections." Nonwhites were threats to Black Consciousness, and activists in turn threatened to "destroy" their collaborating opponents.[32]

Some observers worried about this escalating rhetoric. Percy Qoboza, a columnist for the *World*, advised Black Consciousness leaders to stop dividing the black community into "relevant Black men and irrelevant Black men." He cited one example by name: "SASO needs Chief Buthelezi as an ally and the sooner students realize this, the better for all."[33] That Qoboza saw fit to defend Buthelezi indicated that attacks on Bantustanism had grown ad hominem, despite SASO's earlier intention not to go directly after the "genius of Zululand." This confrontation came to a head at SASO's third GSC in July 1972—an event that, even more than the founding of the BPC, marked the Black Consciousness Movement's embrace of a political doctrine.

The term of SASO's third president, Themba Sono from the University of the North, had been surprisingly militant. Sono was more of an unknown quantity than his predecessors, Biko and Pityana. The latter had grown enamored of Sono's grasp of Black Consciousness philosophy and suggested that he run, which had assured his election in 1971.[34] One can easily see the attraction. In terms of the sheer weight of his philosophical rhetoric, Sono was indeed, as Nkwenkwe Nkomo put it, "nobody's little boy."[35] Although Sono would later criticize Black Consciousness for being overly intellectual, no other writer could match his dense prose; he once described the world as "a very complex situation, a situation compared to the rigidity of an amoeba when feeding to the flexibility of this amoeboid location . . . a psychedelic colouration where flux is more obvious than fixed purpose."[36] It was all the more striking, then, when Sono defied SASO's traditional caution and issued straightforward attacks against Gatsha Buthelezi while touring campuses during 1971 and 1972. Within a month of his election, he was routinely chastising Bantustan leaders for playing the "politics of powerlessness" and describing Buthelezi not as "erudite" but instead as a "poor visionary."[37] Sono sparked controversy by speaking out against the Zululand government while visiting the University of Zululand, something that, Harry Nengwekhulu suggested, prompted Biko and other activists to join in the attacks rather than risk appearing inconsistent.[38]

One might imagine the audience's surprise, therefore, when Sono did a very public about-face in his presidential address at Hammanskraal in July 1972. Rather than press the attack against collaborators, he instead counseled reconciliation, suggesting that "we have to talk to our enemies." Notwithstanding his own role in the process, he contended that SASO had grown inflexible, to the degree that it risked "stagnating in the certitude of ideology." SASO had built Black Consciousness first by defining *blackness* as a counter to liberalism and then by winnowing the population into those who were potential converts and those who were not. Now, Sono urged a return to dialogue: "We then have to seek out people who differ with us and we have to try to convert them to our way of thinking. . . . This includes everybody—black and white whether they are security police, liberals, non-whites etc."[39]

The delegates' response was swift. "As he thundered through his blasphemous speech, I could see Biko sitting with his head supported by both hands and I thought he groaned every now and then as the obscenities hit his ears," Mosibudi Mangena wrote.[40] That this was deemed blasphemy suggests the degree to which Black Consciousness activists had come to associate themselves with this particular political stance, and the record indicates that Biko moved quickly to disavow Sono's sentiments. SASO believed in free speech, a hastily drafted resolution read, but not when it contradicted the "spirit" of SASO policy and threatened to "do damage" to SASO's reputation. Sono's speech had smacked of "sell-out tendencies," and the president was deposed and expelled from the meeting.[41] In the final assessment, a delegate told the *World*, the former president's "personal non-white stand" was more than SASO could bear.[42]

Sono's expulsion marked a critical break. Whereas SASO had begun as a student movement dedicated to the "universal" values of free thought and intellectual exploration, now debate was quashed if it strayed too far from the party line. Observers noted this. The always skeptical *World* editorial page condemned SASO for forgetting itself. The students had become ideological, and "the way they are acting at present smacks of juvenile pig-headedness which will get nobody anywhere," an editorial read. A reader accused SASO of violating the principle at the heart of intellectual exploration: "I am afraid we are beginning to lose confidence in SASO. It seems it is guided by emotions rather than reason."[43] Activists' retorts were simple: Sono had rejected the "whole concept of Black Consciousness"—and he was crazy for doing so. His speech "bordered on the brink of insanity," one member protested, and no "sane" black person could countenance Sono's positions.[44] For his part, Biko followed up Sono's speech with the Movement's most unequivocal statement against collaboration, the article "Let's Talk about Bantustans," which was subsequently published in the first newsletter after the 1972 GSC. Contending that collaborators accepted "a solution given to us by the same people who have created the problem," Biko reiterated the now commonplace party line: no true black could cooperate in any way with "the system."[45]

Although such protests did not stop the government and its allies from making the former homelands into allegedly independent republics, Bantustans remained the Black Consciousness Movement's defining issue within the internal politics of the period. As this discourse developed, a similar combination of intention and accident led the movement to confront the apartheid state. This confrontation was perhaps inevitable; the BPC had, after all, declared its firm opposition to white minority rule and collaboration with the state, while announcing its determination to bring about "total liberation." If adherents of this new thing called the Black Consciousness Movement truly wanted to be counted among the liberators, it could not simply snipe at nonwhite collaborators but needed to follow the ANC and PAC and engage the risks and rewards of direct confrontation. In their official assessment of the third GSC (and in keeping with their often inflated sense of importance), activists noted that as the conference went on, "the eyes not just of BLACK SOUTH AFRICA but indeed the entire world was [*sic*] focused on Hammanskraal."[46] Hyperbole aside, in a few short years the nascent Movement had indeed grown far beyond its university roots. Having a doctrine undoubtedly helped make the transition from the classroom; as Freire had noted, it was easier to create an orthodoxy and lead than it was to promote conversation and listen. From 1972 on, the Movement led toward the more contentious terrain of struggles against the state.

BLACK CONSCIOUSNESS ON TRIAL

On 12 July 1972, Black Consciousness owned the *World,* even if not the attention of people around the globe. The front page carried ongoing reports on both the first BPC convention and the still unfolding aftermath of the Sono affair. On the editorial and letters page, writers urged SASO to cease criticizing Gatsha Buthelezi, and the editors hailed BPC as "the first Black political movement since the banning of our national organisations," devoting space across four columns to assess a SASO policy proposal.[47] The difference from only a few months before—when the paper had reported on SASO's past presidents "Pitjana" and "Diko"—was stark.[48] It took more than just the internal debate within SASO over how best to approach banned groups and Bantustan politics to effect this change. Beginning with a series of student strikes in May and June 1972 and continuing through the Movement's efforts to organize its first major protests following the victory of FRELIMO in neighboring Mozambique—and the SASO/BPC trial (with which this study began) that followed and dragged on for nearly two years—the Black Consciousness Movement assumed pride of place in the narrative of 1970s opposition to apartheid. Here I read selective instances in this process in order to assess how Black Consciousness mutated to fit evolving circumstances and to understand what it was by the time most people outside South Africa became aware of it after June 1976. These years, from 1972 through 1976, were marked by the trial of Black Consciousness, both literally and figuratively, as activists recorded their beliefs in court transcripts and jockeyed for position vis-à-vis both the state and other opposition groups.[49]

Events began to unfold at the University of the North. Turfloop, as the campus was also known, was perhaps SASO's best-organized. From 1971 on, student activists met new students with an array of activities, symposia, and opportunities for community development work.[50] The campus also featured an host of well-known leaders, as its relative proximity to South Africa's media center and its large proportion of students from around Johannesburg lent it a certain veneer. From 1971 through May 1972, the SRC was led by Onkgopotse Abraham Tiro, from Dinokana in the northwestern Transvaal—a name and place not yet associated with Christ and Nazareth. Indeed, in a speech welcoming freshmen to campus in 1971, Tiro betrayed few hints of the militancy that would later earn the comparison. He was a deeply religious man committed to the process of intellectual exploration. "God has give us reasoning powers not to remain inactive or to be perverted on sordid pursuits," he told young SASO members. Instead, they were at university to hone these powers "to the utmost," to "refine" their minds "to be used for the people's lot." Reasoned, committed intellectual exploration was why students went to university. To drive the point home, he went so far as to cite the then minister of Bantu education's warning that "the university is not a place for revolutions." However, Tiro qualified the statement somewhat—"no student can enroll with a university for the *sole* purpose of staging demonstrations and protest marches"—but his conclusion that students were students first was very much in keeping with SASO thinking at that time.[51]

Within a year, however, his thoughts on the subject had changed. The student body chose him to deliver a speech in late April 1972. Before assembled Bantustan and Ministry of Bantu Administration dignitaries, as well as a chancellor and faculty appointed directly by the apartheid government, Tiro launched a broadside against the entire premise of "Bantu" tertiary education and called for "a system of education common to all South Africans." He went on to proclaim students' nationalist role: "The magic story of human achievement gives irrefutable proof that as soon as nationalism is awakened among the intelligentsia, it becomes the vanguard in the struggle against alien rule." The speech veered from detailed complaints—including black students being refused entrance to the campus's segregated bookstore and his father being forced to sit outside the hall, which was crowded with white faces—to grandiose and religiously infused pronouncements. "Let the Lord be praised," he told his audience, "for the day shall come, when all shall be free to breathe the air of freedom which is theirs to breathe and when the day shall have come, no man, no matter how many tanks he has, will reverse the course of events."[52] With that, Tiro asked for God's blessing on the crowd and took his seat.

Such ideas were commonplace in Black Consciousness writing, Black Theology preaching, and conscientizing scripting, but here, Tiro spoke directly to power—and the authorities did not take the affront lightly. Within days, Tiro was expelled and the SRC disbanded. And after the student body staged a sit-in to protest these developments (during which, according to reports, the protestors repeatedly invoked the Lord's Prayer), the police forced all 1,149 students from the campus.[53] The University of the North ceased to function. The white press recorded that the chancellor blamed only Tiro, whose "disgraceful" speech had "endangered the good order of the University," but the *World* focused on the fact that Tiro's "scathing attacks" had earned a "thunderous ovation from the crowd."[54]

Soon, the rest of SASO's campuses erupted in protests and boycotts, events that dominated coverage throughout May. These actions demonstrated the degree to which SASO had successfully organized the black campuses and was now able to present a united front to the wider South African audience. Although there were calls for "adult national organizations" to take over, Black Consciousness activists emerged as the cutting edge in black opinion against the state. SASO delegations made very public trips to negotiate with the authorities, and the organization's grass roots made good on the threat to shut down every university if Tiro and the rest of the Turfloop student body were not reinstated.[55]

Not surprisingly, the government and university authorities were unmoved. After all, there had been little to no overt defiance since 1964, and the apartheid state had little to lose by ignoring the tiny black student population. As May closed, students slowly began to trickle back to campus (110 had returned by the end of the month, slightly more than half over the next couple of weeks), and the SRC president was offered readmission in "two or three years," if he provided evidence that he had "mended his ways."[56] Despite the entire SRC being refused readmission, as winter vacation came and went the universities returned more or less back to normal—only now without the SASO leadership that had been blamed for the trouble.[57]

Tiro lost his case for readmission, but the brief effluence of activity he and his organization caused had at least two important effects. First, Tiro's calls for equality in tertiary education and the authorities' reaction undermined universities as a center of Black Consciousness agitation. This was especially so at Turfloop, where many students, such as Tau Mokoka, simply dropped their studies; others, such as Dan Mogale, a friend of Mokoka's from Pretoria, decided to forgo college and concentrate on organizing in the cities.[58] Although many others continued their studies—and, as we shall see, Turfloop remained, in one student's description, "the hottest place in South Africa"[59]—the influx of relatively educated, politicized, and (in)famous students back into urban townships changed the dynamics there. Tiro himself exemplified this. He resurfaced a few months after his expulsion as a history teacher at Morris Isaacson High School in Soweto. When he taught "off the syllabus," as SASO activists' teachers had done, it resonated in a special way.[60]

Second and perhaps more immediately evident, SASO's ability to pull off simultaneous boycotts contributed to the government's growing perception that Black Consciousness was a threat. It did not act immediately, but in early 1973, the minister of state security followed the banning of eight NUSAS leaders by banning the leadership of SASO and BPC.[61] The banned leaders included Nengwekhulu, Biko, Pityana, Cooper, Moodley, and Mafuna, nearly all of whom had been critical in Black Consciousness's philosophical development from the outset as well as active in Anne Hope's efforts to retain conscientization's original meaning.[62] The banned were Manas Buthelezi's philosophers, self-styled intellectual activists who had warily watched postcolonies and called on consciousness and faith in "true humanity," not mere politics. Banned to their hometowns and forbidden to attend meetings or publish, the founders of Black Consciousness essentially vanished from the public life they had only recently attained. They were still consulted, but these and subsequent bannings paved the way for a new generation of leaders that included people like Tiro, who had made a name for themselves not only by organizing or theorizing but also by confronting the state. Although some still debated whether that was the appropriate course of action, for younger, urban-based (as opposed to campus–based) leaders like Nkwenkwe Nkomo and Zithulele Cindi, confronting authority was simply what the Movement did.[63]

This new generation of leaders expressed glee when the "junta of national salvation" overthrew the Portuguese government in April 1974, especially after the Portuguese military promised to end the conflicts in Mozambique, Angola, and Guinea-Bissau. Thousands of Africans freely celebrated in Lourenço Marques, and Prime Minister Vorster conceded, with considerable understatement, that the events would "affect" white South Africa.[64] South Africa had long relied on the cordon sanitaire provided by stubborn colonial rule on its borders (save for the relatively complacent Swaziland, Lesotho, and Botswana governments); yet in 1974, apartheid was faced with a black-majority, revolutionary government on its frontier. The official transition of power was set for late September, and the Black Consciousness Movement planned to mark it. It was important "to say to our people [that independence] has now happened to our neighbors in Mozambique," then BPC national organizer Nkwenkwe Nkomo explained—to ask, "Mozambique has done it, why can we not be next?"[65] As winter turned to spring, the Movement announced a nationwide series of rallies to commemorate the occasion, in Durban, at the Currie's Fountain Sports Ground, in Johannesburg, and at the still highly organized and militant University of the North. In mid-September, Movement leaders dropped the added bombshell that they were in "secret talks" with FRELIMO to bring representatives of the nascent Mozambican government to address the South African crowds.[66]

Jimmy Kruger, the minister of state security, pledged that these rallies would not take place. The government's incentive was clear. As the transition to black rule in Mozambique approached, newspapers were crowded with reports of impending chaos and "racial violence." By the thousands, white Mozambicans arrived in Johannesburg and reported that "bands of Africans" were roaming that country, "attacking whites" at will. In South Africa, white crowds waved Portuguese and South African flags as they rallied with signs denouncing FRELIMO and announcing their resolve that "terrorists won't rule our lives." Paranoia raged as a white man was sentenced to five days in prison for merely shouting "Up FRELIMO!" on a busy Johannesburg street corner.[67] All the while, SASO and BPC leaders continued to hold meetings, and they announced that delegates had been dispatched to the Mozambican capital, to return with high-ranking FRELIMO officials.[68] This prospect led the government to take the unique step of preemptively banning the SASO/BPC rallies, citing the (white) public's "emotional response" to local groups hosting "terrorists" on South African soil.[69]

The Black Consciousness activists who clustered around Biko during his banishment to King William's Town thought things would end there. The planned commemoration was useful "propaganda," Mpumlwana remembered, but when the government announced the preemptive banning, "we didn't think they [the Movement leaders at that time] would risk people's lives and all get arrested." Furthermore, Black Consciousness had traditionally been skeptical of rallies; in a 1972 interview, for example, Saths Cooper criticized the old mass movements for thinking that such gatherings changed anything.[70] Yet even as King William's Town activists insisted that "there is no way you can mount a revolution on a rally," the national leadership plowed ahead, insinuating that naysayers were "cowards."[71] As these new leaders saw it, defiance in support of a group that had won an armed struggle was revolutionary. "There's that fervor that charges people when they hear that other people have resisted, they've attained their freedom and liberation," Zithulele Cindi explained, and it simply could not be stopped.[72] The decision to continue with the rallies was undeniably defiant and marked an escalation; whereas students in 1972 defied government policies within their universities, activists in 1974 planned to violate a very public Ministry of State Security banning order.

When the dust settled in late September and early October, the fears of the King William's Town contingent had been realized. Police raids broke up rallies of a thousand people each at Currie's Fountain and Turfloop, and dozens of leaders were detained, including previously banned individuals such as Cooper and Moodley, as well as the entire leadership of SASO, BPC, and the University of the North SRC. As 1974 closed, more than sixty Black Consciousness activists remained in detention. In *Pro Veritate*'s estimation, the Black Consciousness Movement had been "crushed."[73] Yet even as the government prepared to bring the Movement's leadership to trial, others felt that change was coming. A British Broadcasting Corporation (BBC) report suggested that the rallies had in fact represented a broader trend, that blacks' "growing confidence in change that one senses was deep flowing rather than frothing down the street."[74] In late November, a group of women aligned with Black Consciousness, including the Christian Institute's Jane Phakati (later known as Oshadi Mangena), marked the detainees sixty-first day of detention by descending on the Union Buildings with a petition demanding their release, signed by hundreds of black women. Recalling the ANC's 1956 women's march on Pretoria, the *World* gave this event a predictably gendered analysis: "It is one of the accepted facts of our society that, when Black women start feeling restless over any issues, this is an indication of the deep anger that must have gripped the community."[75]

Despite the coverage given to Phakati and the other protestors, the real media stars were the thirteen SASO and BPC men who were eventually put on trial in early 1975.[76] Officially known as the *State v. Cooper* (Saths Cooper was defendant number one), the SASO/BPC trial stretched on for nearly two years. In the process, it kept the Black Consciousness Movement in the public eye, while those left behind scrambled to reconstitute their organizations.[77] And for the historian, the trial's records—ten thousand pages and eleven reels of microfilm of testimony, judgment, and evidence on the Movement and its philosophy—provide an invaluable source. Indeed, although Michael Lobban correctly read the trial as a confrontation between "two cohesive but rival ideologies"—one white (apartheid) and one black (Black Consciousness)— beyond the obvious juridical question, the reasoning behind Black Consciousness was itself on trial. The state prosecutor portrayed the accused as terrorists bent on the violent, revolutionary overthrow of the white minority state. Yet as we have seen, by its own admission and development the Black Consciousness Movement had itself been slow to come to such conclusions, if indeed it ever did so. But at the same time, activists had always trusted in transformation and held faith that their methods—intellectual exploration, theological reflection, conscientization, and only recently politicization—would somehow bring change. The trial, therefore, was a paradox. Black Consciousness the ideology was charged with something it had not done, that is, provoking a revolution, while at the same time the Movement's radical credentials demanded that its leaders be found guilty of at least desiring precisely that. If, as Lobban put it, "ideas and aspirations" were crimes, then a guilty verdict validated the Black Consciousness project. This was the intricate drama that played out across the many months of testimony about subjects and people with whom we have grown familiar: James Cone and Paulo Freire, politics versus being, consciousness versus power, conscientization and the Black Messiah.[78]

Yet the trial was more farce than tragedy, and reasoning that some sort of conviction was inevitable, the defendants treated it like theater.[79] They grew matching, unkempt beards and wore uniforms consisting of wool hats and crudely stenciled T-shirts reading "BPC." They sang each day upon entering the courtroom; sympathetic audience members in the gallery joined them, each time forcing the judge and court officials to wait until their song was done.[80] On the first anniversary of the rallies, "Strini Moodley left the dock and amid laughter presented the Prosecutor, Mr. Cecil Rees, with a cake containing one candle. Grinning, Mr. Rees accepted the cake and shook Mr. Moodley's hand. The candle was lit and Mr Rees blew it out to loud applause."[81] The prosecutors and judge "were just ordinary people," Moodley recalled, just actors in the play; there was no special "aura" about the trial, save the realization that no matter what the defense did or said, the accused were going to spend at least some time in prison.[82] So they made use of their time. Detained together in Pretoria, they read newspapers and established a library, ostensibly in order to make their case. Banned people such as Moodley and Cooper were given a voice for the first time in years, and the defense brought Biko from King William's Town to testify on the roots of Black Consciousness. His name and opinions were thus put on record, something that was otherwise illegal under the terms of his ban.[83]

The trial eventually dragged to its conclusion, seven months after Biko took the stand. Despite accusations of terrorism, the judge wrote, "the court is satisfied that neither SASO nor BPC has the characteristics of a revolutionary group."[84] Instead, he argued that their ideology was about something more vague: "total change through total involvement by Blacks in a total liberation struggle."[85] The judge had learned the previous months' lessons well. Black Consciousness had turned political, and politics had brought it to the courtroom, yet at its core, it remained more a philosophy than a political program; more than anything else, it was an "attitude and way of life," characterized by existential commitment to undefined struggle. In one sense, this judgment vindicated the accused, with all nine receiving relatively light sentences, ranging from five to six years of imprisonment on Robben Island. But in another sense, the judge's findings reflected poorly on the Movement's revolutionary potential.

Yet even as the trial concluded, the epoch's revolutionary potential was being tested in entirely new ways. On 17 June 1976, Lybon Mabasa, a former University of the North student leader and current high school teacher in Soweto, testified for the defense. Under cross-examination, he was asked by the state prosecutor if there was anything notable about the day. In keeping with the trial's supposed aura, Mabasa responded somewhat cheekily that it was his birthday. The prosecutor persisted, and Mabasa mentioned what was then focusing the world's attention on South Africa, that the "children" in Soweto were "marching."[86] It was a poignant moment. By 1972, having evolved into a movement, Black Consciousness had become the dominant voice of South African internal opposition to apartheid. Now, it had to share the stage. The children were in the streets and with their presence felt, the trial's debates over whether ideas could bring change took on a new urgency.

SOWETO

There is little doubt that the 16 June protests and subsequent events mark the high point for South Africa in the 1970s, at least in terms of coverage and knowledge about the decade. The disagreements involve how we approach this peak. For some observers, Soweto split the decade, with Black Consciousness irrelevantly falling away to the years before 16 June 1976; for others, Soweto was the highest in a series of ascending heights that Black Consciousness had continued to climb. This debate has dominated the study of the events in Soweto, and only recently have scholars argued for renewed attention to the events themselves and fruitfully examined the historicity of the various claims of responsibility.[87]

The Soweto story is well known and needs only the barest sketch here. In the months leading up to 16 June, students in Soweto and other townships grew increasingly agitated over the Department of Bantu Education's mandate that instruction be half in Afrikaans and half in English. Organized under the aegis of the South African Students Movement (SASM), students at Soweto high schools planned a march to protest "50/50" education on the morning of 16 June. While en route to Orlando Stadium, they were met by police in Orlando West. A scuffle broke out, shots were fired, and two students died—one being Hector Pietersen, whose death was broadcast across the globe thanks to *World* photographer Sam Nzima's famous picture. During the weeks and months that followed, students organized by the Soweto Students Representative Council (SSRC), under the initial leadership of Tsietsi Mashinini, fought pitched battles with the police in townships across the country. Schools were shut, and elders such as Manas Buthelezi formed the Black Parents Association to advocate for reform. By the time the violence stopped around October 1977, thousands of black schoolchildren had fled the country for ANC and other camps, and many hundreds, if not thousands, of young people had been killed.[88]

From exile, the ANC claimed responsibility for the uprising. As fleeing students swelled that organization's ranks, interviews published in *Sechaba* described the student protest as the work of the ANC underground in the country—and certainly not the result of Black Consciousness's spread during the preceding years. In some cases, former SASM leaders wrote the ANC's responsibility back in time with claims that the exiled organization had been planning the demonstration as early as 1974.[89] Black Consciousness had been too intellectual to inspire the students, former student leader Daniel Montsisi insisted: "In their addresses to high school students, they used Latin and all forms of jawbreakers. They were not simple and comprehensible, but were always high and divorced from us."[90] Such claims dovetailed neatly with the government's telling of events; the state was happy to blame outside agitators, communists, and "terrorists" for the troubles rather than acknowledge that the discontent came from within.[91]

From the outset, Black Consciousness supporters were acutely aware of the challenges to their control of the narrative. Press releases from Black

Consciousness organizations complained that "the former South African National Congress should stop misguiding the world, telling the world that all achievements done by black people in South Africa are performed through their influences, this is not correct, its chief officials had skipped the country so they don't feel the present pinch, how can they claim the latest existence?"[92] Many former activists bristled at suggestions that the ANC had been involved. But it must be admitted that for a long time the literature supporting the Black Consciousness perspective was rather thin.[93] This is beginning to change, however; scholarship has begun to move away from organizational debates and returned to close readings of the events themselves. Helena Pohlandt-McCormick has argued for the need to reassert the historicity of the rising by untangling both the various parties' claims and the participants' memories of events.[94] Her conclusions are compelling: that Black Consciousness was essential to students' self-conceptions and worldview; that it structured their understanding of what they were doing and how they did it; and that, contrary to later claims, "the events of the Soweto uprising took both the apartheid government and the ANC by surprise."[95] I might only add that it took Black Consciousness leaders by surprise as well.

The problem stems from language. We call the days after 16 June a rising and cast about for its cause—to return to Chartier, its origins—whether that was the more immediate issue of Afrikaans or the maneuvering of various groups. Yet the so-called rising was itself a reaction not to a revolutionary ideology but to the way the state had subdued the 16 June protest. No one planned for things to turn out that way, least of all the thousands of high school and younger students who assembled on that morning to protest the quality and character of their education. Their identity as students, high school leader Bongi Mkhabela suggested, was critical, as they were instructed to wear their uniforms and they used rhetoric that rang with a love of learning.[96] This was not the 1980s' "liberation now, education later"; this was a protest about the state further inserting itself into young people's minds. It was inspired not by a political doctrine but by the period's increasingly widespread belief that psyches were vital to the process of self-emancipation and therefore that education was the site of both struggle and liberation. Years later, Montsisi dismissed SASO activists for speaking over high school students' heads. Yet before 16 June, his own South African Students Movement had enthusiastically considered the French Revolution's "tennis court resolution" in debating societies and counted among its leaders a student called "Shakespeare's friend in Africa," who was seen quoting William Wordsworth on the eve of the march.[97]

This is not to say that Soweto's students did not enjoy relationships with their elders from the immediately preceding generation. SASM was a Black Consciousness Movement–aligned group. Founded in the late 1960s as the

African Students Movement, by the early 1970s it had acquired the qualifier "South" and affiliated with Black Consciousness thought and organization.[98] This was in part a pragmatic choice. According to the Mashinini family biographer, Tsietsi's older brother's efforts to agitate on behalf of the ANC in the mid-1970s met with little success; that organization was, she wrote, "virtually unknown in the townships [and] . . . could not compete with the Black Consciousness Movement" in Soweto. As Tsietsi himself came of age, he gravitated toward SASM and Black Consciousness and described himself as "embarking on a quest for psychological liberation."[99] Perhaps this was a result of his SASO- and BPC-affiliated teachers—Tiro among them—at Morris Isaacson High School; perhaps not. But at the very least, the ideas were in the air. SASM meetings on the eve of the Soweto uprising were addressed by prominent Black Consciousness activists such as Tom Manthata and former University of Natal medical student Aubrey Mokoena. And on the evening of 16 June, after things had gone rather differently than planned, Mashinini and other leaders sought the counsel of Drake Koka, a longtime Catholic activist and former leader of BPC, a man they called their "godfather."[100] Their language was Black Consciousness, and their symbols—most prominently the raised right fist—were Black Consciousness, even if there is no evidence that some sort of central command or deep, hidden conspiracy had spurred the students to rebel.

In the end, then, Soweto brings us back to the SASO/BPC trial and the Movement's confrontation with the state. The trial was, as Lobban suggested, a trial of ideas. Although the Black Consciousness Movement's potential to bring radical change was found wanting, the judge did find something worrisome in the ideology's tone. Lobban explained that "the judgment . . . laid great stress on the violent aspects of black consciousness," not actual violence but rather "the notion of the martyrdom of blacks who had died in the struggle; [and] the portrayal of Christ as a revolutionary freedom fighter." This notion, the judge concluded, when combined with the Movement's "stress on the violent nature of the whites," could potentially justify blacks' use of force to foment a "revolution," something to which the Movement might have aspired even if it was not undertaken.[101] In this, the state understood things better than many observers and subsequent scholars did. Black Consciousness, Jimmy Kruger told a reporter, gave blacks the "spiritual incentive" to act; it built up the community's "psychological arsenal."[102] The combination of spirit and psychology was potentially explosive, which is why his ministry had harassed church people at Black Theology seminars, banned seminary students like Stanley Ntwasa, raided plays like *Shanti*, and shunted thinkers such as Biko and Pityana away from the public eye—all well before they had done anything to warrant such heavy-handed policing.

This combination of government fear and organizational evolution had seen Black Consciousness emerge from student meetings and the age of politics succeed the age of philosophers. But progress failed to eclipse the Movement's origins entirely. In an aside to his account of Soweto youth culture in the run-up to the uprising, Clive Glaser noted that Christian student groups played a leading role in township high school students' political awakening.[103] Foremost among these was the Student Christian Movement (SCM), which had been transformed from the reactionary organization supplanted in the universities by the UCM into the intellectual home of Methodist Youth Guild presidents such as Tsietsi Mashinini and self-described evangelicals such as Bongi Mkhabela. At SCM meetings, members listened to veterans of the turmoil at the University of the North and talked about Black Theology and the martyrdom of Christ.[104] As with the broader Movement, a particular religiosity informed high school political rhetoric. Some students had seen the DRC ministers conducting services in their schools and rejected Christianity; others, including SASM's president on the eve of 16 June, declared their faith in a God "who is armed with justice, truth and love" and pledged that "we shall not allow ourselves to be separate[d] from Him." In the years since Black Theology had first developed in South Africa, however, things had changed. Activists had been banned, leaders had been imprisoned, and others—as we shall soon discuss—had been killed. And in the weeks following the SASM president's speech, death would be a constant. He sensed it: "We shall rather die in [God's] hands if death becomes the only alternative from sticking to the truth. Any way, death is . . . the necessary end for human life."[105] Perhaps this sort of talk was precisely what both Jimmy Kruger and the judge had feared.

9 ↜ Keeping Faith with the Black Messiah

Suffering, Hope, and the Cost of the Future

THE AGONY in Sam Nzima's photograph is timeless.[1] Hector Pietersen is prone, expressionless, dead. Mbuyisa Makhubo is carrying him, determined, but with eyes betraying a hint of fear. Hector's sister, Antoinette, is dressed in a schoolgirl's uniform, arms raised, wailing. The image continues to strike, like other iconic images of suffering: a naked girl runs from a wall of napalm, vacant eyes stare back from behind barbed fences at any number of times and places. Yet the suffering depicted in these images is not timeless. Rather, it belongs to particular moments and thoroughly historicized emotional experiences. South Africa's 1970s saw their share of emotions: fear and hope and doubt and defiance and determination. As the Black Consciousness Movement increasingly confronted the state, its ideas-cum-ideology were buffeted by powerful forces that activists could not control, especially banning and death. It was one thing to preach faith in a "distant horizon"; it was quite another thing to keep faith that the costs would be worth it.

Soon after attending SASO's organizational meeting in December 1968, Carl Mogale, a UCM activist, wrote to Barney Pityana from Kimberley. Mogale's activities had caught the eye of the local police force. The police "give me no rest," he told Pityana, and "it is generally known in Kimberley that either I am a 'Commie' or an 'agent' of the 'Commies.'" Where we might have expected youthful defiance or bravado, the law's attention in this case resulted in something else. "Barney, believe it or not, life is miserable for me down this end," Mogale admitted. He expressed a litany of frustrations: "I have no parents, no home, no job, no money—agh!" Yet Mogale had not given up. Rather, he wrote, "I am only deflated and not defeated. There is hope although I don't know where. Dawn will surely come." He signed off on a suggestive note, telling

Pityana to "keep the faith baby!" In this one letter, a young South African activist ran a gamut of emotions, from near despair and strained frustration to cautious optimism reminiscent of the Zambian independence movement's cries of "Kwacha! The dawn!" He admitted misery yet counseled faith. Such were activists' experience of the 1970s—the morass of doubt mixed with the confidence that a change would come, in time.[2]

This chapter searches out such moments in order to stake a final claim to the intellectual history of this era by demonstrating how thinking changed in step with setbacks. It begins by considering the earliest "suffering" endured by 1970s thinkers and activists, associated with the banning of UCM leaders and the eventual dissolution of that organization in the face of both government pressure and internal discontent. Black Consciousness organizations learned a great deal from these experiences, and when the first SASO and BPC leaders were banned in 1973, the organizations reacted by renewing their faith in fundamental change in spite of evidence to the contrary. This observation points to a further line of inquiry. Black Consciousness thinkers suggested that an emotion—fear—had long bedeviled the community and compounded its problems. "Fear . . . erodes the soul of black people in South Africa," Biko wrote, and he and others cast it as the prime evil behind The Struggle's loss of momentum in the 1960s.[3] With this in mind, activists countered fear with hope. Hope thrives on a certain ignorance, Charles Taylor reminded us; it "can only exist if you are uncertain about a desired outcome," and it is most potent when accompanied by an earnest effort to make it so.[4] The future South Africans plotted was by no means assured, and this chapter watches as they struggled towards it realization.

Nowhere was the relationship between suffering, hope, and the future more evident than in activists' confrontations with death. Whether it involved a relatively well-known leader such as Tiro or Biko or an anonymous student like Hector Pietersen, each death challenged the Black Consciousness Movement to explain itself. The ideology of sacrifice that resulted was and still is debated. Disagreements aside, Black Consciousness dealt with death differently than previous liberation movements had.[5] As bodies were piled upon bodies, activists' initial attempts to explain what had happened had enduring effect. Given both the Movement's pervasive religiosity and its particular emphasis on Christianity, it is not surprising that that religion, born in death as it was, played a central role. In their rhetoric, Black Consciousness activists attested to German theologian Dietrich Bonhoeffer's powerful conclusion that "when Jesus calls a person, he bids him come and die."[6] South African political practice could not help but change in that idea's wake. This chapter draws to a close by examining the roots and practices of martyrdom in the 1970s and considering how particular deaths lent themselves to an ideology that sanctified loss in pursuit of the political horizon. Not only humans die, however, and this study ends by discussing the demise not just of leaders but also of organizations, ideas, and indeed an epoch.

Justice Moloto, the UCM's first black president, was banned to Mafeking in the northwestern Transvaal in late September 1971, even though his family was from Rustenberg and he himself lived in Soweto.[7] Moloto was charged with "activities which . . . further or are calculated to further the achievement of any of the objects of communism," and the ban was designed to render him mute for three years. In the discourse of the time, banning turned a subject into a nonbeing without the right to speak publicly, to have his or her words read or published, and, in Moloto's case, to "enter any factory, any place where any publication is prepared, printed or published"—as if his mere presence in such an environment threatened to pollute the state's intellectual purity.[8] Given these strictures, it was appropriate that a later activist's ban was met with the pronouncement that he "is no more."[9]

For his part, Moloto met the ban with a combination of resignation and bravado, and the UCM attempted to do the same. Moloto was known as an "outspoken opponent of apartheid," so it undoubtedly stung when the government offered him employment with the Bophutatswana Territorial Authority.[10] Although he initially balked at the offer, he worried about horror stories told of stubborn banned persons shipped even further into the "bundu [bush]." Given that alternative, Moloto gradually resigned himself to "settl[ing] down in my *homeland.*" (The term was underlined in the original, for maximum ironic effect.)[11] For their part, UCM officials and their supporters penned protests and attempted to draw attention to banning's ill effects, as when the Johannesburg office "celebrated" Moloto's marriage with "a wedding cake and two empty chairs for the couple. We invited the press and got some publicity."[12] But irony aside, helplessness dominated. Moloto's ban, Basil Moore wrote to Colin Collins, only underscored what he described as a "Job like catalogue of woes" facing the organization.[13]

Some of the UCM's woes were self-inflicted. Moloto's own term as president had indicated that change was afoot. He linked Christianity exclusively with liberation, and he got there only after touring a speech entitled "Is Christianity White?" in which he had encouraged polarization, with predictable results.[14] As Black Theology became the organization's focus through 1971, internal debates began to undermine the premise of the multiracial, ecumenical organization. This development was laudable and logical, activists suggested, since "the UCM itself has over the past few years advocate [sic] the need for black/white polarization."[15] As 1971 turned to 1972, internal documents portrayed an organization actively willing itself out of existence, on its own terms.

Yet it is clear that such self-inflicted and almost welcomed woes were minor when compared with the deeper machinations of government-induced fatalism. The banning of Stanley Ntwasa and Basil Moore in March 1972—and UCM's inclusion in a government commission of inquiry (along with the Christian Institute, Wilgespruit Fellowship Centre, and NUSAS)—only reinforced the organization's image as a political hot potato. By early 1972, all of the Protestant denominations save the Congregationalists had quietly withdrawn their funding from the UCM.[16] "The U.C.M. is not going to exist for a long time," Chris Mokoditoa wrote to supporters in June 1972, not of its own accord but because of "the attitude of the Gov[ernment] and the severe blows dealt to it."[17]

Moore's and Ntwasa's bans reinforced this prediction. The latter's ban thwarted efforts to publish the collection of Black Theology papers discussed in chapter 6; Ntwasa had been the collection's editor, and the ban carried over to any publications associated with his name.[18] As with Moloto's ban months earlier, UCM met these latest blows with a mixture of defiance and resignation. Ntwasa was banned only three months after returning to Fed Sem to resume his studies; officials there decried the quieting of "one of the most outstanding students the college has had in the past ten years," while his fellow students sang "We Shall Overcome" and other standards.[19] Whites also protested the bannings. James Polley, a former UCM activist, wrote to the *Rand Daily Mail* that, like Ntwasa's, Moore's "only crime is that he considered it his Christian responsibility to oppose racial discrimination in SA and to work for a society more in line with the Christian ethic of love and justice."[20] Like Moloto, Moore was forbidden to enter any place where publishing occurred, as well as any educational institution, except to pick up his small children from school.[21] Yet despite these restrictions, Moore had an out. Holding British and South African passports, he and his family soon left South Africa for England. Colin Collins, long Moore's collaborator, was out of the country when the bannings came. Like Moore, he too chose exile, in Canada, rather than play "Christian martyr [and] go back."[22] This was a difficult decision for Collins. He chafed at my characterization of his departure as "leaving." "I didn't leave," he told me; rather, he had planned a yearlong study trip, adding, "I was fully prepared to come back after one year, but with everyone being banned I had to make a decision." People understood, he claimed, although he remembered Biko urging him to return, since "he said it is easy for whites to stay away and never come back. Blacks always stay and have to face the music."[23]

Blacks did, undoubtedly, have to face the music. Moore went on to organize the Student Christian Movement in England—and, in Collins's words, "radicalize it out of existence"—before emigrating to Australia, where Collins eventually joined him after getting a doctorate in education in Canada. Ntwasa, however, had no option other than to join his uncle—Robert Sobukwe—as a banned person in Kimberley and attempt to meet his situation with defiance. Soon after his arrival, Ntwasa and Sobukwe publicized the banneds' plight with an eight-day fast. "He is enduring his ban boldly and cheerfully," Ntwasa's former assistant Mokgethi Motlhabi assured James Cone in mid-June 1972.[24]

Yet Motlhabi's words betrayed this bravado. The restriction, he continued, was "too strenuous for [Ntwasa's] inquisitive mind and nature," and there was little that the UCM could do to alleviate the pressure.[25] Ntwasa's family was wary of his politics, but he was unable to work and was entirely dependent on them. Aelred Stubbs, Ntwasa's seminary teacher and long-standing champion, visited him frequently in Kimberley, where he found the "gregarious and sociable" Ntwasa under enormous strain, "pent up in a tiny location house."[26] Social death and an enforced return to childhood undermined Ntwasa's hard-won coming of age as a black man; "a black brother has joined the swelling ranks of Black political enuchs [sic]," the SASO Newsletter reported.[27] Ntwasa's correspondence reflected this strained situation. He grew ornery and closed off, and visitors reported that he turned increasingly to drink.[28] Even after his ban lapsed in the late 1970s, its ill effects still manifested themselves. Before his ban, he had been, in John Sebidi's opinion, one of South Africa's "sharpest" theological minds. Motlhabi insisted that banning did not break Ntwasa, yet by the late 1980s, the former traveling secretary had no fixed abode and drank too much, and he was, Sebidi suggested, "so frustrated."[29]

Motlhabi generally presented a more rosy image of Ntwasa's circumstances than did Stubbs and Sebidi. Despite the hardships of the ban, he suggested that Ntwasa met it with resolute "faith that . . . one day we will conquer."[30] Motlhabi thus shifted the focus away from banning's practical effects on individuals to claims that, in fact, bans mattered little. As his example indicates, activists typically sought discursive control by pointing the way forward—Ntwasa was banned, yes, but change was still going to come. SASO took a more militant stance. Its response, issued on the twenty-second anniversary of Sharpeville, rhetorically linked Ntwasa's banning with the 1960 massacre, citing the ban as yet another instance of the government's "violent onslaught" against "the voice of black protest." Like the Sharpeville dead, Ntwasa was no longer on the scene. What mattered now was how those who remained rededicated themselves to struggle in his wake; the ban was not an event to be mourned, SASO concluded, but instead "a challenge to all of us," which called for "more concerted effort and involvement." Banning had caught UCM unprepared, and it turned to protest, irony, and the resignation of Job. SASO instead took control of the discourse and urged its supporters to look forward. Ntwasa had been on the "fore-front of the drive towards self-identity and self-realisation," and his ban demonstrated that the "consciousness . . . of the black community" was "the sure way to liberation."[31]

Beyond this confident veneer, SASO and other Black Consciousness organizations took steps to ensure that bannings would not catch them unprepared. They established layers of leadership. "I used to travel around with . . . Tiro," Harry Nengwekhulu recalled, "he didn't know why. Ben Langa . . . used to move around with Pityana at the office. The idea was that when Pityana is banned, Bennie can take over. With me, when I'm banned, Tiro can take over. He knew my contacts, I brought him with me."[32] Formation schools played a vital role here. They had begun as sites of intellectual exploration, reading, and debate, but with bans looming, the emphasis turned to identifying future leaders. Zithulele Cindi was a high school student and SASM member during the early 1970s. The formation schools that he attended outside Johannesburg were "three or four day affair[s]" at which "you get initiated or trained." "People who were serving would train people who were not serving to be next in line," he explained.[33]

In March 1973, the Movement was forced to enact these plans when the government issued five-year banning orders against Pityana, Moodley, Biko, Cooper, Mafuna, and Nengwekhulu, as well as Sono's replacement as president, Jerry Modisane, and BPC organizer Drake Koka. The World bemoaned the bannings, and Drum dispatched a reporter to visit the new generation of leaders to assess whether the bannings marked a "new dawn or a final sunset" for Black Consciousness. The mood, he observed, "was anything but pessimistic."[34] Instead, new leaders such as the aforementioned Ben Langa strategized to ensure that the Movement did not replicate UCM's experience. A memo penned in May 1973 demonstrated some of their ideas. Anticipating future rounds of bannings, they installed another "shadow executive" and called for a relief fund for the banned (so they were not forced to live off the state). They also organized regular visits to restricted persons, shifting resources to keep the banned active, to whatever degree possible. These ideas took time and money that SASO leaders in particular might not have had—although they had amassed a reasonably endowed trust for banned people by the organization's end in 1977—but on their own, they indicated the practical process of moving forward.[35]

Nowhere was this conviction more evident than in Biko's case. At the time of his banning, he was living in Durban and working with Mafuna and Ben Khoapa at Black Community Programmes, the community development organization that emerged in the wake of SPROCAS. He was restricted to his home district in King William's Town, and, befitting the Movement's rhetorical response, the area around King became BCP's most highly developed locale. This transition did not happen automatically. Indeed, soon after arriving in King, Biko appealed to local officials for modest revisions to his order.[36] Modifications, however, were not forthcoming, and Biko instead assumed a defiant tone. Within two months of being banned, he was returning the stipend checks the government sent to him and asking the local magistrate to "inform the . . . department that I have no use for their [R25] 'mercy wage' which to me is more of an insult than anything else."[37]

Besides, Biko already had a job, as BCP's "branch executive, Eastern Cape." His new title's unruffled tone indicated Black Consciousness's attitude toward state repression. Veterans from the UNNE and elsewhere made their way to King and turned it into conscientization's proving ground—in the term's original sense. They founded a health clinic, published and distributed materials, and helped to organize cooperative industries.[38] Rather than make a big fuss and protest, they acted as if nothing notable had occurred. BCP fund-raising materials showed a beaming Biko-as-middle-management-figure, meeting with "a production supervisor" under the ready-for-business sign "Black Community Programmes Ltd. Eastern Cape Branch Office." That the photographer's presence in the room had in fact violated the terms of Biko's order—he was forbidden to meet with more than one person at a time—received no comment.[39] He was determined, on the one hand, to work around the ban to travel undetected (something that eventually caught up with him) and, on the other hand, to actively court the government's attention. As during the SASO/BPC trial, court cases offered a rare opportunity for the banned to both travel and speak; in 1977, Biko spoke "with evident relish" of deliberately "contravening" traffic regulations so as to provoke court dates.[40] This determination to bend banning to one's own purposes is suggestive of Strini Moodley's account of his own order: "It happened. So what."[41]

It was a question of attitude. Ntwasa's isolation in Kimberley had rendered him mute and frustrated, but SASO learned from early missteps and called instead for "arrogance" in the face of government action.[42] The different approach was evident well before Biko et al. established themselves in King William's Town. Whereas in early 1972, the state had turned Ntwasa into a eunuch and made him "no more," the future mattered more than the loss of any particular person in 1973. SASO celebrated the March 1973 bans with a "Banning Issue" that featured the banned individuals' faces on the newsletter's cover, arrayed in a circle around a defiant black fist. The event was portrayed as an unequivocal dawn, a "milestone accomplished on the road to freedom."[43]

The editors' efforts to turn bans into victories valorized the gendered dimensions of sacrifice. Recall that Ntwasa's 1972 ban had been met with the lament that a "black brother" had joined the ranks of the "political eunuchs." No longer was this the case. The government could not castrate; rather, the banned were targeted precisely "because they wouldn't give in/offer their testicles to be eunuchs."[44] The banned had laid down their lives, in a sense, and in so doing had presented the Black Consciousness Movement not with a crisis of faith but with an opportunity for renewed vigor. Notably, it fell to the spouse of one of the banned to attest to this: as Strini Moodley's wife's put it, her family's loss indicated that "the first sign of victory for Black people [was] recorded."[45]

The conflation of a family's loss with a community's gain demonstrated how Black Consciousness had come to "politicize the personal." As we have seen, 1970s thinkers had trodden a fine line between manly discourse and the prominent role of women in Black Consciousness organizations. Black women "on their own" were not sanctioned, but aggressive, defiant black women in hot pants and Afros were relevant nonetheless. Yet the language deployed here unquestionably put women in their place. The seeds of this had already been sown. Black Theologians celebrated an image of God that was virile, thickly muscled, and male. In her forceful disavowal of "the white world's" feminism in late 1971, Maphiri Masekela argued that although black women were indeed black, they were not exactly the same as men in that they were charged with a unique task: child rearing and the early politicization and "conscientization of the Black children."[46] The maintenance of a conscious home was a woman's appropriate political role. Masekela felt strongly about this. To advocate otherwise, she persisted, was to succumb to the "the power of darkness . . . [the] white women who will come to us parading in *costume* of women's liberation. These are tactics designed by the enemy to divide Black community and we must refuse to be part of a conspiracy against ourselves."[47]

This sentiment was repeated elsewhere. In the early 1970s, Deborah Matshoba had advocated for a separate women's organization as a complement to SASO; by 1973, she too envisioned black women's participation largely within the domestic sphere. Writing in the banning issue of the *SASO Newsletter*, she admonished black women to raise their children in the appropriate way, for "our babies are beautiful and black and they must be brought up in Black truth." This admonition went beyond the mothers, however, to the university students—SASO's constituency, whose female members had been roundly mocked in 1970 and thought worthy of conscientization shortly thereafter. Matshoba knew that students look forward, and she set their eyes on a particular prize. "To the [female] university students I want to say that the young women of to-day are the mothers of tomorrow."[48] They were not the thinkers, the doctors, the activists, the equals; they were not the public face of struggle but the private one, conserving the domestic sphere and yielding the public stage of sacrifice and victory to men. "It is my brother who is on Robben Island; my brother who is running around illiterate and jobless," Matshoba wrote[49]—not her sister who was raped, nor her mother trying to hold a family together with a husband imprisoned. Those were not public experiences: public suffering was to be male, and therefore political redemption would be as well.[50]

With the gendered composition of struggle in mind, it made sense that in the wake of bannings, women were charged not to act but instead to "express Solidarity with these men."[51] Women were reduced to witnesses, watching and celebrating as their men attained a rhetorical victory, which brought the future closer. As Moodley's wife knew, a family's loss was a political movement's gain. "The tears we shed right now" spat flames, a poet wrote, a "fire this time" that would more brightly light the path toward freedom.[52]

"FEAR IS GONE FEAR IS GONE FEAR IS GONE"

In the course of my research, I conducted dozens of interviews, many of which were with people who had been banned or imprisoned or had suffered some other form of government repression. I asked each some variation of the question "Was your faith ever shaken?" or, more fundamentally, "Did you ever lose faith?" My inquiry was open ended. Some interpreted it to mean faith in the struggle, in eventual liberation; some assumed it meant faith in God; and others understood it as something else entirely. But despite the variety of interpretations, the responses were remarkably uniform: no. I have struggled with how to unwrap this uniformity. Perhaps people were ashamed of moments when they, like Ntwasa, broke. Perhaps there were hints in their negative responses: Chris Mokoditoa's "I don't know why I didn't go nuts," for instance, could very well imply an intense internal struggle. Or perhaps, as the banning issue indicated, the dominant discourse did not permit such feelings, even to this day.[53] This may be the most compelling interpretation. After all, as we have seen, Black Consciousness was from the outset a psychological tool, an instrument designed to combat complacence, collaboration, and fear. Fear was the most pernicious of these, and in the face of fear, Black Consciousness put its faith in hope. Discursively, then, banned activists could not be afraid, for they looked forward. Yet countering fear with hope demanded that Black Consciousness address the question of the future—the "not yet" that Biko and others had tried to keep at bay. It demanded developing answers to pressing questions: When would the future come? And at what cost?

Events forced individuals to ask these questions. Rubin Phillip, a classmate of Ntwasa's at Fed Sem and former vice president of SASO, was banned in late 1973, along with the second-level leaders of Black Consciousness organizations. The ban was especially jarring, as Phillip had not been politically active for some time and was instead more involved in the affairs of his rural parish in the Natal hinterland.[54] It shook his faith: "I . . . questioned God. I just wanted to get out of all this." The police handed him his order, and although he put on a brave face in their presence, once they left him alone in his spartanly furnished flat, he "wept for a long time. . . . It was total abandonment." Phillip claimed that he had only told this story to one other person, and his narrative soon shifted to a more conventional tale of trials overcome. As he wept, he continued, he had felt God's presence more strongly than ever: "It was a deeply spiritual thing. Feeling a real sense of real warmth and being affirmed. It was . . . a feeling of well, its ok but you're needed. You need to get on with it." Commitment reasserted itself: "I got up from there and that was it. And became even more committed. If the government thought it was going to muzzle me in any sort of way it didn't."[55]

My interviews elicited many such comments. Zithulele Cindi, for example, could not even fathom the emotion about which I inquired. Did he question his path and balk at the cost? "No, not even once," he said. "There was this drive," he told me, which meant that events such as the SASO/BPC trial and imprisonment "inspired us. So be it. Let's go there." Regarding imprisonment in particular, he noted that "in a morbid way, in a strange way, we were looking forward [to it]." Far from doubting, Cindi and many other activists trusted that whatever the cost, the future was worth it.[56]

This faith in and commitment to the future, this determination to overcome fear with hope, had a history. Recall activists' accounts of the lull that preceded SASO's founding in 1968. "There was a pall of fear," Saths Cooper recollected, that "engulfed every aspect of life."[57] Paranoia had been rampant: "People were fearful of even the walls, there are bugs all over the area so people were not talking about this."[58] Indeed, even after students began to organize, evidence suggests that the pervasive fear could skew interpersonal relations — as when UCM members apparently assaulted a student because they mistook him for a member of the security police.[59] As activists refined their calls for a "psychological intervention," fearfulness "was the psyche that . . . we were trying to overcome."[60] Biko expanded on this in a 1971 piece published in the *SASO Newsletter,* in which he placed fear at the center of South African political relationships. Whites, Biko argued, had constructed a state apparatus based entirely on the *swart gevaar* (fear of the black menace), and blacks' internalization of fear of state repression was responsible for the absurdity of their existential situations. When "no average black man can ever at any moment be absolutely sure that he is not breaking the law," was it not reasonable to be afraid?[61]

It was. And so, Black Consciousness, with its particular definition of blackness and evolving notion of appropriately manifested "beingness," shifted the standards of reason. Consider the response to Sono's apostasy, discussed in the last chapter. Sono had "bordered on the brink of insanity." Similarly, admissions of fear violated the standards of Black Consciousness–infused rational behavior, which called for defiance in the face of fear: "Above all, Teach us to scream out at this pain we feel," a poet wrote, "help us Dear Lord to overcome this fear that . . . fling[s] us into oblivion."[62] Doubt was replaced with certainty: "We've got God and youth on our side. We can't fail."[63] This claim was undoubtedly boastful, a young person's self-conscious bravado in the face of a powerful foe. Yet when repeated again and again, such claims became normative, logical. "We were somewhat incapacitated [this year]," SASO officers reported in the first meeting after the March 1973 bannings; no matter — it was only the "attainment of yet another milestone."[64]

By the mid-1970s, the triumph over fear was unquestioned. "Pre-1970 people were fearful . . . and Black Consciousness got us beyond that"; it was the "key that unlocked everything," activists asserted.[65] "We saw the fear as the oppressor inside you," Itumeleng Mosala explained, and Black Consciousness taught that "we had to learn . . . to be fearless."[66] Given subsequent events, it is notable that high school publications especially manifested this transition. Students wrote poems with titles such as "Fear Not," which urged "Be afraid not / Can there be such a thing like fear? / What is fear for? 'cause imprisonment my breakfast / Banishment, detention . . . are my dinner and supper."[67] And on the morning of 16 June, Soweto's students sang as they marched past the police: "Siyabasaba na? Siyabasaba na?" (Are we afraid of them? Are we afraid of them?).[68] Activists contended that fear had once governed black South Africa's approach to political activities. People had feared prison and banning and scurried away from events such as BPC's founding; now, however, students proclaimed in a phrase repeated across the last page of a 1975 SASM newsletter, "Fear is gone fear is gone fear is gone."[69]

This assertion was the crux of Black Consciousness: with fear gone, change was inevitable. If Biko was right, then these new standards of reason would shape minds into potent weapons with which to pursue the future. "Recent happenings" made the "future appear rosy," a church leader told his audience in early 1976.[70] With the right attitude, demographics would do the work: 18 million black "prophets" were beginning to speak, Manas Buthelezi preached, and their voices would have "a bigger . . . impact than 3 million [whites]."[71] Buthelezi had chosen his word—prophets—carefully. He had used it before, to describe a "growing number of South African Christian prophets who are striving to remind the Church that the Gospel means more than just singing songs about Jesus and saying grace before meals."[72] Prophets were liberated people, fearless people; as Biko had asserted, the students who had initiated Black Consciousness had been prophets in that they, like the prophets of old, stood in judgment of their society and pointed forward.[73]

Yet prophets were not automatically revolutionaries. After all, in the Bible they typically called Israel to account for its moral lapses and warned of God's wrath, not political transition. South Africa abounded in these sorts of prophets, especially in the Zionist and other independent churches that counseled a particular fortitude in expectation of the next world. But that was not how theologians such as Buthelezi or student leaders like Biko used the term. Rather, they agreed with Albert Nolan that "no one can read the prophets without noticing that they are always talking about *ordinary secular events*." Those sorts of prophets revealed God's emotional response to earthly affairs; they demanded attention to the world "around us" and spoke of the will to change in the here and now.[74]

Through prophecy, 1970s thinkers developed a unique eschatology. As early as 1971, UCM officials had tried to spread a particular perspective on faith's future dimension. Just as they assigned seminar papers inexorably linked to black South Africa's political situation, so too did Moore and Ntwasa delimit the form of inquiries into hope. They tasked Buthelezi with writing a "theology of hope for South Africa" and suggested that he consult Jürgen Moltmann's work on the subject.[75] It was an instructive suggestion. Only a few years earlier, Moltmann had charged that mainstream Christianity's greatest flaw was its otherworldly eschatology. He argued that eschatology—traditionally associated with death, resurrection, and the beyond—was in fact not about the end of history but instead about "the historic future," the earthly time that people had not yet lived. The "not yet" was critical, for it was the grounds of hope. "Faith believes God to be true," Moltmann wrote, "hope awaits the time when this truth shall be manifested."[76]

Awaits was too passive a word for what Moltmann described; Christian faith was "impatient," he insisted. "Peace with God means conflict with the world," he continued, "for the goal of the promised future stabs inexorably into the flesh of every unfulfilled present." Curiously, as in early Black Consciousness thought, Moltmann did not bother with the particulars of the historic future; rather, he concentrated on the importance of casting out toward the unseen. Hope was utopian enough on its own. By extending the "bounds of possibility," believers moved themselves closer to the horizon.[77] In 1971, Buthelezi had taken Moltmann's insights to heart. His paper focused on the ethical dimensions of hope. Without hope, he argued, "there is [a] lacking of the . . . appreciation of the value and purpose of life itself." Hope was the foundation of life; as such, it was essential to Black Theology's first step, that of validating blacks as the image of God and blacks as "men" in the fullest sense of the term. Once hopeful, a person might better serve his or her neighbor and humanize the world. The political implications of this were clear: "The struggle against oppression [thus] coexists with the consciousness of victory as a realized eschatological dimension." Struggle in time's current dimension was coeval with victory in the future. Through hope, people could transcend time.[78]

Now, Taylor's observation cited in the introduction to this chapter makes more sense. Hope is always progressive because the present is insecure, prompting human action to make change. It is therefore telling that Black Consciousness discourse was at its most hopeful, boastful, and brave at moments like that which had reduced Rubin Phillip to tears. The *SASO Newsletter's* banning issue waged a discursive struggle by wielding hope in the future against present suffering and fear. The faces of the banned ringed the cover, but through their hopeful talk, their supporters undermined earlier efforts to keep the future at bay. Where Biko had spoken of a second and third stage of struggle at some point, time was now collapsing: "No bannings are going to stop us now. . . . We are on the road to victory!" SASO called. One could not stop to mourn the banned. True, they had suffered and had "laid down their lives," but in the process, they had won "our first victory," and time stretched out ahead.[79]

Over the course of the 1970s, black ministers and laypeople refined this theology of suffering, impatience, and hope to pace the Movement's increasing conflicts with the state. The darker the times, Takatso Mofokeng recalled, the more "I told myself . . . I should . . . preach hope and get them to hope and to develop eyes to see the messiah when the messiah comes. And they should be able to read the signs of the times when the time comes." The Bible told the story: "One day if we look up, the morning star would come."[80] Turfloop activist Ish Mkhabela agreed in similar terms: "Part of the discipline [of] being in those [Black Consciousness] circles" was living "in hope that you'll have your own Exodus." Bongi Mkhabela, who married Ish in the early 1980s, refined his idea. It was not just faith in the liberation revealed in scripture but truly active hope that mattered. Faith that "the things we were doing were going to bring about change." Confrontations might result in loss—and Bongi herself lost years to prison following the Soweto protests in 1976. But to return to the banning issue, such losses were in fact victories, bringing the future ever closer.[81]

By the mid-1970s, the notion that "it might not happen in our lifetime" was no longer thinkable. Instead, Movement leaders began to speak in terms comparable to the ANC's promise of "freedom in our lifetime" and the PAC's "free by '63." Well before his students led the Soweto protests, for example, Morris Isaacson science teacher Fanyana Mazibuko thought in terms of liberation by the end of the 1970s.[82] The mid-1970s were "exciting times," Manas Buthelezi told a *World* reporter; the 18 million black "prophets" had found their voice and felt that they "could do something."[83] There was a sense of possibility; something was going to happen. As Bongi Mkhabela suggested, high school students felt especially empowered. One student argued that his generation would "reap the fruits of our efforts. If we are to attain liberation, we must work for it."[84]

Two remarkable documents from May 1976 reinforced the sense that the future was now. Early in the month, Desmond Tutu, the dean of Johannesburg and recently appointed bishop of Lesotho, wrote to John Vorster, the South

African prime minister. He greeted him as a Christian with a shared affection for their "beloved country" and struck a reconciliatory tone. "Blacks are grateful for all that has been done for them," he wrote, but times had changed, and "now they claim an inalienable right to do things for themselves." The people were beginning to stir, Tutu continued, and white South Africa ignored them at its peril. His words were prescient. The country had been more or less calm since the early 1960s, but, he said, "I have a growing nightmarish fear that unless something drastic is done very soon then bloodshed and violence are going to happen in South Africa almost inevitably. A people can only take so much and no more." He sent his letter on 8 May. That "inevitable" future came quickly.[85]

Tutu's conclusions were not his alone. Later in May, SASM members met at Roodepoort, near Johannesburg. Amid resolutions passed in support of Soweto schoolchildren's protests against Afrikaans and plans for further student strikes, the high school leaders assembled there heard Vusi Tshabalala's presidential speech. Tshabalala spoke confidently about God's favor and about the power and necessity of sacrifice, even death, and he claimed that he himself did not fear life's end. There was something bigger than life, Tshabalala suggested, and he marked it in time. "It is undeniable that change is coming," he declared, since "the bells of history toll louder and louder everyday." A sense of responsibility imbued his rhetoric and informed the moment. This was history, he concluded, and "we are all called."[86]

Tshabalala could not have known what was about to happen. But he nevertheless testified to the historicity of later events, to the ways in which the ideologies and politics of the previous years were poised to win the struggle against fear. Black Consciousness activists countered fear with hope, trusting that if people felt that change was coming, they would be more willing to struggle and sacrifice, to endure bans and silence in expectation of finding and using their voice. Now, high school students participated in the discourse that recognized suffering as triumph and spoke easily of laying down one's life in pursuit of redemption. More than the organization (or lack thereof) of the June 1976 Soweto protests, this was the legacy of Black Consciousness. Biko and his peers had felt a grave responsibility to challenge fear through consciousness, apathy through faith. Events had sped the narrative along; many of the first generation had suffered bannings and imprisonments and some, as we shall see, much worse. Now, a new generation was set to take the stage. Young and optimistic, members of this cohort did not share earlier misgivings about issues of protest and confrontation with the state. Such encounters were realized facts and only served to keep them focused on reaping the fruits of their own efforts, not "at some stage" but sooner than that. Late May 1976 was a moment pregnant with possibility. No longer distant, the horizon was now within reach. It remained only to touch it.

Tshabalala's speech linked elements that we have seen before: the weight of responsibility, the necessity of suffering, and the inevitability of victory. It hinged especially around the idea of death, counseling neither fear nor welcome but instead calm acceptance that death in pursuit of "truth" could reflect the will and shared triumph of God and people. The focus on life's ending would not have surprised his audience, as the rhetorical links between such sacrifices and ultimate victory had been forged years before. Those who were banned in 1973, for instance, had passed a milestone by "laying down their lives." This was to be lauded, since "the struggle . . . demands of us total involvement and our lives."[87] This did not mean, of course, that the banned had literally died. But in keeping with Black Consciousness's focus on the correct way to be, the distance between banning's "social death" and commitment's final test— the struggle unto death—was not great. Indeed, during that same period, the latter sacrifice had at times been called by name, as again in 1973, when the nascent *SASM Newsletter* told its readers to "be ashamed to die until you have won some victory for humanity."[88] The imprecise language was the product of that period's still incomplete shift from consciousness to confrontation and from humanism's distant horizon to political liberation's closer one. But the discursive wedding of death to victory was nevertheless there. As the 1970s progressed and activists began to die, imprecision fell away and literal deaths found meaning in the rapidly unfolding Struggle.

Death epitomized sacrifice, and sacrifice meant victory. Life's end, therefore, was a powerful symbol. But not only that. Black Consciousness had sought a more profound power through theology, and Christianity—and, more specifically, the image of Christ—lent talk of death a resonance it might otherwise have lacked. There was a tension when first we saw Christ in this era's theology. Basil Moore introduced the fighting Christ, who first talked about human worth and then, by associating with Zealots, led by example toward a revolutionary future. Black South African theologians, by contrast, had shied away from this portrayal of the Christian Messiah, preferring to focus on the personal and political import of his message and only then to define their more abstract version of a Black Messiah for their age. Yet with the introduction of death and the progression from fear to hope, Christ evolved into the exemplar of sacrifice grappling toward a political horizon. This was the faith that "lived with" Tiro of Dinokana and saw Jesus of Nazareth.

The connection between Tiro and Jesus linked responsibility for the present with the conviction that setbacks were actually triumphs. In their call for high school students to "reap the fruits" of their own efforts, SASM leaders pushed a theological agenda: "Where do you stand? Waiting for a Messiah of liberation?

But the Miracle Age is past."[89] People made their own miracles, and in keeping with the era's dominant trends, teachings about Christ emphasized the materiality of the Crucifixion far more than his Resurrection and elevation to God's right hand. Albert Nolan, a Catholic priest and UCM activist, brought his so-called Jesus seminars to campuses across the country during the 1970s, in which he reinforced this point.[90] In his seminars, Nolan focused especially on Jesus's seeming paradox, paraphrased from all four Gospels, that "anyone who saves his or her life will lose it; anyone who loses her or his life will save it." Death met well was the ultimate triumph over fear, he explained: "To save one's life means to hold onto it, to love it and be attached to it and therefore to fear death. To lose one's life is to let go of it, to be detached from it and therefore to be willing to die. . . . A life that is genuine and worthwhile is only possible once one is willing to die." Death was its own point—resurrection did not enter into the conversation. Jesus had dwelled repeatedly on the prospect of death, Nolan taught, but not once did he raise the issue of life on the other side. Nolan concluded that, for Christ, resurrection had been irrelevant while people continued to suffer on earth.[91]

Nolan was not the first scholar to make this case. Since the 1960s, South African theologians had demonstrated their debt to Dietrich Bonhoeffer. The cross, as the cost and risk of discipleship, had figured prominently in Bonhoeffer's theology. "[The] image of God is Christ crucified," Bonhoeffer wrote, not Christ born on the wings of angels. The cross was the core of Christianity: "Grace without discipleship, grace without the cross" was "grace without Jesus Christ." True Christians—true disciples—therefore risked an "inglorious martyrdom," rejected and opposed by the powerful, or they were not Christians at all. As he faced death for his own political acts, Bonhoeffer repeatedly returned to this theme, writing poetry that extolled grace found through suffering, hailing the latter as a "wondrous transformation."[92] This, he concluded, was the *imitatio Christi*; notwithstanding the later incursions of dogma and "religion," suffering and death were faith enacted.

Bonhoeffer's emphasis on suffering differed from the South African perspective that evolved across the 1970s. He called his own process from action to suffering to death "stations of the cross" and thereby strove to imitate Christ's suffering by making that suffering his own. South Africans, however, saw their political prospects a bit more optimistically. They described their suffering not as stations of the cross but as "milestones on the road to freedom"; in this way, they domesticated Christian suffering within South African politics. In 1971, Black Theologians had avoided Basil Moore's direct focus on the liberator Christ, even as they declared Christ's church to be the company of liberators. In 1973, after having suffered the banning of its leaders, SASO was prepared to take a more unequivocal stand.

It was in that context that the fourth GSC resolved "to see Christ as the first freedom fighter to die for the liberation of the oppressed." Christ had "pledged his life for the liberation of his subject-race," SASO declared, and he had done so in concert with both "Israeli revolutionary" and "Israeli guerrilla" groups. The resolution mixed Christian and South African idioms. Just as Black Consciousness had only recently embraced the moniker "Movement," SASO now urged all Christians "to follow Christ by involving themselves in liberation movements for the redemption of the oppressed." The language was different from Bonhoeffer's—less personal, more stridently political, with "redemption" something that would happen to the "oppressed"—but the imitation of Christ remained. Christ had fought but not just that. He had first "pledged" his life and then lost it, and in so doing, he had established the connection between sacrifice, liberation, and redemption.[93]

It is perhaps too much of a stretch to compare either Bonhoeffer's or Christ's sacrifice to even the worst banning order—especially given Black Consciousness activists' self-consciously "disciplined" attitude toward such setbacks. Were they not rejecting Christlike suffering, rather than embracing it? Indeed, when the first activist associated with the Movement died, the political-leader-as-Christ paradigm was not yet prepared. BPC's interim vice president Mthuli ka Shezi—*Shanti*'s author—was crushed by a train en route to the first Black People's Convention, meeting in Pretoria in late 1972. Although it was initially reported that he had suffered "multiple fractures as a result of a train accident," it later appeared that this supposed accident had actually been a scuffle with white railway employees after Shezi had taken exception to their treatment of black female passengers.[94] Activists marked his passing in their own way, remarkable as much for what it was not than what it was. SASO and BPC helped his family bury him quietly, with the "laying of wreaths," in Johannesburg's Tembisa township.[95] There, they remembered a fellow student who had "stood tall among his peers." True, he had "shared his life [with] his brothers," but more important, "in his true Blackness THIS WAS A MAN." Shezi had attained what Black Consciousness had been calling for: he had come of age and become a man. At the time, that was enough.[96]

Only a few months later, however, the bannings brought a new urgency to tales of redemptive suffering, and Shezi's image assumed a more Christlike countenance. "Even when we get pushed onto rails and . . . crushed by trains," Nkwenkwe Nkomo wrote in 1973, "we have to preach the gospel of our destiny."[97] Both Shezi and Christ had preached the Gospel; now, in death, Shezi was mourned with a requiem.[98] Xola Nuse was a Johannesburg-based Black Consciousness activist who would later act in *Shanti*. In May 1973, he made the connections between Shezi and Christ and between death and redemption explicit. He applauded Shezi's passing, writing, "Bravo . . . Yours was redemptive / Yes I mean your suffering / And moreso your death / No different from that of Christ." Unlike in either Bonhoeffer's or Nolan's account of the cross, however, Black Consciousness did not stop there. In his discussion of the banned, Nkomo had written about the "spirit" of the Black Messiah, to which Biko et al. had been faithful disciples. Now, Nuse introduced resurrection, imbued with the spirit of those, like Shezi, who had lost their lives. We on earth "see your body depart," he wrote, "yet your soul rises." "This day"—the day on which the author put pen to paper and gave meaning to death—"[is] my easter."[99] The question of perspective is a critical one. "This day"—after the fact—was Easter, just as the most meaningful day on the Christian calendar occurred days after Christ lost his human ability to control events. This was a self-conscious effort to establish the "correct" perspective, to "see" Christ, as the SASO resolution had it, as a freedom fighter, beyond simply declaring him one. Nuse and his allies needed to "explain the meaningfulness of . . . death," and Christ's example showed the way.[100]

Martyrs, Jeremy Cohen has reminded us, are frequently retrospectively made.[101] Black Consciousness activists demonstrated this in the way they treated a victory won through another generation's sacrifice. Beginning in 1971, SASO organized campus commemorations around the March anniversary of the 1960 Sharpeville killings. These were typically emotional affairs, full of bluster aimed at combating the government's own memory of the "incident" at a place it now celebrated as a "model township," where "there is peace and order [and] the events of 10 years ago are largely, and willingly forgotten."[102] Where the government saw ugly, fading memories, SASO remembered the dead's "irrepressible dignity / undying courage / a fervent belief / in themselves."[103] The Sharpeville dead were celebrated as both heroes and martyrs. The young Sowetan artist noted in chapter 7, for example, used his own blood to capture the image of a man shot there, which he then juxtaposed with another painting showing "a black 'saviour or messiah' caught in the chains of death."[104]

The connection between Sharpeville "heroes" and future victories was more a product of SASO's time than of the massacre's aftermath. When the sixty-nine PAC protesters fell in 1960, black South Africa had responded not with steely-eyed determination but with shock. There was a brief effluence of activity, yet when the government countered it, resistance stilled. In his recent study of Sharpeville, Phillip Frankel argued that although the massacre served as a sort of moral witness to the outside world—and in some cases spurred other nations to action—within South Africa and especially within Sharpeville itself, the results were much more mixed. This was not 17 June 1976, when students had returned to the streets prepared to fight another day. Rather, in the aftermath of the 1960 massacre, "guilt and depression" were widespread among survivors, and the PAC's efforts to reorganize the township were met with a "brick wall of collective apathy." If the deaths had had meaning, it was not readily apparent. Sermons preached at mass funerals attested to this. The first funeral, ten days after the killings, was preached from the Book of Job, and it dwelled on "human suffering[,] predestination," and other Old Testament themes. God was capricious and his purposes unknowable. The second funeral, days later, picked up this thread: it "dwelt on [the] transitory nature of human existence" and presaged a decade that was, in Frankel's words, "a period of collective depression for the entire community."[105] Despite quickly exiled liberation movements' efforts to fashion a "martyrology" from these deaths, Sharpeville came to represent the "victimization of people under apartheid," not their ultimate triumph over it.[106] Thinkers in the 1970s blamed this response on the fear that pervaded the prior decade, and in their own time, they were determined to remember the horror of events in a new way, more in keeping with their generation's faith in the future and the belief that martyrs were not victims but victors.[107]

In the wake of both Shezi's death and the 1973 bannings, Sharpeville Day discourse made martyrdom clearer than ever before, countering Job's unknowable suffering with the assured future of God's revelation in Christ. "Sharpeville is a . . . feeling," read the annual Sharpeville Day program for 1973, "it is the Blackest Black." True, black represented mourning, and activists wore it to remember the dead, but this was the era of Black Consciousness, and it could not stop there: "To be dead at Sharpeville [is] yet to be alive [and] well living in the Black community [in] its struggle for liberation . . . Sharpeville is BLACK SUFFERING (which is senonimous [sic] to BLACK LIBERATION)." This parenthetical comment neatly summed up the direction in which Black Consciousness and Black Theology had turned. Suffering and liberation were joined; you could not have one without the other. To underline the point, the unnamed authors pointed out where and when else this had been true. The Sharpeville dead were heroes not just because they fell but because "they fell with dignity," they were black not just because of the color of their skin but because, through Black Consciousness and "black awareness," "they are not dead but alive." The Sharpeville dead were martyrs because they were transformed, by their deaths, into "little-Christs." The dead had suffered, and although "black suffering is not new," the allusion to His suffering was.[108]

But were they truly like Christ? The question of agency dogs discussions of martyrdom.[109] Many of the dead at Sharpeville had been shot in the back as they tried to flee; they died, presumably, full of fright, not the calm acceptance of the imitatio Christi.[110] Here, we return again to the question of belief. Sharpeville was shocking, and black South Africans' reactions to it, manifested in the 1960s lull, reflected their thoughts on laying down their lives for the future.[111] Yet from 16 June until apartheid's end, many thousands died, some almost willingly—MK soldiers, township cadres, and so on. This is not to say that they wanted to die, just that they had weighed the future against their own lives and had decided not to be lulled by fear of death. Perhaps this was nihilism, born of generations of desperation.[112] Certainly, no one, at least to my knowledge, went so far as Bonhoeffer did in leaving letters explicitly comparing themselves to Christ. Yet well before 17 June—a day more remarkable in many ways than 16 June—Black Consciousness's institutional memory of Sharpeville and the posthumous "Christification" of Shezi demonstrated the possibility of a "martyrology" remarkably different from both post-Sharpeville fear and supposed 1980s nihilism.

Which makes the circumstances and discourses surrounding Tiro's 1974 death that much more interesting. According to those who knew him, Tiro had been exceptionally religious. While teaching in Soweto following his expulsion from Turfloop, he served as both a lay preacher and a youth group leader in the Seventh-Day Adventist Church. His friend Eric Molobi noted that the two of them had immersed themselves in church affairs and strove together "for a religious life."[113] At the same time, as we have seen, Tiro was both militant and fearless, and he wanted his fellow SASO members to look at Christ—as he did—as a freedom fighter. In 1973, he was caught up in the second round of bannings and soon left the country to join a small number of Black Consciousness activists (Mafuna and Nengwekhulu among them) in Botswana. He died there in early 1974 when a package ostensibly sent from the International University Education Fund exploded in his hands. Other exiles claimed that Tiro had had an especially keen sense of responsibility, something indicated by his last letter to the SASO office, in which he wrote that "they should be prepared to sacrifice for their ideals."[114] He fervently believed in the freedom fighter Christ who had laid down his life—not been banned but literally died—for liberation. Both Christ and Bonhoeffer had been able to see death approach; Tiro, of course, had lacked the ability to do so. One wonders, though, how differently he would have acted with the foreknowledge of its coming. The possibility is there. Through it, we might venture inside thought, to see something other than youthful bravado in speeches such as Tshabalala's on the eve of Soweto, when the high school student told other youths—some, undoubtedly, who had been taught by and remembered Tiro—to welcome death in a godly struggle.[115]

Willing or not, Tiro as martyr-like-Christ was well established even as commemorative services got under way in both South Africa and Botswana, and activists embraced the South African political modification of the Resurrection. Within the country, SASO and BPC leaders called for Tiro's death to be "redeemed by the blood of 30 million blacks." When a "leader in the black liberation struggle [dies,] his death should be redeemed by the blood of his followers"; this was the *imitatio Tiro*. Compared to the relative calm of Shezi's funeral years before, Tiro's roared: "Son of the soil, your blood has been spilled to irrigate this debauched and outraged land of ours . . . you may be the first but definitely not the last. . . . Some of us may not reap the fruits of liberation but shall always be revered upon in our Martyrdom. So shall you."[116] In Botswana, activists took control of affairs away from Tiro's family: "It was the decision of the movement that you must accept and your family will accept that this was a fighter in the struggle and he must be buried as a fighter," Nengwekhulu explained. Funerals were the ultimate conscientization/politicization tool. "It will politicize people. It will tell people that in the struggle, you will have casualties. It's a struggle and it's never easy."[117] Death, which would figure so prominently after 1976, thus had insinuated itself into The Struggle years before. The message of funerals turned political rallies was that the future would be worth the cost. Many pages back, we saw a poet demonstrate the connection between Tiro and Christ. Now we understand how he got there.

Martyrdom discourse became more commonplace after 16 June. Observers worried about this. The chairman of the African Institute in Pretoria, for instance, used language that resonates in early twenty-first-century ears, as he worried that public deaths in Soweto and across the country could prompt "a holy war for Black peoples throughout the world."[118] Could talk like that at Tiro's and subsequent funerals mean anything less? Commemorations turned political rallies peppered weekends; there were too many for the *World* and other media to keep up with. All of these presented more or less the same public face. Robed priests or ministers delivered a liturgy; the family wore black; and students stood, resplendent in their school uniforms — now uniforms of struggle — leading the crowd in chants and "black power salutes," bearing banners with messages such as "For freedom we shall lay down our lives. The struggle continues."[119] School clothes and closed-fist salutes became the new markers of fearlessness, struggle, and sacrifice. Police shot an eight-year-old girl apparently only for raising her fist as they rode by, an action she had undoubtedly seen older siblings perform time and again in similar situations. Even the cartoon character Jojo — formerly the politically agnostic "most popular man in the townships" — caught the political fever as he mourned an encounter between baton-wielding police and students standing ramrod straight, fists clenched at their sides, striped school blazers both belying and attesting to the seriousness of the situation.[120]

Soweto attracted most of the attention, but the Black Consciousness organizations that were being blamed for the political conflict continued to collect their own martyrs. Mapetla Mohapi was part of Biko's and Mpumlwana's King William's Town circle, where he had been a SASO officer, community development worker, and administrator of the Zimele Trust, which provided support for activists who had been detained or banned.[121] Slightly more than a month after Soweto, he was arrested, and within days, the government claimed that he had committed suicide. None in the activist community believed that Mohapi had actually succumbed to fear, and by now, the path of mourning was well worn. His death, Itumeleng Mosala remembered, was thus "both painful and encouraging."[122]

Readers of *Pro Veritate* could easily pick up on what such sentiments meant. As deaths mounted in Soweto, the Christian Institute's journal published an Easter sermon preached by a Namibian minister. Christ, Zephaniah Kameeta noted, "did not get down from the cross, he did not leave the field before the deciding battle could be fought. But he stood firm until he had won the victory."[123] After Mohapi died, *Pro Veritate* published the sermon Manas Buthelezi preached at his funeral in East London. The juxtaposition of the two needed no elaboration. Buthelezi spoke from Romans 8:31–39 and hailed Mohapi for winning a "victory through death." Regardless of how exactly Mohapi had died, his death in custody marked the "majestic closing of a career of public service." This was a special death, a commendable death, unique in that "many die but few die as a direct result of commitment to ennoble the quality of lives of millions." Far from being mourned, Mohapi and his suffering and sacrifice were only lauded. "In dying," Buthelezi preached, "you pay an installment towards the liberation of others [which] is the crowning of a career with the insignia of victory." He had led his audience to the obvious conclusion and had only to underscore the point. "Of course, Christ's death is the prototype of all deaths that are a mask of victory."[124]

Buthelezi then turned to Nohle Mohapi, Mapetla's widow. What followed marked how far Black Consciousness had come from what the Lutheran minister later described as the age of philosophers, when young students had developed big ideas about being, consciousness, and the challenges of helping the world to discover its more human face. Those student philosophers spoke frequently of manhood; they projected the image of a virile, fighting God to help visualize what that meant. To some extent, I argued, they envisioned a world come of age and urged adults to take responsibility; in that respect, their gendered discourse merely reflected language's limitation.[125] However, as the 1970s closed, the oft-repeated discourse of suffering, sacrifice, and the future marked the point furthest removed from the rarefied air of student debate. Now, there was only The Struggle. Human lives, ways of being more deeply human, more at peace within oneself and one's own identity, mattered less than outwardly militant projections.

Buthelezi spoke to Nohle Mohapi: "Sister, we are aware of the fact that sometimes a national gain means a family loss. All the wives whose husbands are in the struggle for the betterment of the lives of their fellowmen are always threatened by the spectre of widowhood." Adulthood, once in doubt, was now a given, and it had manifested itself in a particular set of human relationships that were to govern being in South Africa's immediate future. The great skepticism—of nationalism, of political activities, of stages two and three—that had marked Black Consciousness before the Movement had been sacrificed to the pressing demands of the struggle for the future. Blackness had once opened the possibility of being more fully human, in the most sacred sense. Now, it meant one thing: a woman, told not to mourn her husband, a child its father, the consolation for lost subjectivity a faith in politics, the knowledge that "as a black woman you are also one of us. If the life and death of your husband has enriched us, it has enriched you as well." The chasm between Sharpeville and Soweto had been effectively bridged, The Struggle was reasserted, the narrative between point A and point B was realigned and pointed resolutely ahead. Contingent moments were woven into the triumphant story of a Movement and the people that it had roused to face the state. They had turned death into victory. How they had gotten there mattered less now, faced with a wave of funerals that fired hope. But the evidence was there, buried in commonplace expressions of faith. Manas Buthelezi, Lutheran minister, student of Black Consciousness and Black Theology, closed: "We can therefore, together with you, thank God."[126]

SEPTEMBER AND OCTOBER 1977

Mohapi's death was, of course, neither the epoch's last nor its most resonant. Events continued at a fever pitch after his funeral; in Soweto, as 1976 ended, funerals turned rallies begot more funerals, as police raided commemorative services and turned more students into martyrs.[127] The Soweto Students Representative Council (SSRC), which had evolved from SASM, remained defiant: "Our struggle will go on until Black people are free or everyone of us has dropped dead."[128] Adults associated with the Black Consciousness Movement gradually aimed to reassert control as 1976 turned to 1977. The Black Parents Association, formed in the wake of the riots, turned into the Committee of Ten, featuring such veterans of previous struggles as BPC leader Thandisizwe Mazibuko; Christian youth leader Tom Manthata; L. M. Mathabathe, the high school principal who had brought Tiro to Soweto; and the Black Messiah's most vocal disciple, Mashwabada Mayatula, who told a reporter that he was motivated by "Christ, the spirit of God, . . . the spirit who tells of liberation."[129] While students, teachers, and Ministry of Bantu Education officials continued to struggle over exams and school attendance, increased coverage was given to Black Consciousness activists during their repeated trips in and out of detention and their testimony to various tribunals on the whys and wherefores of their way of thinking. Along the way, leaders earned their greatest repute, as when the *World* greeted one—whose name they had once misreported—upon his release from detention in late 1976: "Welcome home Steve."[130]

"Steve" featured prominently in the coverage of 1977. He was tried in April for "obstructing justice" in the trial of another activist and appeared in court for violating his banning order in July, when he was described as a founder of the now famous Black Consciousness Movement in South Africa. He was eventually found not guilty on the former charge, the fourth time he had escaped sentencing since 1974.[131] Meanwhile, Donald Woods, editor of the *East London Daily Dispatch*, introduced the white, English-speaking audience to Black Consciousness thinking and to Biko, the man purportedly behind it, through a series of columns published in the *Rand Daily Mail* and elsewhere.[132]

Biko was arrested one final time on 18 August, again for violating the terms of his banning order while traveling with fellow activist Peter Jones. Three weeks later, on 12 September 1977 (perhaps, after 16 June 1976, the decade's best-known date), he died in police custody in Pretoria. The international outcry, conditioned by months of violent news from South Africa, was immediate. For its part, the Movement's response was in keeping with the recent past. Biko had been the "spiritual leader for the whole black consciousness movement," but his followers projected only a "cold, precise, unrelenting and rational" approach to his death. There was no shock; rather, BPC president Hlaku Rachidi reported that Black Consciousness was "immune."[133] Immediate memorial services in Soweto reflected the mood. No "trace of anger or bitterness" was reported, nor were mourners "grimfaced." Do not despair, a crowd gathered at a candlelight vigil in Soweto were counseled, for Biko's death demonstrated only that "we have covered three-quarters of the way."[134]

The ground had been well prepared for such a reaction. Initially, Biko was remembered in concert with previous activists who had died. Pictures of Tiro and Biko flanked a *Rand Daily Mail* analysis, and SASO produced a leaflet that remembered "Tiro, Mapetla, Steve," as well as Hector Pietersen and all others who had suffered and died. In their memory, "all dirges that we have in mind shall be transformed . . . into victory cries."[135] The seeds of Biko's now disproportionate fame were planted, however, as events rapidly transpired. The government aided this. Vorster, recognizing a story in the making, called a general election to reassert the National Party's control. As international supporters began to flood the coffers of Black Consciousness organizations, Kruger further justified Biko's death by charging that his Movement had colluded with the ANC and that although "Black Consciousness" had been acceptable, the "Black Power Movement" that it had become was not.[136] "Ironically," an editorial in the *World* noted, "it has been in death that Steve Biko has attained the fame and renown that should have been his in life."[137]

Biko's swelling influence was in evidence at his funeral, which was unquestionably Black Consciousness's largest and most visible event. Twenty thousand attended the ceremony in King William's Town, leading, it was reported, to panic among that town's whites, who, fearing open rebellion, "flocked to shops to buy firearms and other weapons."[138] They need not have worried. Instead, mourners saw the Black Consciousness Movement bury its dead and demonstrate once more how a "psychological intervention" aimed at the individual had been turned into shock therapy for an entire community. The funeral featured politics "blended with religious sentiments." This was not surprising. Although Biko had been a politician and activist, not a priest, he had nevertheless served his God. Finally laid to rest, he was, others claimed, in fact resurrected, like Christ: "The spirit you have planted in our brains shall remain our precious treasure. . . . The spirit of a martyr does not die, but lingers." Time would bear witness to this fact. "Lord, we are sure we shall win," a funeral oration declared, "because You are on our side." The future was a matter of faith.[139]

Soon, events returned to what passed for normal in 1970s South Africa. Almost reassuringly, the entire student body of the University of the North was expelled in late September, on the same day that over three hundred teachers and principals resigned from their jobs in Soweto to protest repeated government meddling. The government was famously unmoved by Biko's death and claimed that the former student leader had "aimed to deprive the whites of the right of self-determination over their own affairs in their own land" and that Black Consciousness, turned Black Power, posed a grave threat. On 18 October, the *World* covered the continued detention of three of its reporters but little other overtly political news; Jojo weighed in on the government's new seatbelt law, and an editorial condemned "hooligans" who had taken advantage of the unrest in townships outside Pretoria. It was the *World's* last issue. Early the next morning, the government released banning orders against the paper and the Movement whose rise it had covered. SASO, BPC, BCP, SASM, SSRC, the Christian Institute, the *World*, *Pro Veritate*—the newspapers that were able to publish on 20 October 1977 printed a host of acronyms and names, both of organizations and of the dozens of individuals who were now banned. Many, like the Christian Institute and SASO, hearkened back to the beginning of this story, to ideas and debates that had been overshadowed by subsequent events. Activists associated with each had engaged in dialogue with student movements around the world and turned the global awakening of the 1960s into the concrete political struggles of the 1970s. Now, on a Wednesday closing in on 1980, their voices fell quiet.[140]

Two weeks later, twelve black ministers of various denominations gathered in downtown Johannesburg. Some wore clerical robes, others well-appointed suits. Some, such as John Sebidi, had studied at St. Peter's when issues of the appropriate faith for black South Africans had first been raised and debated. Others were veterans of similar experiences at Turfloop, Fed Sem, or Mapumulo. Like Buti Tlhagale, many had officiated at funerals over the past months. They knew people who had been killed, among them Biko, and others who had either been detained, banned or forced into exile, including priests like Clement Mokoka and community workers like Oshadi Mangena. White police followed them as they made their way to John Vorster Square. The ministers walked purposefully and quietly, with placards that bemoaned the crackdown on Black Consciousness and the government's continued plans for Bantu education and Bantustan independence. Some placards bore slogans. Many simply quoted the Bible.[141]

CONCLUSION

Yesterday Is a Foreign Country

THE QUIET did not last. Soon after 19 October 1977, new organizations formed and new movements followed. There was the Azanian Peoples Organisation (AZAPO), followed by the rise of civic organizations. Next came trade unions, antitricameral parliament campaigns, and the United Democratic Front—which courted the old Black Consciousness constituency of Africans, Indians, and Coloureds and counted Movement veterans such as Allan Boesak among its leaders. Then there was the Mass Democratic Movement, soon followed by negotiations, elections, and a "new" South Africa. As AZAPO, Black Consciousness again mutated to fit changing circumstances; it outflanked the UDF's apparent ANC-aligned multiracialism by going further left, to embrace a creed that combined the discourse of blackness, dignity, and adulthood with a more conventional "socialist" approach to South Africa's problems. Symbols marked the transformation. In the early 1980s, a red star was affixed to the familiar black fist. The star, AZAPO explained, stood for "our hope that Black workers, whose blood has been spilled for our liberty, will lead the struggle, and will rule a free socialist Azania."[1] Where once the progression was from nonwhites to blacks, Black Consciousness in the wake of 1977 further winnowed the population—and workers were the blackest of them all.

The 1980s are justly celebrated for the pressure, both internal and external, that activists and their allies exerted on the regime. Yet for some, the 1980s were the darkest years. Political identification by party rose in importance. Funerals abounded, but they were just as often sites of intense internecine conflict as they were sanctifications of the Struggle, the future, and its costs. Whether ANC, UDF, or AZAPO, party identification often trumped simply "being" for liberation. For some, this was a crushing disappointment. Upon her release from prison in the early 1980s, Bongi Mkhabela was met by AZAPO representatives, and "the first thing they wanted to know was which ideology am I going to embrace." The machinations of such questions left her cold; they were too great a departure from Black Consciousness's humanist roots. She ended up marrying AZAPO founder Ish Mkhabela, but the resentment lingered. "For many people this was not simply because two people love each other," she wrote, "but was a political coup for Black Consciousness ideology."[2] Intensified conflict between opposition groups did add to the system's overall instability, however. As the 1980s turned to the 1990s, death remained a constant, a fever pitch of suffering and sacrifice that, young activists were repeatedly assured, would be repaid a thousandfold when that last horizon passed. And in 1994, the new South Africa dawned. Or so the story goes.

Having set the stage, it would be logical to follow events into the present and there join the critics who have rightly begun to question what 1994 meant. Enduring poverty, epidemic AIDS, endemic crime, superficial reconciliation, deep-running racial division, and flagging democracy—all these issues deserve criticism and have received it in spades. I hear and sympathize with writers such as Patrick Bond and Ashwin Desai, and I beg the reader to look to them for discussions of the present. Meanwhile in my few remaining pages, I shall pursue a different tack. Rather than lament the material conditions of the South African present, I want to consider once more the not explicitly political politics with which Black Consciousness began, to test how faith and beingness fare in the "new" South Africa.

So then, with those thoughts in mind, I would ask, Has the horizon been passed? To take beingness first, we might offer a qualified yes. Much of urban South Africa today is a flurry of cultural and economic production, something that has been recently and brilliantly explored by, among others, Achille Mbembe and Sarah Nuttall, who take Johannesburg as their context and the new South Africa as their interrogation.[3] Nuttall in particular focuses on the shopping mall and demonstrates how a trip to Sandton City, Maponya Mall, Rosebank, or similar centers reveals a boldly modern society on the move. There, redoubts of "Afro-chic" package blends of so-called traditional African fashion sensibilities with township style. As part of this latter-day Black Consciousness, the 1970s Movement sells, whether in the form of hip, well-fitting T-shirts that feature the *Drum* cover announcing Biko's death or in more cheaply produced but still stylish shirts decorated with Biko's face, sold amid the Bob Marleys, Ches, and other prepackaged "revolutionaries." That Biko was about consciousness, not "easy" revolution, and that he spent his last years organizing cooperative development enterprises does not figure in the sale. He died for the cause and can be packaged accordingly.[4]

There is ample historical irony at play here—some quite obvious and some less so. Scholars and critics might bemoan consumerism's triumph, but in so doing we fail to note the more subtle ways in which Biko's commodification itself marks a particular sort of revolution. As discussed in chapter 7, culture was a fraught terrain during the apartheid period; government ideology packaged traditional cultures to preserve black-white distinctiveness, while global culture—especially in television and filmic form—was tightly controlled. Now, in post-1994 South Africa, being able to shop for a Biko T-shirt, to watch Oprah every day at 4:00 p.m., to save up for the satellite TV, the smart phone, the designer "takkies" (sneakers), or to pursue an individual aesthetic apart from political solidarity—such activities are a potent sort of revolution.[5] Fashion is, of course, the most obvious way to self-fashion, and any casual visitor to urban South Africa cannot help but be struck by the multitude of styles and voices that fill the airwaves and the streets.[6] Black Consciousness began with the call for undifferentiated subjects to become vocal selves, yet that idea's evolution into an ideology was paced with aesthetic control and restraint. The Struggle having ended, perhaps African existentialism is returning to its modernist, individualist roots.

It would be rather specious to leave things at that, of course. Literal self-fashioning is not necessarily critical selfhood, and conspicuous consumption can be critiqued as only the most superficial sort of change. As far back as 1977, Nelson Mandela condemned the Black Consciousness Movement for renaming the country Azania without bothering to foment an "authentic" revolution.[7] What must Mandela make, therefore, of his own party's efforts to rechristen South African localities without pursuing more fundamental transformation? The area around Johannesburg is no longer the Transvaal, Tshwane has replaced Pretoria, and Jan Smuts International Airport is named after Oliver Tambo, but typically white-controlled capital passes through each more easily than ever. Yet that irony aside, both these efforts and Mandela's 1970s critique misread Azania's function. South Africa's name was not to be changed simply for the sake of change. Although Black Consciousness had been about individual blacks strengthening themselves enough to stand confidently with whites and express themselves, it was not supposed to stop there. "Liberated" persons such as Sabelo Ntwasa and Bokwe Mafuna used their names to mark more fundamental transformations; Black Consciousness was thus an ethic, a way of life, a being for change that was supposed to saturate and fundamentally alter an entire society. Surface transformations would then be born from internal transformation, as Freire taught, not the other way around. AZAPO itself has begun to raise this issue. Recent publications available at its office in Braamfontein rate the respective "dignity" of South Africa's races, and it comes as no surprise that Africans are at the bottom of the list.

Yet I think that there is an ontological problem in these and other attempts to weigh South Africa's present against its past; we who are here now are out of place. When we question South Africa's progress from yesterday to today, we measure it against the Struggle's supposed ideals, marked in past promises that the people would one day touch a given vision of the future. We thus measure today with lessons drawn from a particular past, and as David Scott has recently argued, in so doing we cut off our conversation before it begins. The time on which we draw is past, Scott contended, and "in new historical conditions"—such as our own—"old questions might lose their salience, their bite and so lead the range of old answers attached to them to appear lifeless, quaint, not so much wrong as irrelevant." After all, what do words honed in an anticolonial struggle have to say in a postcolonial age? Rather, Scott continued, we need to go beyond the "romance" of anticolonialism to see the "tragedy" of its ideas, developed as they were within the overwhelming and inescapable rubric of colonial modernity—as platforms for the past, not programs for the future. Rather than wage current struggles with history, he suggested, we should leave the past be. It has suffered enough.[8]

When assessing past political programs, I largely agree. But there are also elements that we today must refuse to leave for history—and AZAPO's dignity scale might show the way. As far back as the early 1970s, Biko understood that society's obsession with horizons, with political solutions, and with members signed up, goals achieved, and votes counted only obscured an ineluctable truth: that the horizon will always be ahead of us, moving away, just out of reach even as we stretch toward it, endlessly and futilely. Biko knew this, and in the rising heat of the political struggle against apartheid, he turned to Kaunda's humanism to set what must have seemed, at that particular moment, to be an altogether improbable goal. "Somewhere on the distant horizon," he wrote in 1971, "we can see the glittering prize . . . of a more human face." A historian's most powerful tool is time, and by separating Black Consciousness from its future, I have sought to preserve something of the ideals that fired those early days, when activists looked warily at postcolonies and called not only for political solutions but also for new ways of being human. To that end, they thought about what makes people people on the most basic level; beyond political slogans about the franchise, about freedom of movement and land, they thought about selves, about community, about dignity and the freedom that lay between the ears. In the mid-1970s, the tide turned away from this vision of politics, however, and by the 1980s, what remained of Black Consciousness had joined the rest of the liberation movements in perhaps their greatest sin—pointing merely at a set of laws and saying, "There, that is your enemy." Collectively, they resolved a political problem—and inaugurated a host of new ones. But we must ask, Does South Africa have a more human face? Or has the quest to be more human in the most sacred sense, to be more ethical, to live in keeping with the cumulative teachings of the "law and the prophets" been lost along the way?

Black Consciousness activists pointed the way toward the distant horizon through faith, and it is thus regrettable to note that the passing of the political horizon seems to have robbed South African Christians of their gift for prophecy. This was initially met with relief by some, including Desmond Tutu, who famously exulted that "at last the Church could go back to being the Church."[9] In the face of life's still multiple challenges, South African Christianity has witnessed an evangelical awakening, with megachurches filled with believers at worship to the gospel of wealth or morality—pietism, of a sort, has been resurrected, as recent scholarship suggests it has all over the African continent and indeed the world.[10] The secular and sacred remain mixed and mutually invested in a world of witches and pending millennia, but apartheid's end seems to have removed some of the incentive to move forward, doing unto others as you would want them to do to you.

Indeed, South Africa remains largely a country of conservative Christians who worry that humanistic concerns have raced too far ahead of the people. This has been the case especially on the issue of same-sex marriage—a right implied by the South African Constitution, upheld by the country's Constitutional Court, enacted (however grudgingly) by the country's Parliament, but still hotly debated. Manas Buthelezi helped to develop the theology that, by the 1980s, saw a multiracial group of South African church people sign the *Kairos Document*, which publicly repudiated the state and declared apartheid a "heresy."[11] Who says the past is past? "I am afraid that time is coming that same sex marriages will be declared a heresy, the same way as Apartheid was," Buthelezi recently wrote in an open letter to his member of Parliament. The new South Africa was not like the old, of course, but by sanctioning same-sex marriage, the entire system of government courted opprobrium for being, once more, "ungodly."[12] The rift between African Theology and Black Theology having healed, the sinfulness of homosexuality appears to be an area where much of the African church establishment agrees, as even a casual survey of recent events reveals.[13]

Yet these broad strokes cover too much. There remain influential Christian prophets—people such as the Catholic bishop of Phokeng, who went against both his church and government inertia to embrace the use of condoms to check the spread of AIDS, and Njongonkulu Ndungane, the past archbishop of Cape Town, who first drew attention for "Africanizing" his clerical robes but is now better known for going against African Anglicanism's increasing conservatism and homophobia and choosing instead to focus on the universal right to dignity rather than on allegedly traditional antipathies to certain ways of living. More recently, another prophetic voice has sounded—that of Rubin Phillip, graduate of Fed Sem and SASO and currently the Anglican bishop of Durban, who spoke out loudly against the Chinese government's efforts to ship weapons to Zimbabwe via Durban in the wake of that country's disputed 2008 elections.[14] Taken together, the coexistence of this variety of perspectives attests to the fact that South Africa, with its myriad problems, is also an open, expansive society, replete with cultural innovations and individuals struggling to find their own way forward. There is still space for prophets in South Africa, and we should all look forward to their jeremiads.

Until then, I think about this. Barney Pityana left South Africa soon after the 1977 bannings; he made his way to London and became an ordained Anglican minister, thereby in some sense validating Nengwekhulu's nickname for him—Bishop. He joined the ANC and, upon his return to South Africa in the early 1990s, served first as commissioner and then as chair of the country's Human Rights Commission. He is now the vice chancellor and principal of the University of South Africa, as well as a sometimes critic of the government and target of ANC Youth League ire. In October 2005, he gave the guest sermon at the Anglican Diocese of Matlosane's annual Family Day commemoration in Krugersdorp. He obviously looks different than he did organizing SASO in the late 1960s but also the same: there is still the same glint in his now-bespectacled eyes, the same unique way of holding his jaw when speaking. He spoke to the huge crowd about the challenge of morality in the heyday of AIDS, about the need to combat poverty, about the manifold demands of life. Then, with a rather mischievous expression that must have exasperated NUSAS leaders, he called on black South Africans to remember the dictates of Black Consciousness, to open their minds and recognize that the quest for true humanity remained ahead of them and that only by embracing their gay sisters and brothers, their political enemies, the poor, the oppressed, the sick—in short, only by facing their deepest fears—might they try once more for the distant horizon. He finished and sat down, accompanied by rather tepid applause. Prophecy, history teaches, always looks clearer from a distance.

Notes

INTRODUCTION: THE SEVENTIES

1. "Minutes," fourth GSC, pt. 3, F753, 21, Karis Gerhart Collection (hereafter cited as KGC). For discussion about this in the trial, see, for example, *S. v. Cooper*, reel 3, 3476–3534, reel 6, 5661, etc., AD1719, Historical Papers, Cullen Library, University of the Witwatersrand (hereafter cited as HP); each of the nine defendants was asked to explain the resolution.

2. *S. v. Cooper*, reel 3, 3534.

3. "Sedibe's Statement," *S. v. Cooper*, reel 10, 1–4, AD1719, HP.

4. It was an ebb, perhaps, but as a recent work has demonstrated, not a full stop. See, for example, Raymond Suttner, *The ANC Underground in South Africa* (Johannesburg, South Africa: Jacana Press, 2008), and Julian Brown, "Public Protest and Violence in South Africa, 1948–1976" (PhD diss., Oxford University, 2010).

5. Chronicles of the 1970s include Gail Gerhart, *Black Power in South Africa: The Evolution of an Ideology* (Berkeley: University of California Press, 1979); Robert Fatton, *Black Consciousness in South Africa: The Dialectics of Ideological Resistance to White Supremacy* (Albany: State University of New York Press, 1986); C. R. D. Halisi, *Black Political Thought in the Making of South African Democracy* (Bloomington: Indiana University Press, 1999); and Craig Charney, "Civil Society vs. the State: Identity, Institutions, and the Black Consciousness Movement in South Africa" (PhD diss., Yale University, 2000). These works share a common teleological bent, which fits Black Consciousness into debates on the theory and practice of resistance to apartheid and on multiracial democracy. The Black Consciousness Movement has also played a prominent role in two sweeping, multivolume collections, each with a revealing title: South African Democracy Educational Trust, *The Road to Democracy in South Africa* (Pretoria: UNISA Press, 2007), and Gail Gerhart and Thomas Karis, *From Protest to Challenge* (Bloomington: Indiana University Press, 1997). Two recent publications marked the thirtieth anniversary of Biko's death: Andile Mngxitama, Amanda Alexander, and Nigel Gibson, eds., *Biko Lives!* (New York: Palgrave Macmillan, 2008), and Chris Van Wyk, *Celebrating Steve Biko: We Write What We Like* (New York: Columbia University Press, 2009). For a more sustained critique of the literature on Black Consciousness, see Daniel Magaziner, "'Black Man, You Are on Your Own!': Making Race Consciousness in South African Thought, 1968–1972," *International Journal of African Historical Studies* 42, no. 2 (2009): 221–41.

6. Malusi Mpumlwana, interview by the author, 9 March 2006, Pretoria.

7. Bongi Mkhabela, interview by the author, 18 April 2006, Johannesburg, South Africa.

8. The past, Paul Cohen has reminded us, is remembered in multiple ways, and the interplay between historical knowledge, experience, and myth exposes the problems of teleology. As he notes, "the degree to which the meaning of the past is hostage to [its] as yet undefined future would appear to belie the common view among historians that, as one of us has enunciated it, 'what comes after cannot influence what came before.'" See Cohen, *History in Three Keys: The Boxers as Event, Experience and Myth* (New York: Columbia University Press, 1997), 62.

9. Roger Chartier, *The Cultural Origins of the French Revolution* (Durham, NC: Duke University Press, 1991), 4. Many thanks to Anatoly Pinsky for suggesting the reference and to Guy Ortolano for steering me toward the French Revolution historiography in the first place. Fred Cooper has recently made a similar argument for colonial and postcolonial studies; see his *Colonialism in Question* (Berkeley: University of California Press, 2004), 18–19.

10. Consider, for example, the differences between Robert Self's *American Babylon: Race and the Struggle for Postwar Oakland* (Princeton, NJ: Princeton University Press, 2003), and Peniel Joseph's *Waiting 'til the Midnight Hour: A Narrative History of Black Power in America* (New York: Henry Holt, 2006). Self did not share Joseph's aspirations to craft a "grand narrative"; instead, he located his study thoroughly in its time and place—postwar Oakland, California—and sought the roots of Oakland's famed Black Power politics in the particular dynamics of urban transformation there. The result is an altogether more satisfying history that takes what became Oakland-inflected Black Power on its own terms, within its own context. Joseph's study is magisterial and exhaustive, but in the end, its does not entirely come together—perhaps because the idea of a unitary Black Power movement owes more to retrospective ideology than to history. See Thomas Sugrue's *Sweet Land of Liberty: The Forgotten Struggle for Civil Rights in the North* (New York: Random House, 2008), for a recent and historicist macronarrative.

11. The lack of explicitly intellectual history in the Africanist canon is at least in part due to the limited source base. South Africa's long colonial and mission histories thus offer a particular advantage, in that interested historians can both trace certain concepts across longer periods of time (as I hope to do in a future project) and watch more tightly bounded intellectual debates at particular moments in the past, as I do here. One other area where such work is possible is in southern Nigeria, where the similarly long history of mission among the Yoruba has yielded the rich source base that Philip Zachernuk explored in his *Colonial Subjects: An African Intelligentsia and Atlantic Ideas* (Charlottesville: University Press of Virginia, 2000).

12. Saul Dubow, *A Commonwealth of Knowledge: Science, Sensibility and White South Africa, 1820–2000* (Oxford: Oxford University Press, 2006), vii.

13. Zimbabwe has a much richer literature on the African middle class than does South Africa. See, for example, Terence Ranger, *Are We Not Also Men? The Samkange Family and African Politics in Zimbabwe, 1920–1964* (Portsmouth, NH: Heinemann, 1995), and Michael O. West, *The Rise of an African Middle Class: Colonial Zimbabwe, 1898–1965* (Bloomington: Indiana University Press, 2002).

14. See, among others, Bhekiziziwe Peterson, *Missionaries, Monarchs and African Intellectuals: African Theater and the Unmaking of Colonial Marginality* (Trenton, NJ: Africa World Press, 2002); Tim Couzens, *The New African: A Study of the Life and Work of H. I. E. Dhlomo* (Johannesburg, South Africa: Ravan Press, 1985); and David Attwell, *Rewriting Modernity: Studies in Black South African Literary History* (Athens: Ohio University Press, 2006). A recent collection that examined these sorts of historical actors is Karin Barber, ed., *Africa's Hidden Histories: Everyday Literacy and Making the Self* (Bloomington: Indiana University Press, 2006).

15. Gary Wilder, *The French Imperial Nation-State: Negritude and Colonial Humanism between the Two World Wars* (Chicago: University of Chicago Press, 2005), 252, 197. Michael Hanchard recently explored black diaspora political theory in light of its development in multiple "non-political venues." See Hanchard, *Party/Politics: Horizons in Black Political Thought* (New York: Oxford University Press, 2006).

16. Among the exceptions to my broad strokes are studies that explore African conceptions of political power; my favorites among them include Steve Feierman, *Peasant Intellectuals: Anthropology and History in Tanzania* (Madison: University of Wisconsin Press, 1990), and Jan Vansina, *Paths in the Rainforest: Towards a History of the Political Tradition in Equatorial Africa* (Madison: University of Wisconsin Press, 1991). Nothing sparked my interest in African intellectual history like John Lonsdale's overwhelming "Moral Economy of Mau Mau," in *Unhappy Valley*, by Bruce Berman and John Lonsdale (Athens: Ohio University Press, 1992), 2:315–467.

17. The concept of domestication was best defined by Jeremy Prestholdt as "the process of making familiar or usable, controlling and bringing into intimate spaces." He wrote about commodities, but I think the idea is equally applicable to ideas. See Prestholdt, *Domesticating the World: African Consumerism and the Genealogies of Globalization* (Berkeley: University of California Press, 2008), 8.

18. Harry Nengwekhulu, interview by the author, 20 March 2006, Pretoria.

19. *SASO Newsletter*, September 1970, 6.

20. The contentious issue of gender figures prominently in Mngxitama, Alexander, and Gibson, *Biko Lives!*

21. See Steve Estes, *I Am a Man! Race, Manhood, and the Civil Rights Movement* (Chapel Hill: University of North Carolina Press, 2005), for a recent example on the civil rights movement, as well as various essays in Peniel Joseph, ed., *The Black Power Movement: Rethinking the Civil Rights–Black Power Era* (New York: Routledge, 2006), especially those by Kimberly Springer and Stephen Ward. See also Springer, *Living for the Revolution: Black Feminist Organizations, 1968–1980* (Durham, NC: Duke University Press, 2005).

22. Michael A. Gomez, *Black Crescent: The Experience and Legacy of African Muslims in the Americas* (Cambridge: Cambridge University Press, 2005), 323.

23. See Robert Morrell, "The Times of Change," in *Changing Men in Southern Africa*, ed. Robert Morrell (Pietermaritzburg, South Africa: University of Natal Press, 2001), 7.

24. The term belongs to Marlon Ross, *Manning the Race: Reforming Black Men in the Jim Crow Era* (New York: New York University Press, 2004), 2.

25. Ibid., 1. For a broad and sensitive study of gendered race relations in South Africa, see Anne McClintock, *Imperial Leather: Race, Gender and Sexuality in the Colonial Contest* (New York: Routledge, 1995).

26. Amrita Basu, ed., *The Challenge of Local Feminisms: Women's Movements in Global Perspective* (Boulder, CO: Westview Press, 1995), 142.

27. The practice of asking open-ended questions about political problems was reminiscent of the early days of the New Left in the United States—the early 1960s before either *new* or *left* had earned its capital letters. The 1962 Port Huron Statement, for example, similarly began from self-consciously *big* questions: "What is really important? Can we live in a different and better way?" Further, it too shied away from ideology in favor of *undetermined* ideas: "Perhaps matured by the past," Students for a Democratic Society members wrote, "we have no sure formulas, no closed theories," only the promise to "search for orienting theories and the creation of human values." Like Black Consciousness, SDS began from an explicitly existentialist and humanist perspective; as we shall see, like SDS, Black Consciousness burst into mainstream historical consciousness bearing a calcified ideological perspective that belied its roots. See "Port Huron Statement," in Jim Miller, *Democracy Is in the Streets: From Port Huron to the Siege of Chicago* (New York: Simon and Schuster, 1987), 331–32.

28. Lewis Gordon, *Existentia Africana: Understanding Africana Existential Thought* (New York: Routledge, 2000), 7, 11.

29. Paul Gilroy, *The Black Atlantic: Modernity and Double Consciousness* (Cambridge, MA: Harvard University Press, 1993), 39.

30. Basil Moore, "President's Report," 1968, 1, AD1126 A4(d), HP.

31. Manas Buthelezi, "Victory through Death," *Pro Veritate*, August 1976, 7–8.

32. Creston Davis, John Milbank, and Slavoj Žižek, eds., *Theology and the Political: The New Debate* (Durham, NC: Duke University Press, 2005). See esp. chap. 1.

33. "Report on Leadership Training Seminar," December 1971, pt. 3, F748, 4, KGC.

34. Steve Biko, *I Write What I Like*, ed. Aelred Stubbs (1978; repr., London: Bowerdean Publishing, 1996), 60; Lindelwe Mabandla, "The Message," 1971, 1, AD1126 J6, HP.

35. Recent works in this regard include Stephen Ellis and Gerrie Ter Haar, *Worlds of Power: Religious Thought and Political Practice in Africa* (New York: Oxford University Press, 2004); Michael Schatzberg, *Political Legitimacy in Middle Africa: Father, Family, Food* (Bloomington: Indiana University Press, 2001); Sean Redding, *Sorcery and Sovereignty: Taxation, Power and Rebellion in South Africa, 1880–1963* (Athens: Ohio University Press, 2006); Clifton Crais, *The Politics of Evil: Magic, State Power and the Political Imagination in South Africa* (Cambridge: Cambridge University Press, 2002); and, most recently, Harry West, *Kupilikula: Governance and the Invisible Realm in Mozambique* (Chicago: Uni-

versity of Chicago Press, 2005), and Harry West and Todd Sanders, *Transparency and Conspiracy: Ethnographies of Suspicion in the New World Order* (Durham, NC: Duke University Press, 2003). Recent scholarship has noted this especially in Pentecostalism. See, for example, Paul Richards, *Ghana's New Christianity: Pentecostalism in a Globalizing African Economy* (Bloomington: Indiana University Press, 2004), and David Maxwell, *African Gifts of the Spirit: Pentecostalism and the Rise of a Zimbabwean Transnational Religious Movement* (Athens: Ohio University Press, 2006), as well as David Gordon's forthcoming *Spiritual Sovereignty and the Political Imagination: A Central African History.* My personal favorite, written by my academic idol, Karen Fields, is *Revival and Rebellion in Colonial Central Africa* (Princeton, NJ: Princeton University Press, 1985). For a trenchant critique of much of the recent literature, see Clifton Crais, untitled, response presented at AHA, January 2009, in the author's possession.

36. Mcebisi Ndletyana, ed., *African Intellectuals in 19th and Early 20th Century South Africa* (Cape Town: HSRC Press, 2008). See also J. B. Peires, *The Dead Will Arise: Nongqawuse and the Great Xhosa Cattle-Killing Movement of 1856–7* (Bloomington: Indiana University Press, 1989), esp. chap. 1.

37. David Attwell, "Intimate Enmity in the Journal of Tiyo Soga," *Critical Inquiry* 23, no. 3 (Spring 1997): 557–77, and Attwell, *Rewriting Modernity;* James Campbell, *Songs of Zion: The African Methodist Episcopalian Church in the United States and South Africa* (New York: Oxford University Press, 1995); Helen Bradford, *A Taste of Freedom: The ICU in Rural South Africa, 1924–1930* (New Haven, CT: Yale University Press, 1987); Robert Vinson, "'Sea Kaffirs': 'American Negroes' and the Gospel of Garveyism in Early Twentieth-Century Cape Town," *Journal of African History* 47, no. 2 (2006): 281–303; and Robert Edgar and Luyanda ka Msumza, eds., *Freedom in Our Lifetime: The Collected Writings of Anton Muziwakhe Lembede* (Athens: Ohio University Press, 1996). For more on Christian identity and the intellectual foundations of South African politics, see Peterson, *Missionaries, Monarchs and African Intellectuals.* For a general restatement of the interpenetrated worlds of religion and nationalism, see Adrian Hastings, *The Construction of Nationhood: Ethnicity, Religion and Nationalism* (Cambridge: Cambridge University Press, 1997).

38. A recent example of this was the remarkable conversation between Philip Benedict, Nora Berend, Stephen Ellis, Jeffrey Kaplan, Ussama Makdisi, and Jack Miles that was published as "Religious Identities and Violence," *American Historical Review* 112, no. 5 (2007): 1433–81.

39. J. D. Y. Peel accused South African Christianity's most celebrated chroniclers—at least in recent days—and others of this; their work is Jean Comaroff and John Comaroff, *Of Revelation and Revolution* (Chicago: University of Chicago Press, 1991). The first two of a projected three volumes have sparked a great deal of debate not just about how the Comaroffs used Christianity as a shorthand to talk about many other things but also about whether they assigned too much power to Christianity in the first place; put another way, debate centered on whether African thought systems had in fact withstood mission and colonialization. Their

primary interlocutor in this regard was Paul Landau, especially in his *Realm of the Word* (Portsmouth, NH: Heinemann, 1995). I will have a (brief) occasion to entertain these ideas in chapter 5.

40. J. D. Y. Peel, *Religious Encounter and the Making of the Yoruba* (Bloomington: Indiana University Press, 2000), 5, 4.

41. Søren Kierkegaard, *Fear and Trembling* (New York: Doubleday Anchor, 1954), 61.

42. Jürgen Moltmann, *Theology of Hope* (London: SCM Press, 1967), 20.

43. For recent reflections on this theme in South African letters, see Jennifer Wenzel, *Bulletproof: Afterlives of Anticolonial Prophecy in South Africa and Beyond* (Chicago University of Chicago Press, 2009).

44. *World*, 23 September 1977, 14.

45. This does not mean that there were not triumphs, only that measured against activists' earliest goals, reinvigorated protest against apartheid's laws was only a particular sort of success. For other successes, see Leslie Hadfield's important work on Black Consciousness community development in the Eastern Cape, "Restoring Human Dignity and Building Self-Reliance: Youth, Women and Churches and Black Consciousness Community Development, South Africa, 1969–1977" (PhD diss., Michigan State University, 2010).

PART I: MAKING BLACK CONSCIOUSNESS

1. Steve Biko, *I Write What I Like*, ed. Aelred Stubbs (1978; repr., London: Bowerdean Publishing, 1996), 27. This selection comes from the article "We Blacks," I Write What I Like (column), *SASO Newsletter*, September 1970. The article was especially significant: it came from the second issue of the newsletter, it was the first Frank Talk column to speak directly to blacks, and it began to articulate the "positive" Black Consciousness philosophy. Biko's first column, published a month earlier, had continued SASO's attack on white liberals. See chapter 2.

2. In his study of black South African culture under apartheid, Rob Nixon suggested that Black Consciousness "attitude" developed in response to the prevailing ideas of the 1950s, at least in some sense. See Nixon, *Homelands, Harlem and Hollywood: South African Culture and the World Beyond* (New York: Routledge, 1994), 39.

3. *SASO Newsletter*, May–June 1972, 18.

CHAPTER 1: SOPHIATOWN AFTER THE FALL

1. David Coplan, *In Township Tonight! South Africa's Black City Music and Theatre* (Johannesburg, South Africa: Ravan Press, 1985); Michael Chapman, ed., *The Drum Decade: Stories from the 1950s* (Pietermaritzburg, South Africa: University of Natal Press, 2001); David Goodhew, *Respectability and Resistance: A History of Sophiatown* (Westport, CT: Praeger, 2004); and Tyler Fleming, "King Kong, Bigger Than Cape Town: A History of a South African Musical" (PhD diss., University of Texas, 2009).

2. Bloke Modisane, *Blame Me on History* (1963; repr., New York: Simon and Schuster, 1990), 106.

3. For more on this period, see Randolph Vigne, *Liberals against Apartheid: A History of the Liberal Party of South Africa, 1953–68* (New York: St. Martin's Press, 1997).

4. For much more on Bantu education and the politics of learning under the state, see Jonathan Hyslop, *The Classroom Struggle* (Pietermaritzburg, South Africa: University of Natal Press, 1999).

5. Only one university retained a multiracial element: the University of Natal Non-European Medical School (UNNE) remained open to the entire nonwhite community.

6. Craig Charney, "Civil Society vs. the State: Identity, Institutions, and the Black Consciousness Movement in South Africa" (PhD diss., Yale University, 2000), 179.

7. Statistics from University Christian Movement archives, pt. 3, F929, UCM, 1, KGC.

8. This visit took place in June 1966. There is a remarkable Web site chronicling this event: http://www.rfksa.org/.

9. Martin Legassick, *The National Union of South African Students: Ethnic Cleavage and Ethnic Integration in the Universities* (African Studies Center, University of California, Los Angeles, 1968), Occasional Paper 4, 56.

10. The classic study, penned while their position was the most fraught, is Leo Kuper, *An African Bourgeoisie* (New Haven, CT: Yale University Press, 1965).

11. Verwoerd's words, cited here, are from William Gumede, *Thabo Mbeki and the Battle for the Soul of the ANC* (Cape Town: Zebra Press, 2005), 20.

12. Can Themba, "The Bottom of the Bottle," in his *The Will to Die* (London: Heinemann, 1972), 115.

13. Students thus occupied the not-quite "liminal situation" explored to great effect by Leo Spitzer in *Lives In Between* (New York: Hill and Wang, 1989), 4. See also Homi Bhabha, "Of Mimicry and Man," in *Tensions of Empire*, ed. Frederick Cooper and Anne Stoler (Berkeley: University of California Press, 1997), 152–60.

14. I pick up this trope in chapter 2.

15. This choice of verb is a careful one. Camus's *The Rebel* was a quintessential text of existentialism and was particularly influential in the theology of James Cone, an African American political and religious thinker whose work was in turn fundamental to Biko (see the latter's "Black Consciousness and the Quest for True Humanity," in his *I Write What I Like*, 87–98) as well as in the wider Black Consciousness "religious project."

16. Interview with Mcebisi Xundu, pt. 1, F41, 11, KGC; Bennie Khoapa, interview by the author, 13 December 2005, Durban, South Africa; Allan Boesak, *Farewell to Innocence: A Socio-ethical Study of Black Theology and Black Power* (Johannesburg, South Africa: Ravan Press, 1977), 45; Fanyana Mazibuko, interview by the author, 18 November 2005, Johannesburg, South Africa.

17. F. Mazibuko, interview. Nthato Motlana, a general practitioner in Soweto during the early 1960s, recalled a man getting arrested for uttering the three letters "ANC"—which in his case meant "ante-natal clinic." The story might be apocryphal,

but it speaks to the remembered atmosphere of the time. Nthato Motlana, interview by the author, 31 January 2006, Johannesburg, South Africa.

18. Nkwenkwe Nkomo, interview by the author, 2 March 2006, Johannesburg, South Africa.

19. Bokwe Mafuna, interview by the author, 30 November 2005, Johannesburg, South Africa.

20. Saths Cooper, interview by the author, 7 December 2005, Johannesburg, South Africa.

21. "Zingisa Educational Project: 1980 Year Report," 1, Haigh Collection Misc., Steve Biko Foundation (hereafter cited as SBF). This project was inaugurated in Biko's hometown after his Ginsberg Education Project was banned along with the rest of the Black Community Programmes in 1977. Its publicity materials referred to his "community bursary" to explain what the project sought to achieve. Regarding his inability to receive a degree, Xolela Mangcu grew up next door to the Biko family and remembers the community hailing Steve's older brother for becoming the first Ginsberg student to earn a postmatriculation degree. Xolela Mangcu, personal communication, 2 March 2006.

22. *World*, 15 February 1972, 3.

23. Letter from Claire Herman United Sisterhood to Snyman Commission, 6 January 1975, Records of the Snyman Commission of Inquiry, K318 K6–3-2, National Archives, Pretoria (hereafter cited as NAP).

24. Letter from Pityana to Collins, 24 February 1971, AD1126 J6, HP.

25. Thandisizwe Mazibuko, interview by the author, 29 November 2005, Johannesburg, South Africa.

26. Chris Mzoneli, interview by the author, 13 December 2005, Durban, South Africa; Mbulelo Mzamane, interview by the author, 16 March 2006, Midrand, South Africa; letter from Stubbs, AB1017 D1 (1969–70), 5, HP.

27. On the subject of banned groups and political backgrounds, there were more overt connections as well—Thoko Mbanjwa, for example, dimly remembered marching with her mother in Durban on the same day that the Congress Alliance women marched to Pretoria in 1956, and Aubrey Mokoape, later a student at the UNNE, was only a teenager when he was arrested with Robert Sobukwe on the morning of Sharpeville in 1960. For the latter, see Benjamin Pogrund, *How Can Man Die Better?* (Johannesburg: South Africa: Jonathon Ball, 1990), 156; for the former, see Thoko Mpumlwana, interview by the author, 22 March 2006, Pretoria. Strini Moodley also remembered protesting the fifth celebration of Republic Day while at the University College for Indians in 1966. He and a small group of others refused to attend the mandatory assembly and instead "marched around" and burned a flag. Strini Moodley, interview by the author, 10 April 2006, Durban, South Africa.

28. Nkomo, interview; T. Mazibuko, interview.

29. This reading of Republic Day (as the holiday was soon known) as "holy" draws from T. Dunbar Moodie, *The Rise of Afrikanerdom: Power, Apartheid and the Afrikaner Civil Religion* (Berkeley: University of California Press, 1975).

30. Cooper, interview.

31. F. Mazibuko, interview; Bonganjalo Goba, interview by the author, 11 April 2006, Durban, South Africa.

32. Tshenuwani Simon Farisani, *In Transit* (Trenton, NJ: Africa World Press, 1990), 33.

33. Tau Mokoka, interview by the author, 28 November 2005, Pretoria.

34. This tension been explored most recently in Mokubung Nkomo, Derrick Swartz, and Botshabelo Maja, eds., *Within the Realm of Possibility: From Disadvantage to Development at the University of Fort Hare and the University of the North* (Pretoria: HSRC Press, 2006), 65–84.

35. The Fort Hare SRC remained informal and off campus until the early seventies, when it was re-formed under SASO's auspices. Barney Pityana, interview by the author, 1 February 2006, Pretoria.

36. Chris Mokoditoa, interview by the author, 9 November 2005, Pretoria; Mogobe Ramose, interview by the author, 6 March 2006, Pretoria; Moodley, interview. The latter's comments are interesting, although perhaps problematic. Until his death in late April 2006, Moodley remained an implacable critic of the ANC. His refusal to accede to the congress's dictates thus might be writing his present-day politics back onto his past. I have decided to include it, however, because it offers hints of individual choice and because, much like the recollections provided by Ramose and Mokoditoa (whose own failure to mention congress boycotts of tertiary institutions might speak to the present day as well), it demonstrates how critical consciousness functioned before entering the university setting.

37. It is worth noting that although Mokoditoa and Pityana both eventually gave up their protest and went to Fort Hare—the former because he saw his younger peers return home with degrees and the possibility of advancement, the latter because the Ford shop floor proved to be unfertile ground for opposition— the issue continued to be debated. This led the *SASO Newsletter* to urge in 1970 that students at Fort Hare reorganize their SRC, since "once you decide to attend [university college] then all the other compromises that you make concerning your presence at the university are logical in terms of the first one." See *SASO Newsletter*, August 1970, 3.

38. "Memo Presented by Black Parents' Vigilance Committee of Soweto," 21 March 1975, K318 K6-3-3, NAP.

CHAPTER 2: "BLACK MAN, YOU ARE ON YOUR OWN!"

1. John Sebidi, "The Dynamics of the Black Struggle and Its Implications for Black Theology," in *The Unquestionable Right to Be Free: Black Theology from South Africa*, ed. Itumeleng Mosala and Buti Tlhagale (Johannesburg, South Africa: Skotaville, 1986), 13.

2. See Craig Charney, "Civil Society vs. the State: Identity, Institutions, and the Black Consciousness Movement in South Africa" (PhD diss., Yale University, 2000), for a more detailed, blow-by-blow account of SASO's founding and institutional politics.

3. "Minutes," 3 May 1968, UCT 1966–80 and undated, 1, SBF.

4. *S. v. Cooper*, reel 11, 1, AD1719, HP.

5. Ibid., and Charney, "Civil Society," 176.

6. Steve Biko, interview by Gail Gerhart, October 1972, Durban, pt. 1, F3, 11, KGC. Biko went on to note, "My own particular hero at that time was [Kenya's] Oginga Odinga." Store this thought, for reasons that will be made explicit later.

7. Letter from Biko to Innes, 8 November 1968, UCT 1966–80 and undated, SBF.

8. "SASO—Its Role, Its Significance and Its Future,"in Steve Biko, *I Write What I Like*, ed. Aelred Stubbs (1978; repr., London: Bowerdean Publishing, 1996), 4, 5.

9. *University Christian Movement [UCM] Newsletter*, third semester, 1969, 1, AD1126 D4, HP.

10. At the 1968 meeting, "the majority of students there were black . . . and the blacks started saying 'we're sick of being the minority group in white organisations where we are told what to do.' That concern [was] so heavy at that conference—Biko and all that crowd, Pityana, they were all there. So we said to them, 'what's your problem? Hive off from us. You go and work out what your role is now'"; see Colin Collins, interview by the author, 19 October 2005, Johannesburg, South Africa.

11. Geoffrey Budlender, "Black Consciousness and the Liberal Tradition," in *Bounds of Possibility: The Legacy of Steve Biko and Black Consciousness*, ed. N. Barney Pityana, Mamphela Ramphele, Malusi Mpumlwana, and Lindy Wilson (Cape Town: David Philip, 1991), 228.

12. Chris Mokoditoa, interview by the author, 9 November 2005, Pretoria.

13. Barney Pityana, interview by the author, 1 February 2006, Pretoria.

14. *UCM Newsletter*, second semester, 1971, 22, AD1126 D4, HP.

15. Collins noted that he and Basil Moore named their black cat Token in recognition of the way integration tended to work; Collins, interview.

16. Steve Biko [Frank Talk], "Black Souls in White Skins," in Biko, *I Write What I Like*, 20, 22. This piece was originally published in *SASO Newsletter*, August 1970. Biko was not the only writer to condemn liberal tea parties; the poet James Matthews memorably did so in his 1972 collection *Cry Rage!* recounting an invitation from "Missus Marshall" of Constantia: "I am invited to view the works of her protégé / another in her collection that numbers a singer, a sculptor / and me / to be displayed when missus marshall / flaunts her liberality / in presenting her cultured blacks"; see Matthews, *Cry Rage! The Odyssey of a Dissident Poet* (Cape Town: Realities, 2006), 50.

17. Harry Nengwekhulu, interview by Gail Gerhart, 17 October 1972, pt. 1, F28, 13, KGC.

18. Transcription, University of Natal–Black Section, 19 March 1972, pt. 3, F282, 19, KGC.

19. Malusi Mpumlwana, interview by the author, 9 March 2006, Pretoria.

20. These headlines are from the 1974 election, when the Progs picked up six seats; *Rand Daily Mail*, 26 April 1974, 1.

21. Peter Randall, interview by the author, 8 December 2005, Johannesburg, South Africa.

22. *World*, 24 April 1970, 1.

23. Ibid., 2.

24. Biko, *I Write What I Like*, 15.

25. Or they would root for the other side. During the 1970s, it became increasingly common for black fans to root against South Africa and for visiting cricket and rugby teams. On one occasion in 1976, black fans actually rushed the field to celebrate the All Blacks' victory over the Springboks. For more on the politics of sport, see Peter Alegi, *Laduma! Soccer, Politics and Society in South Africa* (Scottsville, South Africa: University of KwaZulu-Natal Press, 2004).

26. Biko, *I Write What I Like*, 20.

27. Bennie Khoapa, interview by the author, 13 December 2005, Durban, South Africa.

28. Biko, *I Write What I Like*, 15.

29. *Pro Veritate*, 15 April 1972, 2.

30. *World*, 23 July 1971, 4; 11 January 1972, 4.

31. This was reported in the University of Natal's *Dome* newspaper, 27 March 1969, copy in AD1126 J6, 1, HP. This article also gives a good idea of the disconnect between black and white students. On p. 8, it reported: "Some students have not heard about the third section of our university. UNNE . . . is composed almost completely of Medical students, after the minister has refused to allow non-white studs to study at the University of Natal and at other white universities. Many of the students stay at Alan Taylor Residence at Wentworth, opposite the oil refinery."

32. Nkwenkwe Nkomo, interview by the author, 2 March 2006, Johannesburg, South Africa; Budlender, "Black Consciousness," 231; *Rand Daily Mail*, 14 July 1972, 12.

33. Biko, *I Write What I Like*, 90.

34. Randall, interview.

35. "Minutes," pt. 3, F744, 2–3, KGC; *World*, 22 July 1970, 4. In time, the split from NUSAS transformed white politics as well, as S. Ally and N. Ally demonstrated in "Critical Intellectualism," in *Biko Lives! Contesting the Legacies of Stephen Biko*, ed. Andile Mngxitama, Amanda Alexander, and Nigel Gibson (New York: Palgrave Macmillan, 2008), 171–90. More radical whites gradually seized control of white student organizations, a process that was well under way even as SASO made its move. For more on this, see Ian MacQueen's forthcoming dissertation on Black Consciousness and white students in Durban from the University of Sussex.

36. Letter from Sono to Pretorius, 1 September 1971, pt. 3, F747, KGC.

37. A. L. Mncube, "Taking a Look at IDAMASA," AC623 3.5 1966, 4; "Record of Proceedings of Meeting between Subcommittee SACC and IDAMASA," 1970, 1, HP.

38. *World*, 22 July 1970, 4.

39. M. Mpumlwana, interview.

40. This is from the Alice Declaration, *SASO Newsletter*, May–June 1972, 5.

41. "Communiqué," July 1969, pt. 3, F743, 3, KGC.

42. N. C. Manganyi, *Being-Black-in-the-World* (Johannesburg, South Africa: SPROCAS/Ravan Press, 1973), 24.

43. *SASO Newsletter*, August 1971, 5.

44. Barney Pityana, "Power and Social Change in South Africa," in *Student Perspectives on South Africa*, ed. Hendrik Van Der Merwe and David John Welsh (Cape Town: David Philip, 1972), 189.

45. Kopano Ratele has also discussed the (gendered) implications of this observation in "Men and Masculinities," in *The Gender of Psychology*, ed. T. Shefer, F. Boonzaier, and P. Kiguwa, 165–77 (Cape Town: University of Cape Town Press, 2006).

46. Biko, *I Write What I Like*, 28, 29.

47. *SASO Newsletter*, May–June 1972, 8.

48. *SASO Newsletter*, March–April 1972, 8.

49. *World*, 8 July 1970, 4.

50. Cited in Anne McClintock, "Family Feuds: Gender, Nationalism and the Family," *Feminist Review* 44 (Summer 1993): 62.

51. This observation could find its way into social science as well, as with the famed "Moynihan Report" on *The Negro Family*'s conclusion that the reestablishment of black patriarchy was critical to overcoming black "pathology." Cited in Kimberley Stringer, *Living for the Revolution: Black Feminist Organizations, 1968–1980* (Durham, NC: Duke University Press, 2005), 38.

52. *SASO Newsletter*, August 1970, 7.

53. Bloke Modisane, *Blame Me on History* (New York: Simon and Schuster, 1990), 124, 210–11; Meredith Goldsmith, "Of Masks, Mimicry, Misogyny and Miscegenation: Forging Black South African Masculinity in Bloke Modisane's *Blame Me on History*," *Journal of Men's Studies* 10, no. 3 (2002): 291–307.

54. Mamphela Ramphele, *Across Boundaries* (New York: Feminist Press at the CUNY, 1996), 66, 71.

55. Oshadi Mangena, "The Black Consciousness Philosophy and the Women's Question in South Africa: 1970–1980," in *Biko Lives! Contesting the Legacies of Stephen Biko*, ed. Andile Mngxitama, Amanda Alexander, and Nigel Gibson (New York: Palgrave Macmillan, 2008), 258; Malusi Mpumlwana and Thoko Mpumlwana, introduction to *I Write What I Like*, by Steve Biko, ed. Aelred Stubbs (1978; repr., London: Bowerdean Publishing, 1996), xiii.

56. Julian Kunnie, Review of *I Write What I Like*, H-Net book review, July 2007, available at http://h-net.msu.edu/cgi-bin/logbrowse.pl?trx=vx&list=h-safric a&month=0707&week=b&msg=4QdYMfN6ZNIHoyQ97APpmg&user=&pw=, accessed 16 June 2009.

57. Oshadi Mangena made this point in "Black Consciousness Philosophy" and also in our conversation, interview by the author, 22 November 2005, Johannesburg, South Africa. The argument that this language was merely the convention of the time continues to find favor; at a recent presentation at the University of the Witwatersrand, many in the audience were displeased with my insistence that the "man" in "black man you are on your own" was worth a second look. "Man is just

man!" one audience member protested, to widespread acclaim. Kopano Ratele rejected this argument in *The Gender of Psychology*. To explain away Biko's practices, he wrote, is to fail to grasp "the passion that was present during a life"; see Ratele, "Men and Masculinities," in *The Gender of Psychology*, ed. T. Shefer, F. Boonzaier, and P. Kiguwa (Cape Town: University of Cape Town Press, 2006), 176. Ratele suggested that Biko was examining the mutually constitutive predicaments of "black" and "man." In subsequent pages, I will attempt to go beyond this, to see how "black could overcome "male" (at least momentarily). It is also worth noting that other activists remember Kgware's election as a sham, organized by (male) students who were actually in charge. The correspondence and other documentation that remain seem to corroborate their claims. See Mokoditoa, interview.

58. Amrita Basu, ed., *The Challenge of Local Feminisms: Women's Movements in Global Perspective* (Boulder, CO: Westview Press, 1995), 142.

59. "Black Women and the Black Theology," 11, AD1126[?], HP.

60. Basil Moore, "Freedom Is More," July 1971, 7, AD1126 A4(e), HP.

61. Ibid., 10.

62. Rubin Phillip, interview by the author, 15 December 2005, Durban, South Africa.

63. "Conference Report," July 1971, 37, AD1126 A4(e), HP.

64. Maphiri Masekela, untitled paper, December 1971, F748, 4, KGC,

65. Dan Mogale and Simon Mashiangwako, interview by the author, 20 December 2005, Pretoria.

66. Kimberly Springer, in *The Black Power Movement: Rethinking the Civil Rights–Black Power Era*, ed. Peniel Joseph (New York: Routledge, 2006), 109.

67. Mngxitama, Alexander, and Gibson, *Biko Lives!* 279.

68. Modisane, *Blame Me on History*, 58–59.

69. Bongi Mkhabela, interview by the author, 18 April 2006, Johannesburg, South Africa; *Rand Daily Mail*, 12 October 1970, 11.

70. Biko, *I Write What I Like*, 92, 21.

71. Harry Nengwekhulu, interview by the author, 20 March 2006, Pretoria. See also M. Mpumlwana, interview, and Mosibudi Mangena, interview by the author, 6 December 2006, Pretoria.

72. Phillip, interview. Phillips's phrasing suggestively contrasts the oft-repeated image of illicit multiracial tea parties under apartheid, as noted earlier.

73. Biko, *I Write What I Like*, 5, 7.

74. This idea was perhaps most clearly thought through in Biko's 1977 interview, "On Death," where his discussion of the appropriate response to police violence offered an absolute contrast to Modisane's burning with shame, rubbing the spot where the policeman's playful boot landed. It comes down to a question of agency, something that Modisane evidently disavowed by naming his memoir *Blame Me on History* and that Black Consciousness embraced in its call to be "on your own."

75. Gail Gerhart, *Black Power in South Africa: The Evolution of an Ideology* (Berkeley: University of California Press, 1979), 185.

76. Oginga Odinga, *Not Yet Uhuru* (London: Heinemann, 1967), 314–15.

77. Biko, *I Write What I Like*, 68, 31, 29.

78. "Quo Vadis, Black Student?" *SASO Newsletter*, April–March 1972, 8.

79. Saths Cooper, personal communication, 31 May 2006; Barney Pityana, "The Politics of Powerlessness," *SASO Newsletter*, September 1970, 10. Mark Sanders suggested that SASO thinking about complicity was lifted almost entirely from Fanon, whereas Thomas Ranuga claimed that SASO thought in general was at least "borrowed" from the Martinican. See Sanders, *Complicities: The Intellectual and Apartheid* (Durham, NC: Duke University Press, 2002), chap. 5, and Ranuga, "Frantz Fanon and Black Consciousness in Azania (South Africa)," *Phylon* 47, no. 3 (1986): 182–91. In 1972, David Thebehali asserted that he "used to think that Saso writings were so brilliant and original til [someone] pointed out that it all comes from Frantz Fanon"; interview by Gail Gerhart, 20 October 1972, pt. 1, F38, 2, KGC. SASO activists were enamored with *Black Skins, White Masks*. Saths Cooper recounted that Fanon explained "how people were made to be inferior and even when they had all the accoutrements of achievement, whether intellectual or material, would still be insignificant human beings because the standard in their mind was always something else that they would never be"; Saths Cooper, interview by the author, 7 December 2005, Johannesburg, South Africa.

80. Just as SASO activists reserved the term *nonwhite* to diminish collaborators (see chapters 3 and 8), so too did they deny the collaborators' manhood and adulthood. During a mid-1970s trial, for example, SASO ex-president Pandelani Nefolohodve dismissed Gatsha Buthelezi as nothing more than a "system boy"; *Rand Daily Mail*, 21 May 1976, 2.

81. Thoko Mpumlwana, interview by the author, 22 March 2006, Pretoria. For more on the theoretical underpinnings of cultural action, see chapter 7. See also Leslie Hadfield, "Restoring Human Dignity and Building Self-Reliance: Youth, Women and Churches and Black Consciousness Community Development, South Africa, 1969–1977" (PhD diss., Michigan State University, 2010).

CHAPTER 3: THE AGE OF PHILOSOPHERS

1. "Report of the Commission of Inquiry into Certain Matters Relating to the University of the North," 30 June 1975, 40–41, K318 K7–1, NAP, and "The Student Dean," 13 October 1971, 1, K318 K6–3-1, NAP.

2. Cited in N. C. Manganyi, *Being-Black-in-the-World* (Johannesburg, South Africa: SPROCAS/Ravan Press, 1973), 75.

3. David Attwell, *Rewriting Modernity: Studies in Black South African Literary History* (Athens: Ohio University Press, 2006), 3, 141.

4. Craig Charney, "Civil Society vs. the State: Identity, Institutions, and the Black Consciousness Movement in South Africa" (PhD diss., Yale University, 2000), 82.

5. Manas Buthelezi, interview by the author, 8 November 2005, Johannesburg, South Africa.

6. Frantz Fanon, *Black Skins, White Masks* (New York: Grove Press, 1967), 133, 135.

7. Steve Biko, *I Write What I Like*, ed. Aelred Stubbs (1978; repr., London: Bowerdean Publishing, 1996), 90.

8. "Minutes," 14, and "Amended Constitution," pt. 3, F744, KGC.

9. *SASO Newsletter*, August 1971, 10.

10. Steve Biko, interview by Gail Gerhart, October 1972, Durban, 15–16, pt. 1, F3, KGC.

11. Manganyi, *Being-Black-in-the-World*, 18.

12. James Matthews, interview by the author, 23 May 2006, Cape Town.

13. Indeed, befitting the category's inherent contingency, Cooper suggested that at least some current-day South Africans have recognized this. Speaking of whites, he said, "There are those who just say, hey, I'm a whitey. I'm here and I'm doing this stuff and I'm moving on." They recognize that "the synthesis was not that you would go and live a white life. You'd be who you are." See Saths Cooper, interview by the author, 7 December 2005, Johannesburg, South Africa. This was, it should be pointed out, an inherently external definition of identity, based on a sense of self developed in conversation/contestation with the world outside the mind. Black Consciousness adherents initially argued that this externality needed to follow a wholly interior "conscientization"; over time, however, the broader movement seemed to trade faith in interior transformation for the more easily transmitted surfaces of ideological allegiance. See part 3 for more discussion on this topic. Further, this historically conditioned notion of race recalls Michael MacDonald's discussion of whiteness's mutability after the South Africa War; see MacDonald, *Why Race Matters in South Africa* (Cambridge, MA: Harvard University Press, 2006), 44.

14. *World*, 19 July 1972, 4.

15. *SASO Newsletter*, September 1970, 1.

16. *SASO Newsletter*, September–October 1972, 7, 8. Biko's friendship with Indians and his inclusive political identity were not without their cruder critics. Mamphela Ramphele recalled a fellow student in Durban commenting disparagingly, "Biko . . . your room is full of curry"; see Ramphele, *Across Boundaries* (New York: Feminist Press at CUNY, 1996), 60. Biko's own trajectory was interesting in this regard. He had first been exposed to politics under the auspices of the PAC, when his older brother was arrested for his PAC sympathies. The younger Biko's rejection of multiracial partnership thus resonated with the historical tradition of Africanist resistance to white rule.

17. Robert Edgar and Luyanda ka Msumza, eds., *Freedom in Our Lifetime: The Collected Writings of Anton Muziwakhe Lembede* (Athens: Ohio University Press, 1996), 92. The media picked up on the debate between "African" and "Black" during the early 1970s. *Drum* responded to readers' continued complaints about terms such as *nonwhite* and *Bantu* by commissioning a poll: "What do readers think? Black might be offensive to some groups," October 1971, 59. Responses varied. An African reader from King William's Town insisted that "the only word which is definitely offensive to the non-Whites is 'Black.' It gives you the picture of something ugly," December 1971, 8. Another coined an entirely new term that

he hoped would not carry such baggage, a neologism born of *Afr* (for Africans), *Co* (Coloureds), and *Ins* (Indians), to which the editors responded, I think correctly, "ugh," January 1972, 8. The white press had actually preceded the black to the debate. As early as 1970, the *Rand Daily Mail* reported that the liberal SAIRR had decided to stop using the "offensive term" *nonwhite*, and in early 1971, it too solicited suggestions for a new term. In the course of the paper's survey, one reader summed up the instrumental use of *black, nonwhite, Afrcolins*, or whatever term: *"non-voter," Rand Daily Mail*, 26 November 1970, 4; 10 December 1970, 21. Despite its early attention to the issue, however, the *Rand Daily Mail* continued to toggle between *nonwhite* and *black*, with a preference for the former. This matter finally came to a head in 1972 when the paper was expelled from SASO's third GSC for continuing to use *nonwhite*. *Drum* gloated that it had "a year ago . . . decided the issue through its Letters Page when the Great Debate settled for BLACK," August 1972, 2, *Rand Daily Mail*, 7 July 1972, 8. See also "Minutes," pt. 3, F750, 20, KGC. Readers chastised the *Daily Mail*, with one comparing the term *nonwhite* for people to *nondogs* for cats. Within a few weeks, the paper quietly turned black into its default term. (*Rand Daily Mail*, 13 July 1972, 16.)

18. Biko, *I Write What I Like*, 69, 24.

19. Manganyi, *Being-Black-in-the-World*, 21.

20. *SASO Newsletter*, August 1971, 20.

21. Steve Biko, interview by Gail Gerhart, October 1972, Durban, pt. 1, F3, 35, KGC.

22. All citations in the preceding two paragraphs are from Biko, *I Write What I Like*, 41–47.

23. Kenneth Kaunda, *A Humanist in Africa*, ed. Colin Morris (London: Longmans, 1966), 21–22, 30, 46. See also Kaunda's autobiography, *Zambia Shall Be Free: An Autobiography* (London: Heinemann, 1962).

24. Biko, *I Write What I Like*, 30. Consider this example: "Many a hospital official has been confounded by the practice of Indians who bring gifts and presents to patients whose names they can hardly recall."

25. Ibid., 46. Biko's language here is reminiscent of Deborah Thomas's description of "modern blackness" in Jamaica as "unapologetically presentist and decidedly mobile"; see Thomas, *Modern Blackness: Nationalism, Globalization and the Politics of Culture in Jamaica* (Durham, NC: Duke University Press, 2004), 13.

26. Paul Gilroy, *The Black Atlantic: Modernity and Double Consciousness* (Cambridge, MA: Harvard University Press, 1993), 109.

27. Biko, *I Write What I Like*, 32.

28. Frantz Fanon, *The Wretched of the Earth* (New York: Grove Press, 1968), 209, 225, 221, 223–24.

29. See *SASO Newsletter*, August 1970, 21.

30. *SASO Newsletter*, September 1970, 11.

31. "Composite Report of the Interim-Executive to the 4th GSC," Hammanskraal, 14–22 July 1973, pt. 3, F753, 23, KGC; *Black Review, 1974/1975*, ed. Thoko Mbanjwa (Durban: Black Community Programmes, 1975), 131–32.

32. Steve Biko, interview by Gail Gerhart, 8 November 1973, Durban, pt. 1, F35, 13, KGC.

33. Themba Sono, "South Africa: The Agony of Black Radical Rhetoric 1970–1974" (master's thesis, Duquesne University, [1975?]), 277–78. Note also that this quote was included in the "Dialogue Focuser on Black Power" carried to South Africa by the American UCM; see pt. 3, F762, 6, KGC.

34. Mark Sanders's example is both Biko's and Pityana's use of *Black Skin, White Masks*; see Sanders, *Complicities: The Intellectual and Apartheid* (Durham, NC: Duke University Press, 2002), 186.

35. In the middle of his article, he had written, "In one way or another, both [integrationists and separationists] deplore the fact that white people do not love black people. But love is irrelevant. History is a struggle, not an orgy"; "Liberation," *Ebony*, August 1970, 38–43.

36. Ibid., 42; *South African Outlook*, June–July 1972, 102.

37. Steve Biko, interview by Gail Gerhart, October 1972, Durban, pt. 1, F3, 12, KGC; Malusi Mpumlwana, interview by Gail Gerhart, 16 May 1987, pt. 1, F26, 1, KGC.

38. See, for example, Gail Gerhart's discussion in *Black Power in South Africa: The Evolution of an Ideology* (Berkeley: University of California Press, 1979), and especially George Frederickson's in-depth comparison in *Black Liberation: A Comparative History of Black Ideologies in the United States and South Africa* (New York: Oxford University Press, 1995). See also Peniel Joseph, *Waiting 'til the Midnight Hour: A Narrative History of Black Power in America* (New York: Henry Holt, 2006); William L. Van Deburg, *New Day in Babylon: The Black Power Movement and American Culture, 1965–1975* (Chicago: University of Chicago Press, 1992); and James Cone, *My Soul Looks Back* (Maryknoll, NY: Orbis Books, 1986).

39. Gilroy, *Black Atlantic*, 38–40.

40. Daniel Magaziner, "Christ in Context: Developing a Political Faith in Apartheid South Africa," *Radical History Review*, no. 99 (2007): 80–106.

41. Stokely Carmichael and Charles Hamilton, *Black Power: The Politics of Liberation in America* (New York: Vintage Books, 1967), viii. It is worth noting that although this discussion has focused on Carmichael, SASO writers also "borrowed" from the thoughts and language of other Black Power thinkers, including Malcolm X and Eldridge Cleaver, with occasional symbolism taken from the Black Panthers. The latter's overt Marxism and symbolic embrace of violence, however, did not mesh well with SASO thinking at this stage.

42. It should be noted that SASO activists soon attempted to ensure that it did—see Leslie Hadfield, "Pumping Life Back into the Black Man: SASO Community Projects in 1970s South Africa," paper presented at African Studies Association Annual Meeting, 20 October 2007, New York.

43. Steve Biko, interview by Gail Gerhart, October 1972, Durban, pt. 1, F3, 22, KGC; *SASO Newsletter*, August 1971, 10.

44. *SASO Newsletter*, August 1971, 10.

45. *SASO Newsletter*, June 1971, 18–19.

46. *SASO Newsletter*, May–June 1972, 18.

47. *SASO Newsletter*, September 1970, 7. They eventually retained Carmichael's exact language for the Policy Manifesto.

48. Steve Biko, interview by Gail Gerhart, October 1972, Durban, pt. 1, F3, 4, 5, KGC.

49. *SASO Newsletter*, August 1971, 19.

50. C. R. D. Halisi, "Biko and Black Consciousness Philosophy: An Interpretation," in *Bounds of Possibility: The Legacy of Steve Biko and Black Consciousness*, ed. N. Barney Pityana, Mamphela Ramphele, Malusi Mpumlwana, and Lindy Wilson (Cape Town: David Philip, 1991), 108.

51. There is a great deal of literature on SDS and Port Huron; the citation here is taken from Jim Miller, *"Democracy Is in the Streets": From Port Huron to the Siege of Chicago* (New York: Simon and Schuster, 1987), 331.

52. Barney Pityana, "A Black Viewpoint," address to the SAIRR, July 1971, pt. 3, F746 SASO, 2, KGC.

53. Martin Jezer, "Long Hair Manifest Destiny," *WIN Magazine* 6, no. 4 (March 1, 1970): 17. Many thanks to Keith Woodhouse for revealing the relevance of "relevance" in New Left thought to me.

54. Mogobe Ramose, interview by the author, 6 March 2006, Pretoria; Saths Cooper, interview by the author, 7 December 2005, Johannesburg, South Africa; Bennie Khoapa, interview by Gail Gerhart and Tom Karis, 16 June 1989, pt. 1, F14, 3, KGC; "Report: Conference for Black Church Leaders," May 1972, A835 C1, 9, HP; *World*, 2 July 1972, 4; *SASO Newsletter*, September–October 1972, 16; Biko, *I Write What I Like*, 22.

55. Biko, *I Write What I Like*, 27.

56. Ibid., 48.

PART II: EMERGENT GOSPEL

1. Peter Jones, interview by Gail Gerhart, 21 July 1989, pt. 1, F13, 6, KGC. In this same interview Jones reported that Freire's *Pedagogy of the Oppressed* was the "bible." The implications of this are discussed in chapter 7, below. The Nkomo document is "Memorandum," March 1973, pt. 3, F285, 1, KGC.

2. "Practical Application of the Ideology of Black Consciousness," pt. 3, F744, 1, 2, KGC.

3. Kenneth Kaunda, *A Humanist in Africa*, ed. Colin Morris (London: Longmans, 1966), 36–39.

4. Steve Biko, *I Write What I Like*, ed. Aelred Stubbs (1978; repr., London: Bowerdean Publishing, 1996), 56, 57, 93.

5. See Tim Parsons, *Race, Resistance, and the Boy Scout Movement in British Colonial Africa* (Athens: Ohio University Press, 2004), for more on this.

6. *S. v. Cooper*, reel 8, 8361, AD1719, HP.

7. John Mbiti, *African Religions and Philosophy* (New York: Praeger, 1969), 1. For more on Mbiti, see chapter 5, below.

8. Barney Pityana, "What Is Black Consciousness? And How Is Black Theology

Related to It?" AD1126 D6(a), 1, HP; and reprinted in *The Challenge of Black Theology in South Africa*, ed. Basil Moore, 58–63 (Atlanta, GA: John Knox Press, 1974).

9. Biko, *I Write What I Like*, 93.

CHAPTER 4: CHURCH, STATE, AND THE DEATH OF GOD

1. Roli wa Karolen, "The Casualties," *S. v. Cooper*, reel 11, AD1719, HP.

2. By "mainstream" church, I mean the international denominations' representatives in South Africa—the Reformed Churches, the Catholic Church, the Anglican Church, the Methodist Church, and so forth. The "separatist" or African Independent Churches will be considered in the next chapter.

3. University Christian Movement, "Memorandum," 12 June 1968, AD1126 A1(b), HP.

4. Ibid., UCM, "Constitution of the University Christian Movement of Southern Africa: Article II, Purpose," AD1126 A1(b), HP.

5. Takatso Mofokeng, interview by the author, 28 November 2005, Pretoria.

6. The scholarship mentioned here includes Peter Walshe, *Church versus State in South Africa* (Maryknoll, NY: Orbis Books, 1983); Walshe, *Prophetic Christianity and the Liberation Movement in South Africa* (Pietermaritzburg, South Africa: Cluster Publications, 1995); David Thomas, *Christ Divided: Liberalism, Ecumenism and Race in South Africa* (Pretoria: UNISA Press, 2002); and John De Gruchy, *The Church Struggle in South Africa* (Grand Rapids, MI: Eerdmans, 1979). For a recent reflection on these and other issues, see De Gruchy, *Confessions of a Christian Humanist* (Minneapolis, MN: Fortress Press, 2006).

7. T. Dunbar Moodie, *The Rise of Afrikanerdom: Power, Apartheid and the Afrikaner Civil Religion* (Berkeley: University of California Press, 1975), 265.

8. Colleen Ryan, *Beyers Naudé: Pilgrimage of Faith* (Cape Town: David Philip, 2005), 36.

9. Statement of the 1974 DRC Synod, cited in Allan Boesak, *Farewell to Innocence: A Socio-ethical Study of Black Theology and Black Power* (Johannesburg, South Africa: Ravan Press, 1977), 33.

10. Ryan, *Beyers Naudé*, 43. At one point during the late 1960s, the prime minister's brother was the DRC moderator, as if to underscore this point.

11. So argued Hans Abraham, past commissioner general of the Xhosa in the *Rand Daily Mail*, 16 December 1974, 2. For more on the Covenant, see Leonard Thompson, *The Political Mythology of Apartheid* (New Haven, CT: Yale University Press, 1986).

12. *Rand Daily Mail*, 17 December 1971, 4.

13. *Rand Daily Mail*, 24 May 1972, 4.

14. Ibid., 23.

15. For more on the development—and especially the periodization—of Afrikaner "Calvinism," see Andre Du Toit, "No Chosen People: The Myth of the Calvinist Origins of Afrikaner Nationalism and Racial Ideology," *American Historical Review* 88, no. 4 (1983): 920–52.

16. For a recent discussion, see David Goldenberg, *The Curse of Ham: Race and Slavery in Early Judaism, Christianity and Islam* (Princeton, NJ: Princeton University Press, 2005).

17. Moodie, *Rise of Afrikanerdom*, 4–11.

18. J. A. Loubser, *The Apartheid Bible: A Critical Review of Racial Theology in South Africa* (Cape Town: Maskew Miller Longman, 1987). For more on Kuyper, see Frank Vandenberg, *Abraham Kuyper* (Grand Rapids, MI: Eerdmans, 1960).

19. Ryan, *Beyers Naudé*, 25.

20. Rom. 12:4–6. The Bible version is M. Jack Suggs, Katharine Doob Sakenfeld, and James R. Mueller, eds., *The Oxford Study Bible* (New York: Oxford University Press, 1992), 1443.

21. Loubser, *Apartheid Bible*, 39.

22. The white DRC maintained administrative and financial control over its "daughter" churches, further contributing to blacks' feelings of immaturity.

23. Itumeleng Mosala, interview by the author, 24 April 2006, Pretoria.

24. Allan Boesak, interview by the author, 15 June 2006, Somerset West, South Africa.

25. L. D. Hansen, ed., *The Legacy of Beyers Naudé* (Stellenbosch, South Africa: Sun Press, 2005), 132.

26. "Happening '69, Fact Paper No. 1: Spotlight on the African Colleges," AD1126 A4(c), 4, HP.

27. Mofokeng, interview.

28. Bokwe Mafuna, interview by the author, 30 November 2005, Johannesburg, South Africa.

29. William Temple, *Christianity and the Social Order* (London: Shepheard-Walwyn, 1942), 29. For more on World War II and Christian thinking, see the discussion later in this chapter. For the German Christians, see Doris Bergen, *Twisted Cross: The German Christian Movement in the Third Reich* (Chapel Hill: University of North Carolina Press, 1996).

30. Temple, *Christianity and the Social Order*, 38.

31. "The Purpose and Strategy of the Project," AD1126 I6, 2, 4, HP; Temple, *Christianity and the Social Order*, 114.

32. Peter Randall, ed., *Apartheid and the Church* (Johannesburg, South Africa: SPROCAS, 1972), 42.

33. Dennis Hurley in *Southern Cross*, 22 June 1964, AD1126 M11, HP.

34. Alphaeus Zulu, "The Church Confronts South Africa," 21 May 1964, pt. 3, F348, 2, KGC, and UCM, "Constitution."

35. "Literacy Project," 1970, pt. 3, F928, 2, KGC.

36. Chris Mokoditoa, interview by the author, 9 November 2005, Pretoria; Mokgethi Motlhabi, interview by the author, 3 March 2006, Pretoria; Colin Collins, interview by the author, 19 October 2005, Johannesburg, South Africa.

37. Letter from Hurley to Collins, 14 May 1969, AD1126 A4c, 1–2, HP.

38. Letter from Angela Norman, St. Francis School, to Collins, 25 April 1968, AD1126 A4c, 2–3, HP.

39. Collins, interview, and "Archbishop Whelan's Views on Apartheid," *Southern Cross*, 15 February 1964, AD1126 M11, HP. Whelan contended not only that there was no church teaching opposed to a state maintaining racial groups "in their separate and distinct identity" but also that "the Church has never considered democracy to be the only form of government compatible with Christianity" (1–3).

40. Bonganjalo Goba, interview by the author, 11 April 2006, Durban, South Africa, referring to his experience at a Congregationalist school, and Simon Maimela, interview by the author, 1 February 2006, Pretoria, regarding Lutherans, for example.

41. Annual Conference, 1968, memorandum, AC623 3.5, 1, HP; *World*, 20 January 1969, 4.

42. Testimony of Nkwenke Nkomo, *S. v. Cooper*, reel 8, 8360, AD1719, HP.

43. Mafuna, interview. Fanyana Mazibuko described a similar conflict when he decided not to go to seminary; Mazibuko, interview by the author, 18 November 2005, Johannesburg, South Africa.

44. Dan Mogale and Simon Mashiangwako, interview by the author, 20 December 2005, Pretoria.

45. "Message to the People of South Africa" was reprinted in various media over the course of 1968. Citations here are taken from *Black Sash* 12, no. 3 (1968): 28.

46. Ibid., 29.

47. Ibid., 31.

48. Thomas, *Christ Divided*, 178.

49. "The Purpose and Strategy of the Project," AD1126 I6, 1, HP.

50. Peter Randall, "Brief Memorandum on the Project," A835 Aa 1969, 1, HP.

51. Walshe, *Church versus State in South Africa*, 102.

52. Letter from R. Orr, Presbyterian Church in Pretoria, to National Presbyterian representatives, 24 September 1971, A835 B6, HP.

53. Letter from General Secretary, Presbyterian Church, to Randall, 5 October 1971, A835 B6, HP.

54. Peter Randall, interview by the author, 8 December 2005, Johannesburg, South Africa.

55. Peter Randall, "Press Reaction to SPROCAS," 1 December 1971, A835 Ab, HP.

56. "Twelve Statements: A Christian Election Manifest," circular, Pt. 3, F348, 1, KGC.

57. *Pro Veritate*, 14 February 1970, 17. It certainly did not help that the Progs' most prominent face at that time was Helen Suzman, or, as she was often referred to, "a Jewess."

58. Ryan, *Beyers Naudé*, 68.

59. Beyers Naudé's farewell sermon, in *The Legacy of Beyers Naudé*, ed. L. D. Hansen (Stellenbosch, South Africa: Sun Press, 2005), 25, 27. As John De Gruchy explained, confessing entailed commenting on present practices in light of scripture; it meant that "you publicly said what [scripture] meant in terms of [the] issues of the day," whatever political consequences that might entail.

60. John De Gruchy, "Beyers Naudé and Public Theology," in *The Legacy of Beyers Naudé*, ed. L. D. Hansen (Stellenbosch, South Africa: Sun Press, 2005), 85.

61. Cedric Mayson, interview by the author, 27 February 2006, Johannesburg, South Africa. Scholars such as Ryan and De Gruchy have claimed that the CI was motivated in particular by the example of the German Confessing Church movement that had opposed the Nazis. During the 1930s, a few thousand German church people rejected the church authorities who had aligned with the German state and instead established "Free Synods," or what became known as the Confessing Church; see Ryan, *Beyers Naudé*, 107. Beginning almost immediately after Hitler took power, the Confessing Church issued statements in which it confessed God's absolute authority and therefore reserved the right to struggle against the state. Theologians associated with the movement, such as Dietrich Bonhoeffer, greatly influenced South African Christians who wanted to act in a similar fashion.

62. "The Time Has Come," *Pro Veritate*, 15 October 1972, 2–3.

63. *Rand Daily Mail*, 1 March 1971, 10.

64. Numerous UCM documents bear a policeman's "25/2/71" notation across the top, letting the historian know what was seized in the raid.

65. *Rand Daily Mail*, 1 January 1971, 1, 2; 25 February 1971, 1; 27 February 1971, 1; *World*, 15 March 1971, 12 (see chapter 6); *Rand Daily Mail*, 28 July 1971, 18.

66. *Rand Daily Mail*, 2 April 1971, 18.

67. The latter doubtlessly resonated within the white South African community. Since its founding in 1948, the WCC had grown steadily more critical of white supremacy in southern African, especially as newly independent "Third World" churches filled its ranks. In 1969, its Program to Combat Racism set up a special fund of $200,000 and announced that the money would be distributed among nineteen "organisations of oppressed racial groups," primarily from southern Africa, including the ANC. The government and white South Africa were generally appalled by this; even liberals worried that the WCC was writing off the fates of the white population. However, Zolile Mbali suggested that black students at Federal Theological Seminary "celebrated long into the night on hearing of the WCC grants." See *Rand Daily Mail* 26 January 1971, 10; 10 February 1971, 4; and Pauline Webb, ed., *A Long Struggle: The Involvement of the World Council of Churches in South Africa* (Geneva, Switzerland: WCC Publications, 1994), 11. For more on the WCC and its relationship with South Africa, see Mbali, *The Churches and Racism* (London: SCM Press, 1987).

68. After all, even Christians in public opposition to the state hesitated in the face of the WCC's definitively political act.

69. *World*, 20 January 1969, 4.

70. "Message to the People of South Africa," *Black Sash* 12, no. 3 (1968): 30.

71. Collins, interview.

72. Mayson, interview.

73. "Inauguration of the University Christian Movement of Southern Africa, Report of Grahamstown Conference," AD1126 A4a, July 1967, 6, HP.

74. Basil Moore, "Worship 'Happenings,'" *Pro Veritate*, 15 September 1968, 14.

75. Ibid., 14, 15, 17.

76. Ibid., 14, and letter to James Moulder, President of UCM, from W. J. Ravenscroft, 18 August 1968, 1–2, AD1126 D1, HP.

77. "UCM Inaugural Service, Grahamstown," AD1126 A1(b), 14 July 1967, 3, HP.

78. Letter from Withers, UCM Publications Director, to Falkenberg, 27 April 1968, AD1126 D4, HP.

79. John 2:15–17.

80. "Brother Cairns," "The Catholic Church in the World Today," *Ubunye*, 1970, AD1126 D4, 8–13, HP.

81. Jill Hultin, "A Temporary Arena," *South African Outlook*, July 1967, 99.

82. Colin Collins, "The Church of the Future," AD1126 A4(b), 84, HP.

83. John Davies, "Servant to the University," *South African Outlook*, July 1967, 107.

84. Harvey Cox, *The Secular City* (New York: Macmillan Press, 1965), 16.

85. Along with secularism, atheism and agnosticism would fall into this category.

86. Cox, *Secular City*, 134.

87. Ibid., 16.

88. Ibid., 265.

89. Ibid., 275.

90. Letter from Falkenberg to Detroit Industrial Mission, 4 March 1968, and affirmative reply, Detroit Industrial Mission to Falkenberg, 25 March 1968, AD1126 A4(b), HP.

91. Cox, *Secular City*, 18.

92. G. Kelly and F. Burton Nelson, eds., *Testament to Freedom: The Essential Writings of Dietrich Bonhoeffer* (New York: HarperCollins, 1990), 43.

93. Ibid., 505, 527.

94. Ibid., 43, 517. This call for a Christianity apart from institutions was in some sense reminiscent of Bonhoeffer's contemporary, the Swiss theologian Karl Barth, albeit with a critical modification. Barth described an absolute and qualitative difference between the universe and the divine and argued that it was folly for human institutions to claim divine preference. Thus, like Bonhoeffer, he urged Christians to hold worldly institutions, whether church or state, accountable. Yet whereas Bonhoeffer called for Christians to preach amid history's political reality, Barth cautioned that although the world was God's, it could never be godly. Christians could call human institutions to account only if they preserved the qualitative divide, as "the divine may not be politicized and that which is human may not be divinized." Bonhoeffer disagreed. See Frank Jehle, *Ever against the Stream: The Politics of Karl Barth* (Grand Rapids, MI: Eerdmans, 2002), 42.

95. The program belonged to Christopher Taylor, *Sources of the Self: The Making of Modern Identity* (Cambridge, MA: Harvard University Press, 1989), 216–18.

96. Motlhabi, interview.

97. Basil Moore, "The Theological Stance of UCM," AD1126 A1(b), 1, HP.

98. Ibid., 1–2.

99. Basil Moore, "A 1970 Theological Viewpoint of the UCM," 23 February 1970, AD1126 A1(b), 1, 4, HP.

100. UCM, "Constitution."

101. Basil Moore, "God—How I Think," *One for the Road*, March 1970, 7, 11.

102. Ibid., 8.

103. Ibid., 10.

104. *Pro Veritate*, 16 April 1968, 16.

105. Letter from Simpson to Collins, 9 May 1970, AD1126 D4, HP.

106. Letter from Moore to Simpson, 10 June 1970 AD1126 D4, HP.

107. John Robinson, *Honest to God* (London: SCM Press, 1963), 13; David Edwards, *The "Honest to God" Debate* (London: SCM Press, 1963), 15. For *Honest to God* and Bonhoeffer, see Kelly and Nelson, eds., *Testament to Freedom*, 395.

108. Robinson, *Honest to God*, 139, 64–65, 97, 105.

109. Ibid., 20–21, and Paul Tillich, *The Courage to Be* (1952; repr., New Haven, CT: Yale University Press, 2000), xxv.

110. Tillich, *The Courage to Be*, 66, 178, 190.

111. Moore, "God—How I Think," *One for the Road*, March 1970, 8–9.

112. Goba, interview.

113. Gabriel Setiloane, "Black Theology," *South African Outlook*, February 1971, 30 (italics in original). For African Theology and more on Setiloane, see chapter 5.

114. Barney Pityana, "What Is Black Consciousness?" in *The Challenge of Black Theology in South Africa*, ed. Basil Moore (Atlanta, GA: John Knox Press, 1974), 58.

115. See, for example, Gustavo Gutierrez's critique in *Theology of Liberation* (Maryknoll, NY: Orbis Books, 1974), 224.

116. Albert Nolan, interview by the author, 6 March 2006, Johannesburg, South Africa.

117. "Creative Tensions," *UCM Newsletter*, third semester, 1969, AD1126 D4, 1, HP. Not coincidentally, this was also the height of SASO initiated black-white polarization, as discussed in chapter 2.

118. Collins, interview.

119. "Encounter '70: Conference Report and Assessment," AD1126 A4d, 16, HP.

120. Mokoditoa, interview; "Encounter '70: Conference Report," 17, 27.

121. Mafuna, interview (emphasis mine).

122. D. D. I. Makhatini, "Black Theology—What Is It?" Acc. 153, BT, 2, University of South Africa (hereafter cited as UNISA).

123. At the same time, we must note that for many within UCM, secularization was merely a way station on the road out of the organized church. Many white students moved away from "religion" to "consciousness"; others, including Collins, the movement's general secretary, simply left the church. His example is a suggestive one, not just for the evident power of the secular critique within Christianity but also for the continued challenge South African politics posed to

even a much modified conception of religion. As both a progressive and a Catholic priest, Collins had drawn great energy from the Second Vatican Council of the early sixties. A year before helping to found UCM, he wrote approvingly of the council's "constitution on the Church in the modern world," contending that it dedicated Catholics to the premise that "there must be made available to all men everything necessary for leading a life truly human, such as food, clothing and shelter; the right to choose a state of life freely and to found a family, the right to education, to employment, to a good reputation, to respect . . . to rightful freedom, even in matters religious." This resonated especially in South Africa, he continued, where continuing to ignore the position of nonwhites was "sinful." Yet four years later, after witnessing another brief effluence of liberal efforts to combat the DRC, the "Message," SPROCAS, calls for a confessing community, and the rise of secularization, there had still been no change in the South African political situation. Frustrated, Collins applied for laicization. It was a decision, he wrote, based not only on the South African Catholic Church's failure to respond to Vatican II but also on the changing understanding of faith popular in the UCM. Secular theology gave students the authority to think freely about their faith, and thinkers such as Cox felt that freedom would yield political change. But for Collins and others, the questions of church-state relations and the overwhelming challenge of apartheid remained doggedly unanswered, in spite of liberalism, in spite of calls for a confessing community, in spite of police raids, and in spite of secularization. Faced with this situation, Collins felt he had no choice but to leave the Church. See Colin Collins, untitled, 20 March 1970, pt. 3, F928, 2, KGC; Collins, interview; and Collins, "The Church in the Modern World," *Challenge*, April 1966, pt. 3, F926, 3, 6, KGC.

124. Letter from Ntwasa to Stubbs, 23 December 1971, AB2414 D2 (Ntwasa), HP.

125. Kelly and Nelson, *Testament to Freedom*, 125.

CHAPTER 5: CHRIST IN CONTEXT

1. Lamin O. Sanneh, *Translating the Message: The Missionary Impact on Culture* (Maryknoll, NY: Orbis Books, 1989).

2. John Parratt, *An Introduction to Third World Theologies* (Cambridge: Cambridge University Press, 2004), 8–9.

3. Allan Boesak, *Farewell to Innocence: A Socio-ethical Study of Black Theology and Black Power* (Johannesburg, South Africa: Ravan Press, 1977), 18.

4. Michael Hardt and Antonio Negri, *Empire* (Cambridge, MA: Harvard University Press, 2000), esp. chaps. 2–4.

5. The letter was published in a variety of media. Citations here are taken from "Black Priests' Manifesto: Our Church Has Let Us Down," 23 January 1970, pt. 3, F343, 1–2, KGC. Mokgethi Motlhabi, who was then a student at St. Peter's, recalled reading the manifesto in the newspaper and suddenly awakening to the political problem of his own training for the priesthood; Motlhabi, interview by the author, 3 March 2006, Pretoria.

6. Sabelo Ntwasa, "Why a Black Theology for South Africa?" 1971, AD1126 D6, 3, HP; Clement Mokoka, interview by the author, 19 December 2005, Phokeng, South Africa; Mogobe Ramose, interview by the author, 6 March 2006, Pretoria.

7. "Black Priests' Manifesto," 2.

8. Mangaliso Mkhatshwa [sic], "Africanisation of the Church," Challenge 5, no. 1 (January–February 1968): 2–4.

9. Rand Daily Mail, 23 January 1970, 15; 8 April 1970, 10.

10. World, 24 February 1970, 14.

11. World, 14 December 1970.

12. Letter from Bishop of Cape Town[?] to Stubbs, 9 December 1971, AB1017 D1 1971–2, 1, HP.

13. Black Justice and Peace Vigilante Committee, "Open Letter on Day of Consecration," 22 October 1972, 2, and Rand Daily Mail, 23 October 1972, pt. 3, F343, KGC.

14. Ernest Baartman, interview by the author, 19 June 2006, Cape Town. So famous was Mokitimi's inaction that the Weekend World—a relatively liberal paper at the time—hailed that "he never used the pulpit as a political platform." See Weekend World, 5 December 1971, 1.

15. "Report: Conference for Black Church Leaders," May 1972, A835 C1, 3–4, 10, HP.

16. Rubin Phillip, interview by the author, 15 December 2005, Durban, South Africa; Malusi Mpumlwana, interview by the author, 9 March 2006, Pretoria. The latter's name represented a disjuncture between his background and that of many other Black Consciousness activists: it is the only one he has ever had, not the result of a change in the 1960s or 1970s. It is also worth noting that not everyone was as sanguine about the positive effects of separatism. Oshadi Mangena moved from the AME to the DRC upon marriage and concluded that little separated the two, save for a bit more movement during the former's services. She went on to criticize the political stance taken by Ethiopian and AME churches, a common charge leveled at African independent churches. See the subsequent discussion on this topic. Oshadi Mangena, interview by the author, 22 November 2005, Johannesburg, South Africa.

17. O. Mangena, interview.

18. C. Mokoka, interview.

19. Steve Biko, I Write What I Like, ed. Aelred Stubbs (1978; repr., London: Bowerdean Publishing, 1996), 59.

20. C. Mokoka, interview; Buti Tlhagale, interview by the author, 23 March 2006, Johannesburg, South Africa.

21. Mangaliso Mkhatshwa, "Africanisation of the Church," Challenge 5, no. 1 (January–February 1968). Pt. 3, F343, 2–4, KGC.

22. "Black Priests' Manifesto," 1.

23. David Bosch detailed debates about mission's end in Witness to the World: The Christian Mission in Theological Perspective (Atlanta, GA: John Knox Press, 1980), 5.

24. Jean Comaroff and John Comaroff, *Of Revelation and Revolution* (Chicago: University of Chicago Press, 1991).

25. Paul Landau, *The Realm of the Word* (Portsmouth, NH: Heinemann, 1995). It is interesting to note that Setiloane made a similar argument in the 1970s, for the same region Landau studied. See the later discussion.

26. J. D. Y. Peel, *Religious Encounter and the Making of the Yoruba* (Bloomington: Indiana University Press, 2000), 9.

27. Tlhagale, interview. Anthropology's appeal might have been obvious, but the image of Africans returning to their roots via European/American academics is problematic. Consider Gabriel Setiloane's study *African Theology: An Introduction* (1986; repr., Cape Town: Lux Verbi, 2000). His major source on "African" tradition was Robert Moffat's *Missionary Labours*; indeed, fully half of his cumulative sources were either by white missionaries or white students of "Bantu religion" (Bengt Sundkler, for example). I am not trying to diminish the value of these sources or his skillful use of them; I do think it is important, however, to keep recent scholarship in mind when approaching his text. After all, if missionaries did "invent" (even unintentionally) African "traditional religions" for purposes of conversion, then hortatory references to them in the 1960s and 1970s are rather problematic. Still, they were used, whatever they were, and beg consideration. To that end, I focus in what follows more on their utility—on the questions they helped to ask—than on the nitty-gritty of their content.

28. Chris Mzoneli, interview by the author, 13 December 2005, Durban, South Africa.

29. Tlhagale, interview.

30. Both Gabriel Setiloane and David Thebehali used the word, and innumerable people employed the sentiment. See Setiloane, *African Theology*, 36; Thebehali, interview by Gwendolyn Carter, 11 February 1972, pt. 1, F24, 11, KGC ; Stanley Ntwasa, "Black Theology as Liberation Theology," 1971, AD1126 D6(a), 1, HP. For another example of this argument, see Wesley Mabuza, "Christianity and the Black Man in South Africa Today," 1971, AD1126 D6(a), 2, HP

31. Disapproval was registered in Ntwasa, "Conference Report," [1971?], AD1126 D6(a), 3, HP. For the paper itself, see Lawrence Zulu, "The 19th Century Missionaries in SA: Their Significance for, and Effect on, Black South Africa—A Black Assessment," AD1126 D6(a), HP.

32. Gabriel Setiloane, "Black Theology," *South African Outlook*, February 1971, pt. 3, F348, 29, KGC.

33. Letter from E. Lynn Cragg, Somerset West, *Pro Veritate*, 15 May 1972, 25; "Claims Rejected," *Challenge*, June–July 1968, pt. 3, F343, 24, KGC.

34. John Mbiti, *African Religions and Philosophy* (New York: Praeger, 1969), 1. In her recent translation of Durkheim, Karen Fields suggested that the early twentieth-century sociologist was particularly well suited to Mbiti's task. Durkheim's argument that all religions shared the same basic core, structure, and function—his early cultural relativism—was a bold statement in an academic world that reserved the term *religion* for those more sophisticated (read whiter)

climes. See Emile Durkheim, *Elementary Forms of Religious Life*, ed. and trans. Karen Fields (New York: Free Press, 1995). David Chidester further argued that comparative religion, as a discipline, was born in the colonial context. See Chidester, *Savage Systems: Colonialism and Comparative Religion in Southern Africa* (Charlottesville: University Press of Virginia, 1996).

35. For Setiloane, see the later discussion. For references to God, see Mbiti, *African Religions and Philosophy*, vii–ix and 29, 30, 35.

36. Mbiti, *African Religions and Philosophy*, 3, 4, 15, 219.

37. [Barney Pityana?], "Old Value Systems and Concepts," December 1971, pt. 3, F748, 4, KGC.

38. Bonganjalo Goba, "Corporate Personality in Israel and in Africa—An Assessment of the Significance of This Concept in South Africa Today," 1971, AD1126 D6(a), 1, HP.

39. Gabriel Setiloane, "Ukubuyisa," *South African Outlook*, March 1973, 36–41.

40. It is unclear when this idea acquired the name by which the people I spoke to called it—*ubuntu*—but the sentiments they describe were well established by the early 1970s. A true African was a "man for others" (Goba, "Corporate Personality"); he or she was imbued with "ubuntu . . . a sense of sharing" (Phillip, interview); an African's identity was predicated on "belonging [which is] the root and essence of being" (Setiloane, *African Theology*); "ubuntu: I am because of others. I live, I exist because they also exist" (Mzoneli, interview); Africa's great gift would be in the realm of "human relationships" (Kenneth Kaunda, *A Humanist in Africa*, ed. Colin Morris [London: Longmans, 1966]); and given the chance, Black Consciousness aspired "to be in a position to bestow upon South Africa the greatest gift possible—a more human face" (Biko, 1971).

41. Mbiti, *African Religions and Philosophy*, 5, 4, 27, 212, 216.

42. Gabriel Setiloane, *Image of God among the Sotho-Tswana* (Rotterdam, the Netherlands: A. A. Balkema, 1976), 230.

43. Mbiti, *African Religions and Philosophy*, 271.

44. It is a bit of digression, but this conclusion suggests another, perhaps even more interesting question: was African Theology even about religion? Although Mbiti and others would undoubtedly bristle at the suggestion, recent scholarship contends that so-called religion was not universal, nor sui generis. Derek Peterson and Darren Walhof, for example, argued that the category was a European construct, which missionaries and colonialists employed to represent African societies as unchanging, to "freeze . . . Africans' political thought" and "rope [them] into conversations about contending principles and dogmas" that Africans would surely lose. Religion, they continued, was thus especially implicated in colonial contests' "sociology of power." Comparative religion was the white man's tool, and Mbiti, Setiloane, and others—with their hard-fought discussions of "God" and systematic studies of traditional religion—had been duped. See Peterson and Walhof, "Rethinking Religion," in *The Invention of Religion: Rethinking Belief in Politics and History*, ed. Derek Peterson and Daren Walhof (New Brunswick, NJ: Rutgers University Press, 2002), 5–7. Paul Landau has offered a more subtle discussion of

this that is kinder to African agents but nonetheless unsettling for proponents of "religion." "Africans did not share the European idea that 'religion' was a discrete category of human activity," he wrote. The category's history began and ended with the missionaries, who trusted that "wrongful beliefs offered a toehold to correct ones" and worked assiduously to isolate and identify the "heathen" elements in African societies that might be swapped out. The missionary contest was where the "it" of religion began—not before. See Landau, "'Religion' and Christian Conversion in African History: A New Model," *Journal of Religious History* 23, no. 1 (1999): 8–30. Also see his *Realm of the Word* for more on this topic.

45. Setiloane, *African Theology*, 56.

46. Mbiti, *African Religions and Philosophy*, 15.

47. Setiloane, *African Theology*, 47.

48. Report of the Committee, pt. 3, F755, 2, KGC.

49. "Practical Application of the Ideology of Black Consciousness," pt. 3, F744, 1, KGC.

50. My use of the term *faith* is influenced by both. The former describes faith as something fantastic but indelible, which leaves its mark on history through the *actions* of the faithful. Faith demands subjectivity, Kierkegaard insisted, and it is not merely belief "but an act of freedom, an expression of will"; see M. Jamie Ferreira, "Faith and the Kierkegaardian Leap," in *The Cambridge Companion to Kierkegaard*, ed. Alistair Hannay and Gordon Marino (Cambridge: Cambridge University Press, 1998), 211. Karen Fields put this another way: "When people finally ask themselves, How long? and answer back, Not long! they are already in motion. And they, too, are doing their best to make the prediction so. They go forward with their empirical analysis, whatever its potential, whatever its limits. But in so doing they are not at all dumb objects of the unreachable, as we all are when we ask, How long will the drought continue? or When will the torrent cease?"; see Fields, *Revival and Rebellion in Colonial Central Africa* (Princeton, NJ: Princeton University Press, 1985), 284.

51. John Sebidi, "Cringing Christianity?" *Challenge*, June–July 1968, pt. 3, F343, 12–14, KGC.

52. Barney Pityana, "What Is Black Consciousness?" AD1126 D6(a), 3, HP.

53. Chidester, *Savage Systems*, 4.

54. These are Desmond Tutu's words, cited in John Allen, *Rabble Rouser for Peace: The Authorized Biography of Desmond Tutu* (New York: Free Press, 2006), 48. Of course, we should note Tutu's rather problematic contention that rectangular houses were "normal."

55. Manas Buthelezi, "African Theology and Black Theology: The Search for a Method," Acc. 153, BT, 2, UNISA.

56. Thebehali, interview.

57. Cited in David Bosch, "Currents and Crosscurrents in South African Black Theology," *Journal of Religion in Africa*, no. 6 (1974): 7.

58. "AICA Theological Correspondence Course," pamphlet, 1972/1973, AC623 3.1, 11, HP. There has been, of course, a great deal of debate regarding independent churches' perceived apolitical ways. Jean Comaroff, for example, has argued that

independent churches were in fact political, that the separation and celebration of indigenous theological perspective left a political footprint. Fields also argued that even the most millenarian of movements could be highly political. For our purposes here, however, and for Black Consciousness's purposes in history, politics might be more conventionally defined. In general, AICs did not take an overt political stance; indeed, some, notably the Zionist Christian Church, were profoundly otherworldly and therefore in direct contrast to South African Black Theology's revised eschatology, as described in chapters 6 and 9. For more on independent churches, see Comaroff, *Body of Power, Spirit of Resistance* (Chicago: University of Chicago Press, 1985); Absolom Vilakazi, *Shembe* (Johannesburg, South Africa: Skotaville, 1986); and David Chidester, *Religions of South Africa* (New York: Routledge, 1992). It is also worth noting that the theological materials prepared by the decidedly political Christian Institute for the African Independent Church Association made no mention of politics whatsoever.

59. Joseph Washington, *Black Religion* (Boston: Beacon Press, 1964), 1.

60. Ibid., 21.

61. James Cone, *My Soul Looks Back* (Maryknoll, NY: Orbis Books, 1986), 39.

62. "Black Power: Statement by the National Committee of Negro Churchmen," 31 July 1966, in *Black Theology: A Documentary History*, ed. James Cone and Gayraud Wilmore (Maryknoll, NY: Orbis Books, 1979), 26–27.

63. For a closer reading of Cone, see my "Liberating the Black Messiah," *Maryland Historian* 29 (2005): 23–49. My goal here is to show the development of Cone's thought vis-à-vis the practice of theology and to demonstrate its overlaps and disconnects with both secular theology and African Theology. For more direct point-counterpoint discussions on South African Black Theology, see chapter 6, as well as my *Maryland Historian* article. The argument here proceeds from Cone's first book, *Black Theology and Black Power* (Minneapolis, MN: Seabury Press, 1969). For more, see Cone, *A Black Theology of Liberation* (Philadelphia: Lippincott, 1970), and Cone, *My Soul Looks Back.*

64. Cone, *Black Theology and Black Power*, 1, 7, 9.

65. Ibid., 14, 28, 33.

66. Ibid., 17, 1.

67. Ibid., 35–36.

68. Ibid., 69, 49, 51–52.

69. Ibid., 150, 100–103, 52. Cone's discussion of Judaism is obviously problematic because it excludes the prophets—especially given the use of Jewish prophetic scripture in the Gospels to prove that Jesus of Nazareth was in fact the Christ.

70. John Mbiti, "An African Views American Black Theology," in *Black Theology: A Documentary History*, ed. James Cone and Gayraud Wilmore (Maryknoll, NY: Orbis Books, 1979), 477–82. The article cited here was originally published in 1974, but many of its ideas circulated during the early 1970s. See various issues of *Pro Veritate* during 1972, for instance.

71. As if to underscore this point, during this same period Wilmore published *Black Religion and Black Radicalism* (Garden City, NY: Doubleday, 1972), a historical study of liberation theology (if you will) in African American history.

72. James Cone and Gayraud Wilmore, "The Future . . . and African Theology," *Pro Veritate*, 15 January 1972, 3.

73. Cone, *My Soul Looks Back*, 97–98. It is interesting to note how this played out in 1970s America, with increasing conflicts between radical and cultural liberation movements, the latter of which typically claimed some degree of African identity. Since the late 1960s' radical effluence, politics in the United States have definitely tended toward the cultural/identity politics side of the spectrum and away from the radical change side. See Peniel Joseph, *Waiting 'til the Midnight Hour: A Narrative History of Black Power in America* (New York: Henry Holt, 2006), for more on this topic.

74. David Attwell, *Rewriting Modernity: Studies in Black South African Literary History* (Athens: Ohio University Press, 2006), 144.

75. Untitled poll, 1973, AB2414 B3.1, 2, HP.

76. Desmond Tutu, "Black Theology/African Theology — Soulmates or Antagonists?" in *Black Theology: A Documentary History*, ed. James Cone and Gayraud Wilmore (Maryknoll, NY: Orbis Books, 1979), 490.

77. Buthelezi, "African Theology and Black Theology," 2.

78. [George Motlhabi and Steve Biko?], "Introductory Paper: The Dissolution of the UCM and the Need for an Independent Black Theology Future Structure," [1972?], A2176 8, 13, HP.

79. Ibid., 11. The language here is Manas Buthelezi's; "wholesomeness" was probably "wholeness," a concept that Buthelezi developed to "Africanize" American Black Theology. Buthelezi, interview by the author, 8 November 2005, Johannesburg, South Africa.

80. Biko, *I Write What I Like*, 45.

81. Motlhabi and Biko, "Introductory Paper," 8.

82. Biko, *I Write What I Like*, 31.

83. Cone, *Black Theology and Black Power*, 115.

CHAPTER 6: THE SOUTH AFRICAN VOICE

1. Letter from Stubbs to Bishop of Kimberley and Kuruman, 21 August 1970, 1–2; "Ntwasa: First Year Report," 1; and "Ntwasa: Second Year Report," 2, all in AB2414 D2 (Ntwasa), HP. Also see Mokgethi Motlhabi, interview by the author, 3 March 2006, Pretoria.

2. Colin Collins, interview by the author, 19 October 2005, Johannesburg, South Africa.

3. Motlhabi, interview. Ntwasa was updating John 14:2 — "In my father's house, there are many rooms."

4. For more on Ntwasa and the dictates of relevance, see my "Being Relevant: Towards a History of Political Ethics in South Africa," paper presented at American Historical Association Annual Meeting, New York, NY, January 5, 2009.

5. Letter from Stubbs to Bishop of Kimberley and Kuruman.

6. Justice Moloto, "President's Address, Encounter '70," 10 July 1970, AD1126 A4d, 1, 3–5, HP.

7. As numerous scholars have shown, this was not the first time that South African Christians translated African American Christianity to suit their own purposes.

8. Letter from Ntwasa to Cone, 7 January 1971, AD1126 D6(a), HP.

9. Stanley Ntwasa, "National Seminar on Black Theology," AD1126 D6(a), 1, HP.

10. Manas Buthelezi's invitation, for example, asked him to write on "a theology of hope for South Africa" and suggested that he read Jürgen Moltmann's and Ruben Alves's work on the subject. See Letter from UCM to Buthelezi, [February 1971?], AD1126 D6(a), HP. See also chapter 9.

11. Basil Moore, "What Is Black Theology?" 1971, pt. 3, F929 UCM, 3, KGC.

12. *Pro Veritate*, 15 April 1972, 2–3. Their protest recalled Bennett's (and Khoapa's) discussion of love, in chapter 3, as well as the famed slogan from American Black Power: "Too much love, too much love, nothing kills a nigger like too much love."

13. *Rand Daily Mail*, 23 March 1971, 13.

14. *Pro Veritate*, 15 September 1971, 8. The Transvaal regional seminar's statement on Black Theology was published in a variety of media after its June 1971 meeting. For instance, Bokwe Mafuna was still a reporter at the *Rand Daily Mail* at the time, and his report on the meeting managed to get the entire statement into the paper, 10 June 1971, 3. It was also published, in its entirety, in *Pro Veritate* in mid-July, as well as reproduced in the annual reports of both UCM and SASO.

15. Motlhabi, interview.

16. *World*, 11 March 1971, 4.

17. John Robinson, *Honest to God* (London: SCM Press, 1963), 26.

18. The records of the Snyman Commission, which investigated Black Consciousness activities at the University of the North in 1974 (see chapter 8), contained a flowchart detailing a conspiracy: from SASO to Black Theology to terrorism and an assault on *die Afrikaner volk* and *kerk* (Afrikaner people and church); K318, box 1, NAP.

19. "Minutes of the Executive Committee," 22 March 1971, pt. 3, F929, 2, KGC.

20. This was the flurry of activity that provoked the *Rand Daily Mail's* "atheist" cartoon discussed in chapter 4.

21. *Rand Daily Mail*, 12 March 1971, 1.

22. Reported in the *World*, 14 March 1971, 12.

23. *Rand Daily Mail*, 12 March 1971, 1.

24. Despite being a proud Zulu from a small town, he did admit its potential role "in the cities especially, [where] black people increasingly find themselves insecure and without roots." This and the preceding quotations are from A. Zulu, "Notes on a 'Seminar on Black Theology' at St. Ansgar's Lutheran Mission, Roodepoort, Jo'burg, March 8–12, 1971," KCM 98/3/12, 1–3, Killie Campbell Library, University of KwaZulu-Natal (hereafter cited as KC).

25. *Pro Veritate*, March 1973, 13.

26. A. Zulu, "Notes," 1–3.

27. Basil Moore, "Towards a Black Theology," AD1126 D6(a), 2, HP.

28. Ibid., 1, 4.

29. Ibid., 8.

30. If Christ's world was this heated, then why was theology traditionally so calm? Moore and others blamed Paul. Paul had created Christianity the religion in a context foreign to Christ. Whereas Jesus was a colonized Jew, Paul was a citizen of Rome, a former tax collector with recourse to the system. Therefore, Moore said, "we should be very cautious using Paul as reliable interpreter of Jesus' attitude to the State" ("Towards a Black Theology," 4). In his study *Jesus before Christianity* (Maryknoll, NY: Orbis Books, 1976), the South African theologian Albert Nolan made a similar argument. Yet it is worth noting that the scholarship on the historical Jesus makes the exact opposite argument. Donald Akenson, for example, has contended that Paul's writings are the historical source par excellence. Paul was the only early "Christian" to write at before the destruction of the Second Temple, when "Christianity" (which Akenson called the "Yeshua-faith") was only one of the many subfaiths within "Judahism." The preponderance of quotation marks in the previous sentences hints at the intrigue of Akenson's argument. For more, see Akenson, *Saint Saul: The Skeleton Key to the Historical Jesus* (New York: Oxford University Press, 2002). The question of Christ himself will be considered later in this chapter.

31. Moore, "Towards a Black Theology," 15–17.

32. Ibid., 9.

33. And, of course, there is the question of economics: Christ did not want to see the poor supplant the rich, Moore argued, because "that would have meant accepting that the system of private capital is right, fair and the best for just and liberating human relationships" ("Towards a Black Theology," 18).

34. Ibid., 19.

35. See 1970 and 1971 correspondence from, among others, David Russell and Theodore Simpson in AD1126 D6(a), HP.

36. Letter from Morlan to Moore, 3 February 1971, pt. 3, F929, 1–3, KGC.

37. Stanley Ntwasa, "Conference Report," draft, [1971?], AD1126 D6(a), 2, HP.

38. It is important to note who made this point and when. In early 1971, Ntwasa and the UCM were circulating not only Black Theology and ideas about women's liberation (as seen in chapter 2) but also papers and sentiments that linked both subjects. One paper, entitled "Black Women and the Black Theology" (no author [Basil Moore?], AD1126, unfiled, HP), made this most explicit, and other UCM officials made more subtle references. Justice Moloto, UCM president, offered one of the subtle remarks in a presentation to a group of African church people during this period. South Africans faced many better-known forms of discrimination, he explained, but they needed to be careful to be sensitive to gender discrimination as well. After all, he asked the audience, "do you need strong muscles to be a Bishop?"; see "Notes for IDAMASA Conference," AD1126 A4, [1970–71?], 4, HP.

39. Stanley Ntwasa, "Comments on Cone's Tape," pt. 3, F349, 1–2, KGC.

40. Drake Tshenkeng, "Black and Concerned," undated, AD1126 D4, 1–3, HP.

41. Steve Biko, *I Write What I Like*, ed. Aelred Stubbs (1978; repr., London: Bowerdean Publishing, 1996), 49.

42. Stanley Ntwasa, "The Concept of the Church in Black Theology," 1971, 2, and Ntwasa, "Black Theology as Liberation Theology," 1, both in AD1126 D6(a), HP.

43. Ernest Baartman, "Black Consciousness," *Pro Veritate*, March 1973, 4. In our conversation, Baartman gave the example of a German teacher he had at the University of Chicago Divinity School to demonstrate the power of self-affirmation. This man knew that he did not speak perfect English and was confident enough not to care; when the appropriate English word failed him, he reverted to German and trusted that his students would make themselves understand, rather than expect him to bend over backward to make their task easier. Black Consciousness, Baartman told me, meant blacks finding similar confidence to do the same. Ernest Baartman, interview by the author, 19 June 2006, Cape Town. Recall that Motlhabi described Ntwasa in a similar way, as did Stubbs. It is telling how highly activists of this generation valued self-confidence and commented on those few who manifested it.

44. Moore, "Towards a Black Theology," 9.

45. Mamphela Ramphele, *Across Boundaries* (New York: Feminist Press at CUNY, 1996), 57.

46. James Matthews and Gladys Thomas, *Cry Rage!* (Johannesburg, South Africa: SPROCAS, 1972), 48.

47. *Drum*, October 1971, 59.

48. Matthews and Thomas, *Cry Rage!* 69.

49. Interview with Nkosazana Zuma, pt. 1, F41, 5, KGC.

50. Interview with Deborah Matshoba, in *Biko Lives! Contesting the Legacies of Stephen Biko*, ed. Andile Mngxitama, Amanda Alexander, and Nigel Gibson (New York: Palgrave Macmillan, 2008), 275–84. Mamphela Ramphele also revealed her youthful predilection for such "exceedingly short pants"; see Ramphele, *Across Boundaries*, 58. Much has been written about the racially freighted history and culture of fashion and cosmetics in southern Africa. See especially Timothy Burke, *Lifebuoy Men, Lux Women: Commodification, Consumption and Cleanliness in Modern Zimbabwe* (Durham, NC: Duke University Press, 1996), and Lynn Thomas, "The Modern Girl and Racial Respectability in 1930s South Africa," *Journal of African History* 47, no. 3 (2006): 461–90. See also Thomas, "Skin Lighteners in South Africa: Transnational Commodities and Technologies of the Self," in *Shades of Difference: Why Skin Color Matters*, ed. Evelyn Nakano Glenn (Palo Alto, CA: Stanford University Press, 2009), 188–209.

51. *Drum*, December 1971, 8.

52. Here and in chapter 3, I have suggested that women were seen as being as capable as men, even if Black Consciousness–era activists typically rejected explicitly women's liberation claims. Yet as I will show later in this chapter and in chapter 9, this discursive equality had definite limits, which were soon made abundantly clear.

53. Ntwasa, "Black Theology as Liberation Theology," 1.

54. Manas Buthelezi, "The Relevance of Black Theology," pt. 3, F350, 199, KGC.

55. Manas Buthelezi, "Solidarity as a Means to Peaceful Co-existence," pt. 3, F350, 14, KGC. The image is in *Pro Veritate*, January 1974, back cover.

56. Bonganjalo Goba, in *Pro Veritate*, 15 September 1971, 9–10.

57. This distinction was harder for some to maintain. Moore had already demonstrated this; after all, if Christians were those who struggled and Jesus represented blacks, then he seemed to grant special virtue to blackness. "God has invariably identified himself with the poor, the downtrodden," a reader wrote the *World*, and even though "no one could ever see the . . . complexion of God and live to tell about it," the fact that "Black Africans as a race have suffered the poverty of Jesus' background" suggested that the Son's "face" might be known; *World*, 19 February 1975, 8. If black was beautiful because God had made it so and if blackness was in fact the image of God, then, as UCM members had debated as early as 1970, was God black? Clive McBride, a Coloured minister and Black Theology proponent, recognized the inherent dangers in identifying God with a particular race. "At times I feel morally and racially superior," he admitted, and "I fall victim of nationalist and supremist [*sic*] concepts in my own being—a concept I usually detest in others." This was not how he wanted to feel; rather, he said, God's love ought to mean "the maximum potential of any living Being on his own ability without colour." Yet still, the temptation was there. He cited a poem with a politically current nativity scene: "In silence stands by / the three wise men kneeling / in reverence and prayer / no dark thoughts of colour"—love irrespective of race—"no European near"—simply because whites were nowhere to be found. Colourless-ness was his goal, but in this account of Jesus's birth, it was attained because one race had not been invited to attend. See McBride, "On Seeing Christ as Black," AD1126 D6(a), 2–3, HP.

58. Buthelezi, "Relevance of Black Theology," 198.

59. Barney Pityana, "What Is Black Consciousness? And How Is Black Theology Related to It?" AD1126 D6(a), 3, HP.

60. Motlhabi, interview.

61. Simon Maimela, interview by the author, 1 February 2006, Pretoria.

62. Ibid. Some proponents of Black Theology did use aspects of Jones's critique: an SACC leader, for example, employed Jones's language to explain that whereas white Christianity reflected the "diabolic western concept of divine racism," Black Theology "corrected" the faith. See Ngakane, "The Challenge of Black Theology to the Present South Africa," 6 March 1976, pt. 3, F350, 1–2, KGC.

63. Mark Chapman, *Christianity on Trial* (Maryknoll, NY: Orbis Books, 1996), 24.

64. James Cone, *My Soul Looks Back* (Maryknoll, NY: Orbis Books, 1986), 63.

65. Allan Boesak, interview with the author, 15 June 2006, Somerset West, South Africa.

66. Allan Boesak, *Farewell to Innocence: A Socio-ethical Study of Black Theology and Black Power* (Johannesburg, South Africa: Ravan Press, 1977), 38–39.

67. Recent work has highlighted the messianic thought and the spread of Garveyism in South Africa. See Robert Vinson, "'Sea Kaffirs': 'American Negroes' and the Gospel of Garveyism in Early 20th Century Cape Town," *Journal of African History* 47, no. 2 (2006): 281–303. The description of Garvey as "Black Moses"

was widespread, and significantly, in recent discourse (such as the popular documentary *Amandla!*), Mandela was repeatedly invoked as "our Moses."

68. William Jeremiah Moses, *Black Messiahs and Uncle Toms: Social and Literary Manipulations of a Religious Myth* (University Park: Pennsylvania State University Press, 1982), and Michael Eric Dyson, *I May Not Get There with You: The True Martin Luther King, Jr.* (New York: Free Press, 2000).

69. Dwight Hopkins, *Black Theology USA and South Africa* (Maryknoll, NY: Orbis Books, 1989), 38.

70. Manas Buthelezi, interview by the author, 8 November 2005, Johannesburg, South Africa.

71. Tau Mokoka, interview by the author, 28 November 2005, Pretoria.

72. *World*, 19 March 1973, 12. Graham's visit still resonates. In the recent Geraldine Naidoo play *Hoot*, one character recalls watching an Afrikaans audience respond to Graham's claim. "You would have thought [popular Afrikaans pop singer] Steve Hofmeyr died," he explained. At least one reader of the *World* disagreed with Graham's assertion. In a very odd letter, "Alebone" wrote that "Jesus was certainly White. However, a word of caution here. To be accepted by both colour sides alike, where ought an influential man like Jesus Christ to have been born? Neither side? No sir, it had to be one side or the other—that is indisputable. One had to be either white or black, and Jesus had been born white." That being said, "Alebone" offered the disclaimer that Jesus "never approved of the injustices discharged by his race"; *World*, 19 November 1973, 4. On the subject of popular culture, we should also note Mark Dornford-May's 2006 film *Son of Man*, in which Jesus is a Cape Flats–dwelling umXhosa.

73. *World*, 27 February 1974, 1. See also http://www.soweto.co.za/html/p_scully. htm, accessed on 20 May 2009. The painting, of course, graces the cover of this book.

74. Albert Cleage, *The Black Messiah* (1968; repr., Trenton, NJ: Africa World Press, 1991), 42–43. For more on Cleage, see Thomas Sugrue, *Sweet Land of Liberty: The Forgotten Struggle for Civil Rights in the North* (New York: Random House, 2008).

75. James Cone, *Black Theology and Black Power* (Minneapolis, MN: Seabury Press, 1969), 68. This language pleased no one entirely, whether advocates of the "raceless" Christ or less abstractly inclined black theologians. See Cone, *My Soul Looks Back*, 53.

76. Boesak, *Farewell to Innocence*, 42 (italics in original).

77. Steve Biko, "Black Consciousness and the Quest for True Humanity," in his *I Write What I Like*, ed. Aelred Stubbs (1978; repr., London: Bowerdean Publishing, 1996), 94.

78. Ibid., 98.

79. Basil Moore, "Worship Happenings," *Pro Veritate*, 15 September 1968, 16.

80. Biko, "Black Consciousness and the Quest," 97–98.

81. Biko, "Some African Cultural Concepts," in his *I Write What I Like*, 47.

82. Mashwabada Mayatula, "Presidential Address," December 1972, pt. 3, F282, 1–5, KGC.

83. Nkwenkwe Nkomo, "Memorandum," [1973?], pt. 3, F285, 1, KGC.

84. We should note that Farisani's aggressively postured black man was accompanied by a "young beautiful black woman just about to give birth to a child." (T. S. Farisani, "National Congress Address," 13 December 1975, 4, pt. 3, F286, KGC.) This pairing—of virile, aggressive manhood and fertile womanhood—featured prominently in Black Consciousness gendering as politics unfolded in the 1970s. See chapter 9.

85. Farisani, "National Congress Address," 1–4.

86. "Report on the 1970 SASO Conference," pt. 3, F744, 4, KGC. It is worth noting that dissenting voices were heard. A reader of the *World*, for instance, urged blacks instead to "stand back and give God chance to work on our behalf"; *World*, 11 December 1972, 4.

87. Ntwasa, "The Concept of the Church," 1–4.

88. Anthony Mabona, "White Worship and Black People," AD1126 D6(a), 1, 3, HP.

89. Boesak, *Farewell to Innocence*, 16, 17, 74, 96.

90. Cedric Mayson, interview by the author, 27 February 2006, Johannesburg, South Africa.

91. Bokwe Mafuna, interview by the author, 30 November 2005, Johannesburg, South Africa.

92. John Rees to Peter Randall, 2 August 1972, A835 C9, HP.

93. Biko to Russell, [1974?], pt. 3, F754, 3–6, KGC.

94. Motlhabi, interview.

95. Biko to Russell, 6.

96. Buthelezi, interview.

97. Achille Mbembe and Gayatri Spivak, "Religion, Politics, Theology," *boundary 2* 34, no. 2 (2007): 149–70.

CHAPTER 7: "I WRITE WHAT I LIKE"

1. "Black Community Programmes Year Report 1972," pt. 3, F270, 3, KGC.

2. Steve Biko, *I Write What I Like*, ed. Aelred Stubbs (1978; repr., London: Bowerdean Publishing, 1996), 48.

3. "Literacy Project," pt. 3, F928, 2, KGC. Recent literary theory links "voice"— with its ability to narrate and articulate the desires and experiences of the self— with the spread of a supposedly universal discourse of human rights, the most essential of which is, of course, freedom of speech. In the South African context, the power of speech was fundamental to the conception and methodology of the Truth and Reconciliation Commission, with its argument that victims narrating and perpetrators confessing would hasten reconciliation and renewal. See Elizabeth Anker, "Fictions of Dignity: Human Rights and the Post-colonial Novel," paper presented at Cornell University, 11 March 2008, Ithaca, NY; see also Kay Schaffer and Sidonie Smith, *Human Rights and Narrated Lives: The Ethics of Recognition* (New York: Palgrave Macmillan, 2004).

4. Zithulele Cindi, interview by the author, 13 March 2006, Johannesburg, South Africa; Harry Nengwekhulu, interview by the author, 20 March 2006, Pretoria. For the importance of debating clubs, see also Clive Glaser, *Bo-Tsotsi: The*

Youth Gangs of Soweto (Portsmouth, NH: Heinemann, 2000), chap. 7, and Isabel Hofmeyr, "Reading Debating/Debating Writing: The Case of the Lovedale Debating Society, or Why Mandela Quotes Shakespeare," in *Africa's Hidden Histories: Everyday Literacy and Making the Self,* ed. Karin Barber (Bloomington: Indiana University Press, 2006), 258–77.

5. "Memo: On University Students Work and Study Projects in the Transkei," 3/68, AD1126 D5 (a)(i), 2, HP.

6. Ibid., and "The Educational Method of the Literacy Project of the UCM," AD1126 D5 (a)(i), 1, HP. This same file includes, among other essays on Freire, Thomas Sanders, "The Paulo Freire Method [of] Literacy Training and Conscientization," June 1968, an essay written by an American education student that the UCM sought to distribute, only to be stopped by an American organization's copyright claim. As elsewhere, South African activists responded simply by restating the article's insights in their own voice. See Letter from Moore to Director, American Universities Field Staff, Inc., 15 December 1970, and letter from Spitzer to Moore, 20 January 1971.

7. Anne Hope, interview by the author, 24 May 2006, Cape Town.

8. Biko, *I Write What I Like,* 42.

9. Paulo Freire, *Cultural Action for Freedom* (1970; repr., New York: Penguin, 1972), 42, 51.

10. SASO activists ran not only with Freire's term but also with his method of education as expressed in *Pedagogy of the Oppressed.* Peter Jones, a Coloured activist in the Eastern Cape, for example, referred to the book as "the bible as written by Paulo Freire. . . . It used to be the standard book. You would find it everywhere and everybody read it"; pt. 1, F13, 6, KGC.

11. Hope, interview.

12. Malusi Mpumlwana, interview by the author, 9 March 2006, Pretoria.

13. Testimony of Aubrey Mokoape, reel 4, 4828, AD1719, HP. Walter Rodney's short but insightful study, *The Groundings with My Brothers* (London: Bogle-L'Ouverture Publications, 1969), demonstrates how Caribbean activists tried a similar approach.

14. Freire, *Cultural Action for Freedom,* 67.

15. M. Mpumlwana, interview. It is a bit of a stretch but significant that this argument is still playing out today regarding the Mbeki government's AIDS policy. There is a bit of Black Consciousness in the government's convoluted stance: that charity (in this case from Western drug companies and the like) is not enough and that the people need to build the capacity to solve problems themselves and will never be able to do this if they remain dependent on the wealthy West. Then, however, ostensibly pragmatic NGOs and others are arguing that such theories distract from the real-time struggle.

16. Clement Mokoka, interview by the author, 19 December 2005, Phokeng, South Africa.

17. Testimony of Aubrey Mokoape, reel 4, 4829, AD1719, HP.

18. M. Mpumlwana, interview.

19. Testimony of Strini Moodley, reel 7, 7335, AD1719, HP.

20. Paulo Freire, *Pedagogy of the Oppressed* (1970; repr., New York: Continuum, 1993), 53.

21. Testimony of Strini Moodley.

22. Nengwekhulu, interview.

23. Oshadi Mangena, interview by the author, 22 November 2005, Johannesburg, South Africa. I asked her if these "three c's" were a response to the British Empire's famed three: Christianity, commerce, and civilization. She claimed it was just a coincidence.

24. Hope, interview.

25. Dan Mogale, interview by the author, 6 December 2005, Pretoria, and Dan Mogale and Simon Mashiangwako, interview by the author, 20 December 2005, Pretoria.

26. Vic Mafungo, "Some Aspects of Community Development," undated, pt. 3, F746, 9, KGC.

27. Shun Chetty, interview by SANA, 1979, Gabarone, Botswana, pt. 1, F6, 9, KGC.

28. Mosibudi Mangena, interview by the author, 6 December 2005, Pretoria.

29. Testimony of Simon Farisani, reel 8, 8777, AD1719, HP.

30. Mogale and Mashiangwako, interview.

31. Testimony of Xola Nuse, *S. v. Molobi*, vol. 1, 65, AD1899, HP.

32. Hope, interview; for the PRESO programs, see especially Mosibudi Mangena, *On Your Own: The Evolution of Black Consciousness in South Africa/Azania* (Florida Hills, South Africa: Vivlia, 1989), 25–30. The literacy programs left little evidence in the various archives that I consulted, and my efforts to probe them further met with little success. When I asked Clement Mokoka about the success of the PRESO program that his church had helped to run, he noted only that "everybody that we've trained we always found those people being very useful"; C. Mokoka, interview. Among the precious few documents on the programs was a simple primer in the UCM files; entitled "My Brother!" it described an African man who was coming home from work, robbed, and left for dead. No one offered him assistance—until a "drunk coloured" happened by, fortified him with some brandy, and found help. The primer thus taught both language and Black Consciousness's message of black unity. See "My Brother!" UCM, AD1126 D(a)(iii), HP. For much more on this topic, see Leslie Hadfield, "Restoring Human Dignity and Building Self-Reliance: Youth, Women and Churches and Black Consciousness Community Development, South Africa, 1969–1977" (PhD diss., Michigan State University, 2010). See also Anne Hope's assessment of the same in *Profiles in Diversity: Women in the New South Africa*, ed. Patricia Romero (East Lansing: Michigan State University Press, 1998), 171–76.

33. Freire, *Cultural Action for Freedom*, 66.

34. This is especially well documented in the case of poetry. See, for example, chapters in Anne McClintock, *Imperial Leather: Race, Gender and Sexuality in the Colonial Contest* (New York: Routledge, 1995); David Attwell, *Rewriting*

Modernity: Studies in Black South African Literary History (Athens: Ohio University Press, 2006); and Michael Chapman's oeuvre, especially *Soweto Poetry: Literary Perspectives* (Scottsville, South Africa: University of KwaZulu-Natal Press, 2007). A recent study that addresses these themes is Bhekizizwe Peterson, "Culture, Resistance and Representation," *Road to Democracy in South Africa*, vol. 2 (Pretoria: UNISA, 2007).

35. *The Spear Lives On*, joint publication of the P.E.T. and Shiqomo, September–October [1974?], A2176 14, 2, HP. The demeaning reference to "comical dramas" was doubtlessly aimed as Gibson Kente's, whose occasionally escapist fare was all the rage in the early 1970s. The aesthetic concerns expressed here neatly overlaid with Fanon's, as I briefly considered in chapter 3.

36. Fanyana Mazibuko, interview by the author, 18 November 2005, Johannesburg, South Africa.

37. Thoko Mpumlwana, interview by the author, 22 March 2006, Pretoria.

38. Matthews became prominent with 1972's *Cry Rage*. These apt verses come from a 1981 collection, recently reprinted in Matthews, *Cry Rage! The Odyssey of a Dissident Poet* (Cape Town: Realities, 2006), n.p.

39. Richard Rive, "Poetry in the South African Situation," *Pro Veritate*, March 1975, 22. Rive's words were harsh but, I think, not ill chosen. Much Black Consciousness poetry has failed to inspire more than a superficially historicist reading or offer any historical evidence of Black Consciousness's spreading message. There were, of course, exceptions—Glenn Masokoane's "Black Nana Arise!" was so lyrical as to be almost entirely inscrutable—but Neelan Pillay's "Barefeet" was fairly representative:

> Like the millions of cells that cover my feet
> Are the black cuts on my feet
> Over broken glass, stones and thorns did it travel
> In Winter it did bleed red blood
> like my heart bleeds white hate
> My feet wishes for shoes
> My heart wishes Freedom
> Many died fighting for my shoes
> I don't know exactly when I am going to get my shoes
> It might be the next day
> It might be the next week
> It might be the next year
> But it's definitely before the turn of the century.

> (*The Spear Lives On*, 7)

The same aesthetic judgment might be levied against the fiction from the era; works such as Wally Serote's *To Every Birth Its Blood*, Sipho Sepamla's *Ride on the Whirlwind*, and Mbulelo Mzamane's *Children of Soweto* are more history-by-other-means than transcendent works of fiction. As David Attwell has noted,

Njabulo Ndebele's *Fools and Other Stories* is an exception to this rule, and by concentrating on his characters and lyrical description, Ndebele left himself open to the "accusation of fiddling while the townships burned"; Attwell, *Rewriting Modernity*, 183. Rita Barnard has recently argued that Miriam Tladi also managed to write beyond this aesthetic in her late 1970s work *Muriel at Metropolitan;* see Barnard, *Apartheid and Beyond: South African Writers and the Politics of Place* (Oxford: Oxford University Press, 2007), chap. 5.

40. "There were [once] flutes humming musical patterns in unison with the streams of Africa and the sitar was rising and falling in cadence with the torrential rains of India," he wrote. See Strini Moodley, "Black Consciousness and the Black Artist and the Emerging Black Culture," *SASO Newsletter*, May–June 1972, 20.

41. Andew Apter, *The Pan-African Nation: Oil and the Spectacle of Culture in Nigeria* (Chicago: University of Chicago Press, 2005); Olaniyan, "Thinking Afro-futures: Epistemic Histories," paper presented at Cornell University, 6 March 2008, Ithaca, NY. In a recent article, Barbara Weinstein urged historians to think their way back from the "cultural turn" and instead strive to find the language to discuss politics and economic inequality in new ways. See Weinstein, "Presidential Address—Developing Inequality," *American Historical Review* 111, no. 1 (2008): 1–18. See also the *SASO Newsletter*, June 1971, 14. For Fanon and culture, see chapter 3. One way in which Black Consciousness artists did move through time was by referring to what they increasingly saw as the "sacred" history of past suffering. In 1973, for example, a SASO-sponsored art show near Pretoria featured "Sharpeville," a painting by a twenty-one-year-old Sowetan that depicted "one young man, a victim who was slowly dying from a bullet in his head." The artist apparently used his own blood for the painting—"sucked from a puncture made in my arm"; *World*, 26 July 1973, 12–13.

42. This was recorded in the *Rand Daily Mail*, 17 July 1976, 4.

43. Craig Charney's work demonstrates how Black Consciousness organizations benefited from the expanding literate, urban black public to spread their ideas, which helps explain why poetry and theater were such prominent parts of the movement. See Charney, "Black Power, White Press," University of the Witwatersrand African Studies Centre, 1993.

44. Tau Mokoka, interview by the author, 28 November 2005, Pretoria; C. Mokoka, interview; O. Mangena, interview; Mogale and Mashiangwako, interview.

45. The *World* counted numerous standing ovations; 2 October 1973, 4.

46. *World*, 27 November 1973, 2.

47. Mthuli ka Shezi, "Shanti," in Robert Kavanagh, ed., *South African People's Plays* (London: Heinemann, 1981), 72.

48. *S. v. Molobi*, vol. 1, 35, 191, AD1899, HP; *World*, 6 November 1973, 5.

49. *World*, 27 November 1973, 2.

50. Cited in Kavanagh, *South African People's Plays*, 65.

51. *S. v. Cooper*, reel 10, testimony of Dan O'Meara, 3–4, and reel 8, 7884, AD1719, HP; For more on the circumstances that structured this legal encounter, see chapter 8.

52. From a PET newsletter, undated, *S. v. Cooper*, reel 10, annexure 9, AD1719, HP.

53. Kavanagh, *South African People's Plays*, 77.

54. Thabo Molewa, "On Black Consciousness," undated, 6.2.14, A2177, HP.

CHAPTER 8: THE AGE OF POLITICS

1. James Brennan, "Blood Enemies: Exploitation and Urban Citizenship in the Nationalist Political Thought of Tanzania, 1958–1975," *Journal of African History* 47, no. 3 (2006): 391.

2. *SASO Newsletter*, May–June 1972, 18.

3. Malusi Mpumlwana, interview by the author, 9 March 2006, Pretoria.

4. And various informants claimed that Biko was trying to negotiate a rapprochement between the groups when he was arrested and killed in 1977.

5. Barney Pityana, interview by the author, 1 February 2006, Pretoria.

6. *SASO Newsletter*, September 1971, 1. It is worth noting that as publications director at the time, Biko was most likely the author of this editorial. This editorial exemplified what writing could lend itself to discursive authority; its treatment of Banda resounded with unattributed critiques, such as "someone commented in a heated argument about Banda's visit" or "someone remarked the other day, 'what's so wonderful about this?'"

7. *S. v. Molobi*, 432, AD1899, HP. For Sobukwe, see *S. v. Cooper*, reel 8, 8714, AD1719, HP, when Nkwenkwe Nkomo hailed the PAC leader as a true "black son of Azania." For more on Sobukwe, see the discussion later in this chapter.

8. Letter from Wycliffe Palweni to Justice Moloto re: SASO formation school, 9/10/70, AD1126 J6, HP; "Freedom Struggles of the Past—What Can We Learn from Them to Enhance Grass-Roots Involvement," Transvaal Formation School, September 1974, pt. 3, F756, 1–2, KGC.

9. Testimony of Eric Molobi, *S. v. Molobi*, 402, AD1899, HP.

10. This revision of the coming-of-age narrative was especially prominent among younger activists who joined the ANC after 1976. Nkosazana Zuma described it this way: "I see Black Consciousness as something essential in development, but I also see it as just like a child who is crawling, who has to walk and run and do other things"; pt. 1, F41, 29, KGC.

11. Steve Biko, *I Write What I Like*, ed. Aelred Stubbs (1978; repr., London: Bowerdean Publishing, 1996), 20. Bennie Khoapa also offered this critique, as did Nthato Motlana, who nonetheless remained an ANC supporter even while active in both the PAC and, during the 1970s, the BPC.

12. Report of National Formation School, pt. 3, F752, 13, KGC. It is harder to find a coherent critique of the PAC than of the ANC, beyond the former's failure to include Indians and Coloureds. Robert Sobukwe loomed large in Black Consciousness circles once he was released from Robben Island and banned to Kimberley in 1970. This was especially so two years later when his prominent Black Consciousness–supporting nephew, Stanley Ntwasa, was also banned and joined him there. Various activists recounted trips to visit "Prof." as a favorite initiation into political activism. (For examples, see Tom Manthata, interview by the author,

18 November 2005, Johannesburg, South Africa; M. Mpumlwana, interview; and Drake Tshenkeng, interview by the author, 1 May 2006, Kuruman, South Africa.) Mpumlwana actually distinguished between the PAC under Sobukwe and the more hardened, Africans-only organization that emerged in exile, citing "a total lack of respect for Sobukwe's thinking by the PAC." For his part, Benjamin Pogrund suggested that Sobukwe enjoyed meeting younger activists such as Biko and took heart in the spread of Black Consciousness. See Pogrund, *How Can Man Die Better* (Johannesburg, South Africa: Jonathan Ball, 1990), 350–51. Although it is not exactly relevant to our discussion in this chapter, Sobukwe penned one of the most amusing indications of Black Theology's spread, written to Pogrund soon after the National Seminar in 1971: "A pleasure also was it to hear your voice over the phone, an indication that you did not die over the Easter weekend like that other Jew two thousand centuries ago [*sic*]. It appears that he was quite the agitator—not at all a long bearded Zionist pacifist"; Letter from Sobukwe to Pogrund, 14 April 1971, A2618 Ba10, HP.

13. Harry Nengwekhulu, interview by the author, 20 March 2006, Pretoria. This concern with appearing "adult" eventually saw Mrs. Winnie Kgware appointed as the first president of BPC, even though it was generally agreed that people such as Chris Mokoditoa and Saths Cooper were actually in charge of the organization; see Mokoditoa, interview by the author, 9 November 2005, Pretoria, and Cooper, interview by the author, 7 December 2005, Johannesburg, South Africa. Zuma called Nengwekhulu by name as one who had "never learned to walk"; pt. 3, F41, KGC.

14. M. Mpumlwana, interview; Nengwekhulu, interview; "Presidential Report," pt. 3, F750, 8–9, KGC. The desire for an apolitical "cultural organization" was in keeping with similar movements under way in independent Africa, as noted in chapter 7.

15. Fanyana Mazibuko, interview by the author, 18 November 2005, Johannesburg, South Africa.

16. *Drum*, 22 February 1972, 16. Nengwekhulu, interview.

17. National Organisation's Conference, "Minutes," DOCC, December 1971, reel 10, 1–2, AD1719, HP. It is notable that Biko was not among them, despite Fanyana Mazibuko's recollection that he "happened" upon the meeting when he spotted Biko milling about while he (Mazibuko) was on his way to visit his girlfriend.

18. Ibid., 4, Motion 1. The development of the BPC—as a political "movement"— paced the discursive creation of the Black Consciousness Movement as a singular entity. The *World* regularly used the term in its coverage of the SASO GSC and BPC organizational meeting in July 1972, and the *SASO Newsletter* followed suit in its coverage of BPC's first convention in December 1972. By the March–April 1973 issue of the *Newsletter*, the term *movement* was in regular usage.

19. Ibid., Motion 1, Motion 2.

20. Ibid.

21. *Drum*, 22 April 1974, 6 (emphasis mine). Pages 8 and 9 featured glossy pictures of the leaders in Vorster's company.

22. *World,* 30 July 1971, 4; *Drum,* 22 July 1973, 62.

23. Nengwekhulu, interview.

24. "Reports Presented at 3rd GSC of the SASO—University of Zululand," July 1972, pt. 3, F750, 4, KGC.

25. *Drum,* 8 August 1973, 61. Significantly, an Indian from Cape Town penned this attack.

26. *SASO Newsletter,* August 1971, 2.

27. For coverage of Sledge's visit, see *World,* 20 July 1970, 1; the ad is in *Weekend World,* 3 October 1971, 6.

28. James Matthews, interview by the author, 23 May 2006, Cape Town. See also "say percy dad," reprinted in *Cry Rage! The Odyssey of a Dissident Poet,* ed. James Matthews and Gladys Thomas (Johannesburg, South Africa: SPROCAS, 1972), 77. Matthews contrasted Sledge with Nina Simone, whom he hailed for "her outrage and willingness to fight" and whom he dared Sledge to tell about his exploits in "sunny" South Africa.

29. *World,* 7 October 1974, 4; 5 December 1974, 10. "Uncle Tom's" South African lineage went back further than Black Consciousness. In a letter to Benjamin Pogrund, for example, Sobukwe mocked the Reverend Nxumalo character in *Cry the Beloved Country!* for his "Uncle Tom mentality" (see Pogrund, *How Can Man Die Better,* 251), as did the assembled *Drum* writers in the shebeen scene in Lionel Rogosin's film *Come Back Africa* (1960).

30. *S. v. Cooper,* reel 8, 8714, AD1819, HP.

31. *SASO Newsletter,* August 1971, 2.

32. *SASO Newsletter,* January–February, 1972, 1; "Minutes," July 1972, pt. 3, F750, 10–11, KGC.

33. *World,* 4 July 1972, 4.

34. Nengwekhulu, interview. We have of course seen Sono's name before: as shown in chapter 3, he charged Black Consciousness with being a wholly "imported" doctrine.

35. Nkwenkwe Nkomo, interview by the author, 2 March 2006, Johannesburg, South Africa.

36. *SASO Newsletter,* June 1971, 16–17.

37. *World,* 10 August 1971, 3.

38. Nengwekhulu, interview. For Biko's first foray into such attacks, see *World,* 30 November 1971, 8.

39. Themba Sono, "In Search of a New and Free Society," 2 July 1972, pt. 3, F750, 7–8, KGC.

40. Mosibudi Mangena, *On Your Own: Evolution of Black Consciousness in South Africa/Azania* (Florida Hills, South Africa: Vivlia, 1989), 28.

41. "Minutes," pt. 3, F750, 5, 7, KGC.

42. *World,* 4 July 1972, 1. Sono soon left the country to study in the United States, prompting much speculation of a quid pro quo, since it was "hard to get [a] South African international visa to go and study in the US" at that time; Mangena, *On Your Own,* 29. Whatever the circumstances, Sono went to Duquesne Univer-

sity in Pittsburgh, where he completed his degree with the thesis that chastised Black Consciousness for being entirely foreign. He later returned to South Africa and became active in opposition politics, first with the Democratic Party and then with the Independent Democrats and now with the Alliance of Free Democrats; see http://www.sahistory.org.za/pages/people/sono-t.htm.

43. *World*, 5 July 1972, 4; 17 July 1972, 4.

44. "Memorandum," July 1972, pt. 3, F750, 3, KGC; *SASO Newsletter*, September–October 1972, 9.

45. Biko, *I Write What I Like*, 82. As the 1970s progressed, the Movement was increasingly associated with this point of view. In late 1974, for example, Catholic and other clerics' Black Renaissance Convention flirted with chaos when Black Consciousness Movement delegates loudly protested Bantustan officials' invitations to attend. Collins Ramusi, Lebowa's minister of the interior, was booed when he attempted to speak, and in the end, despite the Convention's calls for unquestioned black unity, "by a wide margin the house voted in favour of excluding homeland leaders and all 'protagonists of Apartheid' from all meetings of Black people" and thus, by extension, from blackness; *Rand Daily Mail*, 17 December 1974, 9; "Report," pt. 3, F289, 6, KGC. As in 1972, critics condemned this as "pathetic" and contrary to "black culture," but ultimately, the Convention's organizer, Smangaliso Mkhatshwa, conceded that "what the SASO/BPC axis clamour for is precisely what Black people want"; *Rand Daily Mail*, 18 December 1974, 9; Mkhatshwa, "Putting the BRC in Correct Perspective," pt. 3, F289, 5, KGC. This incident was also notable for being the apotheosis of a common trope in coverage of Black Consciousness groups: the prominence of outspoken women among their ranks. Female activists such as Mamphela Ramphele spoke often at the Convention and offered their organization's most radical viewpoints. This observation hearkens back to my discussion of gender in chapters 3 and 6; women had a definite place in this era's organizations, but they sometimes had to earn it by being more defiant (more "manly") then men. And even as women such as Ramphele earned great repute, by the mid-1970s women's abilities to be vocal equals was being undermined. See chapter 9 for more on this theme.

46. "Memorandum," pt. 3, F350, 1, KGC.

47. *World*, 12 July 1972, 1, 4.

48. *World*, 22 July 1970, 4; *Weekend World*, 12 December 1971, 10.

49. This section is a critical piece of the overall argument, but it does not purport to offer a comprehensive narrative of these years, which, it must be said, still await their chronicler. Craig Charney, "Civil Society vs. the State: Identity, Institutions, and the Black Consciousness Movement in South Africa." (PhD diss., Yale University, 2002), offered the most comprehensive narrative. See also Julian Brown's dissertation, especially on the turn to confrontation after 1972, chapter 5. I will allude to certain events apposite to my argument, such as Abraham Tiro's death in exile and the banning of Black Consciousness leaders in March 1973; these are handled in much greater depth in the next chapter.

50. Nengwekhulu, interview. University of the North delegates comprised the largest block at SASO GSCs and, according to Nengwekhulu, kept SASO financially afloat during its first years. For the student experience, see Tau Mokoka, interview by the author, 28 November 2005, Pretoria.

51. SASO Newsletter, April–May 1971, 10 (emphasis mine).

52. Tiro, "Speech Delivered on Graduation Day on Behalf of the Graduates," 29 April 1972, pt. 3, F749, 1–2, KGC.

53. Rand Daily Mail, 5 May 1972, 1.

54. Ibid., 3; World, 5 May 1972, 1.

55. Coverage in the World throughout May 1972, esp. 12 May, 1, 16, and 24 May, 6.

56. Rand Daily Mail, 30 May 1972, 3.

57. Indeed, SASO's protest was soon overshadowed by white students' attempts at solidarity. In Cape Town, for example, UCT students blockaded Parliament in the name of academic freedom and suffered repeated police baton charges on the steps of nearby St. George's Cathedral; Rand Daily Mail, 6–9 June 1972, all p. 1. The specter of baton-wielding police battering white students soon pushed SASO from the front page—at least, that is, until they kicked out their president the following month; World, 9 May 1972, 16.

58. T. Mokoka, interview; Dan Mogale, interview by the author, 6 December 2005, Pretoria. This movement away from Turfloop and back to the townships resulted in the founding of PRESO, the organization discussed previously that worked in literacy and cultural education in Pretoria. See chapter 7 for more on this topic.

59. Ish Mkhabela, interview by the author, 3 March 2006, Johannesburg, South Africa.

60. F. Mazibuko, interview. Mazibuko was a science teacher at Morris Isaacson at the time. For more on Tiro's impact, see the trial of Eric Molobi, AD1899, HP.

61. These bans came also in the wake of the 1973 Durban strikes, which many more scholars offer as evidence of a different sort of political awakening under way during this period. Saths Cooper, Strini Moodley, and other Durban-based Black Consciousness activists claimed knowledge of and cooperation with the strikers but little more than that. For more on this, see Sam Nolutshungu, Changing South Africa: Political Considerations (Manchester, UK: Manchester University Press, 1982), and Julian Brown's dissertation, chap. 4.

62. Anne Hope, interview by the author, 24 May 2006, Cape Town.

63. M. Mpumlwana, interview; Nkomo, interview; Zithulele Cindi, interview by the author, 13 March 2006, Johannesburg, South Africa.

64. Rand Daily Mail, 27 April 1974, 1.

65. Nkomo, interview. The fact that Biko named his youngest son Samora after FRELIMO leader Samora Machel further indicates the Mozambican movement's impact.

66. World, 23 September 1974, 1. See also Julian Brown's dissertation, chap. 5.

67. Rand Daily Mail, 9 September 1974, 3; 12 September 1974, 1; 13 September 1974, 1; 14 September 1974, 1.

68. Delegates were sent, including Nkwenkwe Nkomo, who told me about his fence-climbing efforts to pass between South Africa and Swaziland because he lacked a passport. They did manage to meet with some FRELIMO representatives in Lourenço Marques, but with the bulk of the FRELIMO leadership still in the bush, the trip and claims about prominent leaders going to South Africa amounted to little more than propaganda or, as then BPC secretary-general Cindi put it, "bravado." See Nkomo, interview.

69. *Rand Daily Mail*, 25 September 1974, 1.

70. Saths Cooper, interview by Gail Gerhart, 24 October 1972, pt. 1, F8, 2, KGC.

71. M. Mpumlwana, interview. For more on King, see Leslie Hadfield, "Restoring Human Dignity and Building Self-Reliance: Youth, Women and Churches and Black Consciousness Community Development, South Africa, 1969–1977" (PhD diss., Michigan State University, 2010).

72. Zithulele Cindi, interview by the author, 27 March 2006, Johannesburg, South Africa.

73. *Pro Veritate*, December 1974, 7.

74. *World*, 14 November 1974, 6.

75. *World*, 20 November 1974, 1, 24; 21 November 1974, 6. The newspaper itself began to change during this period; it became thicker, with more coverage of politics and liberation struggles in neighboring countries (even if it still referred to groups such as the MPLA [Popular Movement for the Liberation of Angola] and various Zimbabwean organizations as "terrorists") and had fewer sensationalist stories about soccer and crime. For more on the role of women as protesters, see chapter 9.

76. The number was eventually winnowed to nine after four defendants turned state's witnesses.

77. Mpumlwana suggested that immediately following the arrests, activists in King William's Town reasserted control, a contention supported by the fact that the next big conference for either organization took place in King in December 1975; there, activists elected as leader Hlaku Rachidi—a contemporary of Pityana's at Fort Hare—and developed the Movement's most cogent statement on South Africa's political and economic future. For the conference, see pt. 3, F286, KGC, and Hlaku Kenneth Rachidi, interview by the author, 30 March 2006, Johannesburg, South Africa.

78. Michael Lobban, *White Man's Justice* (Oxford: Clarendon Press, 1996), 10, 21.

79. Strini Moodley, interview by the author, 10 April 2006, Durban, South Africa.

80. Nkomo, interview. Both Lybon Mabasa (interview by the author, 20 April 2006, Johannesburg, South Africa) and Clement Mokoka (interview by the author, 19 December 2005, Phokeng, South Africa) recounted going to the trial in solidarity with the accused.

81. *World*, 26 September 1975, 2.

82. Moodley, interview. Cooper, Nkomo, and Cindi agreed with Moodley that the defendants all knew they would be found guilty of at least some of the charges.

83. Biko's testimony over four days in May 1976 was covered extensively by the *World* and later published in Millard Arnold, ed., *Steve Biko: Black Conscious-ness in South Africa* (New York: Random House, 1978). Among other things, this book is notable for continually referring to the work of the educationist "Paul LaFrere"—a transcription error responsible for a great deal of wasted time on my part!

84. *S. v. Cooper*, reel 9, 235, AD1719, HP.

85. *World*, 16 December 1976, 16. The *World* also kept a tally of the trial sta-tistics: South Africa's longest terror act trial to date, 136 court days; 61 state and 21 defense witnesses; cost R250,000; *World*, 14 December 1976, 1.

86. *S. v. Cooper*, reel 7, 7128, AD1719, HP.

87. Helena Pohlandt-McCormick, *"I Saw a Nightmare . . ."* (New York: Colum-bia University Press, 2005). See also Sifiso Ndlovu, *The Soweto Uprisings: Counter-memories of June 1976* (Johannesburg, South Africa: Ravan Press, 1998), and his chapter in *The Road to Democracy in South Africa*, ed. South African Democracy Educational Trust, vol. 2 (Pretoria: UNISA, 2007), 317–50.

88. There is still debate over how many died. See Pohlandt-McCormick, *"I Saw a Nightmare,"* chap. 1, 30. The best blow-by-blow description of events is Alan Brickhill and Jeremy Brooks, *Whirlwind before the Storm* (London: International Defense and Aid Fund, 1980). Pat Hopkins and Helen Grange, *The Rocky Rioter Teargas Show: The Inside Story of the 1976 Soweto Uprising* (Johannesburg, South Africa: Struik Publishers, 2001), is a recent narrative account; short on analysis, it mostly repackages media coverage of events as they unfolded.

89. "How June 16 Demo Was Planned," *Sechaba*, second quarter, 1977, pt. 3, F741, 53, KGC.

90. Daniel Sechaba Montsisi, "Lessons from 1976," July 1983, pt. 3, F742, 39, KGC.

91. Indeed, as the government convened a commission of inquiry during the months that followed, state interrogation repeatedly wove around the figure of Winnie Mandela, with whom high school activists had met and whose association with the ANC looked damning. For testimony, see pt. 3, F797, KGC; for more on Winnie and the rising, see Helena Pohlandt-McCormick, "Controlling Woman: Winnie Mandela and the 1976 Soweto Uprising," *International Journal of African Historical Studies* 33, no. 3 (2000): 585–614.

92. "The Voice of Black People in Southern Africa: The Voice of the People Is the Voice of God," [late 1976?], A2176 12, 3, HP.

93. Cooper, Moodley, M. Mangena, and Mosala were all active either in the Azanian Peoples Organisation (AZAPO) or its offshoot, the Socialist Party of Aza-nia. See Cooper, interview; Moodley, interview; M. Mangena, interview by the author, 6 December 2006, Pretoria; and Itumeleng Mosala, interview by the au-thor, 24 April 2006, Pretoria. The scholarship from this point of view is rather thin, and where it exists, it is so eager to prove Black Consciousness's revolutionary potential that it loses any historical sense of how the movement may have pulled off the Soweto rising. See Robert Fatton, *Black Consciousness in South Africa: The Dialectics of Ideological Resistance to White Supremacy* (Albany: State University

of New York Press, 1986). The situation has worsened with time: as the ANC gradually emerged as South Africa's dominant political force, its leaders embraced 1976 as part of the organization's own narrative of The Struggle years. When the rising's thirtieth anniversary passed in June 2006, the SABC (South African Broadcasting Corporation) documentaries that marked the occasion—under the promotional line "remember why it's all good"—might not have made explicit claims regarding the ruling party's role in events, but they certainly gave Black Consciousness little attention. Indeed, in the 2006 documentary, *Tsietsi, My Hero*, a well-hyped account of SASM and the Soweto Student Representative Council's best-known leader, Tsietsi Mashinini appears more of an ideological orphan than the Black Consciousness exponent he was. See the later discussion on this topic.

94. Here, she followed the lead of fictional accounts of the rising, which still remain some of the strongest narratives. Among the "insider" accounts, Pohlandt-McCormick cited two of my favorites: Sipho Sepamla, *A Ride on the Whirlwind* (Johannesburg, South Africa: A. D. Donker, 1981), and Mbulelo Mzamane, *Children of Soweto* (London: Harlow Essex Longman, 1982). See chapter 7 for the aesthetic limitations of these thinly fictionalized narratives.

95. Pohlandt-McCormick, "I Saw a Nightmare," chap. 1, 160.

96. Bongi Mkhabela, interview by the author, 18 April 2006, Johannesburg, South Africa.

97. Cindi, interview, 13 March 2006; Linda Schuster, *A Burning Hunger: One Family's Struggle against Apartheid* (London: Jonathan Cape, 2004), 41; "Testimony," pt. 3, F797, 4962, KGC.

98. Cindi, interview, 13 March 2006; Clive Glaser, *Bo-Tsotsi: The Youth Gangs of Soweto* (Portsmouth, NH: Heinemann, 2000), 161–62.

99. Schuster, *Burning Hunger*, 56–57.

100. Ibid., 73.

101. Lobban, *White Man's Justice*, 75.

102. Quoted in the *Sunday Times*, 14 November 1976, 2–4-2–79, SBF.

103. Glaser, *Bo-Tsotsi*, 162.

104. Ibid.; Schuster, *Burning Hunger*, 40; B. Mkhabela, interview. Her group leaders included Frank Chikane, a Turfloop student and prominent theological activist. Manthata, formerly of the UCM and then of the SACC, was another prominent adviser.

105. Vusi Tshabalala, "Presidential Speech," May 1976, pt. 3, F740, 1, KGC.

CHAPTER 9: KEEPING FAITH WITH THE BLACK MESSIAH

1. For more on Nzima and the photograph, see Helena Pohlandt-McCormick, "I Saw a Nightmare . . ." (New York: Columbia University Press, 2005), chap. 1.

2. Letter from Mogale to Pityana, 22 January [1969?], UCT 1966–80, 1–3, SBF.

3. Steve Biko, *I Write What I Like*, ed. Aelred Stubbs (1978; repr., London: Bowerdean Publishing, 1996), 76.

4. Charles Taylor, "Review of *Radical Hope* by Jonathan Lear," *New York Review of Books*, 26 April 2007, 6.

5. At least until that point. For martyrdom after Black Consciousness, see Sabine Marschall, "Pointing to the Dead: Victims, Martyrs and Public Memory in South Africa," *South African Historical Journal* 60, no. 1 (2008): 103–23.

6. G. Kelly and F. Burton Nelson, eds., *Testament to Freedom: The Essential Writings of Dietrich Bonhoeffer* (New York: HarperCollins, 1990), 43, 323.

7. Circular from Moore to branches, October 1971, AD1126 G1, 1–2, HP. He was the first Black Consciousness thinker banned, but he already counted banned people among his family. For the family's history with bannings, see Tom Manthata (Moloto's cousin), interview by the author, 18 November 2005, Johannesburg, South Africa.

8. Circular from Moore, 1–2.

9. This was the editorial about Stanley Ntwasa, cited in the discussion of manhood in chapter 2.

10. *World*, 28 September 1971, 6; Circular from Moore, 1.

11. Letter from Moloto to Moore, 26 September 1971, AD1126 G1, 1–2, HP.

12. Letter from Mokoditoa to Collins, 26 May 1972, pt. 3, F930, 2, KGC.

13. Letter from Moore to Collins, 1 October 1971, pt. 3, F929, 1, KGC.

14. Charles Simkins, "Report of the Traveling Secretary to the UCM at Its Conf Held at Wilgespruit from 10 to 16th July, 1970," AD1126 A4d, 1, HP.

15. "Motion of Dissolution of the U.C.M," 1972, AD1126 A1(c), 2, HP.

16. Ibid., 1.

17. Letter from Mokoditoa to Stofile, 7 June 1972, pt. 3, F930, 1, KGC.

18. Letter from Motlhabi to Cone, 24 April 1972, AD1126 D6(a), 1, HP.

19. Clipping from the *Port Elizabeth Weekend Post*, 18 March 1972, AB2414 D2 (Ntwasa), HP.

20. *Rand Daily Mail*, 20 April 1972, 14. Polley also noted that the liturgy Moore preached at the funeral of the former's wife and son was now an illegal document, a particularly biting effect of banning.

21. Letter from Chief Magistrate, Johannesburg, to Moore, 17 April 1972, AD1126 G1, 1, HP.

22. Colin Collins, interview by the author, 19 October 2005, Johannesburg, South Africa.

23. Ibid.

24. *World*, 7 April 1972, 4; letter from Motlhabi to Cone, 28 June 1972, AD1126 D6(a), 2, HP.

25. Letter from Motlhabi to Cone, 28 June 1972, AD1126 D6(a), 2, HP.

26. Aelred Stubbs, "Report," May 1974, pt. 3, F578, 3, KGC.

27. *SASO Newsletter*, March–April 1973, 5.

28. Correspondence in AB2414 D2 (Ntwasa), HP. Also, interview with Drake Tshenkeng, 1 May 2006, Kuruman, South Africa.

29. Mokgethi Motlhabi, interview by the author, 3 March 2006, Pretoria; John Sebidi, interview by Gail Gerhart, July 1989, Johannesburg, South Africa, pt. 1, F33, 7, KGC.

30. M. Motlhabi, interview.

31. National Executive Committee, "Banning of Sabelo S. Ntwasa," 21 March 1972, AD1126 J6, 1, HP.

32. Harry Nengwekhulu, interview by the author, 20 March 2006, Pretoria.

33. Zithulele Cindi, interview by the author, 13 March 2006, Johannesburg, South Africa; Strini Moodley, interview by the author, 10 April 2006, Durban, South Africa.

34. *World*, 5 March 1972, 4; *Drum*, 8 April 1973, 13.

35. Ben Langa, "Bannings and Intimidations," May 1973, pt. 3, F752, 1–8, KGC.

36. Letter from Biko to Magistrate, King William's Town, 11 April 1973, KWT undated, misc. binder, 1–3, SBF. Biko applied for permission to use a library and move between townships to attend sporting events—and promised to obey the ban if these concessions were made.

37. Letter from Biko to Magistrate, King William's Town, 25 May 1973, KWT undated, misc. binder, 1, SBF.

38. Malusi Mpumlwana, interview by the author, 9 March 2006, Pretoria; Thoko Mpumlwana, interview by the author, 22 March 2006, Pretoria; Mamphela Ramphele, interview by the author, 28 July 2006, Cape Town; and Peter Jones, interview by the author, 20 June 2006, Cape Town. For much more on King activities, see Mamphela Ramphele, *Across Boundaries* (New York: Feminist Press at CUNY, 1996), and Leslie Hadfield, "Restoring Human Dignity and Building Self-Reliance: Youth, Women and Churches and Black Consciousness Community Development, South Africa, 1969–1977" (PhD diss., Michigan State University, 2010).

39. "Black Community Programmes: 1974 Report," pt. 3, F270, 2, 11, KGC.

40. Interview with *New York Times*, 1977, A2618 Dc, 10, HP. This admission helps to explain the sheer number of court cases in which Biko participated during late 1976 and early 1977. See coverage in *World*.

41. Moodley, interview.

42. Ben Langa, "Bannings and Intimidations," 3.

43. *SASO Newsletter*, March–April 1973, 1.

44. Glenn Masokoane, "All Saints Day," *SASO Newsletter*, March–April 1973, 6.

45. *SASO Newsletter*, March–April 1973, 8.

46. Maphiri Masekela, untitled paper, December 1971, F748, 5, KGC.

47. Ibid., 6. The social conservatism inherent in such sentiments was reflected in various Black Consciousness activists' rejection of then trendy birth control and other family planning; rather, as one seminar concluded, "family planning must be at all costs discouraged." See "Contextualization of Under-grad studies under Free University Scheme," June 1974, pt. 3, F755, 1, KGC.

48. *SASO Newsletter*, March–April 1973, 5.

49. Ibid.

50. The language here reminds me of Emory Douglas's paintings in the *Black Panther* newsletter, many of which featured women performing supporting roles in the militant black struggle. Perhaps the most remarkable of these shows a woman smiling as she watches her naked son shoulder a toy rifle. It should be noted,

however, that Douglas's art also celebrated armed females, often with babies in tow, a trope featured in MK propaganda as well. Sam Durant, ed., *Black Panther: The Revolutionary Art of Emory Douglas* (New York: Rizzoli, 2007).

51. *SASO Newsletter*, March–April 1973, 5. I will return to the gendered dimensions of sacrifice at this chapter's close.

52. Ibid.

53. Chris Mokoditoa, interview by the author, 9 November 2005, Pretoria.

54. Letter from Phillip to Stubbs, 25 August 1972, AB2414 D2 (Phillip), 2, HP.

55. Rubin Phillip, interview by the author, 15 December 2005, Durban, South Africa.

56. Cindi, interview.

57. Saths Cooper, interview by the author, 7 December 2005, Johannesburg, South Africa.

58. Chris Mzoneli, interview by the author, 12 December 2005, Durban, South Africa.

59. Letter from Edmund Radebe to Colin Collins, 23 July 1969, AD1126 G4, 1, HP.

60. Mzoneli, interview.

61. Biko, *I Write What I Like*, 75.

62. Sipho Magudulela, "Teach Us, O Lord," *SASO Newsletter*, November–December 1972, 18–19.

63. An unnamed delegate after Sono's expulsion, quoted in *Drum*, 8 August 1972, 8.

64. "Composite Report of the Interim-Executive to the 4th GSC," pt. 3, F753, 1, 2, KGC.

65. Malusi Mpumlwana, Thoko Mbanjwa, and Mamphela Ramphele, interview by Thomas Karis and Gail Gerhart, 3 November 1985, pt. 1, F26, 2, KGC.

66. Itumeleng Mosala, interview by the author, 24 April 2006, Pretoria.

67. "Fear Not," *SASM Newsletter*, May–June 1975, pt. 3, F739, 8, KGC.

68. Linda Schuster, *A Burning Hunger: One Family's Struggle against Apartheid* (London: Jonathan Cape, 2004), 66.

69. *SASM Newsletter*, May–June 1975, pt. 3, F739, 9, KGC.

70. Sam Buti, "Views of Black Christians on South Africa's Present and Future," 27 March 1976, AC623 3.9, 1, HP.

71. Manas Buthelezi, "The Christian Presence in Today's South Africa," 27 March 1976, pt. 3, F350, 3, KGC.

72. Manas Buthelezi, "Being Human to Humans," *Parishioner* 73, no. 2 (February 1975): 1.

73. Jennifer Wenzel has recently offered a long-term study of "prophecy" in South African letters. See Wenzel, *Bulletproof: Afterlives of Anticolonial Prophecy in South Africa and Beyond* (Chicago: University of Chicago Press, 2009), esp. chap. 3.

74. Albert Nolan, "The Spiritual Life," *Katurura*, October 1977, Acc. 127, 3, UNISA.

75. Letter from UCM [Moore?] to Buthelezi, February 1971, AD1126 D6(a), 1, HP.

76. Jürgen Moltmann, *Theology of Hope* (London: SCM Press, 1967), 15–16, 20.

77. Ibid., 21, 34–35. My use of *horizon* alludes to Biko's "distant horizon" where "true humanity" might be realized. Although I am not confident that Biko or any other prominent "secular" Black Consciousness leader read Moltmann (none mentioned him to me), the similar ways of thinking are striking. Black Consciousness activist certainly saw themselves as undertaking a task similar to Moltmann's, as indicated by the later choice to title a collection of retrospective essays *Bounds of Possibility*. This sense of hope in the unseen as the most "radical" hope evokes Jonathan Lear's argument in *Radical Hope* (Cambridge, MA: Harvard University Press, 2006).

78. Manas Buthelezi, "A Theological Grounds for an Ethic of Hope," in *The Challenge of Black Theology in South Africa*, ed. Basil Moore (Atlanta, GA: John Knox Press, 1974), 147, 150.

79. *SASO Newsletter*, March–April 1973, 3, 8–9.

80. Takatso Mofokeng, interview by the author, 28 November 2005, Pretoria.

81. Ibid.; Ish Mkhabela, interview by the author, 3 March 2006, Johannesburg, South Africa; and Bongi Mkhabela, 18 April 2006, Johannesburg, South Africa. As struggles mounted, some activists decided that the future had in fact already arrived. They marked this by beginning to use *Azania* in place of *South Africa* and argued that this was going to be the country's future name. The term leapfrogged political transformation in that it symbolically decolonized. "South Africa is a position on a map," the poet James Matthews told me, a relic of European cartography and white control, whereas Azania was an objective, something to fight for. After the March 1973 bannings, the banned were hailed as the "saints" of Azania by Black Consciousness publicists; others invited all "Azanians" to attend a meeting; and perhaps most notably, BPC past president Simon Farisani preached that "Azania will be free and soon"; see Farisani, "National Congress Address," 13 December 1975, pt. 3, F286, 1, KGC.

82. Fanyana Mazibuko, interview by the author, 18 November 2005, Johannesburg, South Africa. The idea of delayed but still certain liberation was present in the poem discussed in chapter 7, where the poet wrote that she would get her shoes "by the end of the century."

83. *World*, 16 January 1975, 6.

84. "To be or not to be?" no author, 1973, pt. 3, F739, 3, KGC.

85. Letter from Tutu to Vorster, 8 May 1976, reproduced in *Ecunews Bulletin*, 26 May 1976, pt. 3, F350, 10, 12, KGC.

86. Vusi Tshabalala, "Presidential Speech," May 1976, pt. 3, F740, 2, KGC.

87. *SASO Newsletter*, March–April 1973, 1.

88. *SASM Newsletter*, May 1973, pt. 3, F739, 1, KGC. The words belonged to the educator Horace Mann and served as the motto for Antioch, the college he founded in Ohio.

89. "To be or not to be?" 4.

90. Harvey Cox has recently penned a fascinating account of his own Jesus-centered teaching at Harvard: *When Jesus Came to Harvard: Making Moral Choices Today* (New York: Houghton Mifflin, 2004).

91. Albert Nolan, *Jesus before Christianity* (Maryknoll, NY: Orbis Books, 1976), 139–42; Nolan, interview by the author, 6 March 2006, Johannesburg, South Africa.

92. Kelly and Nelson, *Testament to Freedom*, 323, 339, 542.

93. "Minutes," fourth GSC, July 1973, pt. 3, F753, 21, KGC.

94. *World*, 16 December 1972, 16; Mosibudi Mangena, *On Your Own: The Evolution of Black Consciousness in South Africa/Azania* (Florida Hills, South Africa: Vivlia, 1989), iii.

95. Cindi Testimony, *S. v. Cooper*, reel 8, 7650, AD1719, HP.

96. "Springs GSC Report," pt. 3, F753, 2, KGC; Barney Pityana, "Obituary," *SASO Newsletter*, November–December 1972, 7.

97. Nkwenkwe Nkomo, "Memorandum," [March 1973?], pt. 3, F285, 1, KGC.

98. "Program: Sharpeville Day," 17 March 1973, reel 11, 1, AD1719, HP.

99. Xola Nuse, "Inkwenkwenkulu," *SASM Newsletter*, May 1973, pt. 3, F739, 19, KGC.

100. Mofokeng, interview.

101. Jeremy Cohen, *Sanctifying the Name of God* (Philadelphia: University of Pennsylvania Press, 2004).

102. The description of the killings as the "Sharpeville incident" comes from the Snyman Commission of Inquiry into Turfloop "Report," 1975, K318, box 5 K7–1, 61, NAP; *Rand Daily Mail*, 21 March 1970, 9.

103. Saths Cooper, "Dedication," *SASO Newsletter*, June 1971, 7.

104. *World*, 26 July 1973, 12–13. The *World* had barely covered the Sharpeville anniversary before SASO focused on it. On the tenth anniversary in 1970, for example, the paper printed a picture of a lone protester in London but otherwise made no mention of the day; *World*, 24 March 1970, 12.

105. Phillip Frankel, *An Ordinary Atrocity: Sharpeville and Its Massacre* (Johannesburg, South Africa: Witwatersrand University Press, 2001), 6, 160–66, 200.

106. Ibid., 119, 218.

107. Nengwekhulu, interview.

108. "Program: Sharpeville Day," 1.

109. See the roundtable discussion in part 2 of Rona Fields, ed., *Martyrdom* (Westport, CT: Praeger, 2004).

110. After all, other than making a fleeting cry, Christ had not tried to save himself.

111. Certain examples of self-conscious martyrdom must, of course, be mentioned, including the Rivonia defendants' willingness to face the death penalty for their MK activities. Mandela exemplified this by declaring himself prepared to die for his ideals.

112. For reflections on this from a slightly different perspective, see Achille Mbembe, "Necropolitics," *Public Culture* 15, no. 1 (2003): 11–40.

113. Molobi, "Autobiography," *S. v. Molobi*, box 2, 16, AD1189, HP.

114. *Drum*, 22 March 1974, 26. Bokwe Mafuna, interview by the author, 30 November 2005, Johannesburg, South Africa; Nengwekhulu, interview.

115. The *World*, 5 February 1974, 2, reported widespread mourning at Morris Isaacson when news of Tiro's assassination reached the school.

116. Cindi Testimony, *S. v. Cooper*, reel 8, 7690–91, AD1719, HP. Such rhetoric was not limited to Black Consciousness activists; editors at the *World* remained skeptical of both Tiro and the "anti-white feelings" that they associated with his movement, yet they too hailed him as a "martyr"; 21 February 1974, 6.

117. Nengwekhulu, interview. The politics of commemoration were being established as well, as Eric Molobi testified that Black Consciousness exiles turned "Thabo Mbegi" [*sic*] and other ANC officials away from the service; *S. v. Eric Molobi*, vol. 4, 403, AD1899, HP.

118. *World*, 13 August 1976, 6.

119. See the coverage in the *World*, especially in August and September 1976. The banner is from the *World*, 18 October 1976, 1. Also see Buti Tlhagale, interview by the author, 23 March 2006, Johannesburg, South Africa. Tlhagale, a Catholic priest, was then assigned to Regina Mundi in Soweto, where numerous funerals and rallies took place. Tlhagale confessed to not being able to tell such occasions apart.

120. *World*, 13 October 1976, 28; 28 July 1977, 2.

121. M. Mpumlwana, interview; "Sananews," 1 September 1976, A2176 13, 4–5, HP.

122. Mosala, interview.

123. Zephaniah Kameeta, "The Cross in the World," *Pro Veritate*, July 1976, 14.

124. Manas Buthelezi, "Victory through Death," *Pro Veritate*, August 1976, 7–8. The journal did not actually identify Buthelezi as the preacher at this funeral, but Aelred Stubbs identified him in his memoir entitled "Martyr of Hope" (itself a suggestive name) in Steve Biko, *I Write What I Like*, ed. Aelred Stubbs (1978; repr., London: Bowerdean Publishing, 1996), 196.

125. This point was also made by Pumla Gqola, "Contradictory Locations: Blackwomen and the Discourse of the Black Consciousness Movement," *Meridians* 2, no. 1 (2001): 149.

126. Buthelezi, "Victory through Death," 7–8. Takatso Mofokeng also suggested his own efforts to preach "victory through death" were greatly influenced by Buthelezi's skill at doing so.

127. See, for example, *World*, 25 October 1976, 1, 24. For more on this, see Pat Hopkins and Helen Grange, *The Rocky Rioter Teargas Show: The Inside Story of the 1976 Soweto Uprising* (Johannesburg, South Africa: Struik Publishers, 2001), chap. 7.

128. Statement in October 1976, cited in *Pro Veritate*, March 1977, 13.

129. *World*, 10 August 1977, 6.

130. *World*, 3 December 1976, 8.

131. *World*, 7 April 1977, 3; 7 July 1977, 5; 14 July 1977, 5; 15 July 1977, 4.

132. *Rand Daily Mail*, 27 August 1976, 20; 3 June 1977, 12.

133. *Rand Daily Mail*, 14 September 1977, 1; 16 September 1977, 2.

134. *World*, 15 September 1977, 1.

135. *Rand Daily Mail*, 20 September 1977, 13; SASO, "A Tribute," September 1977, cover, second to last page (no page numbers), Haigh Collection, SBF.

136. *World*, 3 October 1977, 1.

137. *World*, 23 September 1977, 6.

138. *World*, 23 September 1977, 1.

139. *Rand Daily Mail*, 26 September 1977, 1; *World*, 28 September 1977, 6; 23 September 1977, 14.

140. *World*, 29 September 1977, 1, 2; 30 September 1977, 6; 18 October 1977, 4.

141. Sebidi, interview, 2–3; Tlhagale, interview; see additional coverage in *Voice*, 4 November 1977, 8–9.

CONCLUSION: YESTERDAY IS A FOREIGN COUNTRY

The title is borrowed from Allan Boesak, *Tenderness of Conscience* (Stellenbosch, South Africa: Sun Press, 2005), 1.

1. This material is drawn from conversations with several AZAPO founders; see, e.g., Ish Mkhabela, interview by the author, 3 March 2006, Johannesburg, South Africa, and Dan Habedi, interview by the author, 14 March 2006, Johannesburg, South Africa. For more on the founding of AZAPO, see South African Democracy Educational Trust, *The Road to Democracy in South Africa*, vol. 2 (Pretoria: UNISA, 2007). For more on the 1980s, see Tom Lodge, *All, Here and Now: Black Politics in South Africa in the 1980s* (London: C. Hurst, 1992), and Ineke van Kessel, *"Beyond Our Wildest Dreams": The UDF and the Transformation of South Africa* (Charlottesville: University Press of Virginia, 2000). AZAPO background information is available on the organization's Web site, http://www.azapo.org.za.

2. Bongi Mkhabela, interview by the author, 18 April 2006, Johannesburg, South Africa; Mkhabela, *Open Earth and Black Roses* (Johannesburg, South Africa: Skotaville, 2001), 108.

3. These essays, originally published in *Public Culture*, have just been reissued as Sarah Nuttall and Achille Mbembe, eds., *Johannesburg: The Elusive Metropolis* (Durham, NC: Duke University Press, 2008).

4. For a personal critique of this, see Angela Davis, "Afro Images: Politics, Fashion and Nostalgia," *Critical Inquiry* 21, no. 1 (1994): 37–45.

5. Rita Barnard noted the importance of global media and consumerism at various points in *Apartheid and Beyond: South African Writers and the Politics of Place* (Oxford: Oxford University Press, 2007).

6. See also Sarah Nuttall, "Stylizing the Self," in *Johannesburg: The Elusive Metropolis*, ed. Sarah Nuttall and Achille Mbembe (Durham, NC: Duke University Press, 2008), 91–118.

7. Nelson Mandela, "Whither the Black Consciousness Movement? An Assessment," in *Reflections in Prison*, ed. Mac Maharaj (Cape Town: Zebra Press, 2001), 50–51.

8. David Scott, *Conscripts of Modernity: The Tragedy of Colonial Enlightenment* (Durham, NC: Duke University Press, 2004), 4, 7–11.

9. Quoted in Gerald West, "Don't Stand by My Story," *Journal of Theology for Southern Africa*, no. 98 (1997): 5. Allan Boesak and others have roundly criticized Tutu for this statement, and since the retired archbishop has excoriated the Mbeki, Motlanthe, and Zuma governments in recent years, perhaps he has repudiated it as well.

10. Terence Ranger, ed., *Evangelical Christianity and Democracy in Africa* (Oxford: Oxford University Press, 2006). More recent studies on Christianity focus especially on the rise of Pentecostalism; see, for example, Paul Richards, *Ghana's New Christianity: Pentecostalism in a Globalizing African Economy* (Bloomington: Indiana University Press, 2004), and David Maxwell, *African Gifts of the Spirit: Pentecostalism and the Rise of a Zimbabwean Transnational Religious Movement* (Athens: Ohio University Press, 2006).

11. See Kairos Theologians, *Challenge to the Church: A Theological Comment on the Political Crisis in South Africa: The Kairos Document* (Stony Point, NY: Theology in Global Context, 1985), and Tristan Anne Borer, *Challenging the State: Churches as Political Actors in South Africa, 1980–1994* (South Bend, IN: Notre Dame University Press, 1998).

12. Manas Buthelezi, personal communication, 30 December 2006.

13. See Miranda Hassett, *Anglican Communion in Crisis: How Episcopal Dissidents and Their African Allies Are Reshaping Anglicanism* (Princeton, NJ: Princeton University Press, 2007), for a blow-by-blow account of this. For a particular perspective on faith and politics in postapartheid South Africa, see André Czégledy, "A New Christianity for a New South Africa: Charismatic Christians and the Post-apartheid Order," *Journal of Religion in Africa* 38, no. 3 (2008): 284–311.

14. See the article about Ndungane in the *New York Times*, 10 February 2007, 4. For Phillip, see *Church Times*, 2 May 2008, available at http://www.churchtimes.co.uk/content.asp?id=55976, accessed 18 June 2009.

Bibliography

ARCHIVAL MATERIALS

Historical Papers, Cullen Library, University of the Witwatersrand, Johannesburg, South Africa (HP)

A825	Study Project on Christianity in Apartheid Society
A1888	Benjamin Pogrund
A2176	South African Students' Organisation
A2177	Black People's Convention
A2618	Robert Sobukwe
AB1017	Federal Theological Seminary
AB2414	St. Peter's Theological College
AC623	South African Council of Churches
AD1126	University Christian Movement
AD1450	Trials—*State v. Twala et al.*
AD1719	Trials—*State v. Cooper et al.*
AD1899	Trials—*State v. Molobi*
AK2525	Trials—*State v. Twala et al.*
KGC	Karis-Gerhart Collection

Killie Campbell Library, University of KwaZulu-Natal, Durban, South Africa (KC)

KCAV	Oral History of the Zulu
KCM	Alphaeus Zulu Collection

National Archives, Pretoria, South Africa (NAP)

1–4-614	Staatspresident
K318	Snyman Commission

Steve Biko Foundation, Johannesburg, South Africa (SBF)

DOJ	Department of Justice
ELDD	*East London Daily Dispatch*, clippings
KWT	King Williams Town, misc.
UCT	University of Cape Town collection

University of South Africa, Pretoria, South Africa (UNISA)

Acc. 153	Black Consciousness, misc.

NEWSPAPERS AND JOURNALS

Drum	1968–77
Parishioner	1975–76
Pro Veritate	1967–77
Rand Daily Mail	1970–77

SASO Newsletter	1970–77
S'ketsh'	1972
Voice	1976–77
Weekend World	1968–77
World	1968–77

ORAL INTERVIEWS CONDUCTED
AND TRANSCRIBED BY THE AUTHOR

Baartman, Ernest, 19 June 2006, Cape Town, South Africa
Biko, Nkosinathi, 3 April 2006, Johannesburg, South Africa
Boesak, Allan, 15 June 2006, Somerset West, South Africa
Buthelezi, Manas, 8 November 2005, Johannesburg, South Africa
Cindi, Zithulele, 13 March 2006, Johannesburg, South Africa; 27 March 2006,
    Johannesburg, South Africa
Collins, Colin, 19 October 2005, Johannesburg, South Africa
Cooper, Saths, 7 December 2005, Johannesburg, South Africa
Goba, Bonganjalo, 11 April 2006, Durban, South Africa
Habedi, Dan, 14 March 2006, Johannesburg, South Africa
Hope, Anne, 24 May 2006, Cape Town, South Africa
Jones, Peter, 20 June 2006, Cape Town, South Africa
Khoapa, Bennie, 13 December 2005, Durban, South Africa
Lamola, John, 10 November 2005, Johannesburg, South Africa
Mabasa, Lybon, 20 April 2006, Johannesburg, South Africa
Mafuna, Bokwe, 30 November 2005, Johannesburg, South Africa
Maimela, Simon, 1 February 2006, Pretoria, South Africa
Mangena, Mosibudi, 6 December 2006, Pretoria, South Africa
Mangena, Oshadi, 22 November 2005, Johannesburg, South Africa
Manthata, Tom, 18 November 2005, Johannesburg, South Africa
Matthews, James, 23 May 2006, Cape Town, South Africa
Mayson, Cedric, 27 February 2006, Johannesburg, South Africa
Mazibuko, Fanyana, 18 November 2005, Johannesburg, South Africa
Mazibuko, Thandisizwe, 29 November 2005, Johannesburg, South Africa
Mkhabela, Bongi, 18 April 2006, Johannesburg, South Africa
Mkhabela, Ish, 3 March 2006, Johannesburg, South Africa
Mofokeng, Takatso, 28 November 2005, Pretoria, South Africa
Mogale, Dan, 6 December 2005, Pretoria, South Africa
Mogale, Dan, and Simon Mashiangwako, 20 December 2005, Pretoria, South Africa
Mokoditoa, Chris, 9 November 2005, Pretoria, South Africa
Mokoka, Clement, 19 December 2005, Phokeng, South Africa
Mokoka, Tau, 28 November 2005, Pretoria, South Africa
Moodley, Strini, 10 April 2006, Durban, South Africa
Mosala, Itumeleng, 24 April 2006, Pretoria, South Africa
Motlana, Nthato, 31 January 2006, Johannesburg, South Africa
Motlhabi, Mokgethi, 3 March 2006, Pretoria, South Africa

Mpumlwana, Malusi, 9 March 2006, Pretoria, South Africa
Mpumlwana, Thoko, 22 March 2006, Pretoria, South Africa
Mzamane, Mbulelo, 16 March 2006, Midrand, South Africa
Mzoneli, Chris, 13 December 2005, Durban, South Africa
Nengwekhulu, Harry, 20 March 2006, Pretoria, South Africa
Nkomo, Nkwenkwe, 2 March 2006, Johannesburg, South Africa
Nolan, Albert, 6 March 2006, Johannesburg, South Africa
Phillip, Rubin, 15 December 2005, Durban, South Africa
Pityana, Barney, 1 February 2006, Pretoria, South Africa
Rachidi, Hlaku Kenneth, 30 March 2006, Johannesburg, South Africa
Ramose, Mogobe, 6 March 2006, Pretoria, South Africa
Ramphele, Mamphela, 28 July 2006, Cape Town, South Africa
Randall, Peter, 8 December 2005, Johannesburg, South Africa
Russell, David, 12 May 2006, Cape Town, South Africa
Tlhagale, Buti, 23 March 2006, Johannesburg, South Africa
Tshenkeng, Drake, 1 May 2006, Kuruman, South Africa

SELECTED PRIMARY AND SECONDARY MATERIALS

Adam, Heribert. *Modernizing Racial Domination: South Africa's Political Dynamics.* Berkeley: University of California Press, 1971.
———. "The Rise of Black Consciousness in South Africa." *Race* 15, no. 2 (1973): 149–65.
———. *South Africa: Sociological Perspectives.* New York: Oxford University Press, 1971.
Adhikari, Mohamed. *Not White Enough, Not Black Enough: Racial Identity in the South African Coloured Community.* Cape Town: Double Storey Books, 2005.
Akenson, Donald. *God's Peoples.* Ithaca, NY: Cornell University Press, 1992.
———. *Saint Saul: The Skeleton Key to the Historical Jesus.* New York: Oxford University Press, 2002.
———. *Surpassing Wonder: The Invention of the Bible and the Talmuds.* New York: Harcourt Brace, 1998.
Alegi, Peter. *Laduma! Soccer, Politics and Society in South Africa.* Scottsville, South Africa: University of KwaZulu-Natal Press, 2004.
Allen, John. *Rabble Rouser for Peace: The Authorized Biography of Desmond Tutu.* New York: Free Press, 2006.
Ally, N., and S. Ally. "Critical Intellectualism." *Biko Lives! Contesting the Legacies of Stephen Biko,* edited by Andile Mngxitama, Amanda Alexander, and Nigel Gibson. New York: Palgrave Macmillan, 2008.
Anderson, Gerald, and Thomas Stransky, eds. *Third World Theologies.* New York: Paulist Press, 1976.
Apter, Andrew. *The Pan-African Nation: Oil and the Spectacle of Culture in Nigeria.* Chicago: University of Chicago Press, 2005.
Ashforth, Adam. *Witchcraft, Violence and Democracy in South Africa.* Chicago: University of Chicago Press, 2005.

Attwell, David. "Intimate Enmity in the Journal of Tiyo Soga." *Critical Inquiry* 23, no. 3 (Spring 1997): 557–77.
——. *Rewriting Modernity: Studies in Black South African Literary History.* Athens: Ohio University Press, 2006.
Badat, Saleem. *Black Student Politics, Higher Education and Apartheid: From Saso to Sansco, 1968–1990.* Pretoria: Human Sciences Research Council, 1999.
Barber, Karin, ed. *Africa's Hidden Histories: Everyday Literacy and Making the Self.* Bloomington: Indiana University Press, 2006.
Barnard, Rita. *Apartheid and Beyond: South African Writers and the Politics of Place.* Oxford: Oxford University Press, 2007.
Barth, Karl. *The Epistle to the Romans.* Oxford: Oxford University Press, 1933.
Basu, Amrita, ed. *The Challenge of Local Feminisms: Women's Movements in Global Perspective.* Boulder, CO: Westview Press, 1995.
Bediako, Kwame. *Jesus and the Gospel in Africa: History and Experience.* Maryknoll, NY: Orbis Books, 2004.
Bergen, Doris. *Twisted Cross: The German Christian Movement in the Third Reich.* Chapel Hill: University of North Carolina Press, 1996.
Biko, Steve. *I Write What I Like.* Edited by Aelred Stubbs. 1978. Reprint, London: Bowerdean Publishing, 1996.
——. *Steve Biko: Black Consciousness in South Africa.* Edited by Millard Arnold. New York: Random House, 1978.
Boesak, Allan. *Black and Reformed: Apartheid, Liberation and the Calvinist Tradition.* Maryknoll, NY: Orbis Books, 1986.
——. *Farewell to Innocence: A Socio-ethical Study of Black Theology and Black Power.* Johannesburg, South Africa: Ravan Press, 1977.
——. *Tenderness of Conscience.* Stellenbosch, South Africa: Sun Press, 2005.
Bond, Patrick. *Elite Transition.* London: Pluto Press, 1998.
——. *Looting Africa: The Economics of Exploitation.* New York: Palgrave Macmillan, 2006.
——. *Unsustainable South Africa.* Pietermaritzburg, South Africa: University of KwaZulu-Natal Press, 2002.
Borer, Tristan Anne. *Challenging the State: Churches as Political Actors in South Africa, 1980–1994.* South Bend, IN: Notre Dame University Press, 1998.
Bosch, David. "Currents and Crosscurrents in South African Black Theology." *Journal of Religion in Africa* 6, no. 1 (1974): 1–22.
——. *Transforming Mission: Paradigm Shifts in the Theology of Mission.* Maryknoll, NY: Orbis Books, 1991.
——. *Witness to the World: The Christian Mission in Theological Perspective.* Atlanta, GA: John Knox Press, 1980.
Boyarin, Daniel. *Dying for God: Martyrdom and the Making of Christianity and Judaism.* Palo Alto, CA: Stanford University Press, 1999.
Bozzoli, Belinda. *Theatres of Struggle and the End of Apartheid.* Johannesburg, South Africa: Witwatersrand University Press, 2004.
Bradford, Helen. *A Taste of Freedom: The ICU in Rural South Africa, 1924–1930.* New Haven, CT: Yale University Press, 1987.

Bradstock, Andrew, and Christopher Rowland, eds. *Radical Christian Writing.* Oxford: Blackwell Publishers, 2002.

Brennan, James. "Blood Enemies: Exploitation and Urban Citizenship in the Nationalist Political Thought of Tanzania, 1958–1975." *Journal of African History* 47, no. 3 (2006): 389–413.

Brickhill, Alan, and Jeremy Brooks. *Whirlwind before the Storm.* London: International Defense and Aid Fund, 1980.

Budlender, Geoffrey. "Black Consciousness and the Liberal Tradition." In *Bounds of Possibility: The Legacy of Steve Biko and Black Consciousness,* edited by N. Barney Pityana, Mamphela Ramphele, Malusi Mpumlwana, and Lindy Wilson, 228–37. Cape Town: David Philip, 1991.

Buis, R. *Religious Beliefs and White Prejudice.* Johannesburg, South Africa: Ravan Press, 1975.

Buntman, Fran. *Robben Island and Prisoner Resistance to Apartheid.* Cambridge: Cambridge University Press, 2003.

Burke, Timothy. *Lifebuoy Men, Lux Women: Commodification, Consumption and Cleanliness in Modern Zimbabwe.* Durham, NC: Duke University Press, 1996.

Campbell, James. *Songs of Zion.* New York: Oxford University Press, 1995.

Carmichael, Stokely [Kwame Ture]. *Ready for the Revolution.* New York: Scribner's, 2003.

Carmichael, Stokely, and Charles Hamilton. *Black Power: The Politics of Liberation in America.* New York: Vintage Books, 1967.

Césaire, Aimé. *Discourse on Colonialism.* 1955. Reprint, New York: Monthly Review Press, 1972.

Chapman, Mark. *Christianity on Trial.* Maryknoll, NY: Orbis Books, 1996.

Chapman, Michael. *Art Talk/Politics Talk.* Scottsville, South Africa: University of KwaZulu-Natal Press, 2006.

———, ed. *The Drum Decade: Stories from the 1950s.* Pietermaritzburg, South Africa: University of Natal Press, 2001.

———. *Soweto Poetry.* Johannesburg, South Africa: McGraw-Hill, 1982.

Charney, Craig. "Black Power, White Press." African Studies Centre, University of the Witwatersrand, 1993.

———. "Civil Society vs. the State: Identity, Institutions, and the Black Consciousness Movement in South Africa." PhD diss., Yale University, 2000.

Chartier, Roger. *The Cultural Origins of the French Revolution.* Durham, NC: Duke University Press, 1991.

Chidester, David. *Christianity: A Global History.* San Francisco: Harper San Francisco, 2000.

———. *Religions of South Africa.* New York: Routledge, 1992.

———. *Savage Systems: Colonialism and Comparative Religion in Southern Africa.* Charlottesville: University Press of Virginia, 1996.

———. *Shots in the Streets.* Boston: Beacon Press, 1991.

Chikane, Frank. *No Life of My Own.* London: Catholic Institute for International Relations, 1988.

Cleage, Albert. *Black Christian Nationalism.* New York: William Morrow, 1972.

———. *The Black Messiah.* 1968. Reprint, Trenton, NJ: Africa World Press, 1991.

Cleaver, Eldridge. *Soul on Ice.* New York: Dell, 1970.

Coetzee, P. H., and A. P. J. Roux, eds. *The African Philosophy Reader.* London: Routledge, 1998.

Cohen, Jeremy. *Sanctifying the Name of God.* Philadelphia: University of Pennsylvania Press, 2004.

Cohen, Paul. *History in Three Keys: The Boxers as Event, Experience and Myth.* New York: Columbia University Press, 1997.

Comaroff, Jean. *Body of Power, Spirit of Resistance.* Chicago: University of Chicago Press, 1985.

Comaroff, Jean, and John Comaroff. *Of Revelation and Revolution.* 2 vols. Chicago: University of Chicago Press, 1991 and 1997.

Cone, James. *Black Theology and Black Power.* Minneapolis, MN: Seabury Press, 1969.

———. *A Black Theology of Liberation.* Philadelphia: Lippincott, 1970.

———. *My Soul Looks Back.* Maryknoll, NY: Orbis Books, 1986.

Cone, James, and Gayraud Wilmore, eds. *Black Theology: A Documentary History.* Maryknoll, NY: Orbis Books, 1979.

Cooper, Frederick. *Colonialism in Question.* Berkeley: University of California Press, 2004.

Cooper, Frederick, and Anne Stoler, eds. *Tensions of Empire.* Berkeley: University of California Press, 1997.

Coplan, David. *In Township Tonight! South Africa's Black City Music and Theatre.* Johannesburg, South Africa: Ravan Press, 1985.

Couzens, Tim. *The New African: A Study of the Life and Work of H. I. E. Dhlomo.* Johannesburg, South Africa: Ravan Press, 1985.

Cox, Harvey. *The Secular City.* New York: Macmillan Press, 1965.

———. *When Jesus Came to Harvard: Making Moral Choices Today.* New York: Houghton Mifflin, 2004.

Crais, Clifton. *The Politics of Evil: Magic, State Power and the Political Imagination in South Africa.* Cambridge: Cambridge University Press, 2002.

Cuthbertson, G. C. "Christians and Structural Violence in SA in the 1970s." In *Views on Violence,* edited by W. S. Vorster, 43–60. Pretoria: University of South Africa Press, 1985.

Czégledy, André. "A New Christianity for a New South Africa: Charismatic Christians and the Post-apartheid Order." *Journal of Religion in Africa* 38, no. 3 (2008): 284–311.

Davis, Angela. "Afro Images: Politics, Fashion and Nostalgia." *Critical Inquiry* 21, no. 1 (1994): 37–45.

———. *Women, Culture, Politics.* New York: Random House, 1989.

Davis, Creston, John Milbank, and Slavoj Žižek, eds. *Theology and the Political: The New Debate.* Durham, NC: Duke University Press, 2005.

De Gruchy, John. *Church Struggle in South Africa.* Grand Rapids, MI: Eerdmans, 1979.

————. *Confessions of a Christian Humanist.* Minneapolis, MN: Fortress Press, 2006.

————. "Beyers Naudé and Public Theology." In *The Legacy of Beyers Naudé*, edited by L. D. Hansen, 81–90. Stellenbosch, South Africa: Sun Press, 2005.

De Gruchy, John, and Charles Villa-Vicencio. *Apartheid Is a Heresy.* Grand Rapids, MI: Eerdmans, 1983.

————. *Resistance and Hope: South African Essays in Honor of Beyers Naudé.* Grand Rapids, MI: Eerdmans, 1985.

De Gruchy, John, and Steve De Gruchy. *Church Struggle in South Africa.* Minneapolis, MN: Fortress Press, 2005.

Desai, Ashwin. *We Are the Poors.* New York: Monthly Review Press, 2002.

Diseko, Nozipho. "The Origins and Development of the South African Students Movement." *Journal of Southern African Studies* 18, no. 1 (1992): 40–62.

Dubow, Saul. *A Commonwealth of Knowledge: Science, Sensibility and White South Africa, 1820–2000.* Oxford: Oxford University Press, 2006.

Durant, Sam, ed. *Black Panther: The Revolutionary Art of Emory Douglas.* New York: Rizzoli, 2007.

Durkheim, Emile. *Elementary Forms of Religious Life.* Edited and translated by Karen Fields. New York: Free Press, 1995.

Du Toit, Andre. "No Chosen People: The Myth of the Calvinist Origins of Afrikaner Nationalism and Racial Ideology." *American Historical Review* 88, no. 4 (1983): 920–52.

————. "Puritans in Africa? Afrikaner 'Calvinism' and Kuyperian Neo-Calvinism in Late Nineteenth-Century South Africa." *Comparative Studies in Society and History* 27, no. 2 (1985): 209–40.

Dyson, Michael Eric. *I May Not Get There with You: The True Martin Luther King Jr.* New York: Free Press, 2000.

Edgar, Robert, and Luyanda ka Msumza, eds. *Freedom in Our Lifetimes: The Collected Writings of Anton Muziwakhe Lembede.* Athens: Ohio University Press, 1996.

Edwards, David Lawrence, ed. *The "Honest to God" Debate.* London: SCM Press, 1963.

Edwards, Tim. *Culture of Masculinity.* New York: Routledge, 2006.

Ellis, Stephen, and Gerrie ter Haar. *Worlds of Power: Religious Thought and Political Practice in Africa.* New York: Oxford University Press, 2004.

Elphick, Rodney, and Rodney Davenport, eds. *Christianity in South Africa.* Berkeley: University of California Press, 1997.

Engelke, Matthew. *A Problem of Presence: Beyond Scripture in an African Church.* Berkeley: University of California Press, 2007.

Estes, Steve. *I Am a Man! Race, Manhood, and the Civil Rights Movement.* Chapel Hill: University of North Carolina Press, 2005.

Etherington, Norman. *The Great Treks.* New York: Longman, 2001.

Evans, Ivan. *Bureaucracy and Race: Native Administration in South Africa.* Berkeley: University of California Press, 1997.

Fanon, Frantz. *Black Skins, White Masks*. New York: Grove Press, 1967.

——. *The Wretched of the Earth*. New York: Grove Press, 1968.

Farisani, Tshenuwani Simon. *In Transit*. Trenton, NJ: Africa World Press, 1990.

Fassin, Didier. *When Bodies Remember: Experiences and Politics of AIDs in South Africa*. Berkeley: University of California Press, 2007.

Fatton, Robert. *Black Consciousness in South Africa: The Dialectics of Ideological Resistance to White Supremacy*. Albany: State University of New York Press, 1986.

Feierman, Steven. "Colonizers, Scholars and the Creation of Invisible Histories." In *Beyond the Cultural Turn*, edited by Lynn Hunt and Victoria Bonnell, 182–216. Berkeley: University of California Press, 1999.

——. *Peasant Intellectuals: Anthropology and History in Tanzania*. Madison: University of Wisconsin Press, 1990.

Ferguson, James. *Expectations of Modernity: Myths and Meanings of Urban Life on the Zambian Copperbelt*. Berkeley: University of California Press, 1999.

——. *Global Shadows: African in the Neo-liberal World Order*. Durham, NC: Duke University Press, 2006.

Ferm, Deane. *Third World Liberation Theologies: An Introductory Survey*. Eugene, OR: Wipf and Stock, 1986.

Fields, Karen. *Revival and Rebellion in Colonial Central Africa*. Princeton, NJ: Princeton University Press, 1985.

Fields, Rona, ed. *Martyrdom*. Westport, CT: Praeger, 2004.

Ford, David, ed. *The Modern Theologians*. Malden, MA: Blackwell Publishers, 1997.

——. *Theology: A Very Short Introduction*. Oxford: Oxford University Press, 1999.

Frankel, Phillip. *An Ordinary Atrocity: Sharpeville and Its Massacre*. Johannesburg, South Africa: Witwatersrand University Press, 2001.

Fredrickson, George. *Black Liberation: A Comparative History of Black Ideologies in the United States and South Africa*. New York: Oxford University Press, 1995.

——. *The Comparative Imagination*. Berkeley: University of California Press, 2000.

——. *White Supremacy*. New York: Oxford University Press, 1981.

Freire, Paulo. *Cultural Action for Freedom*. 1970. Reprint, New York: Penguin, 1972.

——. *Pedagogy of the Oppressed*. 1970. Reprint, New York: Continuum, 1993.

Geiger, Susan. *TANU Women: Gender and Culture in the Making of Tanganyikan Nationalism, 1955–1965*. Portsmouth, NH: Heinemann, 1997.

Gerassi, J., ed. *Revolutionary Priest: The Complete Writings and Messages of Camilo Torres*. New York: Vintage Books, 1971.

Gerhart, Gail. *Black Power in South Africa: The Evolution of an Ideology*. Berkeley: University of California Press, 1979.

Gerhart, Gail, and Thomas Karis, eds. *From Protest to Challenge: Nadir and Resurgence*. Vol. 5. Bloomington: Indiana University Press, 1997.

Gibellini, Rosino. *Paths of African Theology*. Maryknoll, NY: Orbis Books, 1994.

Gifford, Paul. *Ghana's New Christianity: Pentecostalism in a Globalizing African Economy.* Bloomington: Indiana University Press, 2004.

Gilroy, Paul. *The Black Atlantic: Modernity and Double Consciousness.* Cambridge, MA: Harvard University Press, 1993.

Glaser, Clive. *Bo-Tsotsi: The Youth Gangs of Soweto.* Portsmouth, NH: Heinemann, 2000.

———. "'We Must Infiltrate the Tsotsis': School Politics and Youth Gangs in Soweto, 1968–1976." *Journal of Southern African Studies* 24, no. 2 (1998): 301–23.

Glenn, Evelyn Nakano, ed. *Shades of Difference: Why Skin Color Matters.* Palo Alto, CA: Stanford University Press, 2009.

Goba, Bonganjalo. *An Agenda for Black Theology: Hermeneutics for Social Change.* Johannesburg, South Africa: Skotaville, 1988.

Goldenberg, David. *The Curse of Ham: Race and Slavery in Early Judaism, Christianity and Islam.* Princeton, NJ: Princeton University Press, 2005.

Goldsmith, Meredith. "Of Masks, Mimicry, Misogyny and Miscegenation: Forging Black South African Masculinity in Bloke Modisane's *Blame Me on History.*" *Journal of Men's Studies* 10, no. 3 (2002): 291–307.

Gomez, Michael A. *Black Crescent: The Experience and Legacy of African Muslims in the Americas.* Cambridge: Cambridge University Press, 2005.

Goodhew, David. *Respectability and Resistance: A History of Sophiatown.* Westport, CT: Praeger, 2004.

Gordon, Lewis. *Existentia Africana: Understanding Africana Existential Thought.* New York: Routledge, 2000.

Graybill, Lyn. *Religion and Resistance Politics in South Africa.* Westport, CT: Praeger, 1995.

Guha, Ranajit. *Elementary Aspects of Peasant Insurgency in Colonial India.* Delhi, India: Oxford University Press, 1983.

Gumede, William. *Thabo Mbeki and the Battle for the Soul of the ANC.* Cape Town: Zebra Press, 2005.

Gutierrez, Gustavo. *A Theology of Liberation.* Maryknoll, NY: Orbis Books, 1974.

Gutterman, David. *Prophetic Politics: Christian Social Movements and American Democracy.* Ithaca, NY: Cornell University Press, 2005.

Hadfield, Leslie. "Restoring Human Dignity and Building Self-Reliance: Youth, Women and Churches and Black Consciousness Community Development, South Africa, 1969–1977." PhD diss., Michigan State University, 2010.

———. "Pumping Life Back into the Black Man: SASO Community Projects in 1970s South Africa." Paper presented at the African Studies Association Annual Meeting, New York, 20 October 2007.

———. "'We Salute a Hero of the Nation': The Place of Steve Biko in South Africa's History." Master's thesis, Ohio University, 2005.

Halisi, C. R. D. "Biko and Black Consciousness Philosophy: An Interpretation." In *Bounds of Possibility: The Legacy of Steve Biko and Black Consciousness,* edited by N. Barney Pityana, Mamphela Ramphele, Malusi Mpumlwana, and Lindy Wilson, 100–110. Cape Town: David Philip, 1991.

———. *Black Political Thought in the Making of South African Democracy*. Bloomington: Indiana University Press, 1999.

———. "Dividing Lines: Black Political Thought and the Politics of Liberation in South Africa." PhD diss., University of California–Los Angeles, 1988.

Hanchard, Michael. *Party/Politics: Horizons in Black Political Thought*. New York: Oxford University Press, 2006.

Hannay, Alistair, and Gordon Marino, eds. *The Cambridge Companion to Kierkegaard*. Cambridge: Cambridge University Press, 1998.

Hansen, L. D., ed. *The Legacy of Beyers Naudé*. Stellenbosch, South Africa: Sun Press, 2005.

Hardt, Michael, and Antonio Negri. *Empire*. Cambridge, MA: Harvard University Press, 2000.

Harries, Patrick. *Butterflies and Barbarians: Swiss Missionaries and Systems of Knowledge in South-East Africa*. Athens: Ohio University Press, 2007.

Harvey, David. *Spaces of Hope*. Berkeley: University of California Press, 2000.

———. *The Urban Experience*. Baltimore, MD: Johns Hopkins University Press, 1989.

Hassett, Miranda. *Anglican Communion in Crisis: How Episcopal Dissidents and Their African Allies Are Reshaping Anglicanism*. Princeton, NJ: Princeton University Press, 2007.

Hassim, Shireen. "Nationalism, Feminism and Autonomy: The ANC in Exile and the Question of Women." *Journal of Southern African Studies* 30, no. 3 (2004): 433–55.

———. *Women's Organizations and Democracy in South Africa*. Madison: University of Wisconsin Press, 2006.

Hastings, Adrian. *The Construction of Nationhood: Ethnicity, Religion and Nationalism*. Cambridge: Cambridge University Press, 1997.

———. *A History of African Christianity, 1950–1975*. Cambridge: Cambridge University Press, 1979.

———. *A World History of Christianity*. Grand Rapids, MI: Eerdmans, 1999.

Higgs, Catherine. *The Ghost of Equality: The Public Lives of D. D. T. Jabavu of South Africa, 1885–1959*. Athens: Ohio University Press, 1997.

Hill, Shannen. "Iconic Autopsy: Post-mortem Portraits of Bantu Stephen Biko." *African Arts* 38, no. 3 (2005): 14–25.

Hirson, Baruch. *Year of Fire, Year of Ash*. London: Zed Press, 1979.

Hoehler-Fatton, Cynthia. *Women of Fire and Spirit*. New York: Oxford University Press, 1996.

hooks, bell. *Ain't I a Woman? Black Women and Feminism*. Boston: South End Press, 1981.

Hopkins, Dwight. *Black Faith and Public Talk: Critical Essays on James Cone's "Black Theology and Black Power."* Maryknoll, NY: Orbis Books, 1999.

———. *Black Theology USA and South Africa: Politics, Culture, and Liberation*. Maryknoll, NY: Orbis Books, 1989.

———. *Heart and Head: Black Theology—Present, Past and Future*. New York: Palgrave, 2002.

Hopkins, Pat, and Helen Grange. *The Rocky Rioter Teargas Show: The Inside Story of the 1976 Soweto Uprising.* Johannesburg, South Africa: Struik Publishers, 2001.

Horrell, Muriel, ed. *Bantu Education to 1968.* Johannesburg: South African Institute of Race Relations, 1968.

Houston, William J. "A Critical Evaluation of the University Christian Movement as an Ecumenical Mission to Students, 1968–1972." Master's thesis, University of South Africa, 1997.

Hyslop, Jonathan. *The Classroom Struggle.* Pietermaritzburg, South Africa: University of Natal Press, 1999.

Jacobs, Nancy. "Consciousness, Liberation and Revolution: Black Theology in South Africa." Master's thesis, University of California–Los Angeles, 1987.

Jehle, Frank. *Ever against the Stream: The Politics of Karl Barth.* Grand Rapids, MI: Eerdmans, 2002.

Jones, William. *Is God a White Racist?* Garden City, NY: Anchor Press, 1973.

Joseph, Peniel. "Black Liberation without Apology: Reconceptualizing the Black Power Movement." *Black Scholar* 31, no. 3 (2001): 3.

———, ed. *The Black Power Movement: Rethinking the Civil Rights–Black Power Era.* New York: Routledge, 2006.

———. *Waiting 'til the Midnight Hour: A Narrative History of Black Power in America.* New York: Henry Holt, 2006.

Juckes, Timothy. *Opposition in South Africa: The Leadership of Z. K. Matthews, Nelson Mandela and Stephen Biko.* Westport, CT: Praeger, 1995.

Kairos Theologians. *Challenge to the Church: A Theological Comment on the Political Crisis in South Africa: The Kairos Document.* Stony Point, NY: Theology in Global Context, 1985.

Kallaway, Peter, ed. *The History of Education under Apartheid.* Cape Town: Pearson Education South Africa, 2002.

Kane-Berman, John. *Soweto: Black Revolt, White Reaction.* Johannesburg, South Africa: Ravan Press, 1978.

Kaunda, Kenneth. *A Humanist in Africa.* Edited by Colin Morris. London: Longmans, 1966.

———. *Zambia Shall Be Free: An Autobiography.* London: Heinemann, 1962.

Kavanagh, Robert. *South African People's Plays.* London: Heinemann, 1981.

Kee, Alistair. *The Rise and Demise of Black Theology.* Burlington, VT: Ashgate, 2006.

Kelley, Robin. *Freedom Dreams: The Black Radical Imagination.* Boston: Beacon Press, 2002.

———. *Race Rebels.* New York: Free Press, 1996.

Kelly, G., and F. Burton Nelson, eds. *Testament to Freedom: The Essential Writings of Dietrich Bonhoeffer.* New York: HarperCollins, 1990.

Khilnani, Sunil. *The Idea of India.* New York: Farrar Straus and Giroux, 1997.

Kierkegaard, Søren. *Fear and Trembling.* New York: Doubleday Anchor, 1954.

Koyama, Kosuke. *Water Buffalo Theology.* 1974. Reprint, Maryknoll, NY: Orbis Books, 1999.

Kretzschmar, Louis. *The Voice of Black Theology in South Africa*. Johannesburg, South Africa: Ravan Press, 1986.

Krikler, Jeremy. *The Rand Revolt*. Johannesburg, South Africa: Jonathan Ball, 2005.

Kritzinger, J. J. *Black Theology in South Africa*. Pretoria: UNISA, 1989.

Kunnie, Julian. *Models of Black Theology: Issues in Class, Culture and Gender*. Valley Forge, PA: Trinity Press International, 1994.

Kuper, Leo. *An African Bourgeoisie*. New Haven, CT: Yale University Press, 1965.

Lamola, John. "Towards a Black Church." *Journal of Black Theology in South Africa* 2, no. 1 (1988): 5–14.

Landau, Paul. *Realm of the Word*. Portsmouth, NH: Heinemann, 1995.

——. "'Religion' and Christian Conversion in African History: A New Model." *Journal of Religious History* 23, no. 1 (1999): 8–30.

Langa, Mandla. *Memory of Stones*. Cape Town: David Philip, 2002.

Langley, J. Ayo, ed. *Ideologies of Liberation in Black Africa, 1856–1970*. London: Rex Collings, 1979.

Lear, Jonathan. *Radical Hope*. Cambridge, MA: Harvard University Press, 2006.

Legassick, Martin. "The National Union of South African Students: Ethnic Cleavage and Ethnic Integration in the Universities." African Studies Center, University of California, Los Angeles, 1968.

Lewis, Desiree. "Introduction: African Feminisms." *Agenda*, no. 50 (2001): 4–10.

Likupe, Raymond. "The Unfolding of African Christology since 1919." PhD diss., University of Notre Dame, 2005.

Lindsay, Lisa, and Stephen Miescher, eds. *Men and Masculinities in Modern Africa*. Portsmouth, NH: Heinemann, 2003.

Lobban, Michael. "Black Consciousness on Trial: The SASO/BPC Trial, 1974–1976." African Studies Centre, University of the Witwatersrand, 1990.

——. *White Man's Justice*. Oxford: Clarendon Press, 1996.

Lodge, Tom. *All, Here and Now: Black Politics in South Africa in the 1980s*. London: C. Hurst, 1992.

Lonsdale, John. "Moral Economy of Mau Mau." In Bruce Berman and John Lonsdale, *Unhappy Valley: Conflict in Kenya and Africa*, 2:315–467. Athens: Ohio University Press, 1992.

Loubser, J. A. *The Apartheid Bible: A Critical Review of Racial Theology in South Africa*. Cape Town: Maskew Miller Longman, 1987.

MacDonald, Michael. *Why Race Matters in South Africa*. Cambridge, MA: Harvard University Press, 2006.

Macey, David. *Frantz Fanon*. New York: Picador USA, 2000.

Magaziner, Daniel. "'Black Man, You Are on Your Own!': Making Race Consciousness in South African Thought, 1968–1972." *International Journal of African Historical Studies* 42, no. 2 (2009): 221–41.

——. "Christ in Context: Developing a Political Faith in Apartheid South Africa." *Radical History Review*, no. 99 (Fall 2007): 80–106.

——. "Liberating the Black Messiah." *Maryland Historian* 29 (2005): 23–49.

——. *One Word: Listening to Violence in Early Colonial Sierra Leone*. Madison: University of Wisconsin–Madison African Studies Program, 2006.

———. "Removing the Blinders, Adjusting the View: A Case Study from Early Colonial Sierra Leone." *History in Africa* 34, no. 1 (2007): 169–88.

Maharaj, Mac, ed. *Reflections in Prison.* Cape Town: Zebra Press, 2001.

Maimela, Simon, ed. *Culture, Religion and Liberation.* Pretoria: Penrose, 1994.

———. *Proclaim Freedom to My People: Essays on Religion and Politics.* Johannesburg, South Africa: Skotaville, 1997.

Maimela, Simon, and Dwight Hopkins. *We Are One Voice.* Johannesburg, South Africa: Skotaville, 1989.

Majeke, N. [Dora Taylor]. *The Role of Missionaries in Conquest.* Johannesburg, South Africa: Society of Young Africa, 1953.

Mama, Amina. *Beyond the Masks: Race, Gender and Subjectivity.* New York: Routledge, 1995.

Mama, Amina, and Elaine Salo. "Talking about Feminisms in Africa." *Agenda,* no. 50 (2001): 58–63.

Mamdani, Mahmood. *Citizen and Subject.* Princeton, NJ: Princeton University Press, 1996.

Manganyi, N. C. *Being-Black-in-the-World.* Johannesburg, South Africa: SPRO-CAS/Ravan Press, 1973.

Mangena, Mosibudi. *On Your Own.* Florida Hills, South Africa: Vivlia, 1989.

Mangena, Oshadi. "The Black Consciousness Philosophy and the Women's Question in South Africa: 1970–1980." In *Biko Lives! Contesting the Legacies of Stephen Biko,* edited by Andile Mngxitama, Amanda Alexander, and Nigel Gibson, 253–67. New York: Palgrave Macmillan, 2008.

Marschall, Sabine. "Pointing to the Dead: Victims, Martyrs and Public Memory in South Africa." *South African Historical Journal* 60, no. 1 (2008): 103–23.

Marx, Anthony. *Making Race and Nation.* Cambridge: Cambridge University Press, 1998.

Mattera, Don. *Gone with the Twilight: A Story of Sophiatown.* London: Zed Books, 1987.

Matthews, James. *Cry Rage! The Odyssey of a Dissident Poet.* Cape Town: Realities, 2006.

Matthews, James, and Gladys Thomas. *Cry Rage!* Johannesburg, South Africa: SPROCAS, 1972.

Masuzawa, Tomoko. *The Invention of World Religions.* Chicago: University of Chicago Press, 2005.

Maxwell, David. *African Gifts of the Spirit: Pentecostalism and the Rise of a Zimbabwean Transnational Religious Movement.* Athens: Ohio University Press, 2006.

Mbali, Zolile. *The Churches and Racism.* London: SCM Press, 1987.

Mbembe, Achille. "Necropolitics." *Public Culture* 15, no. 1 (2003): 11–40.

Mbembe, Achille, and Gayatri Spivak. "Religion, Politics, Theology." *boundary 2* 34, no. 2 (2007): 149–70.

Mbiti, John. *African Religions and Philosophy.* New York: Praeger, 1969.

———. "An African Views American Black Theology." In *Black Theology: A Documentary History,* edited by James Cone and Gayraud Wilmore, 477–82. Maryknoll, NY: Orbis Books, 1979.

———. *Concepts of God in Africa*. London: SPCK, 1970.

McClintock, Anne. "Family Feuds: Gender, Nationalism and the Family." *Feminist Review*, no. 44 (1993): 61–80.

———. *Imperial Leather: Race, Gender and Sexuality in the Colonial Contest*. New York: Routledge, 1995.

Meyer, Birgit. *Translating the Devil: Religion and Modernity among the Ewe in Ghana*. Trenton, NJ: Africa World Press, 1999.

Mikell, Gwendolyn. *African Feminism: The Politics of Survival in Sub-Saharan Africa*. Philadelphia: University of Pennsylvania Press, 1997.

Miller, Jim. *"Democracy Is in the Streets": From Port Huron to the Siege of Chicago*. New York: Simon and Schuster, 1987.

Miner, Edward. "Common Ground in Black American and Black South African Theologies: James Cone and Allan Boesak." Master's thesis, Emory University, 1991.

Mkhabela, Bongi. *Open Earth and Black Roses*. Johannesburg, South Africa: Skotaville, 2001.

Mngxitama, Andile, Amanda Alexander, and Nigel Gibson, eds. *Biko Lives! Contesting the Legacies of Stephen Biko*. New York: Palgrave Macmillan, 2008.

Mochechane, Steve. "The Implications of the Ethics of Dr. Martin Luther King, Jr.: The Case of South Africa." Master's thesis, Garrett Evangelical Seminary, 1990.

Modisane, Bloke. *Blame Me on History*. 1963. Reprint, New York: Simon and Schuster, 1990.

Mofokeng, Takatso. *Christ among the Crossbearers: Towards a Black Christology*. Kampen, the Netherlands: Uitgeversmaatschappij J. H. Kok, 1983.

Mokoka, G. Clement. *Black Experience in Black Theology*. Zeerust, South Africa: Geboren te Sesobe, 1984.

Molobi, Masilo Sonnyboy. "African Theology, Black Theology and the AIC: A Vision for Mission." Doctoral diss., University of South Africa, 2004.

Moltmann, Jürgen. *Religion, Revolution and the Future*. New York: Scribner's, 1969.

———. *Theology of Hope*. London: SCM Press, 1967.

Moodie, T. Dunbar. *The Rise of Afrikanerdom*. Berkeley: University of California Press, 1975.

Moore, Basil. "Black Theology Revisited." Available at http://www.sorat.ukzn. ac.za/theology/bct/moore.htm (accessed on 17 June 2009).

———, ed. *Black Theology: The South African Voice*. London: C. Hurst, 1973.

———, ed. *The Challenge of Black Theology in South Africa*. Atlanta, GA: John Knox Press, 1974.

Morrell, Robert, ed. *Changing Men in Southern Africa*. Pietermaritzburg, South Africa: University of Natal Press, 2001.

Morrow, Sean, Brown Maaba, and Loyiso Pulumani. *Education in Exile: SOMAFCO, the ANC School in Tanzania, 1978–1992*. Pretoria: HSRC Press, 2004.

Mosala, Itumeleng. *Biblical Hermeneutics and Black Theology in South Africa*. Grand Rapids, MI: Eerdmans, 1989.

Mosala, Itumeleng, and Buti Tlhagale, eds. *The Unquestionable Right to Be Free: Black Theology from South Africa*. Johannesburg, South Africa: Skotaville, 1986.

Moses, William Jeremiah. *Black Messiahs and Uncle Toms: Social and Literary Manipulations of a Religious Myth*. University Park: Pennsylvania State University Press, 1982.

Mpumlwana, Malusi, and Thoko Mpumlwana. Introduction to *I Write What I Like*, by Steve Biko, edited by Aelred Stubbs, x–xxiv. 1978; repr., London: Bowerdean Publishing, 1996.

Mukuka, George. "The Impact of Black Consciousness on Black Catholic Clergy and Their Training." Master's thesis, University of Natal–Pietermaritzburg, 1996.

Mzamane, Mbulelo. *Children of Soweto*. London: Harlow Essex Longman, 1982.

——. *The Children of the Diaspora and Other Stories of Exile*. Florida Hills, South Africa: Vivlia, 1996.

Ndebele, Njabulo. *Fools and Other Stories*. New York: Readers International, 1983.

——. *Rediscovery of the Ordinary*. Scottsville, South Africa: University of KwaZulu–Natal Press, 2006.

Ndletyana, Mcebisi, ed. *African Intellectuals in 19th and Early 20th Century South Africa*. Cape Town: HSRC Press, 2008.

Ndlovu, Sifiso. *The Soweto Uprisings: Counter-memories of June 1976*. Johannesburg, South Africa: Ravan Press, 1998.

Nicolson, Ronald. *A Black Future? Jesus and Salvation in South Africa*. Philadelphia: Trinity Press International, 1990.

Nixon, Rob. *Homelands, Harlem and Hollywood: South African Culture and the World Beyond*. New York: Routledge, 1994.

Nkomo, Mokubung. *Student Culture and Activism in Black South African Universities*. Westport, CT: Greenwood Press, 1984.

Nkosi, Lewis. *Home and Exile*. London: Longman's, 1965.

Nnaemeka, Obioma, ed. *Sisterhood, Feminisms and Power: From Africa to the Diaspora*. Trenton, NJ: Africa World Press, 1998.

Noble, Vanessa. "Doctors Divided: Gender, Race and Class Anomalies in the Production of Black Medical Doctors in Apartheid South Africa, 1948 to 1994." PhD diss., University of Michigan, 2005.

Nolan, Albert. *God in South Africa*. Cape Town: David Philip, 1988.

——. *Jesus before Christianity*. Maryknoll, NY: Orbis Books, 1976.

Nolutshungu, Sam. *Changing South Africa: Political Considerations*. Manchester, UK: Manchester University Press, 1982.

Nuttall, Sarah, and Achille Mbembe, eds. *Johannesburg: The Elusive Metropolis*. Durham, NC: Duke University Press, 2008.

Nyerere, Julius. *Man and Development*. Dar es Salaam: Oxford University Press, 1974.

Odinga, Oginga. *Not Yet Uhuru*. London: Heinemann, 1967.

Ohnuki-Tierney, Emiko. *Kamikaze, Cherry Blossoms, and Nationalisms*. Chicago: University of Chicago Press, 2002.

O'Malley, Padraig. *Shades of Difference: Mac Maharaj and the Struggle for South Africa*. New York: Viking, 2007.

Oosthuizen, G. C. "Black Theology in Historical Perspective." *South African Journal of African Affairs* 3 (1973): 77–94.

Papendorff, Adrienne. "A General History of the Development of Education at Mariannhill Monastery from 1884–1988." Bachelor's thesis, University of Natal, 1989.

Parratt, John. *An Introduction to Third World Theologies*. Cambridge: Cambridge University Press, 2004.

———. "Marxism, Black Theology, and the South African Dilemma." *Journal of Modern African Studies* 28, no. 3 (1990): 527–33.

———. *Reinventing Christianity*. Trenton, NJ: Africa World Press, 1995.

Paul, Samuel. *The Ubuntu God: Deconstructing a South African Narrative of Oppression*. Eugene, OR: Pickwick Publications, 2009.

Peel, J. D. Y. *Religious Encounter and the Making of the Yoruba*. Bloomington: Indiana University Press, 2000.

Peffer, John. *Art and the End of Apartheid*. Minneapolis: University of Minnesota Press, 2009.

Peires, Jeff. *The Dead Will Arise*. Bloomington: Indiana University Press, 1989.

Peterson, Derek. *Creative Writing: Translation, Bookkeeping and the Work of the Imagination in Colonial Kenya*. Portsmouth, NH: Heinemann, 2004.

Peterson, Derek, and Darren Walhof, eds. *The Invention of Religion: Rethinking Belief in Politics and History*. New Brunswick, NJ: Rutgers University Press, 2002.

Pithouse, Richard. "The Tool Never Possesses the Man: Taking Fanon's Humanism Seriously." Seminar paper presented at the University of KwaZulu-Natal, 2003.

Pityana, N. Barney, Mamphela Ramphele, Malusi Mpumlwana, and Lindy Wilson, eds. *Bounds of Possibility: The Legacy of Steve Biko and Black Consciousness*. Cape Town: David Philip, 1991.

Pogrund, Benjamin. *How Can Man Die Better?* Johannesburg, South Africa: Jonathan Ball, 1990.

Pohlandt-McCormick, Helena. "Controlling Woman: Winnie Mandela and the 1976 Soweto Uprising." *International Journal of African Historical Studies* 33, no. 3 (2000): 585–614.

———. "I Saw a Nightmare . . ." New York: Columbia University Press, 2005.

Prestholdt, Jeremy. *Domesticating the World: African Consumerism and the Genealogies of Globalization*. Berkeley: University of California Press, 2008.

Ramphele, Mamphela. *Across Boundaries*. New York: Feminist Press at CUNY, 1996.

Randall, Peter, ed. *Apartheid and the Church*. Johannesburg, South Africa: SPRO-CAS, 1972.

Ranger, Terence. *Are We Not Also Men? The Samkange Family and African Politics in Zimbabwe, 1920–1964*. Portsmouth, NH: Heinemann, 1995.

————, ed. *Evangelical Christianity and Democracy in Africa*. Oxford: Oxford University Press, 2006.

Ranuga, Thomas. "Frantz Fanon and Black Consciousness in Azania (South Africa)." *Phylon* 47, no. 3 (1986): 182–91.

Ratele, Kopano. "Men and Masculinities." In *The Gender of Psychology*, edited by T. Shefer, F. Boonzaier, and P. Kiguwa, 165–77. Cape Town: University of Cape Town Press, 2006.

Redding, Sean. *Sorcery and Sovereignty: Taxation, Power and Rebellion in South Africa, 1880–1963*. Athens: Ohio University Press, 2006.

Rich, Paul. *Hope and Despair: English Speaking Intellectuals and South African Politics, 1896–1976*. London: British Academic Press, 1993.

————. "Liberals, Radicals and the Politics of Black Consciousness." African Studies Centre, University of the Witwatersrand, 1989.

Roberts, J. Deotis. *Black Theology in Dialogue*. Philadelphia: Westminster Press, 1987.

Robinson, John. *Honest to God*. London: SCM Press, 1963.

Rodney, Walter. *The Groundings with My Brothers*. London: Bogle-L'Ouverture Productions, 1969.

Romero, Patricia. *Profiles in Diversity: Women in the New South Africa*. East Lansing: Michigan State University Press, 1998.

Ross, Marlon. *Manning the Race: Reforming Black Men in the Jim Crow Era*. New York: New York University Press, 2004.

Rossinow, Doug. *The Politics of Authenticity: Liberalism, Christianity and the New Left in America*. New York: Columbia University Press, 1998.

Ryan, Colleen. *Beyers Naudé: Pilgrimage of Faith*. Cape Town: David Philip, 2005.

Sanders, Mark. *Complicities: The Intellectual and Apartheid*. Durham, NC: Duke University Press, 2002.

Sanneh, Lamin O. *Translating the Message: The Missionary Impact on Culture*. Maryknoll, NY: Orbis Books, 1989.

Schaffer, Kay, and Sidonie Smith. *Human Rights and Narrated Lives: The Ethics of Recognition*. New York: Palgrave Macmillan, 2004.

Schatzberg, Michael. *Political Legitimacy in Middle Africa: Father, Family, Food*. Bloomington: Indiana University Press, 2001.

Schlebusch, Alwyn. *South Africa: Commission of Inquiry into Certain Organisations*. Pretoria: Government Printer, 1975.

Schofeleers, J. Matthew. "Black and African Theology in South Africa." *Journal of Religion in Africa* 18, no. 2 (1988): 99–124.

Schuster, Linda. *A Burning Hunger: One Family's Struggle against Apartheid*. London: Jonathan Cape, 2004.

Scott, David. *Conscripts of Modernity: The Tragedy of Colonial Enlightenment*. Durham, NC: Duke University Press, 2004.

Sebidi, John. "The Dynamics of the Black Struggle and Its Implications for Black Theology." In *The Unquestionable Right to Be Free: Black Theology from South Africa*, edited by Itumeleng Mosala and Buti Tlhagale, 1–36. Johannesburg, South Africa: Skotaville, 1986.

Self, Robert. *American Babylon: Race and the Struggle for Postwar Oakland*. Princeton, NJ: Princeton University Press, 2003.

Seidman, Gay. *Manufacturing Militance*. Berkeley: University of California Press, 1994.

Sepamla, Sipho. *A Ride on the Whirlwind*. Johannesburg, South Africa: A. D. Donker, 1981.

Serote, Wally. *To Every Birth Its Blood*. 1978. Reprint, Johannesburg, South Africa: Picador Africa, 2004.

Setiloane, Gabriel. *African Theology: An Introduction*. 1986. Reprint, Cape Town: Lux Verbi, 2000.

———. *Image of God among the Sotho-Tswana*. Rotterdam, the Netherlands: A. A. Balkema, 1976.

Simone, Abdou-Maliq. *For the City Yet to Come: Changing African Life in Four Cities*. Durham, NC: Duke University Press, 2004.

Sobino, Jon. *Christ the Liberator: A View from the Victims*. Maryknoll, NY: 2001.

———. *Jesus the Liberator: A Historical-Theological Reading of Jesus of Nazareth*. Maryknoll, NY: Orbis Books, 1993.

Sono, Themba. *Reflections on the Origins of Black Consciousness in South Africa*. Pretoria: HSRC Press, 1993.

———. "South Africa: The Agony of Black Radical Rhetoric 1970–1974." Master's thesis, Duquesne University, [1975?].

South African Democracy Educational Trust. *The Road to Democracy in South Africa*. Vol. 2. Pretoria: UNISA, 2007.

Spitzer, Leo. *Lives In Between*. New York: Hill and Wang, 1989.

Springer, Kimberly. *Living for the Revolution: Black Feminist Organizations, 1968–1980*. Durham, NC: Duke University Press, 2005.

Stanley, B., ed. *Missions, Nationalism and the End of Empire*. Grand Rapids, MI: Eerdmans, 2003.

Suggs, M. Jack, Katharine Doob Sakenfeld, and James R. Mueller, eds. *The Oxford Study Bible*. New York: Oxford University Press, 1992.

Sugrue, Thomas. *Sweet Land of Liberty: The Forgotten Struggle for Civil Rights in the North*. New York: Random House, 2008.

Summers, Carol. "Catholic Action and Ugandan Radicalism: Political Activism in Buganda, 1930–1950." *Journal of Religion in Africa* 39, no. 1 (2009): 60–90.

Sundermeier, Theo, ed. *Church and Nationalism in South Africa*. Johannesburg, South Africa: Ravan Press, 1975.

Suri, Jeremi. *Power and Protest*. Cambridge, MA: Harvard University Press, 2003.

Suttner, Raymond. *The ANC Underground in South Africa: A Social and Historical Study*. Johannesburg, South Africa: Jacana Press, 2008.

Taylor, Christopher. *A Secular Age*. Cambridge, MA: Harvard University Press, 2007.

———. *Sources of the Self: The Making of Modern Identity*. Cambridge, MA: Harvard University Press, 1989.

Temple, William. *Christianity and the Social Order*. London: Shepheard-Walwyn, 1942.

Themba, Can. *The Will to Die*. London: Heinemann, 1972.

Thomas, David. *Christ Divided: Liberalism, Ecumenism and Race in South Africa*. Pretoria: UNISA Press, 2002.

Thomas, Deborah. *Modern Blackness: Nationalism, Globalization and the Politics of Culture in Jamaica*. Durham, NC: Duke University Press, 2004.

Thomas, Linda E., ed. *Living Stones in the Household of God: The Legacy and Future of Black Theology*. Minneapolis, MN: Fortress Press, 2004.

Thomas, Lynn. "The Modern Girl and Racial Respectability in 1930s South Africa." *Journal of African History* 47, no. 3 (2006): 461–90.

Thompson, Leonard. *A History of South Africa*. New Haven, CT: Yale University Press, 2001.

———. *The Political Mythology of Apartheid*. New Haven, CT: Yale University Press, 1986.

Thurman, Howard. *Jesus and the Disinherited*. 1949. Reprint, Richmond, IN: Friends United Press, 1969.

Tillich, Paul. *The Courage to Be*. 1952. Reprint, New Haven, CT: Yale University Press, 2000.

Tutu, Desmond. "Black Theology/African Theology—Soulmates or Antagonists?" In *Black Theology: A Documentary History*, edited by James Cone and Gayraud Wilmore, 483–91. Maryknoll, NY: Orbis Books, 1979.

———. *Crying in the Wilderness*. Grand Rapids, MI: Eerdmans, 1982.

———. *Hope and Suffering*. Johannesburg, South Africa: Skotaville, 1983.

———. *The Rainbow People of God*. New York: Bantam Books, 1995.

Van Deburg, William L. *New Day in Babylon: The Black Power Movement and American Culture, 1965–1975*. Chicago: University of Chicago Press, 1992.

Van de Merwe, Hendrik, and David Welsh, eds. *Students Perspectives on South Africa*. Cape Town: David Philip, 1972.

Vandenberg, Frank. *Abraham Kuyper*. Grand Rapids, MI: Eerdmans, 1960.

Vanek, Monique. "Wilgespruit Fellowship Centre, an Ecumenical Island of Multiracialism in Apartheid SA from 1949–1979, with a Particular Focus on the 1960s and 1970s." Bachelor's thesis, University of the Witwatersrand, 2002.

van Kessel, Ineke. *"Beyond Our Wildest Dreams": The UDF and the Transformation of South Africa*. Charlottesville: University Press of Virginia, 2000.

Vansina, Jan. *Paths in the Rainforest: Towards a History of the Political Tradition in Equatorial Africa*. Madison: University of Wisconsin Press, 1991.

Van Wyk, Christopher. *Celebrating Steve Biko: We Write What We Like*. New York: Columbia University Press, 2009.

Vigne, Randolph. *Liberals against Apartheid: A History of the Liberal Party of South Africa, 1953–68*. New York: St. Martin's Press, 1997.

Vilakazi, Absolom. *Shembe*. Johannesburg, South Africa: Skotaville, 1986.

Villa-Vicencio, Charles, ed. *On Reading Karl Barth in South Africa*. Grand Rapids, MI: Eerdmans, 1988.

Vinson, Robert. "'Sea Kaffirs': 'American Negroes' and the Gospel of Garveyism in Early Twentieth-Century Cape Town." *Journal of African History* 47, no. 2 (2006): 281–303.

Volz, Stephen. *Chief of a Heathen Town: Kgosi Sechele and the Arrival of Christianity among the Tswana.* Madison, WI: African Studies Program, 2001.

Waetjen, Thembisa. *Workers and Warriors: Masculinity and the Struggle for Nation in South Africa.* Urbana: University of Illinois Press, 2004.

Walker, Cherryl. *Women and Resistance in South Africa.* 1981. Reprint, New York: Monthly Review Press, 1992.

Walsh, Denise, with Pamela Scully. "Altering Politics, Contesting Gender." *Journal of Southern African Studies* 32, no. 1 (2006): 1–12.

Walshe, Peter. *Church versus State in South Africa.* Maryknoll, NY: Orbis Books, 1983.

——. *Prophetic Christianity and the Liberation Movement in South Africa.* Pietermaritzburg, South Africa: Cluster Publications, 1995.

Ware, Frederick. *Methodologies of Black Theology.* Cleveland, OH: Pilgrim Press, 2002.

Washington, Joseph. *Black Religion.* Boston: Beacon Press, 1964.

Webb, Pauline, ed. *A Long Struggle: The Involvement of the World Council of Churches in South Africa.* Geneva, Switzerland: WCC Publications, 1994.

Weinstein, Barbara. "Presidential Address—Developing Inequality." *American Historical Review* 111, no. 1 (2008): 1–18.

Wenzel, Jennifer. *Bulletproof: Afterlives of Anticolonial Prophecy in South Africa and Beyond.* Chicago: University of Chicago Press, 2009.

West, Cornel. *The Cornel West Reader.* New York: Basic Books, 1999.

West, Gerald. *Biblical Hermeneutics of Liberation: Modes of Reading the Bible in the South African Context.* Maryknoll, NY: Orbis Books, 1995.

——. "Don't Stand by My Story." *Journal of Theology for Southern Africa,* no. 98 (1997): 3–12.

West, Harry. *Kupilikula: Governance and the Invisible Realm in Mozambique.* Chicago: University of Chicago Press, 2005.

West, Harry, and Todd Sanders. *Transparency and Conspiracy: Ethnographies of Suspicion in the New World Order.* Durham, NC: Duke University Press, 2003.

West, Michael O. *The Rise of an African Middle Class: Colonial Zimbabwe, 1898–1965.* Bloomington: Indiana University Press, 2002.

Wilde, Melissa. *Vatican II: A Sociological Analysis of Religious Change.* Princeton, NJ: Princeton University Press, 2007.

Wilder, Gary. *The French Imperial Nation-State: Negritude and Colonial Humanism between the Two World Wars.* Chicago: University of Chicago Press, 2005.

Wilmore, Gayraud. *Black Religion and Black Radicalism.* Garden City, NY: Doubleday, 1972.

Witz, Leslie. *Apartheid's Festival: Contesting South Africa's National Pasts.* Bloomington: Indiana University Press, 2003.

Woods, Donald. *Biko*. New York: Paddington Press, 1978.

Wright, H. *The Burden of the Present: Liberal-Radical Controversy over Southern African History*. Cape Town: David Philip, 1977.

Wright, Michelle. *Becoming Black: Creating Identity in the African Diaspora*. Durham, NC: Duke University Press, 2004.

Wylie, Diana. *Art and Revolution: The Life and Death of Thami Mnyele, South African Artist*. Charlottesville: University Press of Virginia, 2008.

———. *Starving on a Full Stomach*. Charlottesville: University Press of Virginia, 2001.

Young, Cynthia. *Soul Power: Culture, Radicalism and the Making of a U.S. Third World Left*. Durham, NC: Duke University Press, 2006.

Yuval-Davis, Nira, Floya Anthias, and Jo Campling, eds. *Woman-Nation-State*. New York: St. Martin's Press, 1989.

Zachernuk, Phillip. *Colonial Subjects: An African Intelligentsia and Atlantic Ideas*. Charlottesville: University Press of Virginia, 2000.

Žižek, Slavoj. *The Puppet and the Dwarf*. Cambridge, MA: MIT Press, 2003.

Zulu, Alphaeus Hamilton. *The Dilemma of the Black South African*. Cape Town: University of Cape Town, 1972.

Index

Abraham, Hans, 209n11
activists: agency and maturation of, 36–39, 203n74; appearance and fashion choices of, 111, 224n50; background of, 5–6, 13, 18–20, 23, 93; codes used by, 132, 133; friends and enemies named by, 140, 144–48; as historical subjects and conscious selves, 41–42, 44–45; liminality of, 197n13; memories and experiences of, 21–25; as men, adults, and black, 51; reflections on, 185–90; strikes, protests, and rallies of (1972–76), 148–54. *See also* Black Consciousness ideology; Christianity; conscientization; gender issues; masculinity; prophets; selfhood and self-fashioning; voice; *specific individuals and organizations*
Africa: human community as gift of, 45–46, 88–89, 91, 117; idealization of precolonial, 88; independence successes in, 1, 27, 46, 148, 151–52, 160; South Africa's perspective compared with rest of, 80, 91–92; "soil of," 44, 84, 87, 93; true humanity in culture of, 45–46; worldview of, 89. *See also* African diaspora; African intellectual history; Africanism; Africanization; African Theology; African traditional religions; *and specific countries*
African Americans: borrowings from, 46–48; Christianity of, 80, 113–14; dialectics of religion, 93–97; name-calling against, 144–45; translations from, 48–50, 53, 207n41. *See also* Black Power (US); Black Theology
African diaspora: American Black Theology and, 80; black intellectuals and, 6; Black Messiah and, 114–15; as counterculture, 49; gender issues in, 7; music of, 46; white existentialism and, 8–9
African Dutch Reformed Church, 62, 210n22
African existentialism: attitude toward future, 51–53; being "black" in, 42–50, 205n13; beingness and humanity in, 41–42; ethical questions in, 8–9; influential text in, 197n15; liberation in, 10; questions about "I" and blackness, 110–11. *See also* beingness; human community and humanism
African Independent Church Association, 219–20n58
African Independent Churches (AICs): apolitical stance of, 65, 219–20n58; Christianity translated in, 84–87; similarities shared with mainstream church, 216n16; traditional practices in, 87–90, 93. *See also* African Theology; Black Theology

African intellectual history: approach to, 6–8; domestication of ideas in, 193n17; ethical questions in, 8–9; limits of, 5–6, 192n11; predecessors of, 10. *See also* African existentialism; Black Consciousness ideology; theology
Africanism: black (term) vs., 45–46, 205–6n17; exclusions of, 140, 142, 144, 232–33n12; fears of, 43–44. *See also* Pan-Africanist Congress (PAC)
Africanization: of Christianity, 84–90; of clerical robes, 189; debates on, 80–84, 104
African National Congress (ANC): attitudes toward SASO, 141–42; banning of, 18; criticism of, 199n36; failed promises of, 17, 51, 171; identification with, 185–86; leaders exiled or imprisoned, 21; Pityana in, 190; politics of enmity and, 140, 144; practical project of, 142; Program of Action of, 38; responsibility for Soweto claimed by, 155–56, 157, 239n93; student group aligned with, 28; supporters arrested, 68; WCC's support for, 212n67; Youth League of, 38
African Theology: Christianity translated in, 84–87; faith defined in, 91; ideas underlying, 79–80, 85–86; problems caused by, 91–93, 97; reexamination of, 97–99; traditional practices in, 87–90. *See also* Black Theology; theology
African traditional religions: characteristics of, 91; Christianity merged with, 84–90; included in worship practices, 83–84; past as inspiration for future-oriented focus in, 98; reconsideration of, 79
Afrikaners and Afrikaner nation: "as chosen people," 62, 104; Roman rulers compared with, 108; sacralization of events, 23–24, 60–61. *See also* apartheid; Dutch Reformed Church (DRC)
agency: claims of, 36–39, 203n74; martyrdom discourse and, 177–78
agnosticism, 213n85
AIDS policy, 189, 190, 228n15
Akenson, Donald, 223n30
Alves, Ruben, 222n10
Amin, Idi, 38, 43–44
ANC. *See* African National Congress
Anglican Church: criticism of, 82–83; current challenges to, 189; training for priesthood, 100–101
Angola, political change in, 151
anthropology, appeal of, 85–86, 217n27

10, 11, 98; fear, 160, 168, 169, 172; human relationships and consciousness, 52, 55, 117, 188; ideas in books, 49; indigenization, 83; liberal politics, 29, 200n16; missionaries, 85, 91; oppression and race, 38, 43, ix; precolonial history, 88; Progressives, 30; prophets, 170; response to police violence, 203n74; stages of BC project, 51, 108, 142; women's liberation, 36
See also dialectics of political progress
birth control, attitudes toward, 241n47
black and blackness: African (term) vs., 45–46, 205–6n17; as attitude and way, 124; contingency and experience in being, 42–50, 111–12, 205n13; definition of, 140, 146; determinacy of, 107; ideas about, 2–3, 6–7; images of, 112, 120, 227n84, 241–42n50; implications for Christians, 102–3; political definition and implications of, 92–99; questions about being and God's role in, 110–11; as special virtue to God, 225n57; victory in, 180–81. *See also* Black Messiah
Black Community Programmes (BCP), 164–65, 183
Black Consciousness ideology: aesthetics of, 133–38; "black" as used in, 92; Black Messiah as underpinning, 117–19; contingent nature and sources of, 42–50, 111–12, 205n13; divisiveness of, 144–48; domestication of ideas in, 193n17; ethical questions in, 8–9; "fear is gone" and change is inevitable (idea) in, 167–72; future envisioned in, 51–53; lull preceding, 3, 15, 21, 53, 168, 191n4; maturation of, 140–44; Ntwasa as exemplar of, 100–101; other organizations' attitudes toward, 141–42, 232n10; political and institutional background of, 18–25; political turn of, 12–13, 146–48, 233n18; process of doing, 130; questions of "I" in, 110–13; rebellion as essential to, 20–21; as religion, 55–57, 131–33; religion as envisioned in, 90, 98–99; remembered, 190; sacrifice and suffering in, 173–81; secular and sacred intertwined in, 10–11, 214–15n123; selfhood and dignity claimed in, 2–3, 6–8; sources of, 41–50; stages of, 46–50, 51, 108, 125, 131, 142; Western traditions as "irreconcilable" with, 41. *See also* Black Consciousness Movement (BCM); Black Theology; Christianity; conscientization; gender issues
Black Consciousness Movement (BCM): adjusting thinking in, 160–61; alternative stories of, 4–6; banning of, 4, 164, 167–68; Biko's death and, 182–84; collaboration rejected in, 147, 235n45; emergence of, 12–13, 140–48; historiography of, 3–4, 14, 191n5; ideas underlying, 6–9; male domination of, 33–34; media outlet of, 148; organizations in, 1; reflections on, 185–90; revolutionary potential of, 154, 238–39n93; selfhood and dignity claimed in, 2–3, 6–8; on trial with SASO/BPC, 148, 153–54, 157–58. *See also* Black Consciousness ideology; Christianity; theology

"Black is beautiful," 111–13
Black Madonna, 115
black men: dignity of, 2–3, 6–8; multiplicities within category, 7; political liberation of, 32–36; significance of term, 26, 32, 36, 42. *See also* gender issues; masculinity; selfhood and self-fashioning
Black Messiah: changing ideas about, 173–74; Christ as, 114, 115; faith in, 103; ideas underlying, 59, 115–18; images of, 120, 227n84; meanings of, in apartheid context, 118–24; opening for, 69; "spirit" of, 176. *See also* Christianity; theology
Black Panther newsletter, 241–42n50
Black Parents Association, 155, 181
Black People's Convention (BPC): banning of leaders and organization, 150–51, 160, 183; Black Messiah idea in, 118–19; confrontational stance of, 147–48; founding of, 140, 143; leadership changes in, 150–51; objectives and program of, 143–44; officers tried, 1; Shezi's death and, 175; Tiro's death and, 178–79; women's roles in, 7, 34, 233n13
Black Power (US): borrowings and translations from, 47–50, 53, 207n41; Christ in, 94–96; processual approach to, 5; significance of, 94–95; slogan of, 222n12; South African fears of, 183; specific vs. grand narratives of, 192n10; women's images in, 241–42n50. *See also* African Americans
Black Renaissance Convention (BRC), 235n45
Black Theology: abstraction in, 119–20; African twist to, 97–99; blackness/God as good/ apartheid tensions in, 110–14; Christ in, 95–96; "church" (concept) in, 120–21; concerns about, 109–10, 113–14; context of, 80, 97; as correction of faith, 225n62; divisions over inherently political nature of, 103–6; existential nature of, 94–95; godly, human, and liberating unified in, 123–24; as "going black," 105; ideas underlying, 93–94, 96–97; National seminar (at Roodepoort) on, 102–6, 109–10; personal and political bridged in, 106–7, 124, 166; problem of Genesis in, 110–13; spread of, 233n12; suffering and victory in struggles, 173–81; tensions of horizontal vs. vertical faith in, 121, 123; Transvaal seminar on, 222n14; treatise on, 107–9; universalism of, 117–18; women's liberation in context of, 223n38. *See also* African Theology; Black Messiah; Christianity
black women: appearance and fashion choices of, 111, 224n50; BCM roles, 7–8; birth control attitudes, 241n47; BPC roles, 7, 34, 233n13; defiance of, 235n45; images of, 241–42n50; martyrdom discourse and, 180–81; organizational realities for, 233n13; petition and protest of, 152–53; responsibilities of, 166–67; SASO's dismissal of, 33–34; women's liberation and, 35–36, 223n38, 224n52. *See also* gender issues; women's liberation

Boesak, Allan: in 1980s activities, 185; background of, 13; Black Messiah of, 114, 115, 116–17; on faith, 121; on theological teaching, 62

Bond, Patrick, 186

Bonhoeffer, Dietrich: British church fears of, 78; on Christ's sacrifice and the cross, 160, 174, 175; compared himself to Christ, 178; on faith, 72–73, 74, 75; on Incarnation, 72–73, 85–86, 95; on worldly institutions, 213n94

Botswana, Tiro's commemoration in, 178–79

BPC. See Black People's Convention

BRC (Black Renaissance Convention), 235n45

Brennan, James, 140

British Broadcasting Corporation (BBC), 152

Broederbond, 29

Brown, James, 46, 47

Brown, Julian, 235n49

Bureau of Literacy and Education, 128

Buthelezi, Gatsha, 22, 144, 145–46, 204n80

Buthelezi, Manas: on African Theology, 92; on "age of philosophers," 42; on black and nonwhite terms, 112; on Christ as black, 115; on hope, 170; Kairos Document and, 189; on Mohapi's death, 180–81; on past as inspiration, 98; on prophets, 169–70, 171–72; seminar invitation for, 124, 222n10; Soweto uprising and, 155; on "wholeness," 221n79

Buthelezi, Peter, 82, 83

Buthelezi, Sipho, 144

Cabral, Amilcar, 5

Calvinism, 60–63

Camus, Albert, 8, 197n15

Carmichael, Stokely, 47, 50, 51

Catholic Church: apolitical stance of, 64–65; current challenges to, 189; priesthood of, 80–84, 81, 215n5; schools of, 22, 23, 64–65, 81; Vatican II, 81, 83–84, 214–15n123

Césaire, Aimé, 8

Chapman, Mark, 113–14

Charney, Craig, 27, 231n43, 235n49

Chartier, Roger, 5, 156

Chidester, David, 92, 218n34

Chikane, Frank, 239n104

Christ. See Jesus Christ

Christian Institute (CI): apolitical materials of, 219–20n58; banning of, 183; Easter sermon for, 180; government investigation of, 162; multiracialism of, 103; police raids against, 68; study project of, 63, 66, 67. See also Pro Veritate (journal)

Christianity: Black Theology as broader than, 113; colonialism entwined with, 55–56; definition of, 93; implications for black South Africans, 102–3; as justification and rebuttal, 2–3; liberation linked to, 9–11, 56–57, 101, 161; neo-Calvinist version of, 60–63; otherworldly eschatology of, 170; Paul's role in, 223n30; politics entwined with, 56–57, 58–59; present focus of, 96; promise of change in, 124; secularization of, 69–78; translation and indigenization of, 84–90,

98–99. See also Bible; Black Consciousness ideology; Black Consciousness Movement; church-state relationships; death and martyrdom; faith; God; hope; Incarnation; Jesus Christ; missionaries; suffering; theology; and specific denominations

"church," concept of, 120–21. See also African Independent Churches; confessing church; mainstream churches

Church of Scotland, Lovedale College, 23, 28

church-state relationships: apartheid supported in, 59; colonialism and, 55–56; neo-Calvinist theology in, 60–63; secularization of religion and, 69–78; Transvaal Black Theology seminar and, 105–6

CI. See Christian Institute

Cindi, Zithulele, 137–38, 151, 152, 164, 168

civil rights movement (US), 93–96

Cleage, Albert, 116

Cleaver, Eldridge, 207n41

Cohen, Jeremy, 176

Cohen, Paul, 192n8

collaboration, opposition to, 147, 235n45

Collins, Colin: departure from church, 214–15n123; exile of, 162; interracial meeting and, 64; literacy program under, 128; Ntwasa's relationship with, 101; on SASO's founding, 28, 200n10; on secular religion, 71, 73

colonialism: Christianity entwined with, 55–56; comparative religion implicated in, 217–18n34, 218–19n44; de-brainwashing after, 92–93; missionaries implicated in, 86, 123, 218–19n44

Coloured Dutch Reformed Mission Church, 62, 210n22

Coloured Federal Party, 43

Coloured Labour Party, 43, 145

Coloureds: Africanism as excluding, 140, 142, 144, 232–33n12; name-calling against, 144; terminology of, 43

"colourlessness," problems of, 27

Comaroff, Jean, 195–96n39, 219–20n58

Comaroff, John, 195–96n39

Come Back Africa (film), 234n29

Committee of Ten, 181

Communism, 71

comparative religion: colonial origins of, 217–18n34, 218–19n44; concept of, 84–85, 87

Cone, James: on African Theology, 97; Black Theology of, 93–96; on Christ, 99, 114, 116; influences on, 197n15; on Judaism, 220n69; Moore influenced by, 107–9; taped address for seminar, 102, 103, 106; UCM influenced by, 101–2

confessing church: calls for, 59, 68; function of, 67, 211n59; in Germany, 72, 212n61; image of God revised in, 69

Congress Alliance, 25, 198n27

Congress of Democrats, 30

Connolly, Bob, 68

conscientization: approach to, 125–26; artistic creativity and, 133–38; of children, 166–67; concept of, 128–29; in definition of blackness, 140; documents on, 229n32; goals and process of, 129–33; interior identity and, 205n13; in King William's Town, 165; orthodoxy vs., 148; political shift of, 138–39

consciousness, 50, 130. *See also* Black Consciousness ideology; conscientization

consumerism, 186–87

conversion: conscientization as, 132–33; politicization as, 142

Cooper, Saths: arrest and trial of, 152, 153–54; banning of, 150, 164; childhood memories and experiences of, 21; organizing by, 39

topical comments: contingency and identity, 205n13; Durban strikes, 236n61; Fanon, 204n79; fear, 168; "laconic exclamations," 23–24; "psychological intervention," 38, 108, 168, 183; rejection of racism vs. being branding as racist, 27; selfhood, 38

Cox, Harvey, 71–72, 73–74, 89, 244n90

cross, suffering and responsibility symbolized in, 173–81

Cry the Beloved Country! (Paton), 234n29

cultural forms: conscientization and renaissance of, 133–38; packaging revolution in, 186–87; timeliness and present in, 46–47, 135

Currie's Fountain, rally at, 152–53

Curry, David, 43

Curtis, Neville, 30

death and martyrdom: agency and, 177–78; BCM challenged by, 160–61; of Biko, 4, 182–84, 232n4; discourse on, 173–81; examples of self-conscious martyrs, 244n111; iconic images of, 155, 159, 182; roots and practices of, 160; of Tiro, 58–59, 79, 80, 173–74, 178–79

De Gruchy, John, 67, 211n59, 212n61

Desai, Ashwin, 186

dialectics of political progress: contingent nature of, 42–50, 111–12, 205n13; liberal politics rejected in, 31–32. *See also* Black Consciousness ideology; theology

Diggs, Charles, 144

dignity, 2–3, 6–8. *See also* selfhood and self-fashioning

Diop, David, 47

domestication: of Christian suffering, 174–75; definition of, 193n17; of global movements, 8–9

Donaldson Orlando Community Centre (DOCC), 136, 142, 143

Dornford-May, Mark, 226n72

Douglas, Emory, 241–42n50

Drum (periodical), 111, 144, 164, 205–6n17

Dubow, Saul, 5

Durban strikes (1973), 236n61

Durkheim, Emile, 87, 88, 217–18n34

Dutch Reformed Church (DRC): apartheid supported by, 59; "as chosen people," 62, 104; liberal critique dismissed by, 66; neo-Calvinism of, 60–63; separate churches controlled by, 62, 210n22. *See also* Afrikaners and Afrikaner nation

Ebony magazine, 48–49

educational system. *See* Bantu Education; schools; universities

Enlightenment, religion and secular separated in, 90

Enloe, Cynthia, 33

Episcopalianism, Ethiopian order of, 83

Erasmus, J., 74

Essays on Black Theology (collection), 112, 127, 162

Ethiopia, ancient traditions of, 86

Expansion of University Education Act (1959), 19

faith: antidetermination linked to, 130–31; Black Theology as correction of, 225n62; Bonhoeffer's view of, 72–73, 74, 75; definitions of, 11–12, 91, 167, 219n50; implications for black South Africans, 102–3; as liberating Christianity, 9–11; past as inspiration for future-oriented, 98; as path to liberation, 10, 107–8; in people and in God, 55; as personal, 63; politics connected to, 68–69; realities of, 12–13, 159–60; renewal despite bannings, 160–61; suffering and fear juxtaposed to, 167–72; tensions of horizontal vs. vertical, 121, 123; translation of, 79–80. *See also* future; hope

Fanon, Frantz: on cultural present, 46–47, 135; on identities, 8, 42–43; as influence, 55, 204n79

Farisani, Tshenuwani Simon: on Azania, 243n81; Biko compared with, 121; Black Messiah of, 119–20, 227n84; on conscientization, 133; education of, 24

fear: of Africanism, 43–44; of Black Power, 183; faith in face of, 167–72; of FRELIMO, 136, 137, 151–52

Federal Party, 43

Federal Theological Seminary, 82, 100, 212n67

Feierman, Steve, 193n16

feminism (women's liberation), 35–36, 223n38, 224n52

Fields, Karen, 91, 217–18n34, 219n50, 219–20n58

formation schools, 164

Frankel, Phillip, 176, 177

Freedom Charter, 30, 143

"Freedom Is More" (Sunday worship play), 35

Freire, Paulo: as influence, 125, 208n1; on literacy and cultural education, 128, 133, 137, 148, 187, 228n10. *See also* conscientization

FRELIMO (Front for Liberation of Mozambique): BCM contacts with, 151–52, 236n65, 237n68; Essenes compared with, 1; victory of, 148; white fears of, 136, 137, 151–52

French Revolution, 5, 156

Fugard, Athol, 138

funeral rites, traditional components of, 89. *See also* death and martyrdom

future: faith in, 167–72; horizon and, 170, 243n77; human relationship envisioned for, 51–53, 55, 117, 188; past as inspiration for, 98; renaming in, 243n81; uncertainty of, 160–61

Garvey, Marcus, 114, 225–26n67
gender issues: bannings and, 165–67; birth control attitudes, 241n47; Black Messiah images and, 120, 227n84; contentiousness of, 7–8, 193n20; images of black women and, 241–42n50; SASO discourse on, 32–36; women's liberation, 35–36, 223n38, 224n52. *See also* black men; black women; masculinity
General Students' Council (GSC): Christ as freedom fighter for, 175; on dogmatism, 32; growing popularity of, 50; political turn of, 146–47; terminology of, 43
Gerhart, Gail, 38, 43, 45, 51
Gilroy, Paul, 6, 46, 49
Ginsberg Education Project, 22, 198n21
Glaser, Clive, 158
global movements: African domestication of, 8–9; Black Consciousness in context of, 52; radical theological trends in, 59–60, 69; secular theology in, 72–76
Goba, Bonganjalo, 24, 88, 91, 112
God: as black, 115, 116; blacks created in image of, 112–13, 127–28; concept of, 87; as good yet bad things happen, 110–14; images of, 69, 89, 112–13; as particular race, 225n57. *See also* Bible; Christianity; faith; hope; Jesus Christ
Gomez, Michael, 7
Goodwin, Denise, 104
Gordon, Lewis, 10
gospel, 12–13, 85, 114. *See also* Bible; Black Consciousness ideology; theology
Graham, Billy, 115, 226n72
Grahamstown, UCM founded at, 9
Grand Apartheid, 18–20. *See also* apartheid
Great Britain: attitudes toward Bonhoeffer in, 74, 78; church-politics discussion in, 63; Student Christian Movement in, 162
GSC. *See* General Students' Council (GSC)
Guinea-Bissau, political change in, 151
Gwala, Mafika, 134

Hamilton, Charles, 47, 50
Hardt, Michael, 80
homeland, use of term, 161
Hoot (Naidoo), 226n72
hope: doubt juxtaposed to, 159–60; essence of, 11–12; as liberating Christianity, 9–11; radical, 243n77; realities of, 12–13; theology of, 170–72. *See also* faith
Hope, Anne: on activists' codes, 132, 133; background of, 13; conscientization training under, 128–29, 137, 150
Hopkins, Dwight, 115
horizon, use of term, 170, 188–89, 243n77
Huddleston, Trevor, 58–59
human community and humanism: Africa's gift of, 45–46, 88–89, 91, 117; definition of, 4; faith and politics linked in, 68–69, 121–23; future envisioned for, 51–53, 55, 117, 188; "holiness" of, 55; idealization of precolonial, 88; secular religion embedded in, 69–78; selfhood and blackness in, 46–50

Human Rights Commission, 190
Hurley, Denis, 64, 73

IDAMASA (Interdenominational African Ministers' Association of Southern Africa), 31, 65
identities and identifications: as black South African and as Christian, 102–3; contingency and being "black," 42–50, 111–12, 205n13; in defining faith, 79; political nature of, 7. *See also* black and blackness; nonwhite and nonwhiteness; selfhood and self-fashioning; white and whiteness
identity politics: student activists' engagement with, 32–36; in US, 221n73; in wider political sense, 76–77
ideological correctness, emergence of, 137
Inanda Seminary, 39, 134
Incarnation: Boesak on, 114; Bonhoeffer on, 72–73, 85–86, 95; conceptualization of (simultaneous revelation), 85–87, 89, 91, 95; Robinson on, 75; Tlhagale on, 86, 89, 91, 95
Indians: Africanism as excluding, 140, 142, 144, 232–33n12; Biko's friendship with, 205n16; SASO's relationship with, 145
indigenization: of African Theology, 97–98; of Christianity, 84–90, 98–99; of worship practices, 83–84
indoctrination vs. conscientization, 131
Innes, Duncan, 27
Interdenominational African Ministers' Association of Southern Africa (IDAMASA), 31, 65
Israel, Africa's "corporate personality" compared with, 88

Jamaica, blackness in, 206n25
Jesus Christ: in African Theology, 90, 98–99; blackness of, 112, 114–16; in Black Power and Theology, 94–96; centrality of, 9–10; in day-to-day religion, 69–78, 122–23; death of, 160; as freedom fighter/liberator/agitator, 1–2, 12, 104, 109, 114, 157–58, 173–76, 178; fusing one's life with, 120–21; Golden Rule of, 14, 111; Great Commission of, 133; historical context and particularities of, 107–9, 223n30, 223n33; of history vs. of faith, 115–17; humanistic issues of, 110; images of, 69, 125–26, 166; message of love, 9–10, 22, 59, 67, 73, 75, 94–95, 104, 106, 110–11, 113, 162; separate development as betrayal of, 63–64; Sermon on the Mount of, 13, 48, 58, 108; Shezi compared with, 175–76, 177, 178; suffering and victory of, 173–81; teaching centered on, 244n90; Tiro compared with, 58–59, 79, 80, 173–74, 178–79. *See also* Bible; Black Messiah; Christianity; God
Jewish people, 115, 211n57. *See also* Judaism
Johannesburg: consumerism in, 186–87; ministers' protest in, 183–84; SASO activities in, 12. *See also* Sophiatown; *World* (Johannesburg newspaper)
Jolobe, Fikile, 22

Jones, Peter, 182, 208n1, 228n10
Joseph, Peniel, 192n10
Judaism, 95, 220n69. *See also* Jewish people

Kairos Document, 189
Kameeta, Zephaniah, 180
Karolen, Roli, 58–59
Kaunda, Kenneth: on human relations and humanism, 55, 117, 188; as influence, 27, 45–46, 88
Kelley, Robin, 6
Kennedy, Robert F., 19, 197n8
Kente, Gibson, 138, 230n35
Kgware, Winnie, 34, 233n13
Khoapa, Bennie, 30, 48–50, 53, 232n11
Kierkegaard, Søren, 11, 91, 219n50
Kimberley, banned leaders in, 162–63
King, Martin Luther, Jr., 114–15
King William's Town: activists in, 237n77; Biko banned to, 150, 152, 164–65; Biko memorial services in, 183; BPC activities in, 164–65; SASO activities in, 179–80
Koka, Drake, 157, 164
Kruger, Jimmy, 151, 157, 158, 182
Kunnie, Julian, 34
Kuyper, Abraham, 61–62, 63, 84
Kuzwayo, Ellen, 142–43

Landau, Paul, 195–96n39, 218–19n44
Langa, Ben, 164
Langa, Mandla, 134
Lear, Jonathan, 243n77
Lembede, Anton, 10, 38, 44
liberal Christian groups: apartheid opposed by, 63–64, 65–69; raceless Christ preferred by, 116. *See also* mainstream churches; multiracialism
Liberal Party, 18, 20
liberal political groups: multiracial reform efforts of, 18, 27; rejection of, 26–32, 142; tea parties of, 31–32, 200n16. *See also* multiracialism
liberation: arts linked to, 133–38; centrality of, 8–9; Christianity linked to, 9–11, 56–57, 101, 161; faith as path to, 10, 107–8; fluidity of concept, 143; hierarchy of goals in, 32–36; hope for, 171–72; Jesus Christ and, 1–2, 12, 104; philosophy as preparation stage in, 46–50; reflections on, 185–90; secular religion and, 73–78; self-affirmation in, 110–13; suffering joined to, 177–78
liminality, 197n13
literacy programs, 128, 133, 227n3, 229n32
Lobban, Michael, 153, 157
Lonsdale, John, 193n16
Lutheran Theological Seminary, 85

Mabasa, Lybon, 154
Mabona, Anthony, 121
MacDonald, Michael, 205n13
Mafuna, Bokwe: banning of, 150, 164; on Black Theology, 222n14; on daily realities, 122; as "liberated," 187; seminary drop-out of, 65, 77

Mafungo, Vic, 132
Maimela, Simon, 113, 114
mainstream churches: apartheid criticized in, 65–69; apartheid opposed by, 63–64; apolitical stance of, 64–65; neo-Calvinism in, 60–63; questions about, 58–59; secularization of religion and, 69–78; use of term, 209n2. *See also* liberal Christian groups
Majoba (*Drum* reader), 111
Makhitini (rector), 82
Makhubo, Mbuyisa, 159
Mandela, Nelson: activists' attitudes toward, 141; on BCM, 187; Black Messiah and, 114; as Black Moses, 225–26n67; Christ compared with, 108; education decisions of, 19; as self-conscious martyr, 244n111
Mandela, Winnie, 238n91
Mangcu, Xolela, 198n21
Mangena, Mosibudi, 132, 146–47
Mangena, Oshadi (Jane Phakati): on conscientization, 131–32; on gendered language, 202–3n57; petition and protest of, 152–53; on political stance of churches, 216n16; on women in BCM, 34; on women's agency, 38
Mann, Horace, 243n88
Manthata, Tom, 157, 181, 239n104
martyrdom. *See* death and martyrdom
masculinity: banning and, 165–67; of Black Messiah, 120, 227n84; focus on, 32–36, 37; hegemony of, 7; implications of, 42; victory and martyrdom linked to, 180–81
Masekela, Maphiri, 166
Mashiangwako, Simon, 132
Mashinini, Tsietsi, 155, 157, 158, 239n93
Masokoane, Glenn, 230n39
Mass Democratic Movement, 185
Mathabathe, L. M., 181
Matshoba, Deborah, 36, 111, 166
Matthews, James: on appearance and fashion choices, 111; on Azania, 243n81; on liberal politics and tea parties, 200n16; name-calling by, 145, 234n28; poetry of, 134–35, 230n38
Mayatula, Mashwabada, 118–19, 181
Mayson, Cedric, 69, 121
Mazibuko, Fanyana, 21, 171, 211n43, 233n17
Mazibuko, Thandisizwe, 22, 23, 181
Mbali, Zolile, 212n67
Mbanjwa, Thoko, 23, 34, 134, 198n27
Mbembe, Achille, 124, 186
Mbiti, John: African Theology of, 80, 84, 87–88, 92, 97; on Black Theology, 96–97; on defining "religion," 90; on politics and religion, 56, 76; on traditional religions, 89, 91
McBride, Clive, 225n57
memory, reading past through, 5, 192n8
"Message to the People of South Africa" (SACC), 65–66, 67, 68, 69, 103
Methodist Church, 82
Methodist Youth Guild, 158
middle class, 20, 192n13

missionaries: attitudes toward black people, 55–56; Great Commission for, 133; implicated in colonial project, 86, 123, 218–19n44; language of, 87; liberalizing tendencies of, 61; on local practices, 85, 217n27; revising legacy of, 84; undoing mistakes of, 85, 86, 91, 98

mission schools: Catholic hold on, 64–65; government takeover of, 63; questions encouraged in, 23–24; students at, 22–23

Mkhabela, Bongi: disappointments of, 4, 5, 186; on hope, 171; as influence, 158; motivation of, 7; on Soweto uprising, 156

Mkhabela, Ish, 171, 186

Mkhatshwa, Smangaliso, 84, 90, 235n45

modernity: activists' use of texts as counter to, 49–50; Black Consciousness linked to, 41–42; secular religion relevant in, 70–71

Modisane, Bloke, 18, 20, 33, 37, 38, 203n74

Modisane, Jerry, 164

Moerane, M. T., 29–30, 105, 142–43

Moffat, Robert, 217n27

Mofokeng, Takatso, 171, 245n126

Mogale, Dan, 36, 132, 150, 159–60

Mohapi, Mapetla, 179–81, 182

Mohapi, Nohle, 180–81

Mokitimi, Seth, 82, 216n14

Mokoape, Aubrey, 131, 198n27

Mokoditoa, Chris: on Catholic schools, 64; education of, 25, 199n37; on encounter groups, 77; on lack of fear, 167; on SASO's founding, 28; on UCM, 28, 162

Mokoena, Aubrey, 157

Mokoka, Clement, 83–84, 85, 130–31, 229n32

Mokoka, Tau, 13, 24, 115, 150

Molobi, Eric, 136–38, 178, 245n117

Moloto, Justice, 101–2, 161, 162, 223n38, 240n7

Moltmann, Jürgen, 11, 170, 222n10, 243n77

Montsisi, Daniel, 155, 156

Moodie, T. Dunbar, 61

Moodley, Strini: arrest and trial of, 152, 153–54; banning of, 150, 164, 165–66, 167; education of, 25; organizing by, 39; teenage activism of, 198n27

    topical comments: ANC, 199n36; beingness, 51; conscientization, 131; Durban strikes, 236n61; timeliness in aesthetic, 135

Moore, Basil: banning of, 161, 162, 240n7; Black Theology treatise of, 107–10; exile of, 127, 162; feminist play of, 35–36; Ntwasa's relationship with, 101; secular religion of, 73–76, 78, 89

    topical comments: Black Theology seminar, 103; Christ as fighter, 173, 174; Christ's particular context, 223n30, 223n33; hope, 170; Paul's role, 223n30; worship happenings, 117

See also *Essays on Black Theology* (collection)

Morlan, Don, 109

Morrell, Robert, 7

Morris Isaacson high school (Soweto), 134, 150, 157, 171, 245n115

Mosala, Itumeleng, 169, 180

Motlana, Nthato, 197–98n17, 232n11

Motlhabi, Mokgethi: on Catholicism, 64; on daily realities, 123; on faith and theology, 98; on Israelites and blacks, 113; James Cone's correspondence with, 163; Ntwasa's relationship with, 101; on priesthood training, 215n5; on secular religion, 73; on theology and race, 104

Moynihan Report (Daniel Patrick Moynihan), 202n51

Mozambique, independence of, 1, 148, 151. See also FRELIMO

Mpumlwana, Malusi: education of, 23; goals of, 32; motivation of, 4, 5; religious base for, 86

    topical comments: activists in King, 237n77; Biko's gendered language, 34; conscientization, 129–30, 131; faith, 83; liberal politics, 29; other liberation movements, 141; PAC, 233n12; poetry, 134; rallies for Mozambican independence, 152; stages of BC project, 142

Mulder, Connie, 60

multiracialism: apolitical stance on, 64–65; dismissal of, 143; emergence of, 15; hopes for, 103; limits of, 29; reform efforts based in, 18, 27; rejection of, 28, 30–32

music: friends and enemies in, 145, 234n28; renaissance in, 134; soul music, 46, 47

Mzamane, Mbulelo, 22, 135, 230–31n39, 239n94

Mzara, A. Z., 68–69

Mzoneli, Chris, 22, 85–86, 91

Naidoo, Geraldine, 226n72

name-calling, in politics of enmity, 144–48

names: African vs. slave, 111; Azania, 185–86, 187, 243n81; post-1994 changes in, 187–88

Natal Indian Congress, 145

National Bishops' Conference, 65

National Committee of Negro Churchmen (US), 94

nationalisms, 7, 10–11, 33

National Party (NP): Christian involvement with, 59–60; educational restructuring under, 18–19; formation of, 61; liberal politics compared with, 29; reassertion of control by, 182

National Union of South African Students (NUSAS): all-black group's break from, 3; as "black body with a white brain," 27; government investigation of, 162; leaders banned, 150–51; multiracial reform efforts of, 18; racial makeup and divisions of, 20–21, 26–28, 30; rejection of, 31

Nation of Islam, 7, 93

Naudé, Beyers, 59, 62, 67

Ndebele, Njabulo, 231n39

Ndungane, Njongonkulu, 189

Nefolohodve, Pandelani, 204n80

Negri, Antonio, 80

Négritude, 42, 50

Nengwekhulu, Harry: banning of, 150, 164; at Black Theology seminar, 102; on ideas as tools, 6; on liberal politics, 29; on SASO, 236n50; on Sono, 146; on Tiro, 179

Nguni *ukubuyisa*, 89

Progressive Party (Progs), 29–30, 31–32, 211n57
prophets: activists as, 2–3, 4, 6–7, 55; Christ
    as, 108–9; importance of, 220n69;
    incorporation of, 85; ordinary black people
    as, 169–70; in present South Africa, 189–90;
    time for, 171–72
Pro Veritate (journal): banning of, 183; image of
    blackness in, 112
    topics: BCM, 152; Black Theology, 103–4,
    222n14; confessing church, 68; deaths,
    180; poetry, 135; SASO, 30; Twelve
    Statements, 67

Qoboza, Percy: on Black Consciousness
    divisiveness, 145–46; on township
    Catholics, 80–84

race: contingent, experiential definition of,
    42–50, 111–12, 205n13; SASO's definition of,
    143. See also black and blackness; nonwhite
    and nonwhiteness; white and whiteness
Rachidi, Hlaku Kenneth, 182, 237n77
racism and racialisms: clash of, 40–42;
    liberalism and tea parties linked in, 31–32;
    nationalism linked to, 7, 10–11; rejection of
    being branded in, 27; in US, 48–49, 53. See
    also apartheid; oppression; multiracialism
Radebe, M., 30
Radio Zulu, 30
Rambally, Asha, 34
Ramose, Mogobe, 24–25
Ramphele, Mamphela, 34, 111, 205n16, 224n50,
    235n45
Ramusi, Collins, 235n45
Randall, Peter, 31, 66
Rand Daily Mail, topics: bannings, 162; Biko,
    182; blacks as children, 37; Black Theology,
    222n14; Black Theology seminar, 104; black
    vs. African terms, 205–6n17; Old Boys
    Association's declaration, 82; politics and
    religion, 68; Progressive electoral gains, 29
Ranuga, Thomas, 204n79
Ratele, Kopano, 202–3n57
Rees, Cecil, 153–54
Reformation, 72–73. See also Calvinism;
    confessing church
relevance: language of, 52–53; of local practices,
    87–88; of secular religion, 70–71, 74; of
    theology, 98–99
religion: basic core of, 217–18n34; "comparative,"
    84–85, 87, 217–18n34, 218–19n44; definition
    and translation of, 90; politics entwined
    with, 56–57, 58–59, 76, 121–23, 158. See also
    African traditional religions; agnosticism;
    Christianity; Judaism; Nation of Islam
resistance: overt type of, 3–4; theory and practice
    of, debated, 1–2, 8–9, 191n5. See also
    revolution
responsibility: agency of student activists in,
    36–39; of being made in God's image,
    112–13; Christian's call to, 63–69, 71–72;
    for religious practices, 83–84, 85, 89–90;
    suffering linked to, 173–81

revolution: BCM's potential for, 154, 238–39n93;
    Jesus Christ as freedom fighter and, 1–2, 12,
    104, 109, 114, 157–58, 173–76, 178; packaging
    of, 186–87; theater productions and, 137–
    38. See also resistance
Riebeeck, Jan Van, 44, 45
Rive, Richard, 135, 230n39
Robinson, John, 74–75, 78, 105
Rogosin, Lionel, 234n29
Ross, Marlon, 7
Russell, Bertrand, 71
Ryan, Colleen, 212n61

SA. See South Africa
SABC (South African Broadcasting
    Corporation), 239n93
SACC (South African Council of Churches), 31,
    63, 65–66, 67, 123
SAIRR (South African Institute of Race
    Relations), 31, 205–6n17
salvation, 65, 84, 86. See also death and
    martyrdom; faith; hope
Sanders, Mark, 42, 48, 204n79
Sanders, Thomas, 228n6
Sanneh, Lamin, 79
Sartre, Jean-Paul, 8, 42
SASM. See South African Students Movement
SASM Newsletter, 173, 243n88
SASO. See South African Students' Organisation
SASO Newsletter, specific columns: "Black Souls
    in White Skins" (Biko), 200n16; "The
    Chemical Analysis of Women," 33–34;
    "Let's Talk about Bantustans" (Biko), 147;
    "We Blacks" (Biko), 15, 196n11
    topics: Amin's actions, 43–44; bannings, 163,
    165–66, 171; BC as movement, 233n18;
    black political castration, 33; direction of
    movement, 9; fear, 168; Fort Hare SRC,
    199n37; imprisoned leaders, 141; name-
    calling, 144–45; poetry, 134–35; postcolonial
    Africa, 38; voice, 232n6
Schmitt, Carl, 140, 144
schools: "Afrikaners as chosen people" taught in,
    62; formation (type), 164; job reservation
    laws and teachers at, 21–22; Morris Isaacson
    high school (Soweto), 134, 150, 157, 171,
    245n115; poetry in, 134; politicization
    in government-run, 24. See also Bantu
    Education; mission schools
SCM (Student Christian Movement), 158
Scott, David, 188
Scully, Larry, 115
SDS (Students for a Democratic Society), 52,
    194n27
Sebidi, John, 26, 91, 97, 163, 184
Sechaba (periodical), 155
secular theology: African Theology compared
    with, 87–88, 89–90, 93; demise of,
    76–77; move from academia to pew, 105;
    reflections on, 77–78; rejection of, 104; rise
    of, 70–76; in UCM, 69–78, 100–101
Security Branch: BCM as perceived by, 150–51,
    157–58; Black Theology National seminar